# SCORE!

# SCORE!

## My Twenty-Five Years
## with
## The Broad Street Bullies

**Gene Hart**
with
Buzz Ringe

To Marissa —
Shot! Score!

*[signature]*

June 11, 1996

Bonus Books, Inc., Chicago

94  93  92  91                                        5  4

International Standard Book Number: 0-929387-20-1
Library of Congress 90-83079

**Bonus Books, Inc.**
160 East Illinois Street
Chicago, Illinois 60611

*Printed in the United States of America*

To
Ash Can
and
The Gumper

# Contents

# Cast of Characters

# Foreword

A city may possess a world renowned symphony orchestra, it may possess a celebrated museum of art, it may be openly envied for its historical legacies and artifacts, it may be a center of commerce, a port of note, a hub of finance. In short, a city can possess just about all that the critics agree is needed to qualify it as a metropolis of high esteem.

But often all of this largesse is lost on the inhabitants. Instead, more frequently than you might suspect, what quickens their pulse, what puts pride in their stride, is nothing more prosaic than a winning sports team. A city is galvanized by a winner. It rallies 'round a winner. If a city has a team that is winning, no matter what the calendar says, then it is eternal spring, and the citizenry has a sense of continuing rebirth and hope. A winning team implies that its fans are somehow smarter, brighter, sprighter, somehow superior.

All of which explains the unique love affair that has been going on for twenty-five years now between the City of Philadelphia and its ice hockey team.

The Flyers' fortunes may ebb and wane, but the sports fans of the city will be forever indebted to them because they effected a resurrection whose impact upon the psyche of the city cannot be overestimated.

It is necessary to understand that about the time the Flyers came along, in the late 1960s, Philadelphia was wallowing in sporting self-pity and impotence. By the early 1970s, the teams were so horrid that, according to the black humor of the time, a winning streak was when they had back-to-back days off. The Phillies were as consistently unsuccessful as the Chicago Cubs, but without the Cubs' redeeming charm. There was one memorable span of staggering ineptitude in which, in thirty-one years, the Phils managed exactly one winning season. Things weren't any better in football—the Eagles went from 1967 through 1977 without once fielding a winner. But even the phutile Phillies and the fluttering Eagles could not equal the one-season apocalypse rung up by the 76ers of 1972-73. They played eighty-two games and won nine. Which, of course, means they lost seventy-three. It is a ratio of futility that is without peer in any sport. Ever. It is a record, of dubious distinction to be sure, that is quite likely to stand forever.

And Philadelphia was known, far and wide, as the City of Losers. So then, against this background of biblical plague and lamentation and grinding deprivation, there arrived, in the spring of 1974, this fledgling franchise of blade runners, a curious gang of Canadians who, as part of dressing for a game, took out their teeth and put them in paper cups. They played a sport not particularly well known in the States, but on a sunny Sunday afternoon in late May they won the championship of the National Hockey League. The most enduring memory from that day is of Bobby Clarke, the eternal rink rat, hoisting that hunk of hardware they had all spent so much of themselves to get, and then trying to take it on the traditional victory lap skate around the Spectrum through the swirling madness. And then, when they were posing for the picture, Clarke, part imp, part angel, his choirboy curls framing that sweaty fighter's face, looked over at Bernie Parent, who had been so impregnable in goal, and Clarke grinned that fanged grin and gave Parent a wink. A long, slow, exaggerated wink.

And the wink said it all.

All the sacrifice, all the stitches, all the struggle, all the pain and persistence and perseverance that go into the excruciating price demanded to gain possession of Lord Stanley's Cup.

None of us had any way of knowing it at the time, but what the Flyers had accomplished at that moment transcended the mere winning of a championship. They had set into motion the sports renaissance of Philadelphia.

The City of Losers had just become the City of Winners.

It was as though their triumph became an inspiration, and an incentive, for the other teams.

The city itself came unhinged. There was a victory parade the next day, and it was the biggest turnout since World War II ended. The fans were starved for a winner. They poured out into the streets as though they sensed that liberation was at hand. Deliverance had arrived at last. No more civic slurs, no more withering cracks about the losers of Philly. The liberators were swaggering, fearless, combative. They backed down from no one. Philadelphians, accustomed to passive, submissive defeat from their other mercenaries, embraced their new heroes.

The Flyers made the breakthrough, demonstrating with sellout after sellout, how people would support a winner, and very soon the Phillies were winning their division, and the World Series, and the Eagles were winning their division, and getting into the Super Bowl, and the 76ers were winning their division, and playing for the championship, and finally winning it.

In the interim, the Flyers repeated their triumph the very next spring, but have never sipped champagne from Stanley's Cup since. They have come tantalizingly close on occasion. And after an extraordinary run of eighteen consecutive years without a losing season, they succumbed, this past year, to the inevitable cyclical nature of professional sports. They lost more often than they won, they failed to make the playoffs, and there was emotionally wrenching upheaval off the ice, all a reminder that no one, no team, is immune to shifting fortunes.

One constant throughout the Flyers' existence has been Gene Hart. For a quarter of a century he has made that trek up to his aerie in the Spectrum rafters, strapped on his headset, and proceeded to put the lie to the sneering disdainers who claim there is nothing at all exciting about listening to hockey on radio. Those people have never heard Hart's hyperthyroid, thrum-drum, voice-rising, cymbals-crescendo description of "...he shoots...SCORE!" And so there couldn't be a more fitting title for the book that he has written about the Flyers, for that has become his signature line.

For all of their success, the Flyers have also been stalked by tragedy, careers cut short by injury, and two lives snuffed. It is to them—Barry Ashbee and Pelle Lindbergh, Ash Can and The Gumper—that Gene Hart has dedicated this book. That is fitting. Even the Voice of the Flyers has suffered his own personal turmoil. In 1985, Gene underwent bypass surgery. With typical Flyers' resilience and remarkable tolerance for adversity, he barely missed a fraction of a season, and asked, anxiously: "Open-heart surgery, that's a legitimate excuse, isn't it?"

You'd like to think so.

Interspersed through his narrative history of the team are character sketches, and here the operative word is "character." It is the trait the Flyers always have been known for. They have always defined the work ethic. And they have had their share of characters.

This book is replete with them, and my own personal favorite anecdote involves André Dupont, the defenseman known as Moose, who joined the team as it was being remade from small, fast and pacifistic into large, belligerent and pugnacious. The Broad Street Bullies. In a game in Vancouver, the Flyers engaged the home team in a mass punchout, even while threatened with incarceration for earlier fistic transgressions, and then won the game by the whoppingly decisive score of ten to five. In the locker room afterwards, Moose Dupont, naked except for the helmet on his head, sat, smoking. Asked for a summation of things, he said: "Great trip for us. We don't go to jail. We beat up dere chicken forwards. We score ten goal. We win. An' now de Mooze drink beer."

Perfect.

How much easier it would be to deal with life blessed with such an uncomplicated perspective.

At heart, Gene Hart is a raconteur. And so he ties together seasons with anecdotes, and the history of a star-crossed franchise flits past, and in the end you are drawn back to Barry Ashbee, so sturdy, so unbending, dark glasses shielding a horrible eye injury, telling the new Stanley Cup champions in the spring of 1974: "Boys, cherish this group. There'll never be another like it."

He was prophetic, for they were, indeed, pioneers.

*Bill Lyon*
*August 1990*

# Pre-Game
## 1931 to 1967

Usually I don't like to start a story, "Well, it all began..." or "It all started when..." or "This is how it all came to fruition..." but I think before we get fully into the story of the Flyers, a little bit of how I got to where I am might be worth the brief first part of this book, which I'm calling "Pre-Game," to follow the format of having the sections of the book correspond to the periods of a hockey game: Pre-Game, First Period, Second Period, Third Period, Overtime, and possibly even Sudden Death.

So, first permit me, please, to give you a little pre-game background on myself, especially since I am to be one of the characters in this book, as well as the teller of the tale. And I tell it *now*, with the fear that, should I go, most of these stories would go with me; and not so long ago, I almost went! So, before I *do* go, I'd like to tell you my side of the Flyers' saga.

I feel I am well qualified to relate that saga, since the only segment of the entire history of the Flyers that I missed witnessing in person was at the start of the 1985-86 season, when I was undergoing "Open-Hart" bypass surgery, and I had to watch a couple of games on television. I did, however, have a note from my doctor; and since he was the Flyers' team doctor, I hope that constitutes a legitimate excuse.

For most normal people, bypass surgery is a downer, but for me, it was a plus! For, in a game which measures one's courage and involvement by the number of stitches in one's body, I proudly bear the longest scar of them all, and one which, at the drop of a shirt, I am always prepared to show the world.

Now that you know my body so intimately, please allow me to introduce myself. Philadelphia hockey fans know me as Gene Hart, the Voice of the Flyers, but my real and full name is Eugene Charles Hart, and I'm proud to be the son of two immigrants from Europe —a Viennese opera singer named Fritzie Matilda Fischer and a Hungarian acrobat named Charles Eugen (pronounced OY-gan) Hochsander. "Hoch" is Hungarian for "heart," hence my last name —Hart.

My parents met in New York City during World War I and formed one of those European vaudeville teams which played the same act every year, but in different costumes. In the summer, my dad ran the water show on the Steel Pier in Atlantic City, and my mother was billed as "Miss Fritzie," the lady who rode the world-famous High-Diving Horse in the spectacular conclusion of the show. Fittingly enough, my dear wife Sarah was once billed as "Miss Sarah," a later daring rider of the Diving Horse.

I've often been asked how a guy like me could become a hockey announcer. Most careers, I think, are predicated on some logical progression or order. There is usually a desire or an ability to get into a certain field, and then one progresses as one's quality begins to rise and as one learns to make a livelihood in that field. That may be the way it works for *most* people, but unfortunately, or perhaps fortunately, such was not the case with me, as you can easily ascertain from the following crazy-quilt assortment of occupations, vocations, and avocations. In two hundred words, more or less, here is the well-rounded résumé of a well-rounded (some say "fat") person.

Gun boy for lion tamer "Daring Dick" Clemens; Hawaiian high diver; degree in teaching from Trenton State College; member of the Russian linguistic unit of U.S. Army Intelligence; assistant stage manager for Boardwalk water show; one of a bevy of "Binswanger's Bathing Beauties" comedy diving act; bill collector and repossessor of motor vehicles (repo man); high school and college baseball umpire and basketball referee; high school and college basketball and football announcer; foreign sports car salesman; operator of FM radio music station; night shift rock disk jockey; teen talk show host; teacher; teaching principal in three-room school; master of ceremonies for Boardwalk water show; assistant director and announcer for Sea World–style whale and dolphin show; president and chief negotiator for teachers' union; teacher at state prison (no class-cutting or absenteeism, and when you were kept after school, you were really kept!); teacher of learning disability high school students (for seven years); voice of minor-league hockey's Jersey Larks and Jersey Devils (long before the present New Jersey Devils); voice of pro soccer's Philadelphia Atoms (outdoors) and Philadelphia Fever (indoors); voice of box lacrosse's Philadelphia Wings; track announcer at Brandywine Raceway; Board of Directors of Pennsylvania Opera Theatre; Board of Directors of Pennsylvania Hospital's Hospice Program for terminally ill patients; voice of Philadelphia Flyers.

There are times when fate and circumstance play a significant role in determining who does what, and I think that was the case with me, since my twenty-five year career in ice hockey resulted from quite a remarkable series of happenstances. I won't bore you with most of them, you'll be happy to know, but I think that the ones relating to hockey and to sportscasting are worth telling you about.

The first of these incidents occurred back in the year 1937, when as a seven-year-old youngster I returned with my parents from their summer work on the Steel Pier in Atlantic City to our apartment near 100th Street in New York City, where I went to school while my dad plied his trade in the Broadway area. I remember being at home with my mother one evening, bored and with the prospect of nothing to do. There was, of course, no television, only radio, and I was looking through the radio listings in the New York Daily News, hoping to find something like "The Shadow" or "The Green Hornet" to listen to, when I happened to notice a listing at 9:00 P.M. that read: "New York–Detroit." I thought I knew sports, because I knew baseball (the Giants, Dodgers, and Yankees) and I knew football (the New York Giants and Notre Dame), but I didn't know what this "New York–Detroit" could be, as there was no pro basketball in New York at that time. So I tuned in WHN at 9:00 P.M. and what I got was New York Rangers hockey. A new interest was born.

Down on 63rd Street, about three miles south, was the 63rd Street Y.M.C.A., where I would go every Saturday morning for a gym class, a swim, and a little lunch. That was my weekly outing. One time, I recall, they had hockey tickets available. They weren't for the New York Rangers, but for the New York Rovers of the Eastern Hockey League. They played almost every Sunday afternoon at the old Madison Square Garden in a league that contained teams like the River Vale Skeeters, the Atlantic City Seagulls, the Boston Olympics, and the Johnstown Bluebirds. Then they would also have a Metropolitan League game. I didn't understand at the time who the players were in that league, but they were college and semi-pro and amateur players, who made up such exotic teams as the Sands Point Tigers, the Manhattan Arrows, the Brooklyn Armored Torpedoes, the Stock Exchange, and the Jamaica Hawks.

So, for the price of a quarter or fifty cents plus a nickel carfare each way on the Eighth Avenue Subway, it became my routine to get to the Garden at about 12:30, see a game at 1:30, then another game at 3:30, leave at about 5:30, and get home between 6:00 and 7:00. For a total expenditure of less than a dollar, including food, it was certainly a bargain. The worst possible punishment for me, agony really, would be the times when, if I hadn't been good, or for whatever reason, my parents wouldn't give me the money to go.

Of course there were also the even more exotic New York Rangers at night, but because of my age, they existed only in my dream world via radio. My *real* dream was to actually *see* the New York Rangers.

My future career may have been predestined back then, when I was seven or eight or nine, and there seems to be evidence of that in the autograph book I had at that time. It was one of those 1930s satin-covered, multi-hued, slick-paged books that kids of that time kept, and since I worked on the Steel Pier with my dad all summer, it was really a great device to have. For instance, among the signers of my book were stars like Abbott and Costello, Rochester, Betty Grable, Harry James, Eddie Cantor, and Kate Smith.

In the first part of the book there was always a page or two for entries like: My Teachers, My Best Friend, My Motto, and My Favorite Team (which of course in college football was Notre Dame; what else in New York?). There was also a place to complete the statement, "I want to be when I grow up . . ." and I wrote in "*HOCKEY ANNONSER.*" (My spelling has improved since then.) Little did I know then that it would take some thirty years to fulfill that destiny, and with a team that wouldn't even exist until thirty years later.

The first serious setback to the fulfillment of my destiny came with the war scare in 1941, when my father decided to move out of New York City. He bought a home in a place called Absecon Highlands in South Jersey, about fifteen miles outside of Atlantic City, and it was really in the woods. There was our house and then a neighbor about a quarter of a mile down the road, and that was it. To a New York kid, used to freewheeling on the subway from the Polo Grounds all the way to Ebbetts Field, this business of having to walk for perhaps three miles just to say hello to a neighbor was really somewhat of a trauma. And, of course, this also took me away from my new love—hockey.

Worse yet, because of the war there was no electricity out there, so we New Yorkers had to improvise with a gas-fueled generator to produce electricity; but because of gas rationing, we couldn't turn on the lights until 9:00 at night. If I wanted to listen to Giants football, I'd have to rig a radio to a battery, which in those days weighed about eighteen hundred pounds. Portable it was not.

Because I was so isolated, and being a city kid without much affinity for the countrified lifestyle, the only activity with any appeal for me was that radio. I became a fanatic in listening to sports events. At that time WHN was a tremendously wide-ranging sports station in New York, perhaps the first of its kind in the country, and almost every night they had some form of sports. My dream world then included not only the New York Rangers, but also the Brooklyn Dodgers, the baseball and football Giants, local college basketball, and later on the New York Knicks, but particularly the Rangers.

Because I had nothing else to do, I started keeping really detailed score sheets while listening to the radio. Remember, there was nothing to watch, so the hands and mind were free to record these events in red ink and green ink and with whatever other innovations I could think of.

Another big event for me in those days was a trip to a store where New York newspapers were sold, so I could purchase a *New York Times* and update all of the statistics I was keeping for all of the sports that I heard on the radio. Always number one in my priorities were the New York Rangers, since I was a dyed-in-the-wool Ranger fan, who died mostly during the manpower-depleted war years of the 1940s when the Rangers were just an awful club.

For example, I remember in the 1943–44 season a goaltender named Ken "Tubby" McAuley who played the full season of fifty games, allowed 310 goals, and was, I'm quite sure, the only goalie in the history of the N.H.L. to allow an average of more than six goals per game as a full-time starter. It was really that dreadful. In fact, Tubby's (and the Rangers') record that year was 6-39-5. I ached and pained and died with that club during those awful war years.

In 1944 there occurred one of the most important firsts of my young life. My father took us to New York for a few days during Christmas vacation, and I made a beeline for Madison Square Garden, where I bought a $1.25 side-balcony seat for my very first N.H.L. game. Like the first N.H.L. game I had heard on the radio some seven or eight years earlier, it was the New York Rangers versus the Detroit Red Wings, and perhaps my biggest thrill was just seeing the Rangers skate out onto the ice for the first time.

The Rangers, who were seldom winners at that time, won the game six to two, and I was even more thrilled, although it was tough to top the initial excitement of just being in the Garden for a real live Rangers game, instead of a Rovers game. I didn't mind a bit that from where I was sitting in the side-balcony of the old Garden I had to stand up and lean over to see the action along the near boards.

Later on, when I was in high school and college, and even after that, I'd take that 250-mile round trip from South Jersey to Madison Square Garden whenever I had the chance. By then I was splurging on the $2.50 end-arena seats, which were always a good place from which to see my beloved Rangers, and they were still the world's best bargain from my point of view, even though the Rangers were still the N.H.L.'s version of the Dead-End Kids.

Searching through the radio dials one lonely Saturday night in the wilderness of New Jersey, I happened to hear a broadcaster say, "Imperial Oil presents Hockey Night in Canada." I didn't realize it at the time, but that voice belonged to Foster Hewitt—the most legendary voice in hockey. He had begun the first hockey broadcasting in the twenties for the Toronto Maple Leafs, and he was the man who created the vocabulary for a hockey broadcaster.

The voice of Foster Hewitt would become another inspirational force for me, and another of the great thrills of my life would occur when, after twenty years or so of listening to that marvelous voice, I finally got to meet Foster Hewitt in person. I was thirty-six years of age when I met him, and I quite literally felt like the small boy who finally gets to meet his idol, even though I had been a broadcaster myself for about ten years by then. But I'm jumping ahead in the story.

Despite all those years of listening to radio sports broadcasts, in particular to Rangers hockey and later to Foster Hewitt, I never got close to *doing* an actual broadcast until after I'd finished college and my hitch in the Army and I was working as a bill collector and repo man for a finance company in Atlantic City. My job allowed me to have a car and my own hours, as long as I got my work done, so I continued to make those 250-mile round trips to the Garden to see the sixth-best team in the six-team National Hockey League. I also would arrange my work schedule to allow me to travel around the area refereeing high school and college basketball games for a few extra dollars, something I had begun doing while in the Army at Fort Bragg.

After refereeing a Friday night game at undefeated Atlantic City High School, I was changing my clothes in the athletic director's office, where the officials usually change before and after the games. There were some other people in the office at the time, including one of the two members of the Atlantic City radio broadcast team, who offhandedly said something like, "Gee, I guess I'll have to do the Trenton game alone on Tuesday, since Al has another assignment."

I suppose it was at that moment on a Friday night in February of 1958 that my career actually started, when I said, "Well, I'll go along."

At that level of broadcasting the pay is so small that probably if a five-year-old child had said, "I'll go along," the answer would have been the same as it was for me—"Sure!"

At any rate, that Tuesday in Trenton High School's gym I did my first broadcast, which meant keeping the score sheet for the play-by-play man, Ralph Glenn, as well as doing some color and intermission interviews and the post-game wrap-up in order to give Ralph a breather. After the game, he was pleased and I think somewhat surprised that it all came off so well, so much so that I became the third member of the broadcast team of Ralph Glenn, Al Owen, and Gene Hart. As the third man, I mainly kept the score sheet and made comments, which worked out quite well.

Eventually there was an opportunity to make a little more money by moving from WOND to WMID with their play-by-play man Jack Eisenstein. Jack was a school teacher, which is what I had been trained to be, although I hadn't done it yet, since I was still collecting bills and repossessing vehicles between broadcasting assignments. It would have been tough to live on the five dollars I got as a color man for high school basketball and football, although I was eventually raised to the princely sum of fifteen dollars for doing play-by-play.

I had the opportunity to do a lot of games over the next few years, and when Jack Eisenstein was named Superintendent of

Schools in Atlantic City, he was forced to retire from broadcasting, and I became the voice of the Atlantic City Vikings, and the Ocean City Red Raiders, and the Pleasantville Greyhounds. This meant working mainly Saturday afternoons during football season, and Tuesday and Friday nights during basketball season, with the chance to get better and develop some kind of career.

In preparing for those games, I worked very diligently, perhaps more so than most broadcasters at that level. I would drive my finance company car to the rival schools the week before the game to check line-ups, names, and numbers. This was really a necessity in order to do the job properly, because often the game programs were printed with the names in alphabetical order, which makes it impossible to spot players during the game, or the numbers would be left out, or the numbers would be there but they would be the numbers for the jerseys worn *last* week and *not* worn *this* week. There were many difficulties of that kind, but I always worked assiduously on trying to be accurate.

One time I remember driving to Bridgeton to get the background material for the upcoming game against Atlantic City, and one of my colleagues in the business said to me, "What are you making all that fuss for? People here won't know whether you're right or wrong."

That was probably when my broadcasting ethics were solidified, because I remember answering, "Yes, that's true. But *I* know whether I'm right or wrong."

From that time to the present I've always felt better knowing that if I'd done my homework accurately and with the proper discipline, it would be just that much easier to do an accurate and confident broadcast. After all, as a child I had worked meticulously to prepare for games I was only going to be *listening to* on the radio. I wasn't about to stop being diligent then, and I'm not about to stop now.

A lot of crazy situations developed in doing sports broadcasts at the high school level, as I'm sure you can imagine. I can recall doing football games while standing in the back of a pickup truck, with a microphone hung around my neck, and the line-ups in one hand and a commercial book in the other. I can also recall having to compete for air time with a very loud high school band seated directly in front of me, and then not learning until halftime that every time something exciting happened in the game, all that was heard on the air was the BOOM-BOOM-BOOM of a big bass drum.

Competing with a drum was mild, though, compared with having to compete with another human voice. At one school the broadcast booth was like a tree house that was nailed about halfway up one of the light poles, with two large bullhorns attached to either side for the public address system. It would have been bad enough if the P.A. announcer had done the normal job, such as, "Jones carried for four yards, tackle by Smith, first down." But this particular P.A. guy insisted on doing a radio-style play-by-play, so what the listener at home got was a most confusing mixture of two simultaneous play-by-plays.

Probably the nuttiest story in working at this level happened at a September football season opener at Toms River, about sixty miles north of Atlantic City. The field is a typical high school field, with concrete home stands and an open press box behind the last row, beautifully situated under a large oak tree which provided some shade.

A half-hour before the game my partner Bob Richter and I were spreading out our commercials and line-ups when we couldn't help but notice a large, dark, ominous-looking cloud approaching from our left, which we immediately read as one of those late-summer-early-fall thunderstorms. In short, we knew we were going to get blitzed. We really hadn't prepared for rain, other than having brought our jackets along, and we were sitting out in the open.

As the storm approached during the first quarter of the game, the leaves in the tree above us started to rustle, then the branches started going and the acorns started falling on our heads, and then, finally, the rain hit, and it was a torrent. Bob Richter put his jacket over the commercials, because if nothing else, they had to survive. I put my jacket over the amplifier, which was our one piece of equipment to provide the signal back to the studio. We started to get drenched, but we continued with the game.

As usual, there was no two-way communication with the studio engineer, who was sixty miles away. Once we were hooked up to the line in the press box, which was basically a one-way telephone line, we would go somewhere before the game to find a telephone and call the engineer in the studio and say, "Would you put the pot on, please," meaning the volume back in the studio. Then, if we were hooked up correctly, you could hear crowd noise and the band playing, and the engineer would know that everything was properly arranged. Then we would coordinate our watches with the engineer: "O.K., it's 1:10. We'll go on the air in fifteen minutes at 1:25."

When we got back to the broadcast position, we would give the engineer countdowns: "Five minutes to air, four minutes, three, two, one, thirty seconds, ten, nine, eight," etc., down to "one." Then we would pause for three or four seconds and during that delay the engineer would turn up the volume back in the studio, and I would say, "Hi, Gene Hart along with Bob Richter in Toms River." We had no way of knowing after that what was going on back at the studio.

So, there we were in that awful rainstorm doing the first quarter and then the second quarter and then halftime, and, of course, because of the weather we couldn't get anyone to come up and be interviewed for halftime. Bob and I just sat there with water coming out of our eyes, our ears, and even our shoes, but we did the broadcast as well as we could.

All through this I was thinking, "I don't care how bad it is. I don't care how terrible it gets. I'm being a real pro. As bad as the weather is and as bad as the game is, I'm really a pro." And the game *was* as bad as the weather, twenty-six to nothing at halftime, in fact, in favor of Toms River. I was getting clobbered and my team was getting clobbered, but I was being a real pro.

During the third quarter, and by this time the stands were about empty, I happened to notice a man in the aisle in front of me dressed in a yellow slicker like a policeman, and he appeared to be waving to me and trying to yell something, but I couldn't hear what he was yelling. So I said, "With the score twenty-six to nothing Toms River in the third quarter, we'll be right back after this commercial break."

After we broke for the commercial, I leaned out and called to the man in the slicker, "What is it? I can't hear you."

Finally I could hear the man yelling, "I'm from the local police station. Your radio station called us and said they were struck by lightning about two hours ago, and you never got on the air!"

Had I been in the business for a long time and making big money, I probably would have sat back and laughed for about twenty minutes over that true-life shaggy-dog adventure. All that work in all that rain and nobody ever heard us. I was such a hero, and more important, such a pro, and nobody even knew it. So ludicrous and so depressing, but another important lesson learned in the "glamorous" business of sports broadcasting. And remember, the most I was ever paid for a game was fifteen dollars back then, and from that I had to pay my own expenses—gas, tolls, and food, mainly—for a 120-mile round trip which had taken most of the day. I obviously didn't clear a whole lot, but I was learning my trade.

All of those inconveniences and all of those oddities were an important part of my learning process. Through it all I learned to handle my own equipment, to do my own commercials, to keep my own statistics, and to keep on telling the story, no matter what—come hell or Toms River.

In most major sports broadcasting booths today, there are five guys to help the play-by-play man, three assistants for the color man, four engineers, a producer, a director, and some other hangers-on, and I'll look at all those people and say, "Just give me the amp; I'll hook it up myself and do the game with Bob Richter."

Gradually my poise and my confidence were growing, along with the knowledge that it would take a lot to get me flustered during a broadcast. Supporting my confidence were the people close to me who would tell me, "Hey, you do a heck of a job on the radio. You do as good a job as some of those (or them) guys in Philadelphia."

I always took comments like that with a little grain of salt, realizing full well that no one was going to come up and say, "Hi, Gene. I heard you on the radio yesterday, and you were terrible!"

Anyhow, more and more I started to think, "Maybe I do have a flair for this."

While continuing to do as many sports broadcasts as I could in South Jersey, I also worked as a sports car salesman, and as the operator of an FM music station, and finally, as the teacher I had been trained to be. I was making about five thousand dollars a year as a teacher and trying to supplement that as much as possible in radio, when George Hamid, Jr., the man who ran the Steel Pier, had an idea which opened up a whole new geographic area for me.

There had been built in South Philadelphia a beautiful Marineland-type exhibit called Aquarama, complete with a whale and dolphin show, just across Broad Street from where Veterans Stadium now stands. Perhaps it was promoted poorly, or run too extravagantly, or perhaps it was just misplaced in its location all by itself near the South Philadelphia end of Broad Street. At any rate, it went into receivership, and George Hamid, showman that he was, decided to take it over and see what he could do with it.

George asked me to work at Aquarama, at first part-time, and then full-time, and I said "yes" for two reasons: First, my salary jumped from about fifty-five hundred dollars to eight thousand dollars, and second, it gave me for the first time a base in Philadelphia, rather than just in South Jersey. I felt that I had done about as much as I could do in high school sports there, and that maybe with a job in Philadelphia I would at least have a chance to become known there, too.

For the next three years, from 1965 to 1968, I worked full-time at Aquarama as assistant public relations director, show announcer for the seals, whales, and dolphins, and jack-of-all-trades, as was usually the case when you worked for George Hamid. I continued to do games in the Atlantic City area for pin money, but also filled some of the gap between there and Philadelphia by doing high school and college football and basketball for WKDN in Camden, which covered most of that part of South Jersey just across the river from Philadelphia. Two of the high school football stars in that area at the time were Franco Harris and Lydell Mitchell, who of course went on to national fame at Penn State, and later with the Pittsburgh Steelers and the Baltimore Colts respectively.

Announcing for football and basketball, and for whales and dolphins was fine, but my lifetime ambition, remember, was to be a *hockey* announcer. There was, of course, no hockey in Philadelphia, and there was none in Atlantic City, but there was a team in the early sixties in Cherry Hill, New Jersey, just outside Philadelphia, and that team was called the Jersey Larks. So, at least I could see *some* hockey, and I could still travel to New York to see the Rangers.

Then, all of a sudden, in 1966 there was a rumor afoot that the National Hockey League was going to expand. My eyeballs kind of lit up and I was more than a little interested in finding out what teams would be joining the original six: Boston, Chicago, Detroit, Montreal, Toronto, and the Rangers. Remarkably, shockingly, out of the blue came a thousand-to-one shot when an N.H.L. franchise was awarded to a Philadelphia group consisting of Jerry Wolman, Bill Putnam, and Ed Snider, after a knockout razzle-dazzle presentation at the N.H.L. expansion meeting. I was thrilled!

I had always dreamed of being involved with sports at the major-league level, and especially with the National Hockey League, but the odds on that were longer than they had been for Philadelphia to land an N.H.L. franchise. It's that old paradoxical *Catch-22* situation: Nobody wants you at the major-league level unless you have a major-league reputation, and obviously, you can't get a major-league reputation unless you work at the major-league level. Up until the birth of the Flyers, I was just a roly-poly guy who did high school sports in South Jersey and not a whole lot else. What to do?

One of the first things the Flyers organization did was to sponsor a new team at the Cherry Hill Arena called the Jersey Devils, in order to get hockey interest started in the area. I did some politicking at my station in Camden, WKDN, and before I knew it, we were doing the third periods of the Devils' home games. At playoff time we also got to go on the road to Clinton, New York. I was still working at Aquarama, so I'd take Saturday off and drive for five hours to Clinton to do the game on Saturday night. Then, immediately after the game I'd drive back, getting home at five in the morning, just in time to get ready to go to work at Aquarama.

Through the Devils job I got to know some key Flyers' people, like Keith Allen, and some key broadcasting people, like Stu Nahan, who was doing Eagles football and working on WKBS television as "Captain Philadelphia," wearing a silver jumpsuit to match his silver hair. *Despite* his silver suit, Stu appeared to be ticketed as one of the broadcast voices of the new Philadelphia Flyers.

When construction began for the Flyers' new home, the Spectrum, I was right across the street at Aquarama, watching every move. I had no connection with the Flyers at that time, other than knowing some of their personnel through working the Devils games, but I remember how often I would take some time off and walk over and sit in the growing concrete structure and try to visualize where the players' dressing rooms would be and where the press box would be. Now remember, I wasn't a twelve-year-old kid. I was thirty-five, but I still had that hunger: "If only I could get *that* job..."

The next step toward that goal was to record an audition tape to give to the Flyers. Except for a few Devils games, actually just third periods of Devils home games, I had never really *done* hockey before, but I felt that I had enough experience in other sports and a good enough voice, and more importantly, I felt that I had a better knowledge of the National Hockey League than any other broadcaster in the area.

With all of this in mind, I approached John Halligan, who was then the public relations director of my beloved New York Rangers. Through John's good graces, I was permitted to tape the second period of a Rangers-Bruins game from the Garden press box. I had originally been given permission to do a Rangers–Black Hawks game, but as that game approached, it developed that Chicago's Bobby Hull had a chance to break the record for goals in a season, so the demand for seats in the press box precluded any space for me. The Rangers-Bruins game that I *did* get to do proved to be a lot more significant for me, because the star of the two-to-one Boston victory was a young goaltender named Bernie Parent, who was helped on defense by another Bruin youngster named Joe Watson. Both were destined to become cornerstones of the Flyers of the future.

The game was remembered in New York for other reasons. Near the end of the game Bernie Geoffrion of the Rangers became incensed with referee John Ashley, as did the New York fans, who began throwing debris onto the ice. The infamously memorable part of all this was that Geoffrion was ejected from the game for shooting a couple of beer cans at Ashley. Anyhow, I did the audition tape at that game, and with all of my fingers and toes crossed, I took it back to Philadelphia and gave it to the Flyers.

WKBS (Channel 48) had signed up to do the Flyers' telecasts, with Stu Nahan as the voice, but as Philadelphia's first N.H.L. season neared, there was still no word about radio. As long as the Flyers had my tape and no radio deal, I felt that I still had a chance.

Finally I was called in by Bill Putnam, who was the president of the Flyers organization in those early years. Bill asked me if I'd like to be the P.A. announcer for the Flyers' home games. At first, I felt a little bit as though I'd won the consolation prize in a beauty contest. But on the other hand, to be involved with sports, and especially hockey, at the major-league level had been my lifelong dream. And now, suddenly, here I was in the National Hockey League, along with Parent and Watson and the rest of the people acquired by the Flyers in the expansion draft.

# First Period
## 1967 to 1972

# Faceoff
## 1967-68

The first time I, or anyone else, ever saw the Philadelphia Flyers as a team was at their first practice following the expansion draft in 1967. I remember particularly well their first skate on the new Spectrum ice. There were Parent and Watson and Doug Favell and Gary Dornhoefer, all from the Bruins team that I had seen play against the Rangers the season before, as well as Don Blackburn from the Rangers, and Lou Angotti and Ed Van Impe from the Black Hawks, and Brit Selby from the Maple Leafs, along with Coach Keith Allen and a lot of guys I didn't know much about, let alone recognize in their practice uniforms—guys like Jean Gauthier, John Miszuk, Pat Hannigan, Ed Hoekstra, and Forbes Kennedy.

The hard hats were still working on the not-yet-completed Spectrum, and I can recall their looking down from the rafters and saying things like, "You gotta be outta your mind to do something like that for a living!"

The players on the ice would then look up at the guys who were hanging by their heels putting in rivets and say, "You gotta be outta *your* mind to do something like *that* for a living!"

The regular season was to open with a three-game road trip,

the first two games of which were as far away from home as they could possibly be. In their first game the Flyers were beaten badly in Oakland by the Seals, five to one. Their second game wasn't much better, as they blew a two-to-one lead to the Kings during a four-to-two loss in Los Angeles.

Then, on Oct. 18, 1967, the Flyers won the first game in their history by beating the Blues in St. Louis. The Blues scored first and led one to nothing after the first period, but the Flyers tied it in the second period and scored again in the third to win it, two to one. As historically significant as that first victory was, perhaps even more significant was an incident that occurred near the end of the game. Ed Van Impe accidentally or semi-accidentally speared big tough Blues defenseman Noel Picard, who had to be restrained from going after Van Impe as the latter was heading for the penalty box. It was that incident during their very first meeting which sparked the animosity and the truly bitter rivalry that existed between these two teams for the next few years, and which eventually led to the building of a Flyers team that would not and *could* not be intimidated.

The next night the Flyers made their home debut in the Spectrum, which was also my debut as their P.A. announcer. Commemorative coins were given out to the seven thousand or so in attendance as a memento of the occasion. For many Philadelphians, that first Flyers home game was also the first *hockey* game they had ever seen, and as P.A. announcer I tried my best to introduce the new fans to the rules and nuances of this new game in town, ice hockey. I don't mean that I was trying to do play-by-play, like the P.A. guy who did play-by-play through the bullhorns at the high school football game. I just mean that if, for example, the Flyers iced the puck, rather than just saying "Icing," I would briefly explain what the term means. As a result, hopefully I helped a few Philadelphians become knowledgeable hockey fans a bit more quickly.

That first game in the Spectrum was typical of expansion hockey. The Pittsburgh Penguins had a total of fourteen shots and the Flyers had fifteen, one of which became the game's only goal. It was scored by Bill "Sudsy" Sutherland and it was, of course, the first goal ever scored in the Spectrum. The relatively easy shutout was credited to Doug Favell, the "other" goalie who came from Boston in the expansion draft.

So, after losing their first two games, the Flyers had won their next two, but had still scored only six goals in four games. As would so often be the case that first season, tenacious defense, gutty play, and the goaltending of Parent and Favell led the Flyers to low-scoring victory after low-scoring victory, most of those victories coming against the other five expansion teams in the new six-team Western Division of the N.H.L.

As much as I was enjoying the P.A. job, my *full-time* job was still at Aquarama, and as I was driving home from work one night I heard a radio report which really set me back. I wasn't feeling all that strong anyhow, as I was still painfully recovering from surgery for the removal of a gallstone the size of a golfball. Andy Musser, who was then the sports director of WCAU, announced on the air that WCAU had signed a contract with the Philadelphia Flyers to do their radio broadcasts, every game, home and away, including play-offs, beginning with the game on Saturday at Montreal.

I was crushed. No one had said anything to me. Obviously they had found someone else, probably some guy from Canada, or maybe Bill Campbell. I kept waiting for Andy to say, ". . . and it'll be my pleasure to do the play-by-play," but nothing more was said.

I arrived home a beaten thirty-six-year-old man, tired, still sore from the operation, and totally depressed by the thought of having missed out on the biggest opportunity of my life. My wife Sarah greeted me at the door with, "They've been trying to get ahold of you."

I said, "Who? Aquarama?"

She said, "No, Stu Nahan."

Now I would have to listen to Stu telling me something like, "Well, Gene, we signed a big contract, and we had to get Joe Canada from Ottawa because he's a pro, and we really appreciate your help, but maybe you can stay on the P.A."

So I said to my wife, and very weakly, "Oh?"

She said, "Stu's going to call you when he gets back from New York."

Stu obviously had gone to New York to work on the contract arrangements with CBS, and it was nearly midnight when he finally called: "Did you hear the news, Gene? We signed to do the games on WCAU."

"Yes, I heard."

"You don't sound very excited about it."

"Should I be?"

"Sure, you're going to do them."

You just can't imagine how I felt at that instant. Sarah was hanging on my right elbow, wondering what was being said. I put my hand over the receiver and whispered to her, "I'm a star!"

Honest to Heaven, all I could think was that after all those years, beginning with "I'll go along" back in 1957, and through the football games with the drums booming and the horns blaring and the rain pouring down along with the acorns in Toms River, and through all of the hopes and despairs while making five or ten or fifteen dollars a game, and thinking, "Why don't I just give up, because nobody's going to hire a fat guy who's only a high school announcer"—after all of those adventures and travels through the wilds of South Jersey, I had finally made it to where I had always wanted to be and had only dreamed of being. Needless to say, I didn't sleep much that night.

I wish I could say that the reason I was hired by the Flyers was that of all the hundreds of audition tapes that they listened to mine was the best, but I'm quite sure that was not the case. What the Flyers needed was a guy to back up Stu Nahan, to do the radio when Stu wasn't available at home, and to do the road radio when Stu did the television. They also needed somebody who had another job, because fifty dollars a game was not going to sustain a life. Not only that, but the other job would have to be flexible enough to coordinate with the N.H.L. schedule. And it would help if this guy knew something about hockey. Enter Gene Hart from across the street at Aquarama.

It also turned out that WCAU could not sell the radio rights to anyone that first year, so the Flyers wound up paying about seventy-five thousand dollars for their own air time. Obviously the Flyers' budget that year would not allow them to bring in some high-priced import from Canada, so for the time being, they penciled in the naive local high school sports guy from South Jersey, despite his being fat, unknown, and one of the world's worst dressers.

To sum up my good fortune, I was blessed by being in the right place at the right time when one of the great sports franchises of all time was getting started, and when there was a need for some inexpensive temporary help with a new radio deal. I didn't have a whole lot of time to think about all of this that night when I got the call from Stu. It was already early Thursday morning, and we were scheduled to leave for Montreal on Friday to do our first broadcast on Saturday.

Two days later, there I was in the Forum in Montreal—two days after the phone call, that is, and *thirty years* after I'd written in my autograph book that when I grew up I wanted to be a HOCKEY ANNONSER. We broadcast only the third periods of the games that first season, and I can remember praying throughout the pre-game and the first two periods that the team wouldn't get blown out and be embarrassed by this great and famous hockey club, the Canadiens, perhaps before we even got on the air.

Bernie Parent started in goal in his home town of Montreal, and he looked very sharp. The first goal of the game was scored by Leon Rochefort (nicknamed, naturally, "Cheesie"), who had been taken by the Flyers from Montreal in the expansion draft. Pat Hannigan scored a goal in the second period to make it two to nothing, but Montreal scored next to make it two to one, Flyers, after two periods. And that's when the Flyers and I made our first major-league broadcast: "Hi from the Forum in Montreal. It's the National Hockey League, and our debut on WCAU, with the Philadelphia Flyers and the Montreal Canadiens."

I couldn't have asked for a better period of hockey to broadcast. The Flyers had the only two goals of the period, and both were scored by the ex-Canadien Rochefort, which gave him three for the night—a hat trick. It was the first hat trick in Flyers' history, and it came about in the first Flyers' victory over one of the original six teams. And, of course, all of this happened in the Flyers' very first appearance in that most hallowed of hockey buildings, the Forum.

At first, the Montreal fans had looked upon the Flyers with disdain, almost as if they were a composite minor-league club. As the numbers on the Flyers' side of the scoreboard grew from "2-1" to "3-1" to "4-1," the reaction of the fans was one of surprise, and then amazement, and finally, appreciation. In the end, the crowd saluted the young scrappy Flyers with applause, particularly for Rochefort's hat trick and for Parent's goaltending.

My prayers had been answered. I hadn't been nervous, the game was sensational, and I was exhilarated. Before boarding the charter plane that night, I called home and asked my wife, "How was it?"

She gave me a lovely line that I'll always remember: "It was like a symphony."

The next night the Canadiens made their first appearance in the Spectrum, and as if to prove that the night before had not been a fluke, the Flyers led one to nothing until a late Montreal goal made the final score a one-to-one tie. In their first two games against hockey's most glamorous team, the Flyers had earned three out of a possible four points, but an even more important point had been made: The expansion kids could compete on the same ice with the league's greatest teams without the fear of embarrassment.

The National Hockey League has never been noted for its great executive skill or for the promotion of its own game. In fact I've often thought that one of the given proofs of the splendor of the game is that it has survived over all of these years *despite* the N.H.L. In my twenty-some years with the Flyers, the league has done only two things that I consider to be bold moves which worked out brilliantly. One was the eventual merging of two disastrously bad teams, the Cleveland Barons (formerly the Oakland Seals and the California Golden Seals) with the Minnesota North Stars, to form an infinitely improved Minnesota club.

The other bold stroke, and probably the best of its kind ever accomplished by any professional sports league, was the manner in which the N.H.L. expanded in the 1967-68 season. Unlike the other leagues, which would bring in one or two teams at a time and then let those teams flounder for years, the six-team N.H.L. had felt that it should do something exceptional, and it did. In one sweeping motion the stodgy, provincial old N.H.L. doubled the size of its league, adding six major markets across the U.S., including for the first time two on the West Coast.

Los Angeles, Oakland, Minnesota, St. Louis, and Pittsburgh all seemed to be logical choices, and all had suitable arenas of major-league size. And then there was Philadelphia, a "basketball town" with no arena suitable for hockey and no apparent interest in hockey. Somehow the Wolman-Putnam-Snider combine managed to get the Spectrum built, and then another upset occurred: The N.H.L.'s first twelve-team schedule provided a built-in handicap system which assured that the six new teams would be instantly competitive.

The six original teams remained together in the so-called "Eastern Division," while the six new teams were grouped in the "Western Division," which seemed a little silly, since Detroit and Chicago were in the East, while Pittsburgh and Philadelphia were in the West. The clever part of all this was that each club played the teams in its *own* division *ten* times (five home and five away) and played the teams in the *other* division only *four* times (two home and two away). This compromise enabled the home fans in the new cities to see all of the famous teams and famous players, while the fans in the old cities could still enjoy the old rivalries and not have to see the expansion teams too often. It also meant that the relatively impotent new clubs, without any proven goal scorers, would be competing most of the time against teams as impotent as themselves. But at least the level of competition within each division would be fairly even.

The price of an N.H.L. expansion franchise in 1967 was two million dollars, less than some individual athletes of today are paid in annual salary, and for that seemingly bargain price, no league has ever allowed better quality to be drafted by expansion teams. Of the Flyers' original draftees, five went on to have long careers in the N.H.L., those five being Parent, Favell, Dornhoefer, Watson, and Van Impe, and all but Favell were instrumental in winning the Stanley Cup seven years later. In its temporary insanity, or whatever it was back in 1967, the N.H.L. had done something right, and in a big way.

When the Flyers won that first game in Montreal, featuring "home-town boys" Parent and Rochefort, it seemed like an incredible accomplishment, and it really was, especially considering in retrospect how few games the Flyers would win there over the next several decades. Then, just one week after their Montreal debut, the Flyers made their first appearance in the Boston Garden, another building in which Philadelphia victories would be exceedingly rare.

This time Coach Keith Allen's "home-town boys" were former Bruins Parent and Watson, and appropriately, they were the difference in a surprising four-to-two win for the Flyers. Joe Watson, who would never be known for his scoring ability, took the first shot of the game and, of course, it went in. Parent was again excellent, but the Flyers' next debut would be in Toronto, and for that event the "home-town boy" would be Doug Favell. Naturally, he was magnificent in goal as the Flyers were outshot forty-five to seventeen but won two to one.

Montreal, Boston, Toronto, wherever the Flyers went, it seemed that Keith Allen's "home-town boys" would lead Philadelphia to victory. Unfortunately, Allen could not find anyone from Chicago or Detroit or New York to lead Flyers' victories in those cities, but back home at the Spectrum the Flyers did manage to defeat those three teams as well.

With at least one win in four tries against each of the original six teams, the Flyers were proving something to the novice hockey fans of Philadelphia. Somewhat tentative at first, the fans started to become more vociferous and more involved as they learned the game better. I believe the turning point came during the Flyers' first win over the New York Rangers. Some of the New York people had not been particularly kind in their references to Philadelphia as "bush league" and the like. In fact I can recall at that time being a little surprised at my own feelings of fierce loyalty for my new team, the Flyers, at the expense of my former favorites, the Rangers. At any rate, it was sometime during that first three-to-two win over the Rangers that the Philadelphia hockey fans for the first time became real *FLYERS FANS*, and a new and natural rivalry was born.

Later in that first season, Flyers fans were treated to their first big, memorable blockbuster of a weekend. The Flyers were a few games over .500 and were leading the Western Division, when not just one, but *two* of the original six clubs came to Philadelphia in the same weekend. Remember, the old guard teams came to town a combined total of only twelve times all season, so to have two of those in the same weekend was really something. Both games were sold out, and in those days that too was really something, even with the lower ticket prices ($2.00 to $5.50) and lower seating capacity (14,626) of that time. First, on Saturday night, came the Chicago Black Hawks with Stan Mikita, Jim Pappin, Bill White, and the most explosive and exciting player in the league, Bobby Hull. (And before you write me a letter about my spelling of "Black Hawks," let it be known forthwith that the "Black Hawks" did not become the "Blackhawks" until the season of 1986-87, and for what reason I have no idea!)

The voraciously hungry fans were rewarded with a third-period Flyers' rally and a game-winning goal by tough little Forbes Kennedy, and it was sheer bedlam in the Spectrum. Then on Sunday night came the Toronto Maple Leafs, who just happened to be the reigning Stanley Cup Champions, but who also happened to be a team that the Flyers seemed to "own" from the start. Three of the four times they played during that first season the Flyers won, this time four to one, with two of the goals being scored by a guy who is also the answer to the trivia question, "Who was the Flyers' first European-born player?"

The answer to the question and the scorer of the two goals was Polish-born John Miszuk, a big, slow, normally weak-shooting defenseman who typified the Flyers' defensive corps of that era. As Keith Allen used to explain, "We're so good defensively because we're so slow that none of our defensemen can get up the ice fast enough to be caught by the other team's offense." Whatever the reasons, we were all thrilled with that big weekend sweep by *our* first-place Flyers.

Besides Miszuk, Watson, and Van Impe, the Flyers "speedy" defense also included a big, lumbering, often lazy guy from Quebec named Jean Gauthier (pronounced in French, approximately, GO-chay). Whenever Keith Allen would get on him about his work habits, Gauthier would reply, "Don't worry, Coach. When de bell ring, Goach be dere."

Later in the year there was another big weekend series, this time against St. Louis and Minnesota, both of whom were pressing the Flyers for first place. On Saturday in St. Louis and on Sunday in Minnesota the Flyers won each night by one goal, and both winning goals were scored by Jean Gauthier. After the second game, I said, "Way to go, Jean."

He said, "Well, you know, when de bell ring...."

I said, "I know. Goach be dere."

Keith Allen said, "Thank God the bell finally rang."

Another trivia question from the Flyers' first year: What two N.H.L. teams played regular-season games against each other in five different buildings in the same season?

The answer: The Flyers and the Los Angeles Kings. The Forum, or as they prefer to say in Los Angeles, the "Fabulous Forum" was not completed in time for the first meeting of the two teams, and the Los Angeles Sports Arena was unavailable at that time, so the first game was played at the Long Beach Arena. The second game was in the Los Angeles Sports Arena, and finally, on Dec. 30, 1967, Jack Kent Cooke's Fabulous Forum opened with a hockey game featuring the Los Angeles Kings and the Philadelphia Flyers.

During the opening festivities, master of ceremonies Lorne Greene introduced a lovely lady who had been flown in from Canada to sing the Canadian National Anthem. Jack Kent Cooke and his Kings might have surmised that it wasn't *really* going to be their day when the lady walked out to center ice and proceeded to fall flat on her derriere. The only similar moment I can recall was at an All-Star Game in New York when Phil Esposito was introduced, and he went running out and fell on his face, but somehow it probably wasn't as embarrassing for him as that unceremonious pratfall was for the Canadian lady singer. With this good-luck omen behind them, so to speak, the Kings celebrated the opening of their fabulous new home by being shut out by Doug Favell and the Flyers, two to nothing.

Besides opening the Forum and, of course, the Spectrum, on Sunday, Feb. 18, 1968, the Flyers were the first opponents of the New York Rangers in the brand new Madison Square Garden. It was a memorable event for me, and for several reasons. First, Stu Nahan was doing a national telecast that afternoon in Chicago, so I was making my television debut. Unfortunately, whoever designed the new Garden forgot to include facilities for radio and television, so we were placed in a box near the ice with a view of the game not quite as good as what I had remembered seeing as a kid from the side-balcony of the old Garden. But *this* time when I stood up to see what was going on, I'd block the view of the television camera. I could just imagine the people back home yelling at me to sit down every time anything exciting happened.

These were the kinds of problems I thought I had left behind at the high school football games in South Jersey. But the worst was yet to come. Before long we learned that our picture and sound were out entirely, because due to a jurisdictional dispute of some kind, a very strong New York union guy had cut our cable with a hatchet. We were attempting to salvage part of the game over the telephone when Stu Nahan arrived from Chicago to say, "Welcome back to the Big Rotten Apple, Gene!" Oh, yes, I almost forgot, to add insult to injury the Rangers beat the Flyers, three to one.

I suppose the New Yorkers who had earlier called us Philadelphians "bush league" thought all of this to be very amusing. I can recall that during the ninety-mile drive home that night, *this* Philadelphian *ex*-New Yorker was *not* amused.

There are many moods one can experience on a trip back home from a road game: joy, depression, anxiety, tiredness, anticipation, even silliness. The latter may be the best way to describe what was undoubtedly our most *memorable* trip home. We were in Montreal for a Saturday night game and had to be back in Philadelphia for a Sunday night game against the Bruins, but because of a blizzard which had been raging since the day before, there was no way we could take the usual charter flight home. To the rescue came Flyer personnel director and all-around troubleshooter Marcel Pelletier, who had hired a bus for us. Since this was to be a bit longer than the average bus ride, this was no average bus. It was stocked with sandwiches and fruit and soft drinks and beer and coffee and a French-speaking driver by the name of Lucky Pierre.

Once we were out of Montreal and on the lonely two-lane highway which heads south toward the American border, the snow-covered road was so hard to find that Pierre had to guide himself by the tops of the reflector poles on either side of the roadway. I couldn't help thinking, "All we need is to get stuck out here and freeze to death."

At one point Doug Favell was standing at the front window of the bus, trying to see where we were going, when we suddenly hit a huge embankment of snow. That of course sent Favell scurrying madly in retreat to the back of the bus.

Somehow, by early Sunday morning Pierre got us through the snow to the New York Throughway, but because of the weather, it was closed. Many more miles of bad road got us to the Garden State Parkway by mid-afternoon, and by this time things were looking a little clearer and the players were looking a lot punchier. After fifteen hours or so on the bus, it was not surprising to find that Favell and a few others had started playing around with a pillow, which was nothing worth mentioning until the pillow started to come apart. It was an easy step from there to the *next* step, which was to tear the pillow completely open, thereby instantly transferring the blizzard from *outside* the bus to *inside* the bus.

You probably have never been through a blizzard of pillow feathers, as I had not previously, but the best way I can think of to describe it is this: Do you remember as a child watching the dust particles fly around in a sunbeam? Well, try to visualize a bus-sized sunbeam filled with little flying pillow-feather-sized dust particles, and you'll have a rough idea of what the inside of the Flyers' bus looked like.

Doug Favell's first reaction to this emergency situation was to seek out the teammate who was wearing Favell's famous fur coat and to lock him and the coat in the bathroom at the back of the bus, so as to minimize the coat's apparent need for a dandruff shampoo. Next, a few guys started to open the windows, but, as you can imagine, that just made the blizzard more violent. Before long Lucky Pierre was being pulled over to the side of the road by a New Jersey state trooper, who had spotted the feathers coming out of our windows, was convinced that the bus was on fire, and was about to come aboard with a fire extinguisher.

By this time, every person on the bus looked like the San Diego Chicken, and that's just the way every one of us still looked as we pulled into the Spectrum parking lot at six o'clock for the seven o'clock game against Boston. After nineteen hours on that Bus of Two Blizzards, every occupant was feeling more than a little weak, mostly from about four straight hours of hysterical laughter. And imagine what the Flyers' brass—Bill Putnam, Joe Scott, and Ed Snider—must have thought as the bus pulled into the tunnel under the Spectrum and opened its doors in an explosion of feathers, revealing their two-million-dollar investment newly uniformed in the latest thing in feathered finery.

The players giggled and laughed all the way through the process of disrobing in a sort of de-feathering, decompression-chamber room which they had to pass through so as not to contaminate their own dressing room and their *real* uniforms. Fortunately, I also had another suit of clothes to change into before going on the air, so I didn't have to resort to wearing Doug Favell's fur coat over my portly and fine-feathered form.

There was plenty of comedy that first season, and there was a good share of triumph, but there was also tragedy. Three days before the All-Star Game, a twenty-nine-year-old Minnesota North Star player named Bill Masterton was the victim of a freak accident. During a stoppage of play he slipped and fell on the back of his head. The resulting cerebral hemorrhage proved to be fatal. Despite all we hear about the roughness and violence in hockey, Bill Masterton was the only player ever to die as the result of an injury incurred during a hockey game. The night after Masterton died, the moment of silence observed at the All-Star Game seemed to last throughout the game.

Leon Rochefort was the Flyers' lone representative at the All-Star Game, but the next day he was joined in Minnesota by the rest of the team at the services for Bill Masterton. I remember how somber we all felt, certainly not realizing at the time that ten years later we would have similar feelings for one of our own, Barry Ashbee, and ten more years after that for another of our own, Pelle Lindbergh.

The next night, as fate would have it, we were to play the North Stars in Minnesota. It's not hard for me to recall what an uncomfortable feeling there was in the Met Center that night. To be on the ice for the first game following the death of a player is, obviously, a unique experience. The anthem seemed uncomfortable, the moment of silence seemed uncomfortable, and most uncomfortable of all was the Met Center P.A. announcer's customary "Let's play hockey."

Within the first half-minute of the game, Gary Dornhoefer skated down the right side and shot from the blue line. The puck went right through the legs of Minnesota goaltender Gary Bauman, and it was painfully apparent that the players were just not mentally prepared to play. The crowd's reaction was also unique, as it let out a kind of startled sound, "Unh!"—as if everyone had been simultaneously punched in the stomach. The Flyers players did not even celebrate the goal, and the P.A. announcer sounded extra-subdued as he intoned, "Flyers goal by Gary Dornhoefer." Then, with a little more emphasis he repeated his earlier phrase, "Let's...play... hockey."

With that, the crowd slowly started to applaud, and the applause grew in a steady crescendo until it became a full-fledged standing ovation. After that, both teams played a game that looked a little more like hockey, but it may have been the strangest game under the strangest circumstances I had ever seen. The North Stars managed to score two goals, but the Flyers won, four to two, as life went on without Bill Masterton.

Since that time, the Masterton Trophy has been awarded annually to the player who best exemplifies those qualities of which a player, a team, and a league can be proud. It is one of those rare awards for which every player is eligible, whatever his level of ability, and it is one of those rare awards for which even a nomination is a source of great pride.

As strange as the circumstances had been in Minnesota, the Flyers completed their first season under a set of circumstances even more bizarre: With fourteen games left on their schedule, and with the Flyers closing in on their first division title, *the roof blew off the Spectrum*! That's right, *the roof blew off the Spectrum*! Or at least that's what Philadelphians were told by their newspapers and by their city officials.

When the Spectrum had been designed and constructed, it was nicknamed the "Tuna Can," and indeed that's what it looked like in those days before the concessions stands were built into the outside walls. The flat roof was recessed below the level of the "Can's" outside walls and therefore could not be seen from anywhere outside the building. Like most flat roofs, this one had a kind of tar-paper covering in order to waterproof the metal roof which was directly beneath the tar-paper surface. In a severe storm, some of the tar-paper covering had been lifted by the wind to expose a small hole, a small hole in the waterproofing, that is, not in any structural part of the roof.

If the Flyers had been an established team at that time, like the

Flyers of a few years later or the Flyers of today, the Spectrum roof would never have been an issue. If the same thing had happened at the Garden in New York, or at the Spectrum a few years later, the mayor would have had a platoon of policemen or city workers lay their bodies across the hole in order to prevent any further problem. He may even have had them *repair* the hole. But no, the official word was that the building was dangerous and even life-threatening, and the Flyers, who were not drawing spectacularly well and were therefore not yet a political force in town, could do nothing about it.

As a result of this minor roofing problem (but major political problem), the Flyers were kept out of the Spectrum for the entire month of March. In other words, the Flyers were forced by their own city to play their final fourteen games on the road. And no one knows better than a hockey fan that there is no sport in which the home advantage is more important than in hockey.

The next Flyers game after the roof story broke was in Madison Square Garden on a Saturday afternoon. Following a depressing four-to-nothing Rangers' victory, it was announced that the city of Philadelphia had closed the Spectrum because it was a "structural danger." The next night the Flyers were scheduled to play at home against Oakland. That, of course, would be impossible. But in one of the oddest arrangements ever made in the N.H.L., the Rangers offered the use of the Garden for the following afternoon, and since the Flyers and the Seals were already there, the offer was accepted.

It was too late to print and sell tickets, so the Flyers were in the unenviable position of having to play a "home" game without any ticket sales. In order to attract some people to the game, the Rangers announced that anyone holding a ticket for their game Sunday night would be admitted free to the Flyers-Seals game that afternoon. Despite the fact that it was a game between two "foreign" expansion teams, about eleven thousand New Yorkers showed up for the first half of that most unusual day-night double-header. The Flyers first road "home" game ended in a one-to-one tie, with the tying goal scored for Oakland in the third period by Larry "Hank" Cahan, a former Ranger—much to the delight of the "home" crowd.

Next on the schedule was a game in Toronto, to be followed by a home game against Boston. In similar fashion to the two games just completed in New York, both of these next two games were played in Maple Leaf Gardens. By this time the homeless Flyers were hardly scoring at all, and in an aggravating two-to-one loss to the Bruins the frustration of the situation surfaced in the ugliest possible manner.

What stands out most clearly in my mind was the famous, or I should say "infamous," stick-swinging duel between Eddie "The Entertainer" Shack of the Bruins and Larry "The Rock" Zeidel of the Flyers. I can still see Shack with the stick in his hands and Zeidel with the stick in his, and the blood pouring down the foreheads of both, and I can still recall that awful queasy feeling in the pit of my stomach. Probably the only stick fight that was ever as bad (or worse) was the one later on between Ted Green of the Bruins and Wayne Maki of the minor-league Buffalo Bisons. It's unfortunate that Larry Zeidel is remembered more for that one ugly incident than for anything else, because he was worth remembering for so much more. And, in fact, I will tell you more about him later.

With frustration increasing among the nomadic Philadelphia "Gypsies," a temporary home was finally found. The Flyers had held their pre-season training camp in Quebec, which was also the home of their farm team, the Quebec Aces. Le Colisée, now the home of the Quebec Nordiques, had never hosted N.H.L. hockey before, and the time seemed right for the Flyers to give the fans of Quebec a sampling of big-league hockey. The time was certainly right for the Flyers to settle down *somewhere*.

The Flyers' home debut in Le Colisée was a successful one, as they scored twice in the third period to defeat Minnesota, two to nothing. Our television and radio debut from there was another matter. As we had experienced earlier in the new Madison Square Garden, there were *no* television facilities in Le Colisée. We worked in a bucket suspended from one of the columns at the side of the building and dreamed of some day being back in the Spectrum.

Before that first game, I was about to call the engineer back at WCAU when I discovered that our broadcast position had neither a telephone nor anyone nearby who could speak English. We finally found a telephone in the main concourse and worked out a system whereby Marcel Pelletier would call WCAU and then wigwag a signal to one of our scouts who would be standing near an entrance portal. The scout would then wigwag the signal to our traveling secretary Joe Kadlec, who would be somewhere inside the arena where he could see both the scout and me. Joe would then wigwag the signal to me, and after all of that, I would say, "Hi! From Le Colisée in

Quebec this is Gene Hart," and hopefully I got to say that before the folks back home started to search elsewhere on the dial.

All of that wigwagging reminded me of something I had learned from one of the league's senior officials, referee John Ashley, the same referee who had also served as a target for the beer cans shot by Bernie Geoffrion of the Rangers. The lesson was "to get your signals straight," especially if they were signals given by John Ashley. Unfortunately, Ashley's signals did not resemble anyone else's signals. In fact Ashley's signals looked rather like something a man might do if he had a cocktail shaker in each hand and was suddenly overcome by some sort of seizure.

The first time I witnessed this performance, I was doing P.A. at the Spectrum. Ashley came skating over doing shuffling motions with his hands to what appeared to be a Cuban rhythm and said, "Number two."

As he skated away, I didn't have the foggiest notion of what he had called. So, I blew the buzzer to get him to come back over, and I asked him, "What was that call?"

He said, "Well, you ought to be able to figure that out, and if you're around long enough, you will."

I looked at the official scorer and said, "Let's call it high-sticking."

Then, over the P.A. I announced, "Two-minute penalty to number two, Ed Van Impe of the Flyers for . . ." and then with some trepidation, "high-sticking."

John Ashley looked over at me and smiled, and I felt as though I had *really* arrived in the big league. Anyhow, as long as a player serves his penalty, does it really matter what it was for?

All of those wigwag signals in Le Colisée did the trick, because unlike that time in Toms River, we actually did get on the air. Since that time, the building has been expanded from a capacity of about eleven thousand to a capacity of about sixteen thousand, and they have even installed facilities for radio and television!

Our second home game in Quebec was the fifth part of the answer to that trivia question about the two N.H.L. teams that played regular-season games against each other in five different buildings in the same season. The Los Angeles Kings' goalie that night was Hall-of-Famer Terry Sawchuk, who the season before had led the underdog Maple Leafs to the Stanley Cup. Sawchuk had only two shutouts left in him at that point, and his next-to-last one came that night against the Flyers. Fortunately for the Flyers, *their* Hall-of-

Famer-to-be, Bernie Parent, also recorded a shutout, and that masterful double-shutout was one of the season's most memorable events.

The crowds in Le Colisée had been very good, but for the *next* game the place was packed to the rafters. The opponent was Toronto, the automatic natural and mortal enemy of anyone born in La Belle Province, Quebec. The Flyers not only had the so-called "home" crowd on *their* side, they had a crowd which had grown up *hating* the *other* side. And as league champions, the Maple Leafs were easier to hate than ever. Floyd Smith had a hat trick for Toronto, but with the score tied at four in the third period, "hometown boy" André Lacroix, a former Quebec Ace, scored the winning goal for the Flyers, and Le Colisée was suddenly in danger of structural damage far worse than the Spectrum had suffered.

In their final two Quebec home games, the Flyers shut out St. Louis, two to nothing, and were shut out by Pittsburgh by the same score, making their total home-away-from-home record: three wins, two losses, and two ties. That may not sound terribly impressive, but it was good enough to clinch the Western Division title, and finally, after one whole month away from their *real* home, the Flyers flew back to Philadelphia and were welcomed as champions.

The Flyers *were* champions, but they looked more like survivors of the war returning from overseas. They were obviously suffering from battle fatigue after their harrowing march through the month of March, and as they opened their first-ever playoff series under the newly repaired Spectrum roof, their lassitude was apparent, particularly on offense.

The Flyers were shut out by the Blues in Game One, but rallied to win Game Two. In St. Louis the Blues won two more, one of them in overtime, but the Flyers came back to win Game Five in Philadelphia, six to one, with a hat trick by Rosaire Paiement. The Blues led, three games to two, as the series moved back to St. Louis for a most remarkable sixth game.

The Blues scored early in Game Six and then played defense in front of goaltender Glenn Hall. The one-to-nothing lead held up through the first period, and then through the second period, and then through most of the third period. It appeared that the season was over for the Flyers when a bespectacled defenseman named Algernon "Al" Arbour shot for the empty net, which had just been vacated by Bernie Parent with about thirty seconds to play. But the puck hit the post.

With fifteen seconds left, the Flyers came to center ice and dumped the puck behind the St. Louis goal, where Arbour was waiting. This time Arbour whipped the puck around the boards to clear it out of the zone, but the tip of Ed Van Impe's skate stopped it at the blue line. Van Impe then shot toward the goal where Glenn Hall made the save by kicking the puck out to André Lacroix, who put the rebound into the net with just four seconds left. While the Flyers celebrated crazily around him, Glenn Hall remained motionless on his knees for at least a full minute, like a still photograph superimposed on an action movie—the kind of image that's difficult to forget.

It was hot in the un-air-conditioned St. Louis Arena, and as the game stretched into overtime the players became more and more tired, while the fans became more and more restless. One full overtime period produced nothing of consequence, and the game groaned into a second overtime. By this time, fans and players alike were feeling faint, and the shifts on the ice were becoming shorter and shorter. Finally, to get a line change, Don Blackburn of the Flyers flipped the puck in the air from center ice toward the St. Louis end, and then dragged himself over the boards and sat down. Blackburn may or may not have seen with his own eyes that the puck skipped off the ice and deflected off a defenseman and into the net.

After five games and a five-period sixth game, I didn't think there was any way in the world that the Blues could win a seventh game in Philadelphia. But they did, three to one.

And perhaps that was best for the league, which had been severely criticized for guaranteeing not only that an expansion team would win a division title, but also that an expansion team would go all the way to the Stanley Cup Finals. The Blues went on to beat Minnesota in an excellent seven-game semifinal series, with the key game this time a double-overtime *win* for St. Louis. In the finals the Blues were swept by Montreal, but all four games were competitive and interesting one-goal games, one of which went into overtime.

The Conn Smythe Trophy, for the most valuable player in the playoffs, was awarded to a richly deserving Glenn Hall, who became only the second member of a losing team ever to win that award. Some people remember Glenn Hall only as the old goalie whom the Flyers beat in Game Six, or as the old goalie whose nerves were so shot that he became physically ill before every game; I prefer to remember Glenn Hall as the gallant winner of the Conn Smythe Trophy in 1968.

An expansion team did not win the Cup, at least not in the *first* year of expansion, but several new N.H.L. teams certainly did themselves proud, and one of those new teams was the Philadelphia Flyers, Champions of the West.

J *ersey Devils' Advocate*: "Gene, you hinted, and rather broadly I thought, that the Flyers might have gone to the Stanley Cup Finals in their first season if they had not been unfairly forced to become the only semi-permanent-floating-gypsy hockey team in N.H.L. history. Well then, why didn't you and they just hop back across the river to the Cherry Hill Arena where you came from?"

Glad you asked that question, J.D.A., because the old Cherry Hill Arena was one of my favorite places. For a major-league team? I'm afraid not. But that's what made it interesting. And you thought the Spectrum had problems!

When it was first built ("constructed" would be too fancy a word), it was called the Delaware Valley Gardens. (Why are so many hockey buildings called "Gardens"? And the others aren't even in the Garden State.) Next it received the chilling name the Ice House. Through most of its "glory days" ("gory days" would be more appropriate) it was the Cherry Hill Arena, and later the Centrum, before it was ultimately picked up and moved to North Jersey, thus ending the South Jersey hockey era. I don't know what it's called in *North* Jersey—probably the Garden State Gardens.

The *South* Jersey site was about ten minutes away from, and not to be confused with, the Flyers' current training facility, the Coliseum, which is also in South Jersey. Both places were (and the latter still is) about twenty minutes from downtown Philadelphia. The Coliseum was *not* built for spectators, its capacity being the number of people who don't mind standing and freezing in a viewing area about the size of the average family room; it's also possible to *sit* and freeze on a few feet of splintery bleachers, but if you do that, you can't see the ice. Gordie Howe once described the Coliseum as the coldest place he'd ever been in his life, and I would imagine that includes quite a few places.

The Delaware Valley Gardens/Ice House/Cherry Hill Arena/ Centrum *was* built for spectators, but if you were ever a spectator there, you probably wouldn't have thought so. The first team they were able to lure into playing its games there was the Jersey Larks of the Eastern Hockey League in about 1963. They survived only one season, or just long enough to upset their cross-river rivals, the Philadelphia Ramblers, in the playoffs. The Ramblers' home, by the way, was a dingy little building at 45th and Market called the Philadelphia Arena. No "Gardens" there!

One graduate of the Jersey Larks is the popular traveling secretary of the Phillies, Eddie Ferenz. To this day one of Eddie's favorite ploys at check-paying time in a restaurant is to reach into his seemingly otherwise empty wallet and pull out the last check he received from the Jersey Larks.

There was no more hockey at the Cherry Hill Arena until the Flyers initiated the Jersey Devils for the 1966-67 season. Not only were the Larks defunct, but also the Ramblers, and the Flyers were determined to arouse at least *some* interest in hockey in the Philadelphia area. As it turned out, it's probably just as well that not too many prospective Flyers fans came to see the Devils, because if they had, they may have been frightened away forever.

The Devils' uniforms were rather nice, red and black with a devil's head on the jersey (so *that's* where their name came from!), but the playing surface was something else. The ice was so bumpy that it was impossible to shoot from the point (particularly the right point, for some reason) without having the puck land in the seats. There was no glass to protect the spectators, only chicken wire with some holes larger than others, and the holes were, of course, largest where the hardest shots would go. The Devils' defensemen would try to check their opponents into the worst parts of the wire and then skate away leaving them impaled on the ragged metal. It was tough for the referee to detect this kind of deviltry, partly because the lighting was so bad. Despite the conditions, sometimes as many as three or four thousand souls would turn out on a Friday or Saturday night to see an Eastern Hockey League game.

Many of those in attendance had probably seen the movie *Slap Shot* and wanted to see for themselves if such characters really existed. When they came to see the Devils play the Johnstown Jets or the Clinton Comets or the Long Island Ducks, they found out more than they probably wanted to know.

The Eastern League was what is known as a "homer's league." An example of what that means: On Friday night the Devils play the Ducks on Long Island (at the Commack Arena) and are called for nineteen penalties while the Ducks are called for five, and the Ducks win, ten to one; on Saturday night the Ducks come to Cherry Hill and are called for eighteen penalties while the Devils are called for four, and the Devils win, eight to two. You figure it out. It was not only next-to-impossible to win on the road, it was next-to-impossible to lose at home.

Some of the infamously legendary "bad guys" of that league were Blake Ball, Don Perry (later an N.H.L. coach), and the white-haired (even then) John Brophy (later also an N.H.L. coach, now back in the minor leagues). With these guys as competition, Attila the Hun would have won the Lady Byng Trophy. They amassed penalty minutes far beyond Dave Schultz's worst nightmares. But they were gate attractions. One week Brophy would be suspended for life; the next week his suspension would be suspended, but Brophy would not be allowed to play any more Monday afternoon games in Clinton. It was a frightening league in which to be a low-paid official. I wouldn't have done it!

One sample: Jersey Devil and Flyer-to-be Rosaire Paiement was playing in his first professional game, a Devils-Ducks exhibition game before the 1966 season. The puck was dropped to open the game, it went into the corner, and Rosie went after it, only to be cross-checked in the back of the neck by Brophy, as if to say, "Hey, kid, my name is Brophy." Brophy was more formally introduced to Paiement when Rosie turned around and hit him about eight times before Brophy knew a fight was on. The resulting brawl was one of the classics of all time. Forty minutes later, and after reading off penalties for about another six minutes, the P.A. announcer finished with, ". . . and the time: six seconds."

At the other end of the Devils games I can recall the same P.A. guy saying, "Don't forget: Join your favorite players after the game across the street at the Beef 'n' Beer House." Somewhat different from the announcements I was used to making about driving home safely!

The last time I can recall seeing John Brophy as a player was in the fifth and deciding game of a Devils-Ducks playoff series at the Cherry Hill Arena. The Ducks won it in overtime, and as the two teams were shaking hands, the "BOOO's" were cascading down on the Ducks, especially the feared and detested Brophy. Showman that he was, after everyone else had left the ice, John just stood at center ice, smiling serenely and blowing kisses to the entourage. This enraged the crowd to the point of hurling whatever could be found: paper cups, programs, beer cans, even an old man's cane. The more the debris piled up around him, the more kisses John would blow, until finally, like a classic Shakespearean leading man, John was on his knees, while still continuing to blow the most elaborate and affectionate kisses. How long he and the crowd would have kept this up I don't know, probably until the fans could find nothing else to throw. And maybe that's why the last object I can recall skidding across the ice toward Brophy was a toilet seat. When he saw it, John just smiled approvingly and slowly bowed his way off-stage.

While John Brophy's reputation may have been the worst in the league, I think the foulest mouth belonged to a Devils' goaltender whose name I'd better not mention, but it's a name you probably wouldn't recognize anyhow. This guy had to rank number one, or at the lowest two, among the most foulmouthed people ever on the face of the earth. Every other word out of his mouth was an expletive. In fact it may have been because of this guy that the phrase "expletive deleted" was created. If you want to know what this guy looked like, just get out a dictionary, because next to "foulmouth" they show this guy's picture.

Unfortunately, the goaltender in question played in the days before masks were commonplace, so every time a goal was scored against him, it was possible to watch him lip-synch his vile vilification against the opponents, or the officials, or the gods, or the fans, or even his own teammates. One night in Johnstown he was giving it to the fans, and unpopular as he was, the fans were giving it right back to him. As he was skating off after the game, a couple of middle-aged women were taunting him a bit, and he decided to tell them a thing or two or twelve. He skated as close to them as he could and then unloosed upon them a stream of the most obscenely vitriolic filth ever detected by human eardrums.

When goalie and teammates were finally in the dressing room, reports came in that the women had filed a complaint and that the Johnstown police were on their way to arrest the offender. For fear of lynch-mob justice, or for whatever reason, it was quickly decided to spirit the goalie out of the building. So, without waiting for him to change, the goalie was passed through a window into a side alley, where he was then stuffed unceremoniously, but still in full goaltending regalia, into the trunk of Stu Nahan's Cadillac.

Safely out of Johnstown on the Pennsylvania Turnpike, Stu felt it was time to let the goalie get out of the trunk, breathe some fresh air, and maybe even take his skates and pads off. Of course, as soon as he had climbed out of the trunk, who should pull up behind him but a Pennsylvania state trooper. Would justice prevail after all?

And would Stu be arrested for smuggling a felon out of town? Would we all rot in a Johnstown jail?

The trooper looked at the fully-garbed Devils' goaltender standing on the shoulder of the Pennsylvania Turnpike at 12:30 A.M., and fortunately, instead of speaking to our foulmouthed friend, he said to Stu, "What seems to be the problem here, sir?"

Stu explained that the team's goaltender had been injured during their game that night and that rather than wait for the team bus after the game, they had decided to drive him to a hospital in Philadelphia as soon as possible. With that, Stu pushed the goalie into the back seat of the Cadillac and drove off, fortunately before the trooper could hear the goalie's side of the story.

Some of the best Devils eventually became Flyers, including Rosie Paiement and my eventual broadcasting partner, goaltender Bob Taylor. (Before I go any further, let me make one thing perfectly clear: the goaltender in the previous story was *not*, I repeat, *NOT* Bob Taylor.) As the Flyers became stronger, the Devils became weaker and weaker. In their last season they were even more dreadful than the Ranger teams of my youth. I remember a game from that season against a new and equally dreadful team called the Syracuse Blazers. It was, I believe, the ultimate Cherry Hill Arena hockey experience.

The Blazers were traveling down from Syracuse in three cars, but one of the cars had broken down on the way, so, in a league that dressed only thirteen players, three of those were missing. After the first five minutes of the game, the score was seven to five, and you can visualize the mouth of the Devils' goaltender. On second thought, you'd better not.

After countless fights, brawls, and foulmouthing, Syracuse was down to only six players, since two had been ejected and two more were sitting in the penalty box. With one minute left and trailing by sixteen to fifteen, the Blazers couldn't pull the goalie since there was no one left on the bench. The rules state that to prevent a "travesty," the goaltender is not permitted to cross the center-ice red line, but since there was already a travesty taking place, the Blazers' goalie was trying for the tying goal along with everyone else. Shot after shot, including a few by the goaltender, were just wide, or would hit the post, or would be turned aside by the foulness spewing forth from the Devils' goal mouth, until finally, mercifully, the horn sounded, ending the game. The Blazers' valiant effort had fallen short by one goal, sixteen to fifteen.

That night I couldn't wait to get into the Flyers' dressing room to tell about this game of games I had just seen that afternoon. The first guy there was Pat Hannigan, so I gave him the entire story in thrilling full-color detail. His deadpan reaction: "Gee, you score fifteen on the road, you oughtta get a point."

For any who may have *missed* the point, in hockey you get two points for a win and one for a tie, and on the road, particularly in the Eastern League, one point is considered a just reward for a good effort. Unfortunately for the Devils, there were not enough undermanned dreadful teams like Syracuse for them to get points against, and the Cherry Hill Arena became vacant once more.

A team called the Jersey Aces made an abortive attempt to get started there, but they are remembered, if at all, only by their opening night, when the Zamboni machine came out to resurface the ice, but succeeded only in smearing the blue and red lines into large and lovely psychedelic patterns.

The last time hockey came to the Cherry Hill Arena, the building had been renamed the Centrum. The team that played there was called the Jersey Knights, but anyone who cared knew that they, too, had been renamed. The plain blue sweatshirt with the plain white "K" ironed on it (or was it three pieces of adhesive tape in the shape of a "K"?) could not hide the fact that underneath was one of the last surviving members of a World Hockey Association franchise which had given up trying to make it in New York as the "Golden Blades."

It's difficult to conceive now, but among the opponents who came to the woebegone Centrum to play the woebegone Jersey Knights were W.H.A. teams like the Quebec Nordiques and the Edmonton Oilers, with stars like J.C. Tremblay and Bobby Hull. I recall one occasion when the Nordiques were advised to change for the game in their hotel, because the pipes had burst in the Centrum's locker rooms. The players were then transported in an old school bus to the Centrum parking lot, where they had to wait until wooden boards were put down on top of the ankle-deep mud, so that they could walk in their stocking feet to a dark corridor where their skates could be laced on. Once inside, they found more happy news: the Zamboni had broken down, so that the only way to smooth the ice was by hand with shovels and wet towels.

Playing on a surface which looked like a snow-covered vegetable garden didn't seem to appeal to the multi-million-dollar Flying Frenchmen of the Quebec Nordiques, and they lost to the Knights in a miserable display of un-hockey. After the game I looked for Jean-Guy Gendron, a former Flyer who was then with the Nordiques. I felt a little intimidated peering into that school bus full of French hockey stars, but luckily, there in the first seat was Jean-Guy, always a true French-Canadian gentleman. After sharing the usual polite greetings, I asked him how everything was going. Sitting there in that cold school bus, holding his skates on the lap of his cold sweaty uniform, and with cold mud caked on his stockings, Jean-Guy answered in a weary, but dignified way, "Gene, I been een dees game twenty year, and dees league take de cake."

That was the end of hockey in that building, and "Good riddance," you might say. But there were a lot of memories attached to that place for me, and it's a little sad for me to drive by there now and see only a shopping center.

At any rate, Jersey Devils' Advocate, I hope that answers your question as to why the Flyers and I made our home-away-from-home in Quebec, instead of in Cherry Hill.


W e've covered the significant events of the Flyers' first season, as well as the most significant places. Now I'd like to tell you about some of the most significant and memorable characters, and the Flyers have always been a team of character *and characters*. There was, for example, the team's first captain and leading scorer (with a grand total of forty-nine points), Lou Angotti, one of the league's rare Italian players—not a bad idea for a team based in South Philadelphia. But let's start with the man who was most responsible for shaping the image of the Flyers in the minds of Philadelphia's new hockey fans.

He bridged the Delaware River–sized gap between the minor-league Devils and the major-league Flyers in a single bound. He was the wild-mannered first television voice of the Flyers, and their first "star" character. He was not bored. He was not plain. He was Captain Philadelphia, also known as

# The Silver Fox

When I first met Stu Nahan, he held some sort of front office title, vice president perhaps, with the Jersey Devils. (Now wait, a vice president isn't necessarily in charge of vice!) He would sit in the stands at the Cherry Hill Arena along with Keith Allen, Bud Poile, and whatever scouts and other Flyers' personnel were there.

Stu was always quite outspoken and ready to criticize the officials, a trait he later carried with him to Flyer telecasts. The only time I ever saw him close to being speechless was one night when he was harassing the referee from about the eighth row at a Devils game and the ref turned around, pointed, and called a minor penalty on Stu, who just stared back in disbelief. Stu eventually recovered his senses enough to approach the bench and argue his case, but since he officially represented the team, the penalty stood. Stu did not have to sit in the penalty box, but he still holds the record, I believe, for being the only broadcaster in the history of hockey to be penalized for "too much mouth."

Stu was (and still is) a fun-loving extrovert and the most popular guy I've ever known in the business. He was also the only guy I've ever known in the business who had *no* enemies. Maybe the best way to describe Stu's personality is this: He's the only guy I know who could pinch the Queen of England in the rear and she would turn around and say, "Stu, you old son of a gun, how are you?"

Stu smoked big cigars that came in fancy silver tubes. The bands on the cigars read: "Made especially for Stu Nahan." I had always wanted one of those fancy cigars, so one day Stu gave me a tube. It was empty.

Stu got along wonderfully not only with his co-workers, but with the players and owners as well. In fact, I can recall only one time when Stu had a dispute with *anyone*, other than a hockey referee. Frank Dolson, the sports editor of the *Philadelphia Inquirer*, had been giving the Flyers and their management a hard time about the Spectrum roof, the road-circus atmosphere, and the general ineptness of the organization. So, after the famous double-overtime win in St. Louis, Stu said on the air, "I hope *that* game sticks in the craw of Frank Dolson and that fish wrapper he writes for."

When Stu and the team landed back in Philadelphia the next day, Dolson was at the airport to check on what exactly Stu had said. That gave Stu the opportunity to tell him face-to-face, "I said, 'I hope *that* stuck in your craw and that fish wrapper you write for.' " In the next day's *Inquirer*, you can be sure that Dolson got in the last blistering word(s).

Even after Stu moved to Los Angeles to be a television news anchor, he still commuted on the "Red Eye," or by dog sled, or by whatever means possible, to do the Flyers and the Eagles games. As an example, for that game in Montreal when the blizzard struck, Stu flew from Los Angeles to Chicago, then from Chicago to Detroit, and then from Detroit to Toronto, where he rented a car to drive the rest of the way through the snow to Montreal. Twenty minutes before game time I was certain that I was going to be making my television debut that night, but fifteen minutes before game time in walked Stu, fresh as a morning daisy after a mere twenty-hour commute.

The next day, while all the rest of us were enduring that insane bus trip home, Stu was somehow getting himself to New Orleans to do the Eagles-Saints game on CBS. He must have been tired by then, because at the end of the first quarter he delivered a line that he has never been allowed to forget: "That's the end of the first period from New Orleans, with the score Eagles seven, Flyers nothing."

Another time I thought I would be making my television debut was when Stu showed up with the fattest lip I had ever seen, complete with stitches and purple discoloration. It seems that he had volunteered to do a practice stint as a goaltender with the Kings, and he had stopped the first shot (by former Flyer Brent Hughes) with his mouth. We politely suggested that he might look better doing radio that night, but he would have none of that, so he went on television looking like a commercial for Blue Cross and Blue Shield.

In Los Angeles Stu had the opportunity to appear in some Hollywood films. I recall one in which he played the part of a television interviewer and fight announcer. After he finished that picture, Stu was so sure that it would be a bomb that he insisted upon having his name removed from the credits. He couldn't legally have his scenes removed, but having his good name cleared was the next-best thing. That picture was, of course, *Rocky*, and I believe Stu's name *does* appear in the credits of *Rocky II*, *Rocky III*, etc.

When Stu and I last worked together, he did the play-by-play and I did the color on Channel 48. In retrospect, I think that we probably would have been a better team if our roles had been reversed. But he was definitely the star, and the star always did the play-by-play. I'll be forever grateful to Stu no matter what I'm doing and no matter what he's doing, because without him I might still be doing high school football and basketball in South Jersey.

Every time the Flyers play in Los Angeles, I like to call Stu and see how Captain Pismo Beach is doing, and maybe ask him if he has any personalized cigars left.

Naturally, this one's for you,

# Bud

E. Norman "Bud" Poile (rhymes with "boil") was the Flyers' first general manager as well as being the team's first real hard-noser. He was straight, he was severe, and he took his hockey very, very seriously. He had played for five of the six original N.H.L. teams, all but Montreal in fact, and later, as an executive, he had led minor-league clubs to seven titles and seventeen playoff appearances in nineteen years. When he came to Philadelphia from the Seattle Totems of the Western League, he was prepared to take a first-year expansion team to a division title, and anyone who tried to stand in his way had better be prepared to be run over.

One of the players acquired by Poile in the expansion draft was (and is) the answer to another trivia question: Who was the first American-born player to be signed by the Flyers? He was from the state of Washington and his name was Wayne Hicks. He had been a good scorer in the minor leagues at Quebec, but after he produced only two goals in a half-season for the Flyers, Bud Poile traded him to Pittsburgh for a player named Art Stratton, who didn't do much better. Later, when asked his assessment of the Hicks-Stratton deal, Poile answered with acerbity, "That was a trade that hurt both teams."

Poile was a severe critic not only of hockey players, but also of hockey broadcasters. Late in that first season I was doing radio from the Forum in Los Angeles, when during a stoppage of play a huge roar arose from the crowd. To explain what all the commotion was about I said on the air, "The reason for all the yelling in the background is that they've just posted on the Forum scoreboard that UCLA has beaten North Carolina for the NCAA Championship."

At the end of the period, I was handed a note which read, "You are doing a hockey game, not a basketball game. Bud Poile"

When I got back to our hotel that night, Bud called me on the phone to say, "You were doing a hockey game tonight, not a basketball game."

When we got back to Philadelphia, Bud made sure to tell me, "Now remember: You were out there to do a hockey game, not a basketball game."

I said, "Well, the only reason I mentioned it was because of all the cheering."

Bud said, "Tell them the reason they were cheering was that the game was so good. The *hockey* game, not the basketball game."

I was not the only broadcaster to be critiqued by Bud Poile. There was a game in the Spectrum during which the Blues were pounding on the Flyers as only the Blues could do. Bud was so upset and so hot under the collar that he took a little walk away from his seat in the press box to cool down. Before long he was walking behind the Blues' broadcast position, where Dan Kelly and Gus Kyle (one of Bud's former on-ice opponents) were describing the action for the St. Louis television audience. Bud, naturally, could not help overhearing, and soon he was pacing back and forth, muttering, "Tell the truth for Chrissake."

As the muttering continued, and as it increased in volume, Gus Kyle began to look around to see who was making all the noise. When he saw Gus looking at him, Bud said, "You were a lousy player and now you're a lousy commentator," or words to that effect. From that point on, it was up to Dan Kelly not only to fill *all* of the air time, but also to restrain his partner from coming after the general manager of the Flyers. As Gus was being held by the sleeve, the collar, the tie, and whatever else Dan could grab onto while still continuing to do the game, Bud made sure to get in one last line: "I'm an old man, but I'm not afraid of *you*. You were afraid to fight when you played, and you're certainly not going to fight me now!"

Bud Poile was not a diplomat, and he refused to compromise. After two and a half seasons, the man he had brought with him from Seattle, Keith Allen, was moved up from coach to general manager, while Bud Poile took over the minor-league Vancouver Canucks and led them not only to a title, but into the N.H.L. I still think of Bud every time we play the Canucks, or for that matter, the Capitals, because it was Washington's general manager, Bud's son David, who built the Caps into a contender.


**I**n Philadelphia we have a Merry Christmas; in Quebec they have a Joyeux

# Noel

Whenever the Flyers were pounded on by the Blues during those early years, the principal pounder was another hard-noser, Noel Picard, the first true villain in Flyers history. There soon would be other villains to wear the St. Louis (black and) blue note, most notably the Plager brothers, but Noel Picard was the first, and probably the worst. Ever since that incident with Ed Van Impe in the first-ever meeting between the two teams, Noel Picard was the guy Philadelphia fans loved to hate. Even more than Howard Cosell.

It was during a Flyers-Blues game later that first season in Philadelphia that Picard instigated what was probably the ugliest event, other than a stick fight, that I've ever witnessed in a hockey game. From behind, Picard poleaxed and brutalized a little Flyer center named Claude "Pepsi" LaForge, who then lay face down, unconscious in an ever-widening pool of his own blood, while Picard and the rest of the Blues took on the entire Flyers' roster, and quite successfully. It wasn't until about twenty minutes after the game that the two coaches, Lynn Patrick and Keith Allen, were able to entice their respective teams into the dressing rooms.

During their first few seasons, the Flyers' best offensive players were peace-loving French Canadians like Claude LaForge, Jean-Guy Gendron, André Lacroix, and Simon Nolet, all of whom could be intimidated by the un-peace-loving French Canadian "enforcer," Noel Picard. Even the fans in the lower sections of the Spectrum had to be on the alert, because occasionally Picard or the Plagers were known to take their form of "justice" right into the stands. For years, whenever the Blues came to town, a special wooden canopy was placed over the tunnelway leading to the Blues' dressing room to protect Picard and his teammates from the revenge-minded fans, and to protect the fans from the villainous Blues.

After six seasons as the Blues' chief "policeman," Picard retired to the broadcast booth to do color for Dan Kelly. One of Noel's first interviews was with Simon Nolet, formerly one of his Flyer poundees. Neither was noted for his articulation of English, and the interview went something like this:

"Seemone Nolay, een de early eestree of de Flyer an de Blue, dere be many fight. How come?"

"You ought to know, Peecard. You start dem all."

Another time, I happened to catch a Blues' radio broadcast when we were in Chicago. Dan Kelly was trying to get Noel to say something significant about an upcoming St. Louis road trip: "Noel, suppose you tell us about the Blues' three-game road trip."

Following a pause for reflection, Noel said, "Well, Dan, de

Blue dey got de tree-game road trip. Dey gonna go out an dey gonna play de tree game, and den dey gonna come home."

Noel was an admirer of the Blues' owners, Sidney Salomon, Jr., and Sidney Salomon III, and perhaps his most famous broadcasts were the ones in which he referred to "my good friends, Sid Joonyer an Sid de turd." This continued until the Salomons diplomatically asked Noel to refer to them from now on, please, as "the Salomon family."

Noel Picard was not a great hockey player, and he was certainly not a great broadcaster, but he was a tough, honest guy who played a colorful (although too often the color was blood-red) role and a major role in the history of expansion hockey and of the Flyers. For it was because of him, more than anyone else, that the Flyers eventually drafted bigger and tougher forwards—the kind that would make some history of their own.

So that we can remember him for something *other* than that stick fight:

# The Rock

Like his Biblical counterpart, Lazarus "Larry" Zeidel rose from the dead—or at least from hockey oblivion. After a brief N.H.L. career with Detroit and Chicago had ended unspectacularly in 1954, Larry spent the next thirteen seasons establishing himself as the Rock, the legendary bad man of minor-league hockey. He was tough, he was mean, and he terrorized the American Hockey League, mostly as the grizzliest member of the Hershey Bears.

Larry was not chosen in the expansion draft, mainly because he was thirty-nine years old and he had almost no major-league experience. But Larry did not give up. Clever man that he was (and still is, as a successful Philadelphia stock broker), Larry made up his own press-guide type of book and sent it to every N.H.L. team, explaining to them why they needed the Rock. Larry's earnestness, his hustle, and his totally unique approach intrigued Bud Poile and Keith Allen, and after the longest term between major-league jobs in the history of professional sports, Larry Zeidel became a thirty-nine-year-old almost-rookie with the expansion Flyers, and their first real "character."

Larry was also one of the rare Jewish players in the N.H.L., and when asked by a reporter if he were the only Jew in hockey, Larry replied, "I'm the only Jewish guy in hockey who doesn't own a team."

Larry could also say that every time he scored a goal for the Flyers it was like New Year's Eve. Of course he scored only one, and that one bounced in on New Year's Eve during Larry's only full season with the Flyers.

After Larry's moment-of-glory season with the Flyers, like Noel Picard, he experienced some less-glorious moments as a broadcaster. Larry had been hired by the Flyers to do television color along with another broadcasting novice named Pat Shetler, whose experience consisted of being a former N.H.L. linesman. A linesman? Referees are at least interviewed occasionally, but a linesman?

I can recall working with Larry and Pat in pre-season on such basics as how to present themselves: "Hi, I'm Pat Shetler along with Larry Zeidel..."

"No, Larry, you're not Pat Shetler..."

That broadcasting partnership turned out to be less than successful, so Larry was moved over to radio to do color for me. It was then that I found out that Larry carried the same intensity that he had shown on the ice into *everything* he did. That intensity almost ended my career.

Larry was always talking about the hits, and how important they were, because that's the way he had played the game—physically. When he got excited, he would nudge me with his elbow, or if he *really* got excited, he would punch me in the arm. Well, in one game, the Flyers tied the score with about two minutes left and Larry got so excited that he missed my arm and gave me a shot to the ribs that had me slumped over the table. After yelling "Score!" all I could do was breathlessly point to the mike and hope that Larry would say something. I was doubled over in such pain that I can't recall exactly what Larry said, but it was something like, "Well, Gene is so overcome by that goal that he can't talk, but he's thrilled that the Flyers have tied."

Soon after that, I started doing simulcasts with a new guy they brought in from Boston, Don Earle. Larry's days as a hockey broadcaster were over, but I'll certainly never forget that time when I was caught between the Rock and a hard place.

And, finally, here's a champagne toast to you,

# André

The first player about whom the Flyers and their fans (including yours truly) had superstar expectations was a delightful young gentleman named André Lacroix. He had begun that first season in Quebec with the Aces, and later on he would return to Quebec with the Flyers as a conquering hero. But it was his February debut with the Flyers that is most memorable to me. In fact, I doubt that *any* player will *ever* have a more spectacular debut.

The Flyers had been suffering both offensively and with injuries. At Quebec, Lacroix had scored forty-one goals, more than anyone else in professional hockey up to that point in the season. At the risk of incurring the wrath of the hockey fanatics of Quebec, André was called up "on an emergency basis only."

His first N.H.L. game was in Pittsburgh where, with the Flyers trailing one to nothing late in the game, André scored on an artistic break-away to give the Flyers a much-needed point on the road. Then came his even more unforgettable debut in the Spectrum. The story of that game was best told by sportswriter John Brogan in an open letter which appeared in the next day's editions of the *Evening Bulletin*. (In Philadelphia almost everyone used to read the *Bulletin*.) Here is most of that letter:

> Mr. Vic Stasiuk
> Coach, Quebec Aces
> Statler Hilton Hotel
> Cleveland, Ohio
>
> Dear Vic,
>
> Tough luck, old buddy.
> You know we all want to see the Aces make the playoffs, but I'm afraid you're going to have to do it without André Lacroix. The kid's only been in Philadelphia twenty-four hours, but already he's more popular than William Penn.
> You saw him score that beautiful goal in Pittsburgh to give the Flyers a 1-1 tie. Well, Vic, that was nothing compared with what he did last night.

You know the situation. The Flyers had misplaced their offense on their recent seven-game road trip. Their lead over Minnesota in the Western Division was reduced to three points.

I guess you have an N.H.L. schedule in your pocket, but in case you don't, let me tell you that the Flyers played Minnesota at the Spectrum last night. Big game, big crowd—14,392, which was only 254 short of a third straight sellout at home.

Well, to get to the point, Vic, the Flyers bombed them, to up their lead to five points. The final count was 7-3.

That's pretty good news, Vic, because, as coach of the Flyers' top farm team, we know you're rooting for them. The rest of the story may be a little harder for you to swallow. It concerns André.

You know what the kid can do. He scored 41 goals for you in Quebec before a rash of injuries forced the Flyers to recall him, didn't he? Well, Vic, despite your familiarity with him, even you may find this hard to believe.

Would you believe the kid has been in the N.H.L. for two games and already he has five points? No? Well, Vic, you're going to have to face the facts, old pal.

Yep, the kid got another goal last night and added three assists, and even this amateur could see that he clearly dominated the game. He controlled the puck, made the plays. . . well, he did just about everything that's ever been done on a pair of skates, including a between-the-legs back-pass that brought the house down.

That's why I had to pick him as the No. 1 star of the game, even though Leon Rochefort got his second hat trick and Pat Hannigan had a whale of a night.

You should have heard the cheers when they announced him as the Top Star. They almost lifted the roof off the Spectrum! [Editor's note: Hmmm!]

Why, Vic, he could run for office tomorrow and beat Mayor Tate easily.

After it was over, Vic, André was surrounded by reporters who wanted to know about his being one of fourteen children, how he liked the N.H.L., and would he be mad if he were returned to Quebec. He fielded all those questions like a pro.

"I wouldn't be mad if they shipped me back," he

said. "They would be doing it for my own good. Besides, I'd like to help *both* teams."

Can you imagine that, Vic? Wouldn't it be great if it could be arranged?

As you can imagine, your boss Bud Poile has a king-size headache right now. Bud knows the fans in Quebec want Lacroix back for the remainder of the season. And he knows the fans here aren't going to let him go without a fight. And, Vic, there are a lot more people here than there are in Quebec City.

Well, Vic, by now I probably have you crying. So, let me tell you a bit of good news. The Flyers are sending Jean-Guy Gendron back to you in time for tonight's game.

Just keep your chin up, Vic. And good luck. You may need it.

Regards,


John Brogan


After deciding that André was to stay in Philadelphia, Bud Poile remarked, "There goes my summer vacation in Quebec." When asked if it was the toughest decision he had ever had to make, Poile replied, "I've had easier blood transfusions." Then Poile added, prophetically, "No doubt, André will help us. And, he'll get better. But I warned him that there will be plenty of nights when things won't come as easily as they did in his first two games."

Prophetic words indeed. We knew he was small, but what we discovered in time was that he was also a step slow. Once this was widely known, all of the clever moves he could invent would not get him past a smart, experienced N.H.L. defenseman. Then, as the players around him grew larger, and André did not, he became intimidated, as did his linemates.

After three and a half years with the Flyers, André was traded to Chicago for a big defenseman named Rick Foley. And when I say "big," I mean that Rick Foley gave all of us an indication of what Gene Hart would look like in a Flyers' uniform. Unfortunately, he also *played* about as well as Gene Hart would have.

When Chicago coach Billy Reay tried André on a line with Bobby Hull and found that André just could not keep up with Hull (not that *anyone* really could), he moaned, "I've got the only French player in the league who can't skate."

After that, André benefited tremendously by jumping to the W.H.A., where defense was something for the Pentagon to worry about. He put up big numbers for the Philadelphia Blazers (more about them later), the New York Blades, the Jersey Knights, the San Diego Mariners, the Houston Aeros, and the Hartford Whalers. When the Whalers (with father Gordie Howe and sons Marty and Mark Howe) joined the N.H.L. in 1979, André was able to play one last season in the big league before retiring to the Hartford broadcast booth, where he has been considerably more successful than Noel Picard or Larry Zeidel.

Between his brief encounters with the N.H.L., André played a total of 551 games in the W.H.A., scored 798 points, and was (and always will be) the all-time leading point producer in W.H.A. history. More than that, he was an honorable gentleman of the highest order, and the kind of person who, no matter where he went—Quebec, Philadelphia, Chicago, New York, New Jersey, San Diego, Houston, or New England—was a favorite of everyone.

My co-author still keeps a letter he received during the 1968 season, in response to a short note he had sent André wishing him a long and productive career in Philadelphia. It is written in large and beautifully flowing penmanship, and it reads:

Dear Mr. Ringe,

I would like to thank you for your letter. It's very nice of you to wish me to stay here, and I hope that I will. I really like it in Philadelphia, and the people are very nice.

I will do my best to help the team, and also I will try to have a good end of the year. I hope to see you sometimes.

Sincerely,


André Lacroix,
Philadelphia Flyers


Buzz never got to meet André, but he still wishes that he had. I wish that *everyone* could have met André. I am proud to have been able to call him my good friend these past two-plus decades.

A champagne toast to you, André my friend.

**T**he Flyers' first season (1967-68) was really a different entity from the *rest* of the "first period" of Flyers history, with a different concept, different problems, and different rewards. It was a time for getting the organization put together, getting the team on the ice for the first time, and just getting going in every way. All of that was, you might say, only the *faceoff,* which, of course, was won by the Flyers. The reality of trying to figure out how to build a winner came later.

# Remainder of the First Period: 1968 to 1972

On numbers alone, the next four seasons stand out as the four worst seasons in Flyers history. In all four, the Flyers were considerably under the .500 level, and in two of those years they didn't even make the playoffs. It might be fair to term this time as a period of limbo, with very little success to put into the ledger, except at the box office. But, in retrospect, those four years were the most significant and the most important four years in Flyers history, and for a number of reasons.

First, the Flyers' ownership was solidified into the one-man boss-rule of Ed Snider, the intense and marvelously creative man who built the franchise to its current standing. Under Ed Snider, the Flyers acquired control of the Spectrum arena, which had been in bankruptcy with two million dollars in tax debt. With the expertise of Flyers management, the Spectrum became probably the  most used, the most successful, and the most productive sports arena in North America.

More important than the building, the Flyers developed an effective response to free agency, which was then a new and very sticky challenge to all sports ownership. When outfielder Curt Flood left baseball to become a bartender in Spain after being traded from the Cardinals to the Phillies, court rulings made it clear that lifetime control of a player was a thing of the past.

So, the Flyers developed a philosophy which was almost unheard of in professional sports: They would provide for their players working conditions and a tone so positive that they would not *want* to go anywhere else. As a result, Philadelphia was and is considered to be one of the best places to play. Almost no one ever wants to leave, and anyone who *must* leave is inevitably disappointed. Conversely, any player who comes to Philadelphia is inevitably delighted, because he has heard that no matter what the conditions are anywhere else, they will be better in Philadelphia.

It's such a common-sense kind of thought. You would think that the same would apply in any business, in any school, in any relationship. If people are treated the way they like to be treated, they will be more effective and productive people. This has been psychologically proven. And yet, how many times have you seen bosses, or employers of any kind, *not doing that*? When I hear players from other teams complain about how they are "handled," I am always a little surprised, because I really know only the way the Flyers do things, and it's hard to believe that anyone would want to do things any *other* way.

This positive approach has been felt not only by the fans in Philadelphia, but by fans in "enemy" cities as well. The following letter from St. Louis (and no city could have been more of an "enemy" city than St. Louis) serves as an example:

Philadelphia Flyers Hockey Club
The Spectrum
Philadelphia, Pennsylvania 19148

January 8, 1970


Gentlemen:

I would like to take this opportunity to extend mine and my wife's thanks to your organization for considerations extended to my two sons by some of your personnel after the game in St. Louis on January 7, 1970.

After the game, my sons, while leaving the arena, were injured in a freak accident. Fortunately, the injuries are minor and no future difficulties are anticipated. However, at the time of the incident the extent of injuries and damage was unknown.

While they were in the first aid room waiting to be

transported to the hospital, Larry Hillman of your organization came in and presented my boys with his hockey stick. In addition, the gentleman who broadcasts your games came in and gave them what I am sure is the only Flyer year book in the City of St. Louis. Both of these tokens, I can assure you, will occupy a cherished spot in our home.

In a day when the professional athlete is more and more being characterized as nothing more than a salary-oriented individual who thinks of nothing more than himself, it is, indeed, gratifying to know that there are those who can still take that extra effort, and in the tradition of all great sports, recognize the needs of the best of all possible fans, the small boy.

The conduct on that evening of some of your personnel has brought great credit to them and to your organization. I am sure St. Louis fans have not always seemed to be the most hospitable to visiting teams and, particularly, the Flyers, but I would like to state, as a long-time season ticket holder of the Blues, that as devoted as we are to our team, exemplary conduct, whether on or off the ice, does not go unnoticed, even if by a visiting team. It may interest you to know that in the future when you visit St. Louis, you will know that in the stands there are at least two fans harboring mixed emotions about the desired outcome of the contest.

As a more concrete token of our appreciation, I am enclosing a check for fifty dollars which I hope your club will use to purchase a few tickets to some of your games for some worthy boys. I hope this token is taken in the spirit intended and my deepest thanks are extended to all members of your team and your broadcaster.

Very truly yours,


Theodore D. Ponfil


Along with their positive philosophy, the Flyers also developed a team identity during this four-year period. During the first few years, if you were to ask what kind of team the Flyers were, it would be hard to define. They weren't a rip-roaring wide-open shooting-scoring team like Montreal. They weren't a flit-up-the-ice and defense-to-the-winds team like Minnesota. And they certainly weren't a bullying team like the big, bad Boston Bruins. The Flyers were soul-searching for an identity, a signature by which their team could be identified. And with grudging thanks to the St. Louis Blues, a new Flyer identity would be forged during this period.

Also during this period, through the revolving door of a team with growing pains came a new general manager, two new coaches, several new scouts, and numerous new players. Including owner, general manager, and coach, there are about twenty-five essential parts to a Stanley Cup puzzle. At the start of this four-year stretch, the Flyers had only five parts in place, and one of those would be leaving soon. By the end of the four years, all but three would be there.

After thirty-one victories in their first season (first place in the West, although one game under .500), the Flyers regressed in their second season to just twenty wins (third place in the West), and only *five* of those wins were on the road. There was one modest four-game winning string during that second season, but such a streak would not again be matched until four years later, in 1972-73. From the regular season of 1968-69 only two games stand out in my mind. Both were at the Spectrum, and both were downers.

The first was in early November when Jacques Plante of St. Louis (there's that team again!) shut out the Flyers, eight to nothing. The score was bad enough, but the remarkable part of it was that six of the eight goals were scored by one player, Gordon "Red" Berenson. Only once before had anyone scored six, and that was twenty-four years earlier, in 1944, when Syd Howe of Detroit did it to my New York Rangers. Later on, Darryl Sittler would score six for Toronto against Boston, but when I think of the top goal-scoring games of all time, the one that comes to my mind is the night the "Red Baron" put six behind Doug Favell.

The other memorable regular-season game came two months later when a sellout crowd jammed the Spectrum to see whether the Flyers could beat the glamorous Chicago Black Hawks, as they had managed to do during their first "big weekend" of the season before. The souped-up crowd had the Flyers souped up also, and in the early moments Chicago was forced to take a penalty. But before you could say "Flyers' power play," Stan Mikita and Jimmy Pappin had both scored short-handed goals for the Black Hawks, and the rout was on.

After the first nine minutes of the game, the score was six to nothing. At this point Doug Favell was sent to the bench, and Bernie Parent was summoned from *under* the bench, or wherever he was probably hiding. Against Parent the Hawks could score only three in the second period, followed by three more in the third, for a final score of twelve to nothing. That, of course, topped the Blues' eight-to-nothing job, not only as the worst home shutout in Flyers history, but also as the worst in *league* history. (The honor of having the worst shutout on the road again belongs to my Rangers, *fifteen* to nothing, at Detroit in 1944.)

The significant part of the season came a few months later in the first round of the playoffs, when a certain team from St. Louis swept the Flyers in four straight. It wasn't just the fact that the Flyers were swept that was irritating. It was the *manner* in which they were outclassed, overpowered, intimidated, embarrassed, folded, spindled, mutilated, and blasted out in four straight by the likes of Noel Picard and the Plager brothers. After winning the opener, five to two, Jacques Plante allowed only one more goal in the series, and that was a short-handed goal after it was all but over in Game Four. Three goals in four games. Intimidation. Embarrassment.

Following that ignominious series, the identity that the team had been searching for was suddenly formulated when an angry Ed Snider ordered, "I want size, and I want meanness." Flyers scouts listened, and the rest, as they say, is history.

Diminutive "French Connection" gentlemen like Jean-Guy Gendron and André Lacroix would soon be replaced, along with several other memorable characters, one of whom had been just recently imported from New York (in a trade for Leon Rochefort and Don Blackburn) to provide, of all things, some "muscle." That one was Reggie Fleming, whom Flyer fans will best remember by the nickname "Cement Head."

And there was also Allan Stanley, the tall and distinguished defenseman who, after twenty previous seasons with the Rangers, Chicago, Boston, and Toronto, was playing one last season with the Flyers. Only Gordie Howe played more N.H.L. seasons.

And there was future Buffalo Sabres general manager Gerry Meehan, who never scored a goal in his short career with the Flyers, but who will be remembered for one he would score *against* them at the end of this four-year period.

And there was Bob Courcy, a player who was memorable because he did *not* play for the Flyers. After a good training camp,

Courcy had been offered a contract with the Flyers, but he declined, explaining that he had some girlfriends on the West Coast and that perhaps he'd be better off out there. The way things were going for the Flyers at that time, maybe he was right, but that was probably the last time a player would ever turn down an opportunity to play for the Flyers.

These were all players who would *not* be a part of the Stanley Cup puzzle, although some probably thought that the Cup had been *named* after *Allan* Stanley. The five parts of the puzzle that *were* already in place were original draftees Bernie Parent, Joe Watson, Gary Dornhoefer, and Ed Van Impe; plus Simon Nolet, who had been acquired when the Flyers purchased the Quebec Aces franchise.

Then came the 1969 player draft. Since their record in that second season had been so mediocre, the Flyers' first- and second-round picks would be the sixth and seventeenth overall. It is worth noting how those first seventeen selections went, because if they had gone differently, the history of the league would have gone differently also.

## The 1969 Draft

| | |
|---|---|
| **1. Montreal** | **Rejean Houle**—Excellent, although he would eventually have to be lured back from the W.H.A. |
| **2. Montreal** | **Marc Tardif**—Excellent, although he, too, would have to be lured back from the W.H.A. |
| **3. Boston** | **Don Tannahill**—Undistinguished career |
| **4. Boston** | **Frank Spring**—Undistinguished career |
| **5. Minnesota** | **Dick Redmond**—Solid but not great career with six different teams |
| **6. Philadelphia** | **Bob Currier**—Never made it to the Flyers or to any other N.H.L. team |

**7. Oakland**    **Tony Featherstone**—Undistinguished career

**8. N.Y. Rangers**   **André Dupont**—Soon to be traded to St. Louis and then to Philadelphia

**9. Toronto**    **Ernie Moser**—Never heard from again

**10. Detroit**    **Jim Rutherford**—Solid goaltender for four teams, none of them a winner

**11. Boston (their third pick)**  **Ivan Boldirev**—Solid career, but for five other teams

**12. N.Y. Rangers (their second pick)** **Pierre Jarry**—Undistinguished career with five teams

**13. Chicago**    **J.P. Bordeleau**—Undistinguished career, although he lasted nine seasons with Chicago

**14. Minnesota (their second pick)** **Dennis O'Brien**—Only claim to fame was playing for four teams in the same year

**15. Pittsburgh**   **Rick Kessell**—Undistinguished career

**16. Los Angeles**   **Dale Hoganson**—Undistinguished career, mostly in W.H.A.

**17. Philadelphia (their second pick)** **Bobby Clarke**

 Remember, the Flyer scouts were supposed to be after big, mean forwards. One of their scouts was Jerry Melnyk, who, as a player, had been traded from the Blues to the Flyers, but who was then forced to retire because of a heart condition. Melnyk pleaded for Clarke, despite the fact that Clarke was not big and, more importantly, despite the fact that he was a diabetic. When Clarke's stamina as a diabetic was questioned, Melnyk replied, "Stamina?

The kid's been playing forty-five minutes a game, and he's scored over three hundred points in the last two years!"

So, the Flyers selected the kid from Flin Flon, Manitoba, after he had been *passed up* by eleven teams, including the Flyers themselves. Montreal, Minnesota, and the Rangers all passed him by *twice*, and the big, bad Bruins passed him by *three times*. I suppose it's only appropriate that Clarke wound up wearing number sixteen, since that's the number of chances to draft him that were passed up.

It's difficult to imagine what the league would have been like if Clarke had been a Bruin, or a Ranger, or a North Star, or a Canadien. Or a Seal, a Maple Leaf, a Red Wing, a Black Hawk, a Penguin, or a King. He could have been *any* of those, and I guess he *did* become a kind of King in Philadelphia. Jerry Melnyk, the scout who made it possible, is no longer the former Blues player with the heart condition. He's now the Flyers' Chief Scout.

After throwing away their first pick, and after selecting junior-sized playmaker Clarke with their second, the Flyers waited until the fifth round to select, finally, size and meanness, which arrived from Swift Current with one swift kick of a pick named Dave Schultz. In the sixth round they chose another big forward, Don Saleski of Regina.

With their first two N.H.L. seasons behind them, the Flyers had eight parts of their Stanley Cup puzzle in place:

| | |
|---|---|
| **Goaltender** | Parent |
| **Defensemen** | Watson |
| | Van Impe |
| **Forwards** | Dornhoefer |
| | Nolet |
| | Clarke |
| | Schultz |
| | Saleski |

The Flyers' third season (1969-70) was even worse than their second, at least in terms of wins and losses. From thirty-one wins in their first season, the Flyers regressed to twenty wins in the second, and then to just *seventeen* wins in the third, the all-time low point in the team's history. Although they finished in a tie with Oakland for fourth place in the West, the Flyers had fewer victories than the Seals, and therefore missed the playoffs for the first time.

It was during this third season that Bud Poile moved on to Vancouver, Keith Allen took over as general manager, and volatile Vic Stasiuk became the Flyers' second coach, following a year of coaching the Jersey Devils and two years of coaching the Quebec Aces. The Flyers' commitment to youth was taking over (as opposed to the commitment to veterans by the so-far more successful Blues and North Stars), and the growing pains were more severe than ever. Only twice during the season did the Flyers win as many as two in a row, and their lack of offensive punch became more acute with each passing month. Another kind of punch was developing, however, as the Flyers finished second only to the notorious Bruins in penalty minutes.

Total disaster was avoided, at least statistically, when the Flyers set one of the strangest of N.H.L. records with *twenty-four ties*. Lou Scheinfeld of the Flyers' front office was prepared for this event with a unique means of celebration. After the twenty-third tie, Scheinfeld bought up bales of cheap neckties, with the idea that at the conclusion of the record-setting twenty-fourth tie, the Flyerettes (the usherettes at Flyers home games) would rush upstairs in their referee-zebra-striped shirts and mini-skirts, carrying the bales of ties, which they would then let flutter down over the crowd.

I can remember broadcasting the final moments of that tie-breaking tie-game: "Three, two, one, that's the end of the game with the final score Philadelphia Flyers two and the New York Rangers two." As the new record was flashed on the message board, and as the ties started fluttering down, suddenly, from out of the upper deck came a whole *bale* of ties, which then gonged one of the season ticket holders seated directly in front of me. I suppose that Lou Scheinfeld hadn't had time to instruct *every* Flyerette in the intricacies of tie-fluttering, and in the dangers of bale-tossing. At any rate, I can recall that it was most difficult for me to control my mirth during the post-game wrap-up.

Despite their embarrassing lack of victories, the twenty-four ties made it seem as though the playoffs were a fairly safe bet, as the "Tying Flyers" headed into their final six games of the season. But then came a worse belly-flop than the one they had experienced at the hands of the Blues in the previous season's finale. In those final six games, the Flyers' pathetically anemic offense scored a total of just seven goals. Worse yet, needing only a *tie* in either of the final two games, both of which were at home, the Flyers were shut out both times by the identical score of one to nothing.

A short-handed goal by Jim Roberts of the Blues (that team *again*!) won the next-to-last game, which brought the whole season down to the final day, and an afternoon game at the Spectrum against Minnesota. The goalies were Bernie Parent and Lorne "Gump" Worsley, and through one whole period, and then two whole periods, no one could score for either team. Heading into the decisive third period, the Flyers desperately needed to preserve that one last tie in order to make the playoffs.

About midway through the third period, Minnesota defense-man Barry Gibbs wanted a line change and lifted a high pop fly from center ice toward the Flyers' end. The puck was so high, in fact, that Bernie Parent lost it *in the sun*. No, the Spectrum roof had not blown off again, but what did happen is another of those weird occurrences that will probably never happen again, at least not at the Spectrum. Since it was an afternoon game, the setting sun (appropriately) shone through the glass panels around the entrance doors, and through the portals in the stands, and then into the eyes of the goaltender at the opposite end of the ice.

As the puck dropped over the shoulder of poor motionless Bernie and into the net, it occurred to me that if Gibbs tried that same line-changing lift a hundred more times, he probably never again would have been able to accomplish the same feat. Ever since that fateful day, whenever an afternoon game is played at the Spectrum, someone is assigned to make sure that black opaque curtains are drawn across those glass panels.

The only similar happenstance I can recall was during a World Series game, when Billy Loes, a pitcher with the old Brooklyn Dodgers, claimed to have lost a Billy Martin ground ball in the sun. In that case, too, the setting sun had shone through a portal in the stands and into the eyes of the fielder, but that didn't keep the Dodgers out of the playoffs!

To say that the "Game of the Setting Sun" was a stunner to the Flyers and to their fans would be an understatement. But, with their relatively low finish and therefore relatively high drafting position, the Flyers added several more parts to their Stanley Cup puzzle. Drafted number one was Bill Clement from the Ottawa 67's, and drafted number two was Bob Kelly from Oshawa, Ontario.

Also after the season, the Flyers traded two players from the roster of the Quebec Aces to the Hershey Bears for a gangling thirty-one-year-old defenseman named Barry Ashbee, whose previous N.H.L. experience had consisted of a brief and undistinguished fourteen-game stretch with Boston five years before. Ashbee had spent most of his previous seven seasons at Hershey with coach–general manager Frank Mather, who gave the Flyers the following scouting report: "Barry Ashbee deserves to be in the N.H.L. He can play. Barry is better than many of the veterans who are in the league now, and Barry will very much help the Philadelphia Flyers."

So, after their first three seasons, eleven parts of the puzzle were now in place (thirteen, counting owner Ed Snider and general manager Keith Allen):

| | |
|---|---|
| Goaltender | Parent |
| Defensemen | Watson |
| | Van Impe |
| | Ashbee |
| Forwards | Dornhoefer |
| | Nolet |
| | Clarke |
| | Schultz |
| | Saleski |
| | Clement |
| | Kelly |

In their fourth season (1970-71), the Flyers improved from their low of seventeen wins to a more respectable twenty-eight wins, but this was still three less than their total of the first season. Their third-place finish in the West assured a playoff spot this time, but due to another new development in the league, this season also would conclude in the now customarily inglorious fashion.

That new development was another expansion. With Vancouver and Buffalo added to the league, there were now fourteen teams in two seven-team divisions. Logical enough so far, but no farther, because both Vancouver (Bud Poile's team) and Buffalo were added to the *Eastern* Division, while Chicago was shifted into the *Western* Division. The Black Hawks had "courageously" volunteered to leave their colleagues of so many years in the East to create "balance" by joining the six expansion teams in the West. The fact that they would probably dominate their younger compatriots for years to come was, of course, not a factor in their "sacrificial" decision.

The Flyers, who had been treading in the shadow of the St. Louis Blues, now had another and far more formidable shadow cast upon them. Despite their improved performance and record, the Flyers finished *thirty-four points* behind the Black Hawks, who, by finishing first, had won the honor of dispatching the Flyers in four consecutive lopsided first-round playoff games. The Flyers had now lost nine straight playoff games since the double-overtime victory over St. Louis in their first year, and the chasm-wide gap that existed between the Flyers and the N.H.L. elite looked wider than ever, especially now that the elite controlled the "new" division, as well as the "old."

The personnel continued to change during that somewhat hopeless fourth season, and never was there a more dramatic personnel change than the one that occurred on Jan. 31, 1971. Because of the Flyers' inability to score, Bernie Parent, the talented and popular young goaltender, was traded to Toronto for thirty-one-year-old goaltender Bruce Gamble, forward Mike "Shakey" Walton, and the Leafs' number one choice in the upcoming draft. Granted, Parent had a losing record at the time, but that was because he often had to have a shutout in order to earn a tie. To many people, the first blockbuster trade in Flyers history was a depressing one. Fans cried. Bernie cried. His teammates cried. I cried.

"Favell and Gamble" just did not have the same ring to it as "Parent and Favell." I didn't know Gamble, and I didn't know Walton. But there was more to come. Mike Walton was sent on to the Boston Bruins for a youngster named Rick MacLeish, who was playing at the time with the Oklahoma City Blazers. The scout who was pushing to get MacLeish claimed that, despite his undistinguished record, MacLeish would score twenty goals during the remainder of the season in Philadelphia. MacLeish scored only two, and everyone was wondering whether the Flyers had made another blunder, because the scoring they had hoped for in moving Parent was *still* not there.

To make matters worse, the Flyers also struck out in the draft, even though they held the eighth and ninth picks in the first round, one of them Toronto's from the Parent trade. The two players they selected were Larry Wright and Pierre Plante, both with promise that was never to be fulfilled in the N.H.L. The Flyers had no shot at the first two players drafted, Guy Lafleur and Marcel Dionne, perhaps the best one-two punch in draft history, but they did have a shot at some other players who were drafted *after* Wright and Plante. There may not have been any Bobby Clarkes in the group, but any of the following would definitely have looked good in orange and black, and all were chosen later than the Flyers' eighth and ninth picks:

| | |
|---|---|
| **10. N.Y. Rangers** | **Steve Vickers**—After a year in the minors, would beat out the Flyers' Bill Barber for Rookie of the Year |
| **14. Boston** | **Terry O'Reilly**—A giant of a Bruin; and wouldn't he have looked good in a Flyer uniform? |
| **20. Montreal** | **Larry Robinson**—Not only did the Canadiens get Lafleur with Oakland's first pick, but they got *another* future Hall-of-Famer with the twentieth pick; and wouldn't *he* have looked good in a Flyer uniform? |
| **22. Toronto** | **Rick Kehoe**—Would average about thirty goals per year for twelve years, including a high of fifty-five for Pittsburgh in 1980-81; so, Toronto got more from the second round than the Flyers got from the first-round pick acquired from Toronto in the Parent trade |

In a later round the Flyers also drafted a goaltender named Jerome Mrazek, who was a somewhat unusual character. Because of his hippie-style beard, he was nicknamed "Moses," and he definitely skated to the beat of a different drummer. I can recall a bus trip back from New York, when everyone was eating chicken and French fries and sipping beverages, while Moses Mrazek sat in the back of the bus strumming his guitar and singing, "I'm just a poor, way-farin' stranger, travelin' through this land of woe..."

Moses' career with the Flyers was to be mercifully brief, but his song told the sad tale of the Flyers' plight after their first four seasons. The Stanley Cup puzzle count remained stuck on eleven, but this time one of the eleven was *not* named Parent:

Defensemen                Watson
                          Van Impe
                          Ashbee

Forwards                  Dornhoefer
                          Nolet
                          Clarke
                          Schultz
                          Saleski
                          Clement
                          Kelly
                          MacLeish

In their fifth season (1971-72), the Flyers seemed well settled into mediocrity. They won twenty-six games, two fewer than the previous season, and tied for fourth in the West with Pittsburgh, but again missed out on the playoffs, just as they had two seasons before, through the N.H.L.'s tie-breaking procedures.

Some memorable characters arrived during that fifth season, most notably the Flyers' third coach, Fred Shero. Shero had been a defenseman for the Rangers in the 1940s, and then had coached the Rangers' farm team, the Omaha Knights, for years. But Shero had not been given a chance to coach the Rangers, and this may have been the biggest blunder by general manager Emile "The Cat" Francis during his career in New York, a career filled with coaching changes, I might add.

New York's loss was Philadelphia's gain, as the genius stroke of hiring Shero to coach the young Flyers resulted in a marriage made in hockey heaven, or, depending upon your point of view, hockey hell. Shero's nickname was "The Fog," and his appearance was that of a small, bespectacled, withdrawn older gentleman, introverted and even eccentric, quite unlike the Flyers' dignified first coach, Keith Allen, and the antithesis of their rambunctious second coach, Vic Stasiuk.

With the Shero era came a surprising kind of zaniness, some of it instigated by blockbuster trade number two, which occurred on Jan. 28, 1972, almost a year to the day from the Parent trade. To the Los Angeles Kings went four Flyers—Serge Bernier, Larry Brown, Jimmy Johnson, and Bill Lesuk—in exchange for four Kings— Eddie Joyal, Jean Potvin, Bill Flett, and Ross Lonsberry.

Lonsberry (nicknamed "Roscoe" or "The Rabbit") was another player taken from Boston in the expansion draft, and he turned out to be the perfect third member of a line consisting of the freewheeling Rick MacLeish at center, along with the patient and disciplined Gary Dornhoefer on the other wing. The hockey gods could not have sent Philadelphia two better-equipped wingers to complement the broad free-lance talents of Rick MacLeish, and ironically, all three had come out of the Boston organization.

Eddie Joyal's career with the Flyers lasted only until the end of the season, when he joined the brand-new World Hockey Association for their inaugural season.

Jean Potvin would be sent to join his brother Denis with the Islanders during *their* first season, and in return, the Flyers would receive another piece of the Stanley Cup puzzle in the person of Terry Crisp, a smart, feisty, and valuable red-haired centerman.

That brings us to Bill "Cowboy" Flett, who was also being wooed by the new W.H.A. Flett was one of the first truly eccentric characters to play full-time for Philadelphia, and he looked the part, with his long sideburns, his black beard, and a long feather in his ten-gallon hat. Thus suitably attired, Cowboy Flett came riding out of the West (Calgary was his home) to bring to Philadelphia that rarest of commodities—goal-scoring.

Appropriately, Flett saved his first big scoring night as a Flyer for his first return visit to Los Angeles since the trade. With the Flyers trailing three to two in the third period, the Cowboy came up with a natural hat trick (three straight goals) to win it for the Flyers, five to three. He had even set up one of the earlier goals, so after the game we were all waiting for him to be named the number one star of the game. But when the announcements came, not only was he not the number one star, he was not the number two or three star either. We found out later that the reason for his being "overlooked" was that the Kings' owner, Jack Kent Cooke, had been so upset by his former employee's performance, that he had charged down to inform the off-ice officials, "You do not announce Bill Flett."

"But, Mr. Cooke..."

"You announce Bill Flett and I'll fire you."

In the dressing room after the game, Bobby Clarke presented Flett with a spittoon for his performance as the "unspeakable star of the game."

After a game like that, I would interview Flett and ask him

how it happened, and he would say, "Well, Gene, you just keep shootin', 'n' sometimes they go in, 'n' sometimes they don't."

If I had to interview Flett while he was in a slump, I'd ask him what the problem was, and he would say, "Well, Gene, you just keep shootin', 'n' sometimes they go in, 'n' sometimes they don't."

One thing I knew *not* to ask Flett about was the W.H.A., because I knew he had been talking with them, and that the Flyers had to come up with more money to prevent him from taking his ten-gallon hat tricks to "that other league." I also knew that the very *mention* of the W.H.A. was enough to make Ed Snider's blood boil, and I had been repeatedly told as much. Even "basketball" couldn't compare with "W.H.A." in the Flyers' lexicon of forbidden phrases.

After another Flett hat trick, I interviewed the Cowboy, starting with, "Bill, you've never played better, and you've never looked happier..."

Of course, Flett responded *this* time with, "Yeah, Gene, thank God for the World Hockey Association!"

For perhaps the only time in my career, I wanted to point at my interviewee and say, "*I* didn't say it! *He* did!"

Besides Bill Flett and Fred Shero, there were other great stories from the Flyers' fifth season, and one of them had to be one of the most tremendous human-interest sports stories ever. On Feb. 8, 1972, the Flyers were playing in Vancouver, and in goal was the thirty-one-year-old "journeyman" (as the Philadelphia press liked to call him) Bruce Gamble, the man who had come from Toronto in exchange for Bernie Parent, and therefore, a man who had a lot to prove to Philadelphia's fans and press.

Early in the game, the Canucks were pressing, and a shot got through the defense and apparently hit Gamble, knocking him down. Trainer Frank Lewis came out to minister to Gamble, while on the radio I was speculating as to whether Gamble had been hit by the puck or perhaps by someone's stick. I watched the replays on a television monitor, but I still couldn't tell exactly what had happened.

After a short rest and some smelling salts, Gamble played through the first and second periods without allowing a goal. With the Flyers leading three to nothing in the third period, I found myself pulling for Bruce to get his first shutout as a Flyer. In the final minute, a goal-mouth scramble resulted in a cheap Vancouver goal, but the Flyers won, three to one, and we all congratulated Gamble for his performance as star of the game.

On our flight to Oakland that night, Bruce told Frank Lewis that he was not feeling well at all, so when we landed in Oakland, Frank took him to the hospital to be checked out. Not until I awoke the next morning did I receive the shocking news that Bruce Gamble had suffered an apparent heart attack during the game the night before.

Just hours after his *finest* hour with his new team, Bruce Gamble's hockey career was over, and the letters poured in from throughout the hockey world. Here is one of those letters:

Downsview, Ontario
Feb. 11, 1972

Dear Mr. Gamble,

How the world can change in less than a day. In the wee hours of Wednesday morning's broadcast, Gene Hart seemed so happy, so very, very happy. One could not help notice the joy in his voice as the Vancouver game progressed. "It is unbelievable! Bruce Gamble refuses to be beaten!"

It was one of those rare and precious moments in professional sports, so short in time, but so full of the future promise of a young and jelling hockey team. It seemed that the Flyers had finally found a new leader in a quiet, gifted and brave goaltender. From the broadcast it appeared that this was perhaps one of the finest games of your career, and, now, there is little doubt.

Then, as Mr. Hart began his Oakland broadcast, I knew something wrong, very wrong had happened. When he started to talk about the tremendous shock felt throughout the entire Flyer organization, I knew something had happened to you. I guess it must have been the instinctive reaction of being a Bruce Gamble follower over the years. But one learns that in keeping the faith your follower must become ever more and more attached and devoted and, hence, suffer all the more acutely the sadness and disappointment that cut short those moments of triumph. It just doesn't make any sense. Like so many times before, it just seemed too good to last.

But another thing that your follower learns, Mr. Gamble, is the inherent moxie and spirit that is part of your goalie's make-up—a reckless and undauntable resolution to rise again and take whatever fate has in store. We live for those moments, for in them are the stuff of courage always and brilliance often.

Last year I switched from a life-long Toronto allegiance to be a Flyer fan—the date I guess to be about the end of January. I no longer hate the Leafs for trading you; as it turns out it is the best thing that could have happened. Instead, I merely pity them. No one can understand why the Leafs are falling so badly. But I think I may know a good part of the answer: The Toronto team lost its heart last January, and Philadelphia is experiencing its re-birth.

You have been slowed down, and the chanting and praise have ceased for the moment; but you will be back.

Thank you for reading my letter and I realize that you must rest. Thank you also for your efforts again this season. You never stopped trying. Take care, and get well, Bruce Gamble. We keep the faith.

Yours sincerely,


Sheila M. Ryan

The same eloquent person also wrote a shorter letter to me:

Downsview, Ontario
Feb. 11, 1972

Dear Mr. Hart,

May I thank you, Mr. Hart, for really caring about Bruce Gamble. You have displayed a most genuine and deep concern, and this concern can only help spread to the many others who may be prompted to write to him and give the encouragement and re-assurance he is going to need, even if he is never to play hockey again.

Following Bruce Gamble has never been easy, for I have known no player who has suffered so, so many setbacks, and most of them just don't make any sense. This heart attack is just another. Finally, just when Philadelphia was starting to appreciate the talents and presence of Mr. Gamble, so long deserved, this had to happen.

So Mr. Hart, I thank you for your concern. It will be appreciated a good deal more than you can imagine. If he does make it back, I can assure you and the Flyers that the last two weeks were not atypical of his ability. He is still young. Given a chance, he will shine for Philadelphia. For you see, it will be the first clean chance he has ever really had. Quiet men feed on heartfelt encouragement. Thank you again.

Yours sincerely,


Sheila M. Ryan


Without Bernie Parent *or* Bruce Gamble, the Flyers were down to Doug Favell and no one else. Since they didn't know until the morning of the game in Oakland that this would be the case, there was no time to call in a goalie from Quebec, or from anywhere else on the East Coast. Keith Allen remembered a goalie from his days in Seattle, placed a call to him in Spokane, and had him fly in that day to sit on the Flyers' bench and back up Doug Favell. Because he never appeared in a game for the Flyers, and because that was the only time he ever had a Flyers' uniform on, the name of Russ Gillow does not appear in the record books, but here's to you, Russ, and thanks again!

Five days later, for a game in Buffalo, the Flyers called up goaltender Don McLeod from the Richmond Robins to serve as Doug Favell's back-up. That night, Favell, often the victim of injudicious decisions, became involved in some turmoil at the end of the second period, and was ejected from the game. The main problem with that was that Don McLeod had an injured knee and could not play. According to the rules, the Flyers would have to dress one of the skaters on their roster to finish out the game. Gary Dornhoefer volunteered to put on the pads, and he was about to do so, when McLeod decided he'd better give it a try.

McLeod then played the entire third period with his stick in one hand, and with his other hand supporting himself on the crossbar of the goal, so that he wouldn't fall down. Miracle of miracles, the Flyers scored to tie the game at four, and then kept the Sabres away from McLeod well enough to preserve the tie and a well-earned point on the road.

In the season's final two games, goaltending would again become ultra-crucial. In the next-to-last game, the Flyers led Pittsburgh at the Spectrum two to nothing in the third period, and they needed to hold onto the victory to clinch a playoff spot and to knock the Penguins out of the playoff picture. The Penguins, however, scored two late goals, the second with their goalie pulled, and forced the Flyers to face elimination the next afternoon in Buffalo.

It was Sunday, April 2, the season's final day, and the already-eliminated Sabres had nothing to lose, while the Flyers had *everything* to lose. As they had the night before, the Flyers took a two-to-nothing lead, but also as they had the night before, the Flyers let their opponents tie it at two in the third period. That wasn't *too* bad, because a tie would still squeak them into the playoffs, just as had been the case two seasons earlier during the "Game of the Setting Sun" against Minnesota.

I did a lot of counting down on the air that day, counting down to the playoffs, from ten minutes, eight minutes, six, five, four, three, two, one minute to go to the playoffs... Then I was counting down the *seconds*, and I remember looking at the clock with eight, seven seconds left, and I was thinking, "Here come the playoffs!" when I saw former Flyer Gerry Meehan skate down the left side and let go a sixty-footer which sailed over Doug Favell's left shoulder and into the net. I recall saying, "Shot, score, Gerry Meehan. And that just does it for the Flyers. Three–two Buffalo with four seconds left." And I stood up and said, "The Flyers are eliminated from the playoffs for the second time in three years." Then I turned to the side and said to no one in particular, "Son of a bitch!"

If the "Setting Sun" had been a stunner, Gerry Meehan's goal seemed a *disaster*. Or at least until it was time to reap the benefits from the draft. For, drafted number one in 1972 was the player who would become the greatest winger in Flyers history, Bill Barber. Drafted second was Tom "Sparky" Bladon, who would one day set the all-time N.H.L. record for points in a game (eight) by a defenseman. Drafted third was Joe Watson's younger brother Jimmy, eagerly sought after by the W.H.A.; but blood being thicker than money, the Watson brothers of Smithers, British Columbia, were soon to be reunited in Philadelphia.

As disastrous as the previous four seasons had seemed, the Flyers' Stanley Cup puzzle was, for the most part, complete. The owner, the general manager, and Coach Fred Shero all were in place, as were the following seventeen players:

Goaltender

Bob Taylor (called up from
Richmond toward the end
of the season)

Defensemen

Joe Watson
Ed Van Impe
Barry Ashbee
Tom Bladon
Jimmy Watson

Forwards

Gary Dornhoefer
Simon Nolet
Bobby Clarke
Dave Schultz
Don Saleski
Bill Clement
Bob Kelly
Rick MacLeish
Ross Lonsberry
Bill Flett
Bill Barber

Forward Terry Crisp would be joining the team during the next
season, and then the puzzle would be lacking only three more pieces
—one forward, one defenseman, and one goalie. It was time to stop
asking, "Are we having fun yet?" Because the *real* fun was about to
begin, and in more ways than one!

# Second Period
# 1972 to 1979

After the dismal ending to the 1971-72 season, and the failure of the Flyers once again to show any signs of movement towards the upper echelon of the N.H.L., Flyer fans were starting to display some subtle and some not-so-subtle signs of impatience. Indeed, after five consecutive seasons of mediocrity, or worse, one would have to say that the Flyers appeared ripe for a challenge.

That challenge was born in the mind of a handsome, young California entrepreneur and promoter named Gary Davidson, who spawned the idea of another hockey league, another *major* hockey league, to become the first-ever direct competition for the National Hockey League. And so the World Hockey Association was born, with a dozen franchises that most hockey fans could not name: the Alberta (soon to be Edmonton) Oilers, the Chicago Cougars, the Houston Aeros (moved from Dayton before the first season), the Los Angeles Sharks (later to become the Michigan Stags and then the Baltimore Blades), the New England Whalers (later to be moved from Boston to Hartford), the New York Raiders (later the Golden Blades, the Jersey Knights, and the San Diego Mariners), the Ottawa Nationals (later the Toronto Toros and the Birmingham Bulls), the Quebec Nordiques, the Winnipeg Jets, the Minnesota (St. Paul) Fighting Saints, the Cleveland Crusaders (later the Minnesota *New* Fighting Saints), and the reason for telling you all of this—the Philadelphia Blazers (actually born in Florida as the Miami Screaming

Eagles). For you collectors of exotic team names, other franchises which later came (and went) were: the Calgary Cowboys, the Cincinnati Stingers, the Denver Spurs (later the Ottawa Civics), the Indianapolis Racers, and the Phoenix Roadrunners.

As the Flyers (and I) learned the hard way in the case of Bill Flett, salaries were boosted *tremendously,* both for those who stayed in the N.H.L., and, especially, for some who were lured by and gleefully jumped at the big money being dangled by the W.H.A. It's no wonder that "W.H.A." rapidly became a taboo phrase to N.H.L. owners, who were now forced to pay N.F.L./N.B.A./Major League Baseball-level salaries, but without the big TV money of the other three sports.

Some of the N.H.L.'s biggest names took the money and ran, and not just names like Ted Green and J.C. Tremblay, but even bigger names like Gordie Howe and Bobby Hull, the all-time scoring leaders in N.H.L. history. Gordie Howe may have ceased being a force for the Detroit Red Wings, but he could still be a very effective drawing card while playing with his two sons, Marty and Mark, at Houston and later in New England. And Bobby Hull, perhaps the N.H.L.'s most exciting player, would have a golden opportunity to live up to his nickname "The Golden Jet" in Winnipeg, where he signed a multi-million-dollar contract in a civic ceremony held in the middle of the city's main street. The competition in the W.H.A. wouldn't be the same as in the N.H.L., but Hull's signing gave instant credibility to the new league and cast fear into the hearts of N.H.L. executives.

For Philadelphia fans, and for many other N.H.L. fans, the most shocking jump was made by one of the game's most gifted young goaltenders, Bernie Parent. After leaving the struggling Flyers (whose principal dividend from the trade was the now rapidly developing centerman, Rick MacLeish), Parent spent two seasons with the also-struggling Toronto Maple Leafs. While Bernie at that stage was not the player who could make the big difference for either team, at least in Toronto he had the good fortune to work with, talk to, and learn from the man he considered to be the greatest goaltender of all time, Jacques Plante. Because of that association, which would continue until Plante's death during the eighties, it was an immeasurably improved goaltender, in terms of both technique and philosophy, who was advised by his agent to go for the big bucks and sign with the W.H.A.'s Miami franchise, the Screaming Eagles.

The Eagles may have screamed in Miami, but the only time that they took off was to fly (or flee) to the North, where they were reborn as the Philadelphia Blazers. As was the case in several other areas of North America, the W.H.A.-N.H.L. hockey war was on in Philadelphia. Bernie Parent was back in town, not at the Spectrum, but several miles north at the Civic Center (Convention Hall), just off the University of Pennsylvania campus at 34th and Spruce Streets, where he was joined by another former Flyer, André Lacroix, as well as some other big names from other N.H.L. clubs.

There was Danny Lawson from Detroit and there were *three* former Boston Bruins, not counting Parent. After all, the Flyers already had *five* former Bruins on their roster, so why not fight fire with fire? The Blazers signed new Bruins, like top draft choice Ron Plumb, as well as old Bruins, like twelve-year N.H.L. veteran John "Pie" McKenzie. And they signed Boston's answer to Peck's Bad Boy, the man who was supposed to be their saviour, the Moses who would lead the Blazers to the Promised Land—Derek Sanderson.

There was a definite feeling of concern in the Flyers' camp. The Blazers had lined up an appealing cast of characters, they were playing in a well-established Philadelphia building which had been a home-away-from-home for several popular ice shows, and they had to draw only ten or eleven thousand spectators to fill the place. Even four or five thousand might be enough to drain fans away from the fizzling Flyers, and there were at least that many excellent seats in the Civic Center.

The man who was to attract the people into those seats was Derek "Turk" Sanderson, whose self-styled image in Boston was that of "Playboy of the Western World," hockey division, Joe Namath having already claimed New York and the football division. Derek, like Joe, was good looking, reasonably articulate, and generally fun to be around. As he hit the Carson show and the rest of the talk-show circuit, he tended to play the role he thought was expected of him, more clown prince than crown prince, and the more outrageous the better.

As a hockey player, Derek had been a superb player of his role with the Bruins, that of third or fourth center, pesky checker, and defensive strength for one of the lesser Boston lines to play against one of the opposition's better lines. The kind of role Terry Crisp would play so well for the Flyers. It's easy to see, in looking back, that he was *not* the kind of player who would become a great team leader. He was *not* a Bobby Clarke, but then, who else was?

One of the lasting impressions of Derek came out of "Philadelphia Blazers Day," when he was representing the team as their spokesman during an event designed to introduce Philadelphia to its new hockey hero. Somehow, the lead story in the next day's *Daily News* came out, "How I Rate the Broads on the Road," which, of course, ran with an accompanying photo of Derek with a lovely young lady, along with lines like, "My pre-game meal on the road is a steak and a blonde."

In another article, Derek was quoted as having challenged Stan Hochman of the *Daily News* with this question: "You go ask Clarke who's better, him or me?" So, Hochman did just that. He went to Clarke and asked him the question, the kind of question which, if you think about it, is almost impossible to answer diplomatically. As he has since become known for doing, Clarke thought for a moment first, and then gently replied, "I don't want to get into something like that. That's kind of silly. We're all in this, the Blazers and the Flyers, to make a living, and I'm glad we're all doing that. I'm happy for me and I'm happy for Derek. But why don't you ask him if he's *happy* over there?"

Stan Hochman summed up the story pretty well when he stated that the Blazers had pinned their hopes on this spokesman who "probably isn't even the second-best centerman in the city," an obvious reference to Clarke and Rick MacLeish.

Still later, when the Winnipeg Jets made their first appearance in Philadelphia, Hochman noted that the Golden One, Bobby Hull, had spent the afternoon before the game signing autographs in the Blazers' downtown office. Wrote Hochman: "That's the difference between a player like Hull and a player like Sanderson. Hull spent his day here trying to *earn* his big salary, while all Derek could do was try to figure out how to *spend* his."

Sanderson's public image slipped and finally crashed, as did Derek's personal life, sadly, all perhaps because more was unreasonably expected of him than he was able to deliver.

But I'm getting ahead of myself in the story, because at the start, Derek Sanderson and the Philadelphia Blazers, with Bernie Parent in goal, appeared to be something more than a novelty or a curiosity. They were, in fact, a source of growing concern, and even worry, to the Flyers.

Although I wasn't able to be there in person, I'll never forget the Blazers' opening night at the Civic Center Arena. The game was scheduled for a Friday night, but since the Flyers were to play in De-

troit on Saturday night, we flew to Detroit on Friday, thereby missing this once-in-a-lifetime event. We knew that the game was sold
out and that all sorts of city dignitaries, stars, and assorted bigwigs
were to attend, but there would be no way to find out how the game
went until we read the Detroit newspapers the next morning.

Following a somewhat uneasy sleep in my hotel room in Detroit, I awoke early and picked up the morning papers to see what
had happened. I turned to the sports page, and there under
"W.H.A." was the listing "Cleveland (or whoever the visiting team
was) at Phila.—Ppd." As a longtime follower of baseball, I knew
that "Ppd." meant "Postponed," but since hockey games are rarely
rained out, I was quite curious as to why the Blazers' gala opening
had been postponed. I figured that the best way to find out was to
go to Joe Kadlec's room, since he knew the Blazers' public relations
man pretty well, and I thought perhaps Joe could give him a call.

Before I get into that telephone call, I'd better give you some
background on one of this world's most unflappable characters, Joe
Kadlec. And in the job Joe has (and has had since the beginning)
he'd *better* be unflappable, or he'd be in a padded room somewhere.
As the legendary (and original) Flyers' traveling secretary/P.R.
director/arranger of public appearances/"director of team services," Joe is probably next-in-line to the trainers as the man closest
to the Flyers players all these years. He not only handles all the players' travel arrangements (from chartering buses to giving out plane
tickets to planning family travel), he also gives out the road money,
orders the meals, and handles the game tickets.

Joe is thin (gaunt from overwork?), always dapperly dressed,
never with a hair out of place, even when sliding home with the winning run for the Flyers' softball team. The players' nicknames for
Joe range from "Mighty Joe" to "Casper," depending upon the circumstances. No matter what the nickname, Joe is the Flyers' style-
setter, who always wears *great* suits. In fact, to Joe, *everything* is
*great*. If one of Joe's chartered planes ever crashed into a mountain,
the rescuers would find Joe's body smashed, but his hair would still
be perfectly in place, and Joe would be smiling and saying, "Great
crash!"

With so many different responsibilities for so many different
people, it's no small wonder that Joe's optimism and unflappability
are occasionally tested. One such occasion took place on a trip to
Cleveland, where the team stayed in a downtown hotel and then
commuted to the Richfield Arena outside of town, where the Cleve-

land Barons' games were played. Trainer Jim McKenzie had decided that, if the team charter were to arrive late at night, he and his assistant Matt DiPaolo should stay closer to the arena, so that they could be there early in the morning to prepare for the team's 9:00 A.M. skate. Accordingly, Jim had asked Joe to get him a room at the Holiday Inn near the arena, and Joe had agreed to do so.

Naturally, when Jim and Matt arrived at the Holiday Inn, the place was sold out and there was no room for them. It was then too late to go back downtown, so they decided to go directly to the arena and sleep in the dressing room. Unfortunately for them, when they got to the arena the dressing room was not available, so, to make a long story longer, they ended up sleeping in the boiler room of the Richfield Arena, or I should say, they ended up spending the rest of the night in the boiler room.

By the time everything was set up for the morning skate, Jim was not just boiling mad, he was ready to kill. That's when I arrived with the team and, of course, with Joe. Well, when Jim spotted Joe, he let him have a chin-to-chin variation of the kind of verbal abuse usually employed only by the likes of the Devils' goalie in Johnstown. Not quite so vulgar, perhaps, but still the kind of attack which is frightening enough to make you want to remove yourself and your loved ones from the building. After venting his spleen for at least five minutes, Jim, still infuriated, finally turned and stalked away. I was embarrassed to have witnessed this whole scene and was pretending to be going about my business of getting ready to tape a pre-game segment, when Joe, unflappable as ever, calmly straightened his tie (his hair was still perfect) and said, "He was kidding. *Great* kidder!"

I felt a little less amused on another occasion when *I* was the victim of Joe's planning. The Flyers were to play a Saturday night game at Washington, and I figured that would be a good day to drive down early with my son Brian, to do some sightseeing with him in Washington, and then relax with him during the afternoon before doing the game that night. At the game before that, on Thursday night, I asked Joe if my reservation was all set for Saturday, and he said, "Sure, you're all set."

On Saturday morning when I arrived with Brian at the Sheraton Hotel near the Cap Centre, I asked for my room key and was told, "Oh, the Flyers aren't here."

I said, "Yes, I know. I'm just here a little early to do some sightseeing with my son."

The man behind the desk explained further: "No, I mean the Flyers aren't staying here this time because we have a convention, so they had to book rooms elsewhere."

I said, rather helplessly, "Well, do you know where?"

"Sorry, no."

Since it was Saturday, the Flyers' office was closed and there was no way to reach Joe, who was with the team. My next thought was to go straight to the Cap Centre and find out from our trusty trainers where we were staying. When I got there, I found out that there was to be a basketball game there that afternoon and that our trainers wouldn't be allowed in until about four o'clock. By now it was nearing noon and I was feeling more and more the way Jim McKenzie had felt. I was ready to take Joe Kadlec and mash him and bash him and thrash him and lash him.

Someone at the Cap Centre thought that we were staying at the nearby Ramada Inn, so we went there, only to find out that we were staying in a Ramada Inn on the other side of town. By the time we got there, it was about two in the afternoon, our whole day was ruined, and I was seething. Finally I found Joe in the coffee shop and asked him as politely as I could, "Joe, when I was checking with you on Thursday night, why didn't you tell me *then* that we were changing hotels?"

Still and forever unflappable, Joe replied without missing a bite of his hamburger and fries, "All you hadda do was ask."

From that day on, whenever there is an unexpected foul-up in our plans, Bob Taylor, or I, or even Coach Paul Holmgren, will say, "All you hadda do was ask," or another Kadlec standby, "Trust me!"

Here's to you, Joe, and, "*Great* job!"

Anyhow, I went to Joe's hotel suite in Detroit to find out about the Blazers being "Ppd." Kevin Johnson, the Blazers' P.R. man, had worked for Joe with the Devils, so it was not an unnatural thing for Joe to call him now to get the story of the grand opening which had closed before it had opened. While Joe was placing the call, I went into the adjoining bedroom and picked up the extension phone. I'm so glad that I did, because it was a truly remarkable call and a truly remarkable story.

First of all, because of the usual parking problems around the Civic Center, the game had been held up until at least the majority of the sellout crowd could be seated. Then, during the pre-game warm-ups, the players complained that the ice didn't feel or sound quite right. There was still no reason for a postponement, or at least not until the Zamboni machine rolled out to resurface the ice. Unfortunately, instead of smoothing and resurfacing the ice, the Zamboni cracked and then broke the ice into large jagged sections.

At this point I should reassure you that this could not happen in a building designed for ice hockey, because in such a building the refrigeration pipes are set in concrete and water is then sprayed on and frozen in thin layers on top of the solid concrete foundation. In the Civic Center, there being no such arrangement, the refrigeration pipes were set in *sand*. That still would have been all right, but only if the sand were completely *saturated* with water before being frozen. Instead, the water was sprayed on *top* of the sand, so that the traditionally thin coating of ice had nothing to support it from beneath but loose sand. The ice was strong enough to support the weight of the players for a while (despite the strange feel and sound of it), but it was not nearly sturdy enough to withstand the weight of the Zamboni, which assumed a new identity as an icebreaker.

With the Zamboni sitting in the midst of the destruction it had caused, Blazers' president Jim Cooper had to go out and explain to the already disgruntled crowd that the game could not be played. After paying for tickets and parking, and after fighting through traffic and parking delays, followed by a delay of the game, followed by an announcement of postponement, the Philadelphia fans in attendance found a new and novel method of registering their disapproval. Unfortunately for Jim Cooper and the Blazers, upon entering the building each fan had been given a souvenir hockey puck to commemorate the occasion, and most of those pucks were now being returned to the Blazers' management, on the fly, from every part of the building.

After ducking for cover, Cooper found where Derek Sanderson was hiding and "asked" him to serve as team spokesman one more time. So, Derek then had to come out and placate the angry multitude as only he could do: "Well, whatta you gonna do? The ice is bad and we can't play."

The souvenir pucks were already all over the shattered ice, so Derek was spared the indignity of being pelted with any of those. But he was not spared a long and rousing chorus of "BOOO's," to which Derek responded, "Well, if you think *this* is bad, wait till you try and get out of the parking lot!"

Throughout the telling of this tale of disaster and woe by Kevin Johnson, I was holding the receiver to my ear with one hand and covering the mouthpiece with my other hand, all the while rolling on the floor of the bedroom and trying to suppress my hilarity. Joe, meanwhile, after each piece of increasingly horrible news, would say, "Aw, that's a shame," or "Gee, that's really too bad," or "Gosh, what a terrible thing to have happen!"

Everything that could have gone wrong *did* go wrong for the Blazers, not only during their "Ppd." opener, but also later on, when the most popular Blazer, Bernie Parent, broke his foot. In the Blazers' big crosstown shootout with the Flyers, the Blazers' guns were emptying rapidly, while the Flyers were just learning to shoot!

Although the Flyers were still under .500 through late January, for the remainder of the season the war between the W.H.A. Blazers and the N.H.L. Flyers was about as even as a kid with a cap pistol facing Wyatt Earp. And from February on, the memories of the four *worst* years in Flyers history faded quickly, as the buoyant and vigorous young Flyers charged full speed ahead into the four *best* years in their history.

In the final thirty-two games, the Flyers produced their best stretch run to date, 18-9-5, and caught the aging North Stars in a second-place tie, both teams finishing with records of 37-30-11, just nine points behind the now-also-aging and Bobby Hull-less Black Hawks. Suddenly, it was time to celebrate not only the Flyers' first winning season, but many other accomplishments as well.

After five consecutive years of impotent offense, the Flyers of 1972-73 had *five* thirty (or better) goal scorers: Gary Dornhoefer (for the first time), Bill Flett (with a career-high forty-three), Bill Barber (who led all rookies in scoring, but was second to New York's Steve Vickers for the Calder Trophy), Rick MacLeish (who finished with 100 points and became the team's first fifty-goal scorer, including a league-leading twenty-one power-play goals), and Bobby Clarke (who was the *first* Flyer to reach 100 points, and who would be named for the first time as a second-team all-star, behind only league-leading scorer Phil Esposito). At season's end, the N.H.L.'s leading scorers stacked up this way:

1. Esposito, Boston
2. Clarke, Philadelphia
3. Orr, Boston
4. MacLeish, Philadelphia

The Flyers had previously been second to the Bruins not only in scorers, but also in penalty minutes. But that was no longer so, as the Flyers took over the league leadership in "PIM," a dubious honor they would not again relinquish until the decade of the eighties. In fact, the Flyers' identity had been transformed to such an extent that they were now known as well by their aliases as they were by their given name: The Philadelphia Flyers, *a.k.a.* "Freddy's Philistines," also *a.k.a.* "The Mad Squad" (after the popular television police show of that time, "Mod Squad"), also *a.k.a.* "The Broad Street Bullies" (thanks to Jack Chevalier of the *Evening Bulletin*).

The principal perpetrators of the mayhem and molestation which gave rise to these aliases were just four members of the club, but all four were also members in good standing of another club— the "200 Club"—which meant that all four had 200 or more penalty minutes, a first for the Flyers (or for *any* N.H.L. team), and more than enough to make up for the relatively low totals of everyone else. The leader, as always, was Dave "The Hammer" Schultz, who, of course, would set not only all of the Flyers' records for "PIM," but all of the *league's* records as well. But Schultz was far from alone among the "Bullies," as he got plenty of help from Bob "Hound" Kelly (who played hockey as if he were the ball in a pinball machine), and Don "Big Bird" Saleski (who bore an amazing resemblance to the friendly and popular "Sesame Street" character).

In December this trio suddenly became a quartet, with the addition from St. Louis (where else?) of defenseman André "Moose" Dupont. To acquire Dupont, the Flyers gave the Blues two players, first-round bust Pierre Plante (selected with Toronto's choice from the Parent trade) and Brent Hughes, a defenseman who had been extremely popular with the Flyers players. When he first arrived in the Flyers' dressing room, Dupont was a most unwelcome figure, and for several reasons. First, he had suddenly replaced Hughes, one of their best buddies, and second, he still represented in their minds the ugliness of the team they hated the most, the Blues. And it had not been that long since the most recent horror show by the Blues in Philadelphia, which, in fact, had occurred in January of the previous season, shortly after the Blues had acquired Dupont from the Rangers.

That particular brawl, which may have been the most horrendous in the history of the Spectrum, happened this way: The Flyers were leading, two to nothing, late in the second period, and Blues coach Al Arbour was incensed over what he felt was a lack of coherent officiating from referee John Ashley. So irate was the usually mild-mannered Arbour that, at the end of the period, he followed Ashley across the ice and caught up with him in the tunnelway where the Zamboni enters and exits. While Arbour and Ashley were in heated dispute, one of the fans in the seats above the tunnelway quite accurately dumped a large container of beer squarely onto the head of the bespectacled coach, which not only further infuriated Arbour, but also lit the fuse under Arbour's players.

At that time, those players included the likes of Noel Picard, Garry "Iron Man" Unger, the aforementioned Moose Dupont, and the Plager brothers, Barclay and Bob, who decided to serve some vigilante-style justice on the fans of Philadelphia. In a scene right out of the movie *Slap Shot,* both Plagers charged across the ice and up into the stands, scattering patrons, with or without beer, as they climbed up after the culprit. Meanwhile the rest of the Blues were out on the ice being taunted and tormented by the fans, who were safely sheltered behind the glass at the end of the rink while the Blues banged and whacked their sticks at them in frustration.

It looked as though things would quiet down somewhat when the Plagers apparently could not find their man, who was probably out buying another beer to dump. But then, as the Blues were finally heading down the tunnel toward their dressing room, another goonball in the stands took a poke at one of the Blues, and this time the altercation spilled down the tunnelway and all the way *under* the stands.

After about a forty-minute delay to separate the combatants and to assess the damages (the limits of which we would not find out until we read the next day's newspapers), the game resumed with predictable results. The Flyers, who had been sitting in their dressing room the whole time waiting for the trouble to end, were ice cold, while the Blues, with their adrenalin pumping, scored three times in the third period to win the game, three to two.

Some of the Blues, including Coach Arbour, Garry Unger, and the Plagers, got to celebrate their victory by spending the night in the Philadelphia Police Department's "Round House," and while not much else resulted from that "incident," it has to go down in Flyers history as the all-time "Ugliest Performance by a Visiting Team."

It's no wonder, then, that when Moose Dupont walked into the Flyers' dressing room for the first time, he was greeted with less than open arms. Perhaps more of a wonder is the fact that a fight did *not* break out at that moment, especially since Dupont and Hugsy Hughes, the popular Flyer whose place he was taking, had both unknowingly reported first to the wrong dressing rooms. However, it took only a few weeks for Moose Dupont to make an indelible impression upon his new teammates, and also upon fans from, quite literally, coast to coast.

Almost exactly a year from the date of the St. Louis brawl, the Flyers were in Vancouver for a late-December game against Bud Poile's Canucks, when one of those confrontations took place during which every player chooses a dancing partner from the other team and grabs onto his jersey until the dance is over. Don Saleski and his partner were dancing near the player benches when a Vancouver loonie reached over the glass, grabbed Saleski by the hair with both hands, and somehow managed to lift him against the glass in such a way that only the toes of Don's skates were still touching the ice.

Like a cavalry charge, or like a plague of Plagers, the Flyers burst over to the site of the lynching, freed the lynchee, and took on the lyncher and his accomplices. Before long, the brawl was totally out of control, with eight or nine Flyers, including Dupont, Ashbee, Saleski, Schultz, Lonsberry, Flett, Van Impe, Joe Watson, and Bob Taylor, up in the stands looking for reasons to be arrested. The Vancouver Police were, of course, more than willing to comply. Charges were brought against the Flyers in question, and a court hearing was scheduled for the day before the Flyers' next game in Vancouver. Strangely enough, the date of the hearing, Feb. 8, 1973, was precisely one year to the day from the *last* front-page Flyer story in Vancouver—Bruce Gamble's heart attack.

About all that came out of the hearing in February was that the subsequent trial would be delayed until after the hockey season, but the Flyers still had to play the Canucks the next night. With the continuing worry over the pending trial and possible jail sentences, or whatever might be decided in the Vancouver courtroom, I was concerned. No, more than concerned, I was definitely, positively *sure* that the Flyers would tippy-toe around the Pacific Coliseum like little angels, so as not to further incur the wrath of the Vancouver authorities.

Wrong! Within the first two minutes of the game, the now utterly fearless Flyers were involved in *another* full-scale brawl, this time more with the Canucks (who probably thought that they could take advantage of the Flyers' *dis*advantage) than with the fans. And again in the center of the action was the big new defenseman, André Dupont.

My first reaction was shock, then horror, as I thought, "Oh, my God, they're going to be sent to Devil's Island now!" Not only that, but the Flyers had to skate most of the first period two men short. And remember, this was a team struggling to reach the .500 level for the first time. Not to worry. Clarke and MacLeish scored short-handed goals, the super-charged Flyers led six to two after the first period, and they then went on to record the only double-digit road victory in their history, ten to five.

After the game, one of the top reporters for the *Vancouver Sun* sought out the man he considered to be the Flyers' chief villain of the night, André Dupont, and asked him how he viewed the game and the events of the past few days. Moose was sitting by his locker smoking a cigarette, totally naked except for the helmet on his head, as he replied, "Great trip for us. We don't go to jail. We beat up dere chicken forwards. We score ten goal. We win. An' now de Mooze drink beer."

From that point in the season, the fresh and sometimes foolish Flyers would never look back. Trial or no trial, they were hell on skates for the rest of the year, and one of the reasons for that was the new guy who came over from St. Louis, André Dupont. For, despite his goofball antics, Moose was a winner, and it is probably more than coincidence that, after their infamous brawl in the Spectrum, the Blues would not win another game in Philadelphia during Moose's career with the Flyers.

André Dupont was not only a winner, he was (and is) a character of special and endearing qualities, and this is as good a place as any to tell you a little more about the man he/himself called

# Mooze

André Dupont (correctly pronounced dew-POHN, although in Philadelphia it usually came out DOO-pont) was born and raised in Trois-Rivieres, Quebec, and it had to be quite a culture shock when he was drafted by the Rangers and sent to their farm team in Omaha, Nebraska. The change of scene didn't hurt Moose's hockey, as he was named the Central Hockey League's Rookie of the Year in his first season and the C.H.L.'s Most Valuable Player in his second.

But ordering food to put into his 200-plus-pound body was another matter, and the coach of the Omaha Knights, Fred Shero, could not help him with his English as much as he could with his hockey. As the story goes, all Moose ate for the first few weeks he was in Omaha was eggs with toast, because the only meal he felt confident enough to order in English was "two eggs, one side over, and a pair of toast."

When he came out of the Montreal Juniors as a hefty, even overweight winger, Moose more than lived up to his nickname. Fred Shero claims to have taught him to play defense, despite his immobility, by carrying all 250 pounds of him out to center ice and then watching him slash anyone within reach. He must have used this technique fairly effectively, because he collected almost 300 penalty minutes in his first year at Omaha and *over* 300 in his second year. Freddy obviously knew what he was doing, not only when he was teaching the Moose to play defense, but also later on when he pushed to acquire Moose from St. Louis, even though his players didn't like him, or perhaps *because* his players didn't like him.

The same style the Flyers hated the Moose for in St. Louis they loved him for in Philadelphia. I recall one game in particular when the Flyers were leading, three to two, with about two minutes left against the Scouts in Kansas City. The Flyers were two men short, and the Scouts had pulled their goaltender, so it was six skaters against three as Kansas City was desperately going for the tying goal. The three skaters for Philadelphia were forward Bill Barber and defensemen Ed Van Impe and the Moose, who knew perfectly well that no matter what they did, no penalty could make the situation any worse, since three skaters is the minimum allowed by the rules. Well, if you've ever seen one of those slasher movies, that was nothing compared with what Eddie and the Moose dealt out to the poor defenseless Scouts.

Finally, with the Scouts' forwards retreating almost in a deep semi-circle before the grim reapers, Bill Barber scored a shorthanded goal to clinch the outcome at four to two for the Flyers. A team is not often faced with a six-on-three situation, but if it ever comes to that, it certainly helps to have a Moose as one of your three.

Moose's roughhouse style sometimes surfaced at odd times. I can remember when the Flyers obtained a forward named Dennis Ververgaert from Vancouver, and during his first leisurely pre-game skate with the Flyers, Moose welcomed him to Philadelphia by cross-checking him into and almost *over* the boards into the bench area. I was seated nearby and could easily see the puzzled look on Ververgaert's face, and I could also easily hear Moose's deep-voiced explanation: "Dat was just to show dat you're not wit dem pansies anymore in Vancouver."

Moose could take it as well as dish it out, fortunately for him. The worst pain I ever saw him endure was one time when he had dislocated his thumb, and he had to leave the game to have the thumb forced back into place. As this was being accomplished, Bobby Clarke came in and saw Moose looking paler than usual, the cold sweat pouring down from under his helmet, and with a hockey player's traditional disregard for pain, Clarke asked, "Hey, Doc, did Moose cry?"

Before the doctor could answer, Moose said, honestly, "No, but de Mooze make faces!"

Moose's offbeat sense of humor resulted in at least one unique nickname for each and every member of the Flyers' family. For instance, he is the one who gave Bob Taylor the nickname which still sticks with him—"Chef." Everyone assumes that Bob is an expert in the kitchen, which he may be, but the nickname derives from Bob's alleged American Indian heritage, and to Moose an Indian is a chief, and in French "Chief" is "Chef."

Moose loved to prey on ethnic backgrounds, and I recall a game against Toronto when Moose kept yelling at one of the Maple Leafs, "Hey, Swiss Cheese!" At first no one paid much attention, but Moose kept at it: "Hey, Swiss Cheese! Hey, Swiss Cheese!"

Finally, Gary Dornhoefer asked Moose who "Swiss Cheese" was, and Moose answered, "Him!" pointing to defenseman Borje Salming. When it was explained to Moose that Salming was not Swiss, but Swedish, Moose said, "Same ting. Hey, Swiss Cheese!"

Moose scored only fifty-five goals in his eight seasons with the Flyers, but it seemed as though every one of them either tied or won a big game. More important than his goal-scoring, or his sense of humor, or his physical style of play, was his wonderful attitude towards the game. He enjoyed winning, and he enjoyed playing hard and well, but if he had a bad game, or even a bad week, he would simply shake it off and go out and give everything he had in the *next* game. I can recall more than once hearing him say, "Boy, de Mooze was sure horshit tonight!" and then, instead of brooding or worrying, he would find a way to win the *next* night.

Over the years, the Flyers have had a way of weeding out the brooders and the worriers, while seeking to find as many positive-thinking young leaders as possible, no matter what language they spoke. Moose Dupont was one of those leaders.

Moose played out his N.H.L. career as one of the veteran leaders of the young Quebec Nordiques, and then he returned to coach in Trois-Rivieres, where, presumably, he could order a meal of more than "two eggs, one side over, and a pair of toast."

**B**esides Moose Dupont and checker-cheerleader Terry Crisp, the Flyers added "The Little 'O' " to their roster during the 1972-73 season. "O" (for Orest) Kindrachuk was a smart young center who had been signed as a free agent from San Diego, and who was called up late in the season from the Flyers' farm team in Richmond, where he had been the second-leading scorer for the Robins.

Fred Shero also added a five-time American Hockey League all-star from Hershey named Mike Nykoluk, not to play, but to be his assistant coach. By today's standards, that does not sound like an extraordinary move, but at that time, an assistant coach was something football teams had, *not* hockey teams. Hiring Mike Nykoluk demonstrated that Fred Shero was not only an innovator, but also a coach who was not afraid of being replaced by a man most coaches would have considered to be too close for comfort.

With the addition of Dupont, Crisp, Kindrachuk, and Nykoluk, only *one piece* of the Stanley Cup puzzle remained to be filled in—a reliable first-team goaltender. Early in the season, the sad conclusion to Bruce Gamble's career had been recognized with an emotional ceremony, the first such "night" to honor a member of the Flyers. During the season's early going, the Flyers' goaltenders, and they were considered to be equals at that time, were Doug Favell and the "Chef," Bob Taylor.

Unfortunately for Taylor, an early-November start in Pittsburgh would be his last for a while, as a brilliant kick save early in the game cost him a severe hamstring pull in his right leg. Doug Favell, thinking it was not his night to play, had enjoyed a pre-game meal of a pizza, a couple of hot dogs, and a few sodas. When he was forced to enter the game, Dougie spent more time letting out gases than stopping pucks. The Penguins capitalized with three easy goals to put the game away early, and the Flyers' goaltending picture was more muddled than ever.

Bob Taylor came back late in the season, but due to his injury-enforced inactivity, he was not as sharp as he had been early in the year, and he was relegated to a role as a back-up, a role he would have to become accustomed to during his five seasons as a Flyers' goaltender. Perhaps the premature ending to Bob's career as a starting goaltender was a blessing in disguise for him, because it enabled him to become involved in the broadcasting side of the game at a relatively early age. If he had not become involved when he did, I might not have had the distinct pleasure of working with him for the past dozen or so years on Flyers' radio and television. I'm sure the Chef regrets never having had his full shot at success as an N.H.L. goaltender, but I think he realizes that the success he now enjoys may not have come about otherwise. And besides, how many broadcasters *or* goaltenders have their names engraved on the Stanley Cup? Well, Bob Taylor's name is on there *twice*! Here's to you, Chef, my partner and good friend!

While Bob Taylor was out with his injury, a rookie named Michel Belhumeur split the goaltending duties with Doug Favell, and it was with Michel in goal that the Flyers achieved another of their firsts. After six seasons of trying, and thanks to a game-winning goal by Gary Dornhoefer, the Flyers for the first time finally won a game in Chicago.

On the post-game show, I interviewed a still-breathless Michel Belhumeur, who was enjoying the moment that would turn out to be the highlight of his career. After congratulating him for his fine performance as a rookie goaltender defeating the first-place Black Hawks, I said to him, "Probably, of all the Hawks, Dan Maloney gave you the most trouble."

Michel responded with, "Oh? Who ees he?"

I had never anticipated that he wouldn't know, so I said, "He was number nine on the left wing."

Michel concluded this line of in-depth questioning with, "Oh, the big mother with the shot!"

Michel's only season in Philadelphia ended with a respectable record of 9-7-3, but in the playoffs the entire goaltending responsibility was placed on Doug Favell, the sometimes flaky, often spectacular, always entertaining Flip-Flopping Flyer.

This time the first-round playoff opponent would not be St. Louis or Chicago, but Minnesota, the team the Flyers had caught from behind for a second-place tie. Like the Blues, the North Stars had traded most of their high draft choices during their early years for proven veterans, so this would be a good test for the hot, but inexperienced young Flyers. While most of the Flyers were in their early twenties, the North Stars had eight players over the age of thirty-five. I don't believe that there are that many players of that age in the *entire league* today.

During the regular season, the Flyers had the odd home game of the five played between the two teams, and with the three-to-two edge in victories, the home-ice advantage belonged to the Flyers. But only until Game One, because in that game the Flyers were shut out in the Spectrum for their tenth consecutive playoff loss.

Although they won the second game in Philadelphia, the Flyers then had to travel to Minnesota where they were *again* shut out in Game Three, five to nothing. Experience and savvy were getting the better of inexperience and youth, and it looked as though it would be another sad ending for the floundering Flyers.

Then in Game Four, with the Flyers facing the prospect of being down three games to one, Doug Favell shut out the North Stars in their own building, and the series was tied at two games each. Everyone headed back to Philadelphia for Game Five, which turned out to be a classic.

The Flyers led by a goal late in the game, but the Stars tied it and sent it into overtime, and that's when Gary Dornhoefer created a monumental moment in Flyers history. Dornhoefer charged down the left wing, turned the defenseman, skated in on goaltender Cesare Maniago, and shot while being taken down in front of the net. Dornhoefer was still in the air and parallel to the ice when the puck entered the net to give the Flyers their first-ever overtime victory in the Spectrum, and a three-to-two lead in the series. It is that goal by Dornhoefer which is memorialized by the bronze statue "Score!" at the south entrance of the Spectrum, and I can't think of a more appropriate moment to be preserved.

Game Six in Minnesota was *almost* anti-climactic. The North Stars led, one to nothing, after one period, but this game was to be a microcosm of the entire series, and indeed, of the entire season. The big, strong, tough young Flyers dominated the fading Minnesota veterans in the second period, scoring three goals to the North Stars' none. The Flyers won the game, four to one, but more importantly, after six seasons of striving unsuccessfully, the Flyers had finally won their first playoff series. And, after being shut out in two of the first three games of the series, the Flyers had come back to win the next three, with Doug Favell allowing a total of only three goals in those three games. Favell was hot, the Flyers were hot, and now, for the first time, it was "On to the Semi-Finals!"

Before moving on to that next series, I'd like first to pay tribute to the man whose overtime "Score!" won the pivotal game of the Flyers' first victorious playoff series, and that of course would be Gary Dornhoefer, best known to most of us as

# Dorny

Through most of his fourteen-year career in the N.H.L., Gary Dornhoefer's main goal was to get through one whole season injury free. For Gary was the kind of player, perhaps more than any other I've ever seen, who consistently sacrificed his body for the good of the team, usually by screening the opposition's goaltender for a teammate's shot—a custom which made him the target of every defenseman (and goaltender) in the league, save his own. Gary was tall for a forward, but he was mostly skin and bone, and at some time or another everything on his being had been broken, except, that is, his competitive spirit, which was immense.

Like the Moose, Dorny was almost as well known for his acerbic wit as for his razor-sharp elbows. We used to joke that Dorny was in the dressing room between periods sharpening his elbows, when actually he was just sharpening his wit. In fact, he may have been the only Flyer who could get under Moose Dupont's thick skin. I recall one time when he got Moose so upset that Moose, for once, was almost speechless. Finally, all Moose could think of to say was, "Why you...you...Germanshit!"—a term of endearment that several other players repeated and played with until there was a variation for just about every nationality.

Dorny was a fan favorite as well as an athlete's athlete. He was the first Flyer to be given a "night" when retirement was within sight, a night just to honor his contributions as a team man, not a night to sympathize with the tragic conclusion of a career cut short, as had been the case with Bruce Gamble.

Perhaps a more fitting tribute was paid to Dorny by his teammates during his last season. Dorny had just returned from one of his many injuries, I can't recall which injury, there were so many, most of them broken bones. It was during a relatively meaningless game against the Rockies in Colorado, and Dorny managed to score the first of his few goals of the season. It wasn't the kind of goal you'd want to immortalize in bronze. In fact, it took about three bounces and then trickled through the goalie's pads, but it *was* a *goal*, and Dorny had survived some long odds to score it. The reaction of his teammates was marvelous, as every one of them streamed out onto the ice to congratulate their hero and just say, "Welcome back, Dorny."

Dorny had to leave and be welcomed back many times during his years with the Flyers, and he regretted not being on the ice for some of the team's biggest moments. But during the year in which he was able to play *almost* every game, he scored the biggest goal of them all. For that he will be remembered for as long as the bronze on his statue continues to shine. And for those of us who were (and are) honored to know him, he will be remembered for that and so much more. Thanks for the memories, Dorny.

A fter winning the first-round (actually the quarter-final) series in Minnesota, we didn't have a chance to come home before heading for the first game of the semi-finals in (imagine a trumpet fanfare here, if you will) Montreal. And I thought I had been excited the *first* time we were to play there, five and a half years earlier!

This time I had with me some good luck charms that hadn't existed on that first trip, for I had taken to Minnesota with me two German-style army helmets, which some fans had painted orange and black and had inscribed with the players' numbers of the "200 Club," now also known as "Schultz's Army." I thought it might be fun to wear them into Montreal, so I gave one to our television producer, Harlan Singer, and we disembarked right behind Marcel Pelletier, who was the first one off the plane.

The next morning, there on the front page were the three of us, all in our heavy trenchcoats, and Harlan and I in our helmets, under the headline, "Flyers' Army Arrives in City." I don't keep a lot of souvenirs, but I still have those helmets in my den. Although I don't wear them much anymore, they still serve as reminders of the Flyers' first signature, or identity, an identity familiar even to hockey's ultimate fans in Montreal.

The first game in Montreal was true to its build-up. Rick MacLeish scored in overtime to conclude a marvelously exciting contest. Do you remember the goal that Bernie Parent once lost in the sun? Well, on MacLeish's goal, Montreal's Frank "The Big 'M' " Mahovlich claims to have overskated the puck because he had lost it *in a puddle,* thereby allowing MacLeish to skate in alone against goaltender Ken Dryden. You probably had no idea that weather conditions were so important in hockey! For whatever reason, the Flyers had beaten the Canadiens in the Forum, and everyone connected with the team was thrilled, as were the fans back in Philadelphia, who had watched from the edges of their seats via television.

Game Two in Montreal was equally exciting, as again the Flyers took the Canadiens into overtime before a game-winning goal by a rookie defenseman named Larry Robinson, who, amazingly enough, was still winning Cups with the Canadiens in 1986.

Now, finally, after winning their first-ever playoff series in Minnesota, and after splitting two overtime thrillers in Montreal, the Flyers would come home to the Spectrum and to their fans, who had watched, enthralled, as this unprecedented chapter in Flyers history had unfolded on television. And perhaps the most memorable part of this story was the welcome given to the returning Flyers when they first skated onto the Spectrum ice for Game Three. It was beautiful and it was thrilling. The fans stood and they applauded in such a way that the sound of the applause grew, and then it grew some more. No whistling or shouting, no horns or bells, just pure old-fashioned applause, which swelled into the greatest ovation I had ever heard. I remember commenting on the air that I had never heard applause grow and sustain so, and it went on and on, for four, five, six, seven minutes, until it finally *had* to subside under the playing of the national anthem. It was such a wonderful tribute and such a terrific outpouring of love from those fans who had waited so long, and who were now thanking their Flyers for making the wait worthwhile. It was as if they were saying, "You've finally *arrived,* Flyers, and we've arrived, too, and we're with you all the way."

I can recall Gary Dornhoefer telling me later, "Gene, I've been around sports for a while, but I've never heard anything like that in my whole life! What a great feeling!"

The Canadiens won the next three games to win the series, four games to one, an outcome not totally unexpected by most hockey experts. Unfortunately for Doug Favell, his streak of hot goaltending, which had helped the Flyers to defeat Minnesota, had deserted him against Montreal. In the final game of the series, the winning goal was scored from center ice by, appropriately, Frank Mahovlich, and it was a goal all-too-reminiscent of the one Favell had allowed with four seconds left in Buffalo to end the previous season.

Meanwhile, across town at the Civic Center, Bernie Parent had recovered from his broken foot in time for the W.H.A. playoffs, but due to contractual promises not kept, Bernie refused to play for the Blazers, and that was the final humiliating note for the Philadelphia entry of the W.H.A. After the season, the Blazers packed up and moved to Vancouver, in hopes of challenging Bud Poile's Canucks. When the Canucks won that confrontation, the Blazers then moved on to Calgary, before eventually passing into oblivion.

It is said that one "can never go home again," but Bernard Marcel Parent put the lie to that old chestnut when his N.H.L. rights were traded by Toronto to the Flyers in exchange for a number one draft choice and a "player to be named later." At the end of July it was announced that the unnamed player was named Doug Favell.

Not only was the W.H.A. no longer a direct threat to the Flyers, it was now actually *helping* the Flyers, first by leaving Bernie behind in Philadelphia, and almost as importantly, by siphoning off talent from just about every N.H.L. team *except* the Flyers, whose philosophy of making the players happy was now paying off in more ways than one. While upper-echelon N.H.L. teams like Chicago and Montreal were being raided for name players, the growing and strengthening Flyers were now consolidated into a young and spirited, but also talented and deep hockey team—a team with rapport and camaraderie, a team of substance and character.

The Flyers were also a team that was hungry to start the next season. For even though they had lost the semi-final series to Montreal, they knew that they had something special going; they knew that they were ready to challenge for the top; and they knew that they had a coach they could trust and believe in—a coach who was fond of saying, "I don't have the best players; I have the best *team*."

With every part of the puzzle now in place, here is the team with which the Flyers entered the 1973-74 season:

| Goaltenders | Bernie Parent |
| | Bob Taylor |
| | |
| Defensemen | Joe Watson |
| | Ed Van Impe |
| | Barry Ashbee |
| | Tom Bladon |
| | Jimmy Watson |
| | Moose Dupont |

Forwards         Gary Dornhoefer
Simon Nolet
Bobby Clarke
Dave Schultz
Don Saleski
Bill Clement
Bob Kelly
Rick MacLeish
Ross Lonsberry
Bill Flett
Bill Barber
Terry Crisp
Orest Kindrachuk

The two men in charge of developing the battle plans for the Flyers were, of course, assistant coach Mike Nykoluk, and Fred Shero, lovingly known to most of us as

# The Fog

Of all the characters I've known in sports, my most unforgettable character (to borrow a phrase from the *Reader's Digest*) would have to be Fred Shero. Even considering coaches and managers of other sports, from Casey Stengel to Buddy Ryan, Fred Shero is still my choice as the ultimate coaching character. By appearances, you might have thought that he was the absent-minded professor: small, studious, bespectacled, slightly disheveled, eccentric, soft-spoken, even quiet; not just quiet, but quiet to the extent that I often wondered how (or if) he communicated with anyone. Some of his players wondered that, too.

When he first arrived, we all knew that he had been for years a very successful coach in the New York Rangers' farm system. But he was still totally unknown, at least to me, and one had to wonder why he never had been chosen to coach his former team, the Rangers, especially considering all of the coaches they had gone through.

The secrets of Freddy's success were not soon revealed. His disastrous first season had begun with a seven-to-nothing shellacking by Los Angeles, and it had ended with the horrifying Gerry Meehan goal with four seconds left in Buffalo. After that game, a shocked Shero had stated, "I feel as though I've just lost a member of the family."

During his second season, Freddy's mysterious philosophy began to get results, and that is why, despite their playoff loss to Montreal, the Flyers were so anxious to get going with the *next* season, Freddy's third. We'll get to that wonderful year momentarily, but first, an attempt to analyze that mysterious philosophy, the Philosophy of Freddy the Fog.

If I had to summarize Freddy's philosophy in as few words as possible, in college outline form, I would give you first this quote from Freddy himself: "Hockey is a children's game played by men; since it is a children's game, they ought to have fun." And Freddy's players had fun! Oh, my, did *all* of us ever have fun!

Even in practice sessions, Freddy was keenly aware that, to avoid an overdose of stress, things should not be too serious. Still, there was discipline, and there was a point to everything that was done. To avoid becoming stale, or worse yet, bored, the usual drills were *not* repeated over and over. Instead, Freddy would have twelve-on-twelve games, and one-on-one shoot-outs for the ultimate reward of five dollars, a reward fought for in berserk fashion by some rather well-off young men. Once in a while, Freddy would even throw in a drill which seemingly had no purpose. After explaining how he wanted it done, Bobby Clarke would say, "This drill is stupid and meaningless, and I don't think we should do it."

Of course, Freddy would then say, "That's exactly the point, and that's exactly what I *wanted* you to say. Now let's have a five-dollar shoot-out."

Some of the things Freddy insisted upon were at first thought to be a little quirky, or even a little picky. The players didn't think that. *I* did. For instance, when we were traveling, we always heard from Joe Kadlec, "Freddy wants the players on the plane first," and when the beverages were served, "Freddy wants the players to be served first," or when the meals were served, "Freddy wants the players to be served first." Even if the plane were filled with Ed Snider's family and guests, "Freddy wants the players to be served first."

When we were playing at home, Freddy's office was not in the main executive area where everyone else's office had always been, but in what is now the little stick closet by the door of the players' dressing room. Besides a blackboard, the only decoration Freddy ever put up in that "office" was a memo which read, "If you continue to park in the same wrong space in the Spectrum parking lot, your car will be towed."

I once asked Freddy why he did these things, and he answered very simply, "If it comes to a confrontation between management and the players, I want the players to know that I'm on *their* side." I then realized that Freddy's intent was that he wanted the players to know that in his mind, above all else, *the players came first.* All of his subtle little trivialities showed only one thing: It was the players *alone* that mattered to him.

Sometimes Freddy's subtleties were marvelously crafty, and even devious, but ever so effective. On the road, for example, Freddy never set a curfew or held a bed-check. He trusted his players to be the kind of men who knew what was good or bad for them. But he would then set up a schedule which would make staying out late the night before a game almost impossible. Instead of arriving in a new city at night, as most teams did, he would get everyone there in the afternoon, so the players could relax and eat dinner at a proper hour. Then he would hold a team meeting in his room at 10:00 or 11:00 P.M., to go over the next opponents and to announce that there would be a team skate at 9:00 A.M., which would mean leaving the hotel at 8:00 A.M. It was never stated as such, but it was understood that if you still wanted to go out on the town, then "God bless you!"

Because of Freddy and others after him, some one-upsmanship developed in scheduling ice time for the visiting team "before 7:00 A.M. or after 3:00 P.M.," or at some other obviously inconvenient hour. Nowadays, also because of Freddy and others after him, when there is ice available, the visiting team always skates at 11:30 A.M. and the home team skates at any other time it chooses. Freddy's way may have been the best way, because it almost assured, without dictating it, that dinner would be at a sane hour, followed by a good night's sleep during sane hours, followed by breakfast at a sane hour, followed by exercise at a sane hour, followed by lunch at a sane hour, followed by plenty of time to become psyched for the game.

As for the players' diet, Freddy's philosophy was summed up in this statement: "I'm not going to worry about what they eat or drink, or about what they *don't* eat or *don't* drink. They're grown men and they ought to be able to handle themselves. They have a hard enough job just playing a full schedule of games from coast to coast and through two countries, without having to worry about that as well."

This novel attitude of treating the players as men was appreciated by everyone who played for Freddy, as were the times he would give Clarke some money and say, "Take the guys out and buy them dinner."

After a game on the road, the players haven't eaten since noon, and after ten or twelve hours with no food, and following a tough hockey game, they are more than ready to stave off their starvation and quench their thirst. I recall one such time after a game at Chicago Stadium, which is located in an area that looks remarkably similar to what Warsaw looked like after it had been bombed during World War II. In other words, after a game there, you'd better make the team bus or be prepared to spend the night in the team dressing room, because no cab driver is anxious to go there.

On the bus, Freddy would always sit in the right front seat, the one with the view out the front window. Joe Kadlec and I also liked to sit near the front, and on this particular occasion, Freddy leaned over to us and asked, "Where do the players like to go?"

I said, "What do you mean?"

Freddy said, "You know, to eat and drink."

A little hesitant, I said, "Hennessey's."

"Where is that?"

"Downtown."

Then Freddy asked the driver, "Do you know where Hennessey's is?"

"Sure."

"Well, take us there."

When I asked Freddy why he was doing this, he said, "Isn't it kind of foolish to take them back to the hotel, let them flip-flop around the lobby for a while, and then have them all spend money on cab fares to take them to Hennessey's, or wherever, for a few beers and something to eat before bed? We're already paying for this bus, so let's use it to take them some place they like."

When the players realized where the bus was taking them, there were cheers and shouts of "Way to go, Freddy!" and "All right!" and "Let's hear it for Freddy!" And when they were disembarking at Hennessey's, they thanked Freddy appreciatively and asked him if he wanted to join them.

Freddy just said, "No, thanks, I'm going to the hotel."

It was times like that which created the camaraderie, the togetherness, the oneness of that team. Freddy gave the players the tools and the situation in which they could become a really unique team, a team with no cliques and no caste system, no superstars and no hangers-on, a team which mixed together in all possible combinations.

Except for the goaltenders, who always roomed alone, Freddy also made sure that everyone had a chance to room with everyone else during the course of the season, so that everyone could get to know everyone else as well as possible, even the quieter, less outgoing members of the team. And they were all different, with different temperaments, different characters, and with different levels of skills, and of interests, and of intellect. If there was a common bond (other than hockey talent), it was that they were all men of deep-down quality and stature, and they were all being coached and carried to glory by Freddy Shero. And whether they knew it or not, Freddy understood the character of his players better than anyone else. As he put it, "In the first year, I know more about my players than their wives do. And what's more important, I know who's willing to do what it takes to win."

Freddy was so interested in the character of his players that I thought I would throw him a curve one day by asking him, "If you had the chance, would you take Derek Sanderson?" To me, that would have been as difficult a personnel decision as one could possibly make, but Freddy answered without any hesitation at all, "Of course."

"Why?"

"I'll always take talent over no talent. Then it's my job to get the talent to produce."

"Do you ever get involved in the drafting and trading of talent?"

"No, I just take what they give me and do the best I can with those people."

Another example of why Freddy got along so well with his players occurred on another bus, after another game, in another city on the road. This time the bus was to take everyone to the airport, and to help combat the dehydration of the players, cases of beer and soft drinks were placed on the front seat of the bus across the aisle from where Freddy was seated. Joe "Thundermouth" Watson was the first to discover that the occupants of the bus faced serious trouble, because the beer bottles were the old-fashioned kind with untwistable caps. Never one to overreact in a critical situation, Joe turned to Freddy and thundermouthed, "Holy Jeez, Freddy, Holy Jeez! They're not twist-off tops, and they're not cans, and we can't open 'em! What're we gonna do, Freddy? How're we gonna get 'em open? What're we gonna do, Freddy?"

Without even so much as the blink of an eye, and with an expression on his face that made him look as though he had just achieved nirvana, Freddy reached into the breast pocket of his jacket and pulled out a beer opener (affectionately known to some as a "churchkey") and said, "First thing you learn when you turn pro is to carry one of these."

"Way to go, Freddy! All right!"

Who else do you know who carries an opener in his breast pocket? Could Freddy have set up such a scenario? If he did, he certainly couldn't have set it up much better! It was incidents like that which helped to solidify the rapport between Freddy and his players.

Freddy's magic touch was also felt in the way he went about encouraging or congratulating his players. He was not a rump-patter or a "rah-rah-way-to-go" kind of coach. He had more effective ways than that. I recall one game against the Rangers during which the Flyers had let themselves get behind three to nothing during the first two periods. Between the second and third periods, instead of blistering or pleading with his players, Freddy didn't go into the dressing room at all. He allowed the players the time to themselves, to make their own determination as to what had gone wrong.

Since the team had developed the kind of pride which made it extremely distasteful for them to lose to *anyone,* let alone the Rangers, the souped-up Flyers stormed out and chased the Rangers all over the rink in the third period. They didn't win, but with a wonderful comeback effort, they managed to score three goals and accomplish what is known as a "good tie."

After every game, the score sheets are run off and distributed to the media, and one copy is always posted on the dressing room bulletin board, so that the players can check on their shots, assists, goals, penalties, and plus-minus ratings. On this occasion, Freddy intercepted the score sheet before it was posted and wrote across it from lower-left to upper-right: "Money doesn't mean anything to me, but great moments by my team do. Thanks for tonight. Freddy." When that message was hung up in the dressing room, it was gazed upon by the players as if it were a papal encyclical.

Freddy had a great psychological sense about people, especially his own players. With others, he could also be a master of put-on. He never said a whole lot, yet he seemed to *say* a whole lot. And he would take the glare and the criticism of the press on himself, thereby allowing his players to be free to be what they wanted to be. Like a great oriental philosopher, he was often quite cryptic. And like the philosophy from a Chinese fortune cookie, he was often quite funny.

A man who thinks like this can't be entirely crazy, or entirely sane:

"Moose Dupont told me that two men drowned in his home town. I don't understand how two men can drown in Three Rivers."

"I don't like to score too quickly on the power play. I'd rather run 'em around for two minutes."

"There are no heroic tales without heroic tails."

"If Bob Kelly scores twenty goals, I'm not using him correctly."

On Scotty Bowman, then coach of the Canadiens: "I feel sorry for Scotty. It must be tough dealing with twenty-four all-stars."

When Bowman was having a noteworthy verbal battle with Bobby Clarke, Freddy was asked how he was going to handle the situation, so it wouldn't interfere with Clarke's game. Freddy answered that he was going to start Clarke on the right wing, so that he would be on the opposite side of the ice from Bowman. The press had already printed "Clarke Shifted to Right Wing for Montreal" before realizing that in the *next* period the right wing would be on the *same side* as Bowman, skating up and down the ice right in front of him, thus making the situation worse than ever. The headline should have read, "Freddy Fools Press Again."

Freddy also had his fun with the television people. I remember in particular a Sunday afternoon N.H.L. "Game of the Week" on NBC, featuring the Flyers at Boston. All week long the press and, in particular, NBC had been building up the Big Bad Bruins vs. the Broad Street Bullies, Phil Esposito vs. Bobby Clarke, Terry O'Reilly vs. Dave Schultz, and Gerry Cheevers vs. Bernie Parent. Then Freddy threw everyone for a loop when it was announced just before the game that the Flyers' goaltender that day would not be Bernie Parent, but Bob Taylor, who for about forty consecutive games had done nothing but sit on the bench and watch Bernie.

When the NBC announcers, Tim Ryan and "Terrible" Ted Lindsay, heard of this sudden switch, they searched the bowels of the Boston Garden until they finally found Freddy, who was sitting on a wooden folding chair behind the Zamboni, and, as usual, was marking with a pencil on a notepad. "Why Taylor, Freddy? And why now?" asked the men of NBC.

Freddy meditated for a while and then adjusted his glasses for a while, carefully maneuvering them higher onto the bridge of his nose, as he loved to do when anyone was awaiting one of his pearls of wisdom. Finally came the long-awaited answer: "It's his turn."

Freddy had Bob Taylor in goal for another game that I recall very well, a game which I consider to be the most rip-roaring, breathtaking, marvelously zany hockey game that I've ever seen. It was the kind of game that should have been taped and then shown around the world to demonstrate just how exciting a game of hockey can be. This game had a little, or I should say, a *lot* of everything—great plays, costly mistakes, and three fights by Dave Schultz, including a knockout of the Montreal tough guy, John Van Boxmeer, the only *one-punch* knockout I'd ever seen. (I remember Dave standing there, looking embarrassed and not knowing what to do next.) The Flyers beat the Canadiens on the scoreboard also, seven to six, thanks to Bobby Clarke's first hat trick, the third goal of which came on a magnificent play with only a minute left in the game.

After the game, the Montreal press found the mysterious Mr. Shero sitting under a coat rack in the corner of the little room next to the dressing room. "Fred Shero, how do you assess this game tonight?"

Freddy looked down at his note pad and thought and thought. Finally he looked up, adjusted his glasses, and stated matter-of-factly, "Montreal played one goal dumber than us."

The mystique of Fred Shero came in many guises. After another wacky game, I asked Freddy, "What'd you think of the game tonight?"

"I don't think about the games."

"You don't?"

"No. You try to think about all these games, you go goofy."

One of Freddy's greatest strengths was that he didn't dwell upon his defeats, or upon his successes. Even after his most magnificent triumph, winning the Stanley Cup for the first time, Freddy was off to Russia three days later. When asked why he didn't stay around for a while to savor his success, Freddy answered succinctly, "I've already taught them everything I know. The only way they're going to get better is if I get smarter."

Whatever Freddy learned in Russia, it certainly didn't hurt the Flyers' chances when they later had to play against the Russians. Said Freddy, "You don't follow all that fancy looping and circling they do. You just stand up at the blue line, because despite all the looping and circling, eventually they'll have to come to you."

And what Freddy didn't learn from the Russians he would figure out by studying films, or the "fillums," as he called them, and he was the first N.H.L. coach I can recall doing that. Of course, nowadays, studying videotapes is common practice for every team, but Freddy, I believe, started it all with his "fillums" of the Flyers' upcoming opponents, of the Russians, and of his own team.

When the critics complained that his team was too rough, Freddy responded with, "You want to see pretty skating? Go to the Ice Capades." Freddy's teams *were* rough, but they were more *good* than rough. The four members of the "200 Club" were the *only* fighters on the team, and even "Big Bird" Saleski didn't fight much. Schultz, Dupont, and Kelly did more than their share of intimidating, but *everyone* on the team had a role, and *everyone* played. Freddy said, "You must be able to use *all* the players you have. If you can't, you've got to go out and get players you *do* use."

With that philosophy in force, *all* of Freddy's players felt as though they *belonged* and were *wanted,* and perhaps even more important, when crunch time came in the third period, the key players were not worn to a frazzle; they were warmed up and ready to dominate the last part of the game. Under Freddy, the Flyers became known as a team that *"owned* the third period."

And who were these key players who made the big difference? Freddy believed that every great hockey team has six key players, and it may be worth giving up three or four or even five players to get one of those six. The four-time champion Edmonton Oilers of recent vintage were a journeymen group except for their six great players—Gretzky, Coffey, Kurri, Anderson, Messier, and Fuhr. Freddy's first six were: Clarke, MacLeish, Barber, Schultz, Ashbee, and Parent. The others were more than journeymen, but they were still what the opera calls "spear carriers" when compared with the Big Six. I disagree with Freddy a little about the key six. I believe there were seven, the seventh being Freddy himself.

Freddy was concerned about *all* of his players, no matter who they were or where they ranked on the team's depth chart. He was concerned about them on the ice and off, during the season and during the off-season. Freddy's philosophy (begun by the Sniders in the early seventies) was: "As long as you earn your living here in the Philadelphia area, you ought to live here; and if you're going to live here, you ought to become solid citizens of this community." As a result of that philosophy, the homes of most Flyers are in the Philadelphia area, rather than in the Canadian towns of Flin Flon, or Kitchener, or Port Credit. And this also explains the tremendous success of a myriad of off-ice ventures, from charity softball games to the "Flyer Wives Fight for Lives" Leukemia Fund.

To his players, Freddy was like a good father. They didn't always understand him, but they always knew that he cared. And they trusted him. And that made it just that much tougher when the divorce came, and Freddy became coach and *general manager* of the organization he had lived with for most of his professional life, the New York Rangers.

It wasn't that he didn't care about his players anymore, and it wasn't the money that made him do it. It was actually the fulfillment of a dream he had always had, realistic or not, and Freddy accepted the challenge of being his own general manager, not just a coach who "takes what they give me." The unfortunate part, as far as the Flyers were concerned, was that he had a year left on his contract, and when the rumors started about New York, he had said he wasn't leaving. When he left, Bobby Clarke and the others felt betrayed. After seven years of hearing Freddy talk about honesty, integrity, and loyalty, he had lied to them, and he had left, leaving a distinctly sour taste in the mouths of all.

Psychologist that he was, and crafty as he was, I don't believe that Freddy was devious in the nasty sense of the word. His agent had probably worked out the whole deal with the Rangers, getting for his client an advancement in both position and salary, and returning him to the family with which he had grown up, and then told Freddy, "If anyone asks you, you're not going." So, by honoring his agent's request, Freddy had left a dark cloud over Camelot, and the gap between Philadelphia and New York seemed more cavernous than ever.

When Freddy returned to the Spectrum as the coach of the Rangers, he was, of course, booed by the fans who had loved him so much. The New York fans didn't know what to make of him, but when the Rangers made it to the Stanley Cup Finals in his first year, they expected even more in his second year. They didn't get more; they got less, as this time their team was eliminated in the quarterfinals. In his third year in New York, Freddy began losing interest, especially when he realized that he didn't *really* have control of his team. He was disillusioned, he drowned his sorrows in alcohol, and he was fired in mid-season.

Freddy became very sick, and there were even rumors that he might not survive. Freddy not only survived, he was redeemed. Bobby Clarke provided the first bridge to Freddy's glorious past when he asked specifically that Freddy be the primary speaker at Clarke's retirement dinner. Freddy gave a marvelous speech, and he was invited back again to be the coach of the Flyers' old-timers team. This time the fans greeted him with affectionate cheers.

After some television and public relations work for the New Jersey Devils (part-way between New York and Philadelphia), and a year of coaching a team in Holland, Freddy returned to the Flyers' family in the spring of 1990 as a senior advisor. He is a happy man now, and it's always a joy to see him. In fact, the longer he lives, and the healthier he gets, the better I feel.

To paraphrase Winston Churchill, I believe that if the Flyers live a thousand years, there will never be a more shining hour than the term of Fred Shero and the Broad Street Bullies.

Thanks, Freddy.

# That Wonderful Year: 1973-74

After the two original Flyer goaltenders were traded for one another, Doug Favell's inconsistency (five or six great saves followed by a debilitating "bad" goal) was suddenly replaced by the steady brilliance of Bernie Parent, now all the steadier and more brilliant after his association with Jacques Plante in Toronto, and despite his wasted year with the Blazers. It was a sad move for Dougie, who had grown with the Flyers through their first six seasons, and who would now have to struggle with the inept Maple Leafs, a team Bernie wasn't anxious to play for either. But for Bernie and the Flyers, it was a move that meant that the last piece of the Stanley Cup puzzle was now in place.

The entire cast was set: the owners, the front office executives, the coaches, and the players. And there was also one final secret ingredient—a person who would soon become the Flyers' legendary secret weapon. Her name was

# Kate

There have been many versions of "The Legend of Kate," most of them inaccurate. Here's the way it really came about:

Lou Scheinfeld (the Flyers' executive who had conceived the idea of buying the bales of neckties) noticed and was concerned about the growing lack of attention and respect displayed during the playing of the national anthem, a difficult piece of music to sing, even under the best of circumstances. So, Lou tried to shake everyone up by periodically replacing the traditional anthem with a recording of Irving Berlin's "God Bless America," as sung by Kate Smith. Lou succeeded in shaking up some people to the point of inspiring numerous letters of violent protest.

The Flyers weren't winning much when this experiment began, but it was noticed that the first time Kate's voice was heard, the Flyers won. Despite the protests, Kate's recording was tried again, and again, and the Flyers won again, and again. Soon it was recognized by everyone that whenever Kate's "God Bless America" was played, the Flyers won, and it became part of the pre-game ritual to try to figure out whether Kate would be played or not.

Before long it became apparent that Kate was no longer just an experiment to shake up the troops. She was a psychological weapon strategically used only in the big games against Montreal or Boston, or against division rivals like Chicago and St. Louis. Before those games, there was electricity in the air as the announcement came: "Join Kate Smith..." and the rest would be lost in the roar of the crowd, until the music started and everyone sang "God Bless America." After the game, there would be another roar when the scoreboard would display a message something like: "KATE'S RECORD IS NOW 37-3-1!"

In the summer before the Flyers' seventh season (1973-74), Lou Scheinfeld had another idea: Why not have Kate come and sing *live* at the Spectrum before the season's opening game? Contacts were made with Kate's home on Long Island, but all requests were answered with solid "No's." With some further gentle probing, it was learned that Kate had declined because she was sincerely and deeply concerned about how a rough, tough modern-day sports crowd would react to a singer whose career had been totally in eclipse, and who may have been totally unknown to anyone not around in the thirties and forties, when her career was at its peak.

Despite all of her concerns, and despite her previous rejections of the idea, Kate was finally convinced to give it a try. It was agreed by all concerned that this live appearance would not be advertised in any way. This would truly be a secret mission by the Flyers' secret weapon, known only to Kate and her closest associates, a few people in the Flyers' front office, and the chauffeur who would drive a limousine to Long Island and transport Kate to the Spectrum.

When opening night arrived, there was plenty to be excited about. There usually is on opening night, but this time the Flyers were actually *starting* the season that they had been so hungry to start at the end of the previous season. Not only that, but their opponents were the Toronto Maple Leafs, featuring their newly-acquired goaltender, Doug Favell.

When the players were introduced, there were cheers for Favell, and there was a warm welcome-back-home ovation for the goaltender at the opposite end of the ice, Bernie Parent. Meanwhile, quite unobtrusively, a carpet was being unrolled from the Zamboni end of the ice, followed by a small electric organ and a floor microphone, which were set up at the end of the carpet, near Doug Favell.

Then from public address announcer Lou Nolan came these words: "At the beginning of this new season, would you all please rise and join us in the singing of 'God Bless America'..." (a roar from the crowd) "...with Kate Smith..." (a mightier roar) "... LIVE!"

When Kate walked out onto that carpet, the building literally exploded with an ovation that rose in a crescendo until it was absolutely deafening. In all of the great events that I've witnessed, in sports and otherwise, I've never heard a warmer ovation. Anyone who didn't have chills or goose bumps had to be someone who couldn't be inspired by *anything*.

There was still one small question to be answered. At her advanced age, and after having been out of touch for so long, how well would Kate be able to sing? I remembered having heard her live on the Steel Pier in the late thirties, and being thrilled by her voice, but after thirty-five years or so, one had to wonder if the clarity would still be there. It was. She sang beautifully. Another ovation drowned out her final words, and then went on and on, as Kate smiled, and waved, and blew kisses to her enraptured audience.

It was the culmination of the most bizarre, the most unexplainable, and the most wonderful and memorable partnership imaginable, unmatched anywhere in the history of sports—the partnership of a sixty-six-year-old pop singer of thirty years before with a rough and crazy bunch of mostly Canadians called the Broad Street Bullies, all bound together by the singing of a patriotic song about America. It was a partnership which remains unmatched to this day, and will probably remain unmatched always.

I f ever there was an omen that a sports team was due for an extraordinary season of unbelievable excellence and achievement, the first live appearance of Kate Smith at the Spectrum was that omen. As Doug Favell said after the game, "As soon as I saw her, I knew we were cooked."

Kate got some help from Bernie Parent, who shut out Toronto in the opener, and then followed that with a shutout of the New York Islanders in the season's second game. After his rocky year with the W.H.A., Bernie was not only back, he was ready for the finest season of his career.

Offensively, the Flyers did *not* have their finest season. In fact, they didn't match in numbers what they had done the year before. There were no 50-goal scorers and no 100-point players, and this time the league's top four scorers were all Boston Bruins, instead of two Bruins and two Flyers. But with Bernie in the nets, the Flyers didn't *need* to score as much. The latter stages of most games were spent helping Bernie to protect a lead, rather than trying to roll up the score.

After Bernie's shutouts in the first two games, the Flyers won two more games and then lost three straight, two of the losses coming in Vancouver and Los Angeles. The Flyers would not lose again in either of those places for more than a decade. More importantly, for the rest of the season they would not lose more than two in a row, and that happened only once. From a record of four and three after the first seven games, the remainder of the season resembled the spectacular closing drive of the previous season.

The most important game of the regular season took place on March 14 before a Spectrum sellout crowd of 17,007. The Flyers had a chance to clinch their first Western Division title since their inaugural season, six years before, but their opponents on this day were the leaders of the Eastern Division—the Boston Bruins—a team the Flyers had not beaten in their *last twenty-seven tries*. The Flyers had defeated the Bruins three times in the early years, but since their last victory, their record against Boston was an unsightly 0-24-3.

But on this day, with the division championship at stake, and with the growing possibility of meeting the Bruins later on in the playoffs, the Flyers outshot the league's highest-scoring team, forty to twenty-five, and won, five to three, but more convincingly than that score would indicate. The Flyers had proven they could beat the league's best on a given day at home, but they still had only four wins in seven *years* against the Bruins, and if they were to meet them again in the playoffs, they would need four wins in seven *games,* and at least one of those wins would probably have to be *in Boston.*

Such challenging thoughts did not discourage the Flyers in the least. In fact, the celebration in the dressing room following that huge victory was one of the most memorable I can recall. Champagne was flowing freely down everyone's throat and all over everyone's hair and clothing, when, suddenly, some of the players noticed me and thought, for some reason, that it would be a good idea to throw the "Mound of Sound" into the shower. Four guys grabbed me and were trying to pull my 280 pounds away from the locker onto which I was desperately clinging, when I heard Keith Allen's voice above the others' yelling, "Gene, Gene, let them do it! I don't want any players hurt!"

So, that night I took an earlier shower than I'm accustomed to. I thought it was pretty funny until I realized that not only was I soaking wet, but also the sleeve of my jacket was badly ripped and a large hole had been torn in the knee of my pants. I could live with all of that until I also realized that I had promised to appear after the game on a national telethon, the local segment of which was being televised from a studio in Veterans Stadium, across the street from the Spectrum. And, of course, I had no change of clothes with me, since I had planned on going directly to the studio, without first detouring through the shower.

When I arrived at the studio, I explained my situation to the telethon's local host, Bill "Wee Willie" Webber: "Bill, I'm in trouble. My jacket is torn, I've got a hole in my pants, and I'm soaking wet."

Bill said, "Don't worry. Just comb your hair. We'll smooth out your jacket and the wrinkles in your shirt, and we'll shoot you from the waist up. Nobody will see the hole in your pants, and no one will be able to see that you're all wet."

What Bill and I didn't think of was the hot television lights, and the fact that heat causes moisture to evaporate. As Bill was interviewing me, a steamy mist of water vapor began to envelop me, and it became quite obvious to the television audience that I was not a normal-looking 280-pound guest. Bill said, "This is the first time, Gene, that I've ever seen a guest of mine stand in an aura. You actually look holy!"

"Well, Bill, I'm holy all right, but only on the knee." Then they showed the knee in question, and I told the "hole" truth about the Flyers' unique victory celebration.

For the remainder of the season there would be many *other* reasons for celebration. The Flyers finished the regular season with an even better stretch run than the one of the previous season, losing only two of their final twenty games, and those two losses came after all of the league standings had already been clinched. The Flyers lost only sixteen games all season, while winning fifty for the first time. They not only won the West, but they set a new Western Division record with 112 points, 7 more than the 105 accumulated by the Black Hawks, who had one of *their* best seasons. Unfortunately for the Flyers, their total of 112 was still 1 point shy of Boston's 113, which meant that the Flyers would have the home-ice advantage over every possible playoff opponent *except Boston.*

In the season's next-to-last game, with the final standings already determined, Fred Shero decided to rest Parent, Clarke, and a few others, and the Flyers lost to Pittsburgh, six to one, thereby apparently eliminating their chance to win the Vezina Trophy for fewest goals allowed during the season. But, on the last day, the Flyers beat Minnesota, while in Chicago Marcel Dionne of the Red Wings scored a goal in the season's final minute, with the result being that the Flyers (and Bernie Parent) wound up in an exact tie with the Black Hawks (and Tony Esposito) for the Vezina. Interestingly enough, the Flyers scored one more goal than Chicago during the season, which meant that after a combined total of 156 games, those two teams finished only one goal apart.

And speaking of goalie Tony Esposito, the brother of Boston's all-star center Phil Esposito, I am reminded of one of my favorite trivia questions: Of all the famous brother combinations in hockey, other than the Hulls, the Richards, and the Mahovlichs, which two brothers scored the most combined goals? The answer, of course, is the Espositos, with 717 (778, including playoffs); Phil had 717 (or 778), and Tony had zero (or zero).

Bernie Parent didn't score any goals either, but what an extraordinary year his first Vezina season was. And when I say "season," I mean that almost literally, since Bernie played all but six games. He lost only thirteen of his seventy-two starts, tying twelve, and winning *forty-seven,* the most wins ever in one season for an N.H.L. goaltender. He also collected a personal and league high of twelve shutouts, and he finished the season with a remarkable goals-against average of 1.89 per game.

Of all the staggering statistics of that great season, perhaps the most significant was this one: The Flyers sold out seventy of their seventy-eight games, including *every* home game—at a Spectrum capacity of some 2,400 more than could have been squeezed in a few years earlier. Seats had been added in every conceivable location—in a new third deck, in some areas which had previously been used only for press, radio, and television, as well as in the old concessions stands, which had been moved to the outside walls so that their spaces could be transformed into "super boxes." There were even folding chairs added in some of the aisles, and new ingeniously designed rows of hanging seats were suspended from the concrete arches over the entrance/exit portals. And wherever it was located, *every one* of those seats was occupied by a paying patron for *every one* of the Flyers' home games.

Of the eight road games which did *not* sell out, one was the season's second game on Long Island, one was *almost* sold out in Atlanta, one was in Pittsburgh where sellouts were rare, and five were in California (three in Oakland, two in Los Angeles), where no one *ever* sold out. During the final one-third of the season, *every* Flyers game was a sellout, even though fourteen of the final twenty-nine were on the road.

The purpose of hockey, or any other sport, is entertainment, and the Flyers were a hit in more ways than one. As their fame and notoriety increased, the response of the ticket-buying fans around the N.H.L. increased as well, even if only because they wanted to root against the team they loved to hate. And no team ever had more detractors than the Flyers, unfairly so, I believe. In fact I've always resented the many writers and even league officials who said that the Flyers were bad for the game, and that they intimidated and fought their way to the top, and that this couldn't happen today, and that the Flyers were just lucky that they were allowed to get away with everything they got away with.

Hogwash! These same pious and hypocritical "experts" condemn the Flyers and then call the fierce, nasty, ugly wars between Montreal and Quebec—"Battles for Provincial Honor." Hogwash and doublespeak! There were excesses among the Flyers, just as there are, and probably always will be, with Montreal and Quebec. And what about Montreal and Calgary during the 1986 Stanley Cup Finals? And speaking of Montreal, isn't it ironic that the Canadiens became one of the *most* penalized teams in the league, while the Flyers became one of the *least* penalized?

Condemning the Flyers for the actions of Dave Schultz and a few others is like condemning the great Pittsburgh Steeler teams of the seventies for the actions of "Mean Joe" Greene and the "Steel Curtain" defense. Hockey, like football, is a collision sport. It is not like dancing, which is, or used to be, a contact sport. Besides, condemning *any* great team detracts from and, in effect, condemns the entire sport.

In all of the condemnation of the Flyers' "brutality" and "viciousness" (terms which were thrown at the whole team, but which could have been meant for, even loosely, only four individuals at the most), overlooked was the fact that the Flyers were an exciting, wonderfully alive, brilliantly talented hockey club, a club which possessed every element necessary to win *any* kind of hockey game. They had great goal scorers in MacLeish, Barber, and later, Reggie Leach. They had great leadership and inspiration from the league's three-time Most Valuable Player, Bobby Clarke, and from their coach, Fred Shero. They could play three or even four excellent lines, two of which were high-scoring lines. They had strength "up the middle," as they like to say in baseball, with five superior centermen and a defensive corps featuring the solidarity and spunk of Van Impe, the Watsons, and all-star Barry Ashbee. And backing up all of that talent was the world's greatest goaltender of that time, and one of the greatest of *all* time, Bernie Parent. "Great defense wins championships," as they like to say in football. Well, the same applies in *any* sport, and the Flyers had the best defense in hockey.

While the Flyers had excessive amounts of penalties called against them, they were also excessively excellent at killing those penalties, and at just about any other aspect of the game that you would care to discuss. Most teams preferred to talk about their fighting, but as Fred Shero put it, "Fighting and talking are both part of the game. Hockey is just a love affair when you don't have any fighting. And as for talking, you show me a team you can talk to, and I'll show you a team you can beat."

The Flyers didn't win them all. No one does that. But the teams which somehow managed to beat them had so much physical and psychic energy drained from them in the process, that they were inevitably impotent for the next game or two afterward.

Perhaps Montreal captain Henri Richard best summed up how "lucky" the Flyers were to finish ahead of the Canadiens, when he said, "We need to work harder, that's all. Now look at Philadelphia. They work harder than any other team in hockey."

Lucky? Bullies? All things considered, I hope you'll agree with me, and with former all-star and network television commentator Ted Lindsay, who stated simply enough, "The Flyers play the game the way it was meant to be played."

Whatever you want to call what the Flyers were doing, they must have been doing something right, because they were setting new attendance records everywhere they went. I also had a *personal* attendance record of which I was rather proud: In the Flyers' seven-year history, I had never missed a game. But, three days from the end of the season, I was sure that my streak was over. I noticed a lump inside my thigh, just above the knee, and I thought it was just a pulled muscle, but my doctor was very concerned and ordered me into the hospital. Instead of a pulled muscle, I was diagnosed as having phlebitis, or a blood clot, which might have occurred from sitting in one position for too long with my knee bent, as would happen on one of those long nonstop charter flights that the Flyers make so frequently.

So, there I was in my hospital bed, with my consecutive-game streak in severe jeopardy, since the Flyers were 350 miles away in Pittsburgh. But, to the rescue came Harlan Singer, who arranged a microphone hook-up from my bed to the Pittsburgh Civic Arena, where Don Earle was to do the play-by-play, assisted by Bobby Clarke, who was sitting out the game. It was an odd feeling lying there watching my television monitor and saying, "Hi, Gene Hart from Jefferson Hospital in Philadelphia, along with Don Earle and Bobby Clarke at the Civic Arena in Pittsburgh..."

Before long my loud voice had attracted some curiosity seekers to my partially opened door, and they were obviously intrigued by the sight and sound of a large man in a hospital gown, with heat packs around his leg, lying in bed and talking loudly into a microphone about a game he's watching on television. Eventually quite a crowd gathered in my room, and soon there was more cheering going on in there than there was in Pittsburgh, at least for the Flyers. It didn't help them win, but it bolstered my spirits, and my streak was still alive.

The doctors wanted me to stay in the hospital for a week, but I said, "No way!" since the playoffs were to start in three days. I promised to broadcast standing up, through most of the first game at least, to avoid further complications with the leg. Nothing short of a general anesthetic was going to keep me away from those playoffs!

Round One of three best-of-seven playoff rounds was to be against the Atlanta Flames, who believed that they could upset the Flyers, even though the first two games were in Philadelphia. The Flyers may have been ready to be upset, too, because they seemed to have a case of first-game jitters, as did I, especially since I wasn't supposed to sit down for most of the game. With the Flames on a power play near the end of the first period, good old reliable Gary Dornhoefer scored a short-handed goal in the last half-minute of the period, and suddenly the nervousness was gone. Dornhoefer's goal got everyone going, Orest Kindrachuk added two more goals, and the Flyers then breezed, five to one.

In Game Two, Barry Ashbee had three second-period assists, Rick MacLeish had three second-period goals, and the Flyers won again, five to one.

In Atlanta for Game Three, tempers flared for the first time in the series. Goalie Dan Bouchard became enraged over a MacLeish goal which should not have been allowed, and he was ejected from the game. Even though the site and tone had changed, the Flyers still won rather easily, four to one.

Then, with the Flyers holding a three-games-to-none lead, one of the most memorable events of the series (and the season) occurred, but it did *not* occur on the ice. In fact no one is sure to this day exactly *what* occurred or *where* it occurred, but it *is* known that Fred Shero was missing for one whole night in Atlanta, and that when he reappeared, it was apparent that he had been mugged, or had been in a heck of a fight, or had been run over by an Atlanta street-cleaning machine. Whatever had happened to him was never clarified by Freddy, possibly because he himself wasn't too sure. At any rate, that was probably the most bizarre of all the bizarre escapades attributed to Freddy during his coaching career, and it was certainly the one which earned him his nickname, "The Fog."

In Freddy's place behind the bench for Game Four in Atlanta was Assistant Coach Mike Nykoluk. The Flyers played at the start as if they had been following in Freddy's nocturnal footsteps, and the Flames led, three to nothing, after one period. In the second period, Atlanta rabble-rouser Bryan (father of Ron) Hextall was pounded in a fight, and the Flyers came alive, scoring once in the second and twice more in the third to send the game into overtime. About five minutes into the extra period, Bobby Clarke picked off a pass and fed Dave Schultz, who was all alone as he put the puck past goaltender Phil Myre (a Flyer-to-be) to win it for Philadelphia, four to three. With, and then without, Fred Shero, the Flyers had swept the Flames, allowing just six goals in the four games.

Where there were Flames, there may have been smoke, but no "Fog." For the *next* series, Round Two—the Stanley Cup Semi-Finals—Freddy would be ready, and so would his team, because the opponents this time would be the New York Rangers.

The Rangers were a great team that year, and they were favored to beat the Flyers and then give Boston a battle for the Cup. The Rangers, in fact, had all the qualities necessary to *win* the Cup. They had three excellent lines, the most glamorous of which was their top line of Jean Ratelle, Rod Gilbert, and Vic Hadfield. They had superior defense, featuring smart, staunch, solid veterans Brad Park and Dale Rolfe. And they had a wonderfully clever and active goaltender in Eddie Giacomin. They hit, they were tenacious, and they were well balanced. They were just plain *good.*

In many ways the Rangers and the Flyers were perfectly matched against each other, but there was a major difference in team personality. The Rangers were the stylish, gray flannel suit and rep tie guys from Madison Avenue, with the perfectly coiffed hair and the attaché cases, while the Flyers were the blue-collar team, a bunch of guys who would scramble, grab your skate, bite your ankle, and dive into the goal post head first. If the Flyers were to have any kind of edge against the Rangers, it would have to be their willingness to allow their hair to be mussed. And, of course, the Flyers had the home-ice advantage.

The Rangers had been through a tougher first-round series than the Flyers had, and at the start they were no match for the well-prepared Flyers, who won the first two games in the Spectrum, four to nothing and five to two.

Jolted by the relative ease of the Flyers' first two wins, the Rangers won the next two in New York, five to three, and then two to one in overtime. The Rangers had tied the series at two games each, but far more important was an incident which occurred early in the overtime period. A shot from the point by Ranger defenseman Dale Rolfe was deflected directly into the eye of Flyer defenseman Barry Ashbee, and what a horror it was to see! Even from the distance of the Garden broadcast booth, I could see the blood fly, and my first thought was, "Oh, my God! How serious is it? Will he be blinded? Will this put him out for the series? For the season? Forever?"

We later learned that Barry would be lost to the team for an undetermined period of time, and then it was as though an epidemic hit the Flyers, as Bob Kelly, Bill Clement, and later, Gary Dornhoefer all joined Barry on the injured list. With Flyers dropping right and left, and with the series now tied, there was no way the Rangers could lose, and there was no way the Flyers could win. Was there? I must admit that I had my doubts.

The next two games were not close, the Flyers winning at the Spectrum, four to one, and the Rangers winning in the Garden by the same score. Now the series was tied at three apiece, with each team having won all of its home games.

The seventh and deciding game was played at the Spectrum on Sunday afternoon, May 5, before a wildly anticipatory sellout crowd and a national television audience. The game was as even and as tension-packed as one might expect from these two teams, but if ever one incident defined the Flyers' edge, it came in the third period, with the Flyers leading three to two. There was a battle for the puck in the corner, involving Brad Park, Dale Rolfe, and Dave Schultz. When Schultz felt that he had been challenged, he started in on Dale Rolfe. It was a terribly one-sided confrontation, but the most significant part was that as poor Dale Rolfe was being hammered into the ice by Dave Schultz, not one Ranger made a move to come to his aid, not even Brad Park, who later was quoted as saying, "If I had to win that way, I don't want to win." He got his wish not only that day, but later on during his brief tenure as coach of the Detroit Red Wings, when he was suspended because of the brawls in which his team was involved.

Less than a minute after Rolfe and Schultz had been removed from the ice, Gary Dornhoefer scored to give the Flyers a four-to-two lead. But then, with five minutes left, Peter Stemkowski scored for the Rangers, and it was four to three, and time for the nail-biters to chew on their fingertips. With time running out on them, the Rangers then made a tactical blunder which eliminated their last real chance to tie; they were assessed a two-minute penalty for too many men on the ice. Instead of going on to the finals and to the

Cup they thought they deserved, the Rangers were going nowhere but home for the summer.

Despite their injuries, the Flyers had scrapped and checked and then checked some more, and they had survived. The season was already far more successful than anyone had dared to hope for, because the Flyers had upset the Rangers and were now going on to the Stanley Cup Finals—one step beyond anything they had ever accomplished before. And like the semi-final series against Montreal the season before, it would be good experience to play in the finals for the first time, even if they did have to face Boston, the team they had beaten just four times in seven years, and even if Boston did have the home-ice advantage. Maybe they could steal one win somehow, as they had done against Montreal the year before, and that would be enough incentive to make them hungry for the start of the *next* season.

Against the Eastern Division Champion Bruins, the Flyers were given *no* chance—none. And now they would have to go to Boston without some of their key players, and in particular, without the man they called

# Ash Can

On paper, Barry Ashbee's career statistics look like those of a thousand other journeyman defensemen, and perhaps that is why he remained buried in the minor leagues for so long. When he finally made it to the Flyers at the age of thirty-one, my first impression of him was that he was a loner, an unhappy man, even an *angry* man. That may have been *because* of all those years in the minors, including seven years at Hershey during which he was given only one brief trial by the Boston Bruins, and that had been five long years before. Or it may have been because of the pain that was always his companion, the pain that made it necessary for him to wear a padded "horse collar" around his neck when he played, to prevent further nerve damage.

At first I thought he might not make it with the Flyers, but was I ever wrong! He played magnificently for four seasons, and at the conclusion of his fourth season, he became the first Flyer defenseman ever to be named to the N.H.L. All-Star Team. Over those four seasons, Barry learned to relax and to enjoy his teammates, and eventually he lost most of his angry-man demeanor. That was the result of the way Fred Shero treated him, and of the quality people around him, and of the sheer joy of winning at the major-league level.

What a leader he turned out to be, and what a battler! Not a fighter, a battler! He had battled through all of that pain for all of those seasons in the minors, and he wasn't about to stop just because he had made it to the big time. He was always direct, never subtle, and occasionally his directness would get him in trouble. I recall a game in Pittsburgh, when referee Bryan Lewis called a penalty on Barry, who reverted to his angry-man self. I marked down the penalty and then looked up to see what call Lewis would make, but I couldn't find him, and I couldn't figure out where he had gone. Finally my partner Don Earle pointed to the monitor, and I then realized that Barry had decked Lewis with a right hand and that Lewis wasn't making any calls at the moment, and he wasn't taking any calls either!

Barry was, of course, suspended for being so direct with his critique of the officiating. The only similar incident I can remember was years later when Paul Holmgren contacted an official and was suspended, but Barry Ashbee was the only guy I can recall ever belting a referee.

Barry's unsubtle approach was also effective with non-officials. I remember in particular a time in Oakland, when we were preparing to leave our hotel for the airport, which was only about five minutes away. The team bus was scheduled to leave at 7:30 A.M., but as always, if all the players were on board before the scheduled departure time, the bus would leave earlier. Since the bus was primarily for the players, they might wait for another player, but certainly not for anyone else. So, as a rule, unless you're a player, it's smart to be on the bus about fifteen minutes before the scheduled time.

Well, on this particular morning, all of the players were on board, and the bus was pulling away from the hotel just as Don Earle was coming out of the lobby. Since the hotel frequently shuttles courtesy vans to and from the airport, it was assumed that Don would soon catch one of them and be at the airport at almost the same time as everyone else. As it turned out, that's exactly what happened. But unfortunately, Don took it as a personal affront that the team bus had not been held for him. When he arrived at the airport, Don took his two bags and marched purposefully up to the front of the long line of players, who were all patiently waiting to check their own bags. When he reached the head of the line, Don plunked down his bags, as if to say, "How dare you leave me behind!"

When Barry Ashbee saw what Don had done, he walked with equal vigor and purpose to the front of the line, picked up both of Don's bags, walked all the way to the other side of the terminal, and unceremoniously heaved both bags through a window and into the street. Without saying a word, and without laying a finger on Don, Barry had made an eloquent statement indeed. Don didn't talk to Barry, or to me, or to anyone else, for two days after that, but he wasn't late for the team bus, either.

Barry's direct, unsubtle, honest approach enabled him to battle successfully against the longest of odds, but when Dale Rolfe's million-to-one shot deflected into his eye, he was suddenly faced with the end of his career as a player, and a different kind of battle began. When he realized and accepted the fact that his playing days were over, he was, of course, disappointed and sad, especially since he and his team were both at the peak of their hockey lives. But I have never seen such a look of shimmering pride in a man's face, even through the dark glasses he had to wear, as when Barry told the teammates he loved so much, "Boys, cherish this group; there'll never be another one like it."

The following year Barry was offered the opportunity to join Fred Shero and Mike Nykoluk as an assistant coach. Barry was extremely cautious and reluctant to accept, because deep down he was concerned that a bone was being thrown to a handicapped guy. Barry knew that even *one* assistant coach was unprecedented, and his pride would not allow him to accept any kind of handout. But Barry and the Flyers battled through all of that, too, at least psychologically, and Barry became the Flyers' second assistant coach.

Being a coach eventually developed into something special for Barry. I remember seeing him just before a major road trip, and just after a particularly tough loss at home. I said, "It's going to be a tough road trip now, Barry."

His eyes just glittered as he answered, "Yeah, it'll be great to see how good this club really is."

He was right. It *was* great, and partly because of him.

If ever a player deserved a "night" in his honor, it was Barry Ashbee, but Barry battled against that, too. The Flyers kept pitching the idea to him, and Barry kept rejecting it. "Condescending," he said. Finally the Flyers convinced him, but Barry agreed to go along only if there were *no gifts.* "I'm telling you right now," Barry insisted, "I'll go through with this, but if you give me one gift, I'll walk right the hell off the ice."

When the big night arrived, it was like a combination of the two previous nights the Flyers had held for Bruce Gamble and for Gary Dornhoefer. As the ceremonies proceeded, I sneaked a peek at Barry, who was standing alongside his wife Donna and his two children, Heather and Danny, and I could see that this battle was won, and that Barry was beginning to melt a little, and maybe even enjoy himself.

Then the big secret which had been kept from him was driven onto the ice—a beautiful new camper from all of the players. Again I looked at Barry and I could see a little smile, as if to say, "Those sonofaguns! They gave me a gift!" and his eyes glistened with pride, and the tears welled, but he battled them back.

The next day, Assistant Coach Ashbee drove his new camper to practice, and everyone took turns admiring his magnificent gift. After practice, Barry invited the whole team inside the camper, and it was only then that they realized that Barry had stocked, no, make that *filled,* the whole thing with beer and soft drinks. What a glorious finish to a glorious episode!

I honestly think that, despite all of his protestations to the contrary, Barry might have become a head coach, and a good one. He certainly had the respect of every player. But that was one battle that Barry would never have a chance to fight.

At the beginning of April 1977, the Flyers were preparing to meet Toronto in the first round of the playoffs, and I had come to the Spectrum to watch practice when I noticed that the players seemed uncharacteristically serious, even somber. I remember feeling a little surprised that they were taking the first game of the playoffs so seriously, especially since Toronto did not figure to give them too much trouble. I saw Marcel Pelletier nearby and I asked him, "What's wrong with them, Marce? Why are they so tight?"

I'll never forget Marcel's words: "They just told the players that Barry has leukemia."

Needless to say, I was staggered, even though at that time I wasn't sure of the exact implications. There was a press conference, during which it was announced that Barry would undergo chemotherapy, and that he would battle through this thing the way he had beaten all of the other obstacles in his life. And there had been plenty of those.

During the playoffs, Barry stayed in contact with his defense-men from his hospital bed, trying his best to keep them going, even though their coach couldn't be with them in person.

To check on Barry's condition, I kept calling the Flyers' office from Lenape High School, where I was teaching, until one morning when I was told, "Barry died this morning."

I said, "I don't think I can teach any more today," and I drove to the Flyers' office, where a lot of the guys were gathered. I don't remember most of what was said, but I do remember thinking, "Gee, the Cup doesn't seem so important any more."

I remember talking with my wife about going to Toronto for Barry's funeral services. Then a call came from the Flyers' office in-forming us that Mr. Snider had chartered a plane, and that all of the Flyers family was invited to join him, including wives and all of Barry's neighbors and friends. It was a marvelous gesture, and I was reminded of the services for Bill Masterton ten years before in Minnesota, but this was different, because Barry was one of our own.

It was a quiet trip on the charter, unlike any other I'd ever been on. I remember it well, including the unfortunate farewell over the intercom, "Thank you for flying with us this morning, and we hope you enjoy your day in Toronto." When the uninformed stewardess who said that realized the situation, I think she felt as awful as the rest of us.

Two buses took us to the church, which was surrounded by tel-evision and news people, along with numerous other people from the neighborhood. I recognized Barry's father, and when he saw ev-eryone getting off those buses, it appeared that some of his pain was lifted, because Barry's friends were there with him. And probably nothing that can be said in words can mean as much to the bereaved as just *being there*. At a time like that, what can one say, anyhow, that makes much sense?

Barry's friends came not just from Philadelphia and Ontario, but from everywhere. There were former Hershey Bears, former op-ponents, and about a half-dozen former Flyers, including Doug Favell and Dave Schultz, who was then a member of the Los Angeles Kings. There were also a number of representatives from the Toronto Maple Leafs, both executives and players. I've always had a closer feeling for two of those players, Darryl Sittler and Lanny McDonald, just because they were there.

All of us were in an anteroom of the church, waiting to be told what to do. The Flyers players were lined up together on one side of the room, while the former Flyers were on the other side, not quite sure where their place was. Bobby Clarke looked over at them, and with just one gentle gesture, he drew them into line with the Flyers.

I remembered when Bobby Clarke was a "yes" and "no" guy, very polite, but not very articulate, and I was, therefore, somewhat concerned when I learned that Clarke, as the team's captain and leader, would deliver the eulogy for Barry. I should have known better. As with so many other duties, Bobby performed in a manner far superior to what anyone else could have done. He delivered a stunning eulogy, staggering in its simplicity and accuracy. The tears were flowing from me, and from many others, when Bobby finished with, "Barry, you were a heck of a man."

Barry was that. How many could have survived all of those personal defeats? Or even one or two of them? Barry not only survived, he battled to the end, and in such a way that makes me feel that if I moan over lesser things, I demean him in doing so.

Barry is a permanent part of the Philadelphia community now, not only because of his number "4" banner which hangs from the Spectrum rafters, but, more importantly, because of the Barry Ashbee Leukemia Research Fund and the Barry Ashbee Research Laboratories at Hahnemann University Hospital. It is my understanding that, unlike a few years ago, fifty per cent of those who contract leukemia today have some hope of survival. And the battle continues.

Barry, you were a great hockey player, a great competitor, a great friend, and as Bobby said, a heck of a man. I'll always cherish you, because there'll never be another one like you.

T he Flyers were up against the league's best offense in the Stanley Cup Finals without Barry Ashbee, their all-star defenseman. The top four scorers in the N.H.L. were all Boston Bruins, and three of them had over 100 points. They had the "World's Greatest Center" in Phil Esposito; in fact, Boston's favorite bumper sticker read, "Jesus saves, but Espo scores on the rebound!" They had the "World's Greatest-Ever Defenseman" in Bobby Orr, who was also the greatest defenseman *offensively* in the history of the game. They had Johnny Bucyk, and Ken Hodge, and Wayne Cashman, and Terry O'Reilly, and Carol Vadnais, and Dallas Smith, and you just couldn't beat them. At least the Flyers couldn't.

Not only had the Flyers won only four games in seven years

against the Bruins, but *in Boston* they had won only *one* in seven years, and that was in the first game ever played between the two teams. And since the Bruins had the home-ice advantage, all they had to do was win their four home games and the Cup would be theirs. Conversely, the Flyers had to win at least one game in Boston to have any chance at all.

During the first two games in the steamy Boston Garden, the Bruins played as though they were in a shooting gallery, with Bernie Parent as the target. In both games, they blew out to early two-to-nothing leads, and in both games the Flyers fought back to tie, while Bernie turned aside shot after shot, any one of which could have been a game-winner for Boston.

In the final minute of regulation in the first game, it appeared that overtime was a certainty, since neither team was threatening at the moment, and both teams appeared to be sagging from the oppressive heat. Then came a highly unusual and controversial play. The Bruins dumped the puck down the right wing into the corner, and Moose Dupont and Wayne Cashman went after it. The two collided, and Cashman's skate hooked onto Dupont's sock, pinning the Moose to the spot and allowing Boston's other forward, Ken Hodge, to reach the puck first. Hodge then pivoted and sent the puck back to the right point, where Bobby Orr gathered it in, took one stride, and shot a bouncer that skipped past Parent to win it for Boston with a half-minute left, three to two.

It was the kind of goal and the kind of loss that can crush a team. Just as the Flyers were about to go into overtime and perhaps steal the first game on the road, as they had done in Montreal the season before, they were victimized by a fluky game-winning play by Boston. I was crushed, and the fans watching on television back in Philadelphia were crushed, but the Flyers themselves were *not* crushed. They were *angry.* It had been their game to win, they should have won, and only a break on a penalty-not-called had cost them the game. Far from crushed, or even down, they were determined to even the score in Game Two, which turned out to be one of the greatest games in Flyers history.

Despite the Flyers' great effort in Game Two, it looked as though the Bruins' two early goals would be enough to win it for them, two to one. With time running out, I was heading downstairs to do the post-game show, and I was thinking post-game thoughts, like, "The Flyers gave it a heck of an effort here in Boston, and they gave the Bruins all they could handle, but they're now down, two games to none, and we're heading back to Philadelphia..."

As I got to the bench area, I realized that Bernie had been pulled for an extra skater, and then, just as I reached rinkside, the puck came out to Moose Dupont, who shot and scored. It was tied at two, and this time we *were* going to overtime. I didn't mind at all having to climb all the way back upstairs.

There were no tremendous scoring opportunities for about the first ten minutes of overtime, but then, suddenly, Johnny Bucyk was all alone on a break-away, and I thought, "This is it." But Bernie smothered the shot, and the Flyers were still alive. Freddy then sent Dave Schultz out for his first shift of the overtime period. The Flyers threw the puck down the right side, and Ed Van Impe wound it around the boards into the left-wing corner, where Schultz banged his way clear and got the puck to Bill Flett. Flett saw Bobby Clarke in front of the net and slipped the puck to him. Clarke shot, but it was blocked by goaltender Gilles Gilbert. As Gilbert scrambled for the rebound, and before Terry O'Reilly could cover for him, Clarke shot again and hit nothing but net. The building was stunned into silence, except for a few delirious yelps from the Flyers, who swarmed around Bobby Clarke as he leaped about the ice in joyous celebration.

Just as I was saying, "Score! The Flyers win a game in Boston!" Harlan Singer pounded me on the back, and my headset popped off. So, while I was trying to talk about this most glorious moment in Flyers history, I was also trying to reach over the side of the broadcast booth to retrieve my headset. I didn't care, because I was so thrilled that the Flyers had what they needed, and what had seemed so impossible just a few days before—even a few *hours* before—a win in Boston.

The feeling was different than it had been after splitting the first two against Montreal the year before. This time the Flyers were confident that they could win three games in Philadelphia, no matter *who* they were playing. As Freddy said, "We can beat Boston." Most people still didn't believe him.

Game Three in Philadelphia was relatively easy, as Orest Kindrachuk and Ross Lonsberry scored third-period goals to lock up a four-to-one Flyer victory.

Game Four was a pivotal one. Either the Flyers would take a three-games-to-one lead, or the Bruins would tie the series at two and regain the home-ice advantage. As the Bruins had done in Boston, the Flyers took an early two-to-nothing lead, the second goal coming on an end-to-end rush by, of all people, Dave Schultz. But by the eleven-minute mark of the first period, the Bruins had tied it at two.

It stayed that way until there were about five minutes left in the third period, when Bill Barber came up with an electrifying play. Barber skated down the left wing, and from an angle along the left boards his thirty-five footer beat Gilbert on the long side, and the Flyers led, three to two. (Bobby Orr later called it "the best wrist shot I've ever seen.") A minute or two later, Moose Dupont made a steal at the left point, cut inside a check, and blew a shot past Gilbert to ice the game for the Flyers, who went crazy in the corner while Dupont did the "Moose Shuffle" in celebration of his second big goal of the series. This incomparable and incorrigible team, which no one had predicted could get this far, was now within one game of the Stanley Cup.

When we returned to Boston for Game Five, I was in a state of euphoria. Before the game, some fans were yelling to us in their New England accents, "We're gonnar beat you! The Flyahs can't beat the Broons! We'll show you!"

I turned to the hecklers behind me, and very calmly replied, "It makes no difference what happens tonight. The Bruins could win, fifty to nothing. It doesn't matter, because there's no way you're going to win that sixth game in Philadelphia on Sunday." I not only said that, I *believed* it. The Flyers had won eight playoff games in the Spectrum, and they had been playing as if possessed in that building. Of course, if the Bruins somehow managed to win Game Six, there probably would be no way the Flyers could win Game Seven in Boston. And there I was, already assuming the worst for Game Five, so that we would return to Philadelphia for the concluding victory.

My assumptions were realized in Game Five. Bobby Orr scored a couple of goals in the second period, and the Bruins won easily, five to one. But as usual, the Flyers did not die easily. There were forty-three penalties called during the game, and the Flyers were angry that they had been beaten, and beaten for the *first time* really, at least in *their* minds. But they also felt that they had left their calling card, inviting the Bruins to Philadelphia for a Sunday afternoon picnic.

On Saturday night, I was so keyed up in anticipation of the next afternoon's game, that I knew I wouldn't be able to sleep. I watched the late show, the late-late show, the late-late-late show, and the early-early-early show. At about 5:00 or 5:30 A.M., I didn't know what to do with myself. There was nothing on television, there was no place open yet for breakfast, and it was still dark outside. So, for something to do, I climbed onto my rider-mower and started cutting the lawn, using a flashlight to see where I was cutting.

Pretty soon, a police car came by and pointed its spotlight at me. The policeman must have thought I'd gone loony for sure, but all he said was, "Good luck, Gene."

All I said was, "Thank you."

When I got to the Spectrum, and that fateful hour of May 19, 1974, was finally at hand, I was terribly concerned that I would become so wrapped up in the game as a fan, that I might not be able to do a proper professional job. It's difficult to explain, but I forced myself into a very deliberate consciously unconscious state, divorcing myself from my emotions, so that I wouldn't lose control of the sense of the game. And having had no sleep at all seemed to make that somewhat easier to do.

The crowd in the Spectrum was unbelievably souped up, realizing, along with everyone else, that this was really a one-game series for the Flyers. NBC's people were excited, too, not only because of the huge national audience that they were sure to attract, but also because Tim Ryan, Ted Lindsay, Scotty Connal, and the rest were fans, too, and for *any* hockey fan, this game was IT!

If the excitement in the building was tremendous during warm-ups, it was nothing compared with the crowd's reaction to the second live appearance in the Spectrum of Kate Smith. She had been electrifying at the season's opening game, and she was electrifying again. And again her final words, "God bless America, my home sweet home," were drowned out by another explosion of an ovation. When she had finished, Bobby Orr and Phil Esposito skated over to her and shook her hand, as if trying to find a little good luck for themselves, but as they skated away again, Kate gave them her own little jinx sign, and the crowd loved that, too.

The referee that day was the league's senior official, Art Skov, who had become more than a little irritated when a writer had noted that the Flyers had not lost when Skov was the referee. To Skov, and to any other good official, favoritism is never a consideration, and I was sure that he would call this game without any regard for past history. And after all, the Flyers couldn't have both Kate Smith *and* the referee as good luck charms, could they?

Finally Art Skov dropped the puck and the game was actually under way. And what a game! The Bruins obviously felt that they had to come on strong and early, and they did, outshooting the Flyers, sixteen to eight, in the first period. The Bruins had so much the better of the early going that it looked almost like the first two games in Boston, but Bernie Parent made save after save, and the game remained scoreless through the first fifteen minutes.

During a Flyer power play late in the first period, there was a scramble in front of the Boston goal, and Bobby Orr covered the puck while Bobby Clarke chopped away. Suddenly both Bobbys were winging rights at each other, and as they were being separated, Orr threw one of his gloves, and then the other, at Clarke. Art Skov gave each two minutes for roughing, and in those days that meant that each team lost a man, so the Flyers would now be skating four men on three.

With Clarke in the penalty box, Rick MacLeish took the face-offs, and on his third one, he got the puck from the right faceoff circle back to Moose Dupont at the left point. Instead of unloading a big shot, Moose anticipated MacLeish coming across in front and got off a two-thirds-speed wrist shot. Just as the puck was about to reach goaltender Gilbert, MacLeish lost Dallas Smith's check by a half-stride, got his blade on the shot, and directed it into the net. Despite being outshot, the Flyers led, one to nothing, after the first period.

Obviously, goals were going to be about as hard to come by as Flyer victories had been during their string of twenty-seven consecutive winless games against Boston. It had been unbelievable to expect that the Flyers could beat the Bruins four time in seven games, let alone four times in *six* games, or really, *five* times in seven games. So, how much more unbelievable would it be to shut them out for the rest of this game? Just because they had *never* shut them out before. . . ? And just because *no one* had shut them out all season long. . . ?

Through the second and third periods, the Bruins' shots diminished, as the Flyers' checking took over. The drama and tension were nearly unbearable as the realization of this enormous upset sneaked into the consciousness: "Gee, this could really happen. . . Control yourself!. . . 'It doesn't matter, there's no way the Bruins are going to win in Philadelphia on Sunday'. . ."

There is absolutely no professional rationale or sound justification for feeling this way. And it's not thinking, it's *feeling*—a fan's gut feeling. But we could have played until midnight, or through eight periods, or until Tuesday afternoon, and the Bruins not only would not have won, they would not have scored. It was almost as if it had been preordained.

In the third period, the Bruins' shots diminished to five, and for the last five minutes of the game, the Spectrum was absolutely in bedlam. With just over two minutes left, Terry Crisp stole the puck and led Bobby Clarke with a blue-line-to-blue-line pass just ahead of Bobby Orr. Clarke was heading in alone on Gilbert when Orr caught up with Clarke, grabbed him, and spun him around. Art Skov called a two-minute holding penalty on Orr, who erupted in anger and charged at Skov, but just in time Orr was bear-hugged out of danger by Ken Hodge.

During the ensuing power play, without Orr on the ice, the Flyers attacked, but they couldn't score. By the time Orr returned, there were only seconds left, and Orr desperately fired the puck down the ice from beyond the red line. Joe Watson touched up, but no icing was called, and the scoreboard clock ticked down the final seconds, between the Flyers' "1" and the Bruins' "0."

With about three seconds left, I said, "Ladies and gentlemen, the Flyers are going to win...the Stanley Cup!" And as the final buzzer sounded, "The Flyers win the Stanley Cup! The Flyers have won the Stanley Cup!"

Unbelievably, the "Miracle of Broad Street," the impossible dream, had come true. As Don Earle carried on with, "The Flyers have become the first expansion team to win the Stanley Cup..." I was just incredibly exhilarated. I looked down and saw Simon Nolet climb up on the bench and slam his stick down so hard that the blade broke off. I saw Orest Kindrachuk jump into the arms of Dave Schultz, wrapping his legs around Schultz's waist and his arms around his neck, and thus knocking Schultz over like a felled tree. I saw the ecstatic Flyers mobbing Bernie Parent, while the shell-shocked Bruins waited uneasily for the traditional handshake, and for the traditional fraternal hug by the two goalies.

Someone had given me a small bottle of champagne, just in case it might be needed, and I thought that there could not have been a better time to open it. So, I popped it open. But since it was warm, it sprayed all over everywhere, including all over the people in the seats in front of me. It also sprayed all over my score sheet, causing my red and blue ink markings to run together in new patterns of their own design. I never did enter the third-period statistics, but I still keep and treasure that score sheet.

The Cup was awarded to Bobby Clarke and the Flyers by league president Clarence Campbell, who had previously criticized the Flyers' style of play. On this day, he graciously congratulated the Flyers, and then said, "They have now proved that expansion was a success."

Clarke and Parent and the others tried to take the traditional victory lap around the ice, with the Cup upheld for all to see, but the ice was so flooded with young fans, it was more like trying to carry the Cup through the Broad Street Subway. It would have been better if the team could have skated the Cup around by themselves, while the fans applauded and cheered them from the stands, but Ed Snider had not wanted to post extra guards around the ice, for fear of jinxing the team. So, the victory lap became almost as much of a battle as the game had been.

The dressing room was pandemonium also. By the time I got there, it was literally impossible to move. I remember the smile on the face of Bill Clement, who had just returned from ligament damage to play brilliantly in the last game. And I remember Terry Crisp describing the action, like the coach he was destined to be. And I remember the Watsons, Joe and Jimmy, yelling over and over, "Can you believe it? Can you believe it?"

Joe Watson offered some champagne to Bobby Orr, who had been the best man at Joe's wedding, but Orr declined, saying, "I don't deserve this."

Joe said, "You deserve it more than anyone else in hockey."

"But the Bruins are only number two," said Orr.

Fred Shero's strategy had worked perfectly: "We're a hitting team, but always before we made the mistake of treating Orr as an untouchable. As a result, he's killed us. This time, the idea was to let Orr have the puck in his own end, and then make him work harder than he normally has to work. And whether it's Orr or anyone else, you should always take the shortest route to the puck carrier, and then be sure to arrive in an ill humor!"

I remember all of that as if it were yesterday. And I remember the dressing room blackboard, where Fred Shero had written before the game, "Win today and we'll walk together forever."

The celebration lasted well into the night. When my wife and I arrived home, both of us still a little teary-eyed, some of our neighbors came over and just stood there and applauded.

When Bobby Clarke got home, he found that some of his shrubbery had been torn out and taken away as souvenirs. I wonder where those bushes are now. Does someone point to them with pride and say, "Those are the bushes Bobby Clarke gave us the day the Flyers won the Stanley Cup"?

I had savored that Sunday afternoon and evening, but it didn't really get to me until early Monday morning, when I was driving to Lenape High School. I was listening to the sports on WCAU, and they played the tape of the finish of the game: "Thirteen seconds left...The Flyers are going to win...the Stanley Cup!...The Flyers win the Stanley Cup!...The Flyers have won the Stanley Cup!"

Then it hit me! I was no longer the professional who was saying those words. I was a fan who had tears in his eyes and goose bumps all over, as I realized what an extraordinary thing that team had done.

I got to school early that morning, so that I could smuggle a bottle of champagne into the faculty room, and so I could explain that nothing, not even my beloved students and fellow faculty members—*nothing* could keep me away from the Flyers' victory parade, which was to be held that morning. Everyone understood, and the students were warned not to cut school, but two-thirds of the school went to the parade anyway.

We who were to be in the parade met at the Spectrum, where we were to form up. There were open cars for the principal participants, and a bus or two at the end for the children of the participants. Don Earle and I were to be in the lead car, so that after we rounded City Hall and reached Independence Mall, we could get to the microphones first and introduce everyone else. The Cup was in the second car, followed by Mayor Rizzo in the third car, and then the players in the rest of the cars, with the buses bringing up the rear of the motorcade.

Don and I were to sit on the rear deck of the convertible, with our wives in the seat in front of us. Sarah and I agreed that our children were small enough to fit in the car with the Earles and us, so instead of sending them off to the buses, eight-year-old Lauren, six-year-old Sharon, and four-year-old Brian got to ride in the first car with us.

Since a parade like this had never happened before, we didn't know quite what to expect. We certainly didn't expect what we got! It was, as some people like to say, awesome! Two million people flooded the wide sidewalks, and the medial strips, and all of the ten lanes or so of the city's widest street, toe to toe and shoulder to shoulder, all the way from the Spectrum to City Hall. It was the greatest turnout of humanity in the history of the city, and there were representatives of every phase of life in Philadelphia, from brain surgeons to sanitation engineers, from stockbrokers to fish mongers, from the Main Line to the Italian Market, and from Chestnut Hill to Cherry Hill. It was a mob so densely packed together that we couldn't travel more than three or four miles per hour, and even then we were constantly concerned that we might be running over people's feet. Some players, Bobby Clarke for one, couldn't get through at all, so thick were the crowds around them.

About every third person would hand me a bottled beverage of some kind, and not being a big drinker, I would take a small swig and then hand the bottle to some very grateful person a little further along our route. Before long my left shoulder was black and blue from the pounding of many hands in this parade to top all parades, but I didn't mind a bit!

As we approached the taller buildings of center city, there was confetti, and there were streamers, and bands, and airplanes trailing banners, and mummers, and bandaged-up hospital patients, and I remember one guy in a body cast with a Flyer logo painted on his chest. And everyone was yelling to me, "Way to go, Gene!" Once, when the parade had stopped for a few minutes, I thought, "If I don't look behind me, I can imagine that this whole darned parade is for me!"

I'm told that one man in a downtown hotel was astounded by the number of people who were running around saying, "Isn't it wonderful?" and by the several girls who gleefully kissed him. When he asked one of them what was so wonderful, the answer, of course, was, "Oh, you've never been in Philadelphia on a Monday?"

Finally we arrived at Independence Mall, and the adoring mobs greeted their Broad Street Bullies individually, as we introduced them. And were those blue-collar guys from north of the border ever adored! It was an unparalleled outpouring. No other team in any sport or in any city has ever had anything like the reception given that Flyers team by the City of Brotherly Love.

The Flyers had brought pride back to the city of Philadelphia, a city which for years had been known as a city of losers. As *Sports Illustrated* headlined it, "That often-mocked city enjoyed sweet victory, as its audacious Flyers, a mere seven years in existence but blessed with a singing talisman, a superb goalie and a tooth-shy whirlwind, won hockey's title." Soon, with the Flyers leading the way, Philadelphia would be known as the "City of Winners." On this day it was hard to imagine that it had ever been any other way, especially when, at the end of the mall overlooking the Liberty Bell and Independence Hall, the Birthplace of Liberty, everyone stood and joined Kate Smith, live, in the singing of "God Bless America." If Irving Berlin himself had written such an ending for such a story, everyone would have said, "Too hokey! No one would ever believe it!"

With all of the turmoil of that time—the war in Vietnam, hippies and flower children, animosity and the generation gap—here was something that everyone, no matter who they were, could enjoy and savor as just something really good. What a day and what a year was had by Philadelphia! And what a future lay just ahead!

Four months later, I was broadcasting a Flyer pre-season exhibition game, and Ed Snider asked me to come to his office after the first period. I thought, "Uh, oh! What did I say now? I didn't mention basketball, and I didn't mention the W.H.A., and I don't think I said anything bad about any of our prospects..."

When I got to his office, Mr. Snider handed me a little box and said, "Here, Gene. You deserve it."

I opened the box, and I got goose bumps all over again when I saw what was inside. It was a beautiful ring, inscribed "Stanley Cup Champion" and "Philadelphia Flyers" and "Gene Hart."

I thanked Mr. Snider and hurried off to where my wife was seated in Section "Z." I gave her the box, and she, too, was thrilled. We shed a few more tears together, and then it was back to work in the broadcast booth.

No one had to tell me what to say on the air this time. I knew the same thing that everyone else knew. Outside of the Delaware Valley, where they were loved, the Flyers were detested by almost everyone, especially now that they were Stanley Cup Champions. The next challenge—and it's the toughest challenge in sports—was to repeat, to do it *again,* to prove that the first time was no fluke.

Yes, winning it all again would be sweet, but there's nothing like the *first* time for anything. And that wonderful year 1973-74 is indelibly etched in my mind, like no other year I've ever known.

There were many individuals who were responsible for, and who deserve credit for, the winning of that first Cup, but none more than the Flyers' *other* secret weapon (besides Kate, that is)—the man his teammates called, not Bernie, but

# Bennie

Bernard Marcel Parent was born in Montreal, Quebec, but he will always be a Philadelphian. He loved (and loves) Philadelphia, and Philadelphia loved (and loves) him, and in a different way from any other athlete I've known. Bobby Clarke was the laborer and leader whom everyone loved to revere and admire; Bernie Parent was the artist and charmer whom everyone loved to cherish and adore. If you had a chance to see Bernie in the first car behind the Cup during the victory parade up Broad Street, you would know what I mean. He was the good king who had just delivered his people from the evil invaders, and his loyal subjects loved him all the more for his latest heroics.

On the ice, he played a glamorous position, but the manner in which he played it made it all the more glamorous, especially after his two and a half years of apprenticeship with the Master, Jacques Plante. Bernie was the *new* Master, whose every nimble move had style, and grace, and meaning, almost as if he were performing a classical ballet. With a minimum of movement—a flick of an elbow, a flash of a skate—Bernie achieved the maximum effect. He was a purist. He was special. And the fans of Philadelphia knew it and loved him for it. Sometimes he suffered hard luck, but that just made him even more endearing. And when he made one of his classic saves, who could forget the sound of the crowd, with its roar of "Bernie! Bernie! Bernie!"

When he was traded to the Toronto Maple Leafs, Bernie cried, and it was the first time I had ever seen that happen, but I understood, because Bernie didn't want to leave all his friends and the city he loved. I cried, too, because I didn't want him to leave either.

After the Maple Leafs, and the Screaming Eagles, and the Blazers, it seemed that Bernie might be one of those athletes who have brilliant talent and no kind of luck but *bad* luck. When he recovered from his broken foot, but refused to perform in the W.H.A. playoffs, it seemed so uncharacteristic of Bernie. But when it was learned that he had not been paid, it was suddenly understandable, especially when it was also learned that his agent got more out of the deal than Bernie did. And then again, if he *had* been paid, he might not have been able to return to the Flyers.

And what a return he made! Actually, he was shelled out by the Rangers in the second period of his first pre-season game back in the Spectrum, but by the time the *real* season started, Bernie and Kate were both ready. Together they started the season with a shutout, and together they ended the season with a shutout. And even without Kate's help, Bernie picked up twelve other shutouts along the way.

The magnificent masked hero of the Flyers swept almost every possible award—the Vezina Trophy (for fewest goals allowed during the regular season), the Conn Smythe Trophy (for the most valuable player in the Stanley Cup Playoffs), and selection as the N.H.L.'s First-Team All-Star Goaltender. The following year, Bernie proved that none of that was a fluke, as he swept all of the same awards, and again concluded with a shutout as an exclamation point. For those two back-to-back seasons, no goaltender was ever better, and no goaltender *could have been* any better.

Bernie had already accomplished what no other goaltender in the history of the N.H.L. had accomplished, and he was sitting on top of the world. But then, suddenly, Bernie's world began to disintegrate. First, there was pain in his arm. Then it was discovered that the problem was with a disk and nerve at the base of his neck. A serious operation sidelined Bernie for most of the 1975-76 season, and when he returned, he was not nearly so effective as he had been before. He looked weak during the playoffs against Toronto and Boston, giving up eight goals (five of them by Darryl Sittler) in one game against the Maple Leafs, and even knocking in a game-winner with his own stick against the Bruins. He was still capable of flashes of his brilliant former self, but he would never again be the uniquely glorious goaltender of the past.

In the spring of 1979, Bernie's career ended as suddenly as Barry Ashbee's had, against the same team, and in a frighteningly similar manner. Jimmy Watson and Ranger forward Don Maloney were positioned in front of the Flyers' goal when their sticks went up, and suddenly Bernie was coming out of the net and skating toward the bench in obvious pain. He took off his mask and held his eye, and although no one knew at the time what had happened, we knew that it couldn't be good.

It was later determined that the corner of the butt end of Maloney's stick had entered Bernie's mask through the eye slit, and it had protruded just far enough to cause damage to the eye similar to what Barry Ashbee had suffered. On a goaltender's body, the eye is the *only* uncovered spot, assuming the goaltender is wearing a mask of the Jacques Plante–Bernie Parent style, and try as they might in experiments with Bernie's mask, no one could force-fit any part of a hockey stick through the narrow eye slits. An unforeseeable freak accident. And a sad and disappointing end to a marvelous career. At the press conference to announce the doctors' bad news, Bernie cried for the second time since I had known him. I did, too.

Other than his family, Bernie had only two interests in his whole life—hockey and fishing. And those were the only subjects he ever really wanted to talk about. But he loved both, and he loved talking about both. He was building a new fishing boat, which was his greatest pleasure, when he discovered that his agent hadn't properly taken care of his taxes and his finances, and the boat-building project had to be abandoned.

Instead of being a financially well-off ex-athlete, Bernie was suddenly not in good financial shape at all. The Flyers gave him a job as a coach, and they restructured his contract to give him more financial security. However, like Fred Shero, Bernie tried to find solace in liquid form. But he wasn't a "Lost Weekend" kind of guy, and he recognized his dependence, came to grips with it, fought it valiantly, and defeated it. Of all the great victories in Bernie's life, that had to be one of the most rewarding.

Bernie was the fourth Flyer to be given a "night," and the second to have his number retired, as his "1" joined Barry Ashbee's "4" in the Spectrum rafters. Bernie is still a presence with the Flyers, not just in the form of that banner above us, but also in his continuing work with the Flyers' goaltenders. A few years ago, his prize pupil was a boy who had idolized Bernie as a child in Sweden. One of the great moments of both of their lives was the moment when Bernie was able to present the Vezina Trophy to Pelle Lindbergh, who said, "I've got to tell you...I want to thank the man who taught me everything I know about goaltending in the N.H.L., my friend, Bernie Parent."

As Bernie and Pelle embraced at the podium that night, it was beautiful to see the pride in their eyes. A few months later, when Pelle died, Bernie said, "It's as if I have lost a son."

To paraphrase what Red Barber once said about baseball, "It's only a game to the people who watch it. To the people in it, it's not only a very serious business, it's their life."

Bernie's life in hockey will always be special to the people around him, not only because of his love for the game and for the people who play it, but also because of his Gallic charm and his impish sense of humor. Many will remember his post-game interviews, which invariably began with, "Some fun, eh?" I recall one of his first interviews, following his first start in Chicago. I had noticed that he had been chatting with Bobby Hull before the game, and I asked him what he had said to Hull. Bernie's answer was, "I said to heem, don't mess wit' *me*, Baldy."

"And what do you try to do when Hull shoots, Bernie?"

"I try not to get hit!"

I recall another time later on, when I was trying to get Bernie to say something nice, perhaps even sentimental, about Ed Van Impe, who was standing next to him during the interview. I said, "Bernie, what has it meant to you all these years to have a defenseman like Ed Van Impe in front of you?"

Bernie said, "It means you get screened a lot!"

"But Bernie, what is it that makes Eddie so effective in front of the net?"

Very seriously, Bernie answered, "Well, he farts a lot!" Then he laughed his wonderful laugh, knowing that his part of the interview was over, and that my next question would be for Ed Van Impe.

Bernie will always be special in hockey, and he will always be special to me. I was blessed to have known this man of strength and character, and to have called him my friend, and to have seen him survive so well.

Another key member of the Cup-winning Bullies was the biggest Bully of them all, the man they called

# The Hammer

Looking back at the seventies, the most significant players of that decade were Orr, Esposito, Lafleur, Dryden, Clarke, Parent, and some people may be surprised, or even laugh, when I add to that list a six foot, one inch, 190-pound winger from Waldheim, Saskatchewan, named David William Schultz.

Dave Schultz was unique, because, more than anyone else in that decade, he changed the face of the game, while changing the faces of many of the game's players. He changed not only the record book, but the rule book, and he changed the thinking of most of the teams in the league. And for one of those teams, the Flyers, he created an aura and a signature unlike any other in the league's history.

From a total lack of identity in the sixties, two players gave the Flyers character in the seventies. Bobby Clarke gave them their hard-working, tenacious, never-give-up quality, while Dave Schultz gave them their sneering, cocky, even arrogant "Broad Street Bullies" temperament. It was a personality akin to that of the "Big Bad Boston Bruins," but it was also uniquely the Flyers' own.

Dave Schultz's philosophy was simple: "I'll fight anybody or do anything, but nobody's going to fool with my team." In that sense, Dave was a leader of Freddy's Philistines, the Mad Squad, the Bullies, and, of course, Schultz's Army, complete with German helmets. As opposition tough guy Jerry "King Kong" Korab once said, "The Flyers don't want to fight you one on one; they want to fight you *nineteen* on one." The other side of that thinking is that no Flyer would have allowed another Flyer to be pounded into the ice, like a nail by a hammer, the way Dale Rolfe of the Rangers was hammered by Dave Schultz.

Wherever the Flyers went, the fans would be beside themselves in anger, and they would hoot, and boo, and in New York some sickies even threw sugar packets at Bobby Clarke, the diabetic. Most of the vilification was unloaded on the team as a whole, not just on Clarke or Schultz, and brash and cocky as they were, the Flyers as a team *loved* the negative attention. The louder the noise, the more they enjoyed it, and laughed at it, and were even inspired by it. I remember an All-Star Game when all of the players were being introduced, and when they got to "...and now the representatives of the Philadelphia Flyers..." 15,000 people booed, and the Flyers who were being introduced just lit up with smiles.

To hockey fans around the world, the most noticeable Flyer was Dave Schultz, and *not* because he was given so much room to operate in the offensive zone, which he invariably was! No, it was, of course, because he was breaking unheard-of records for penalty minutes. Schultz rewrote the book for penalty minutes in a period, in a game, in a series of games, in a season, in a series of seasons, and in a career. One season he had more than 500 penalty minutes. There was a time when whole teams didn't have that many.

And the Hammer's notoriety was truly *world*-wide. I recall a luncheon before the Flyers were to play the Russians, and all of the players were introduced and asked to stand. More than any other Flyer, except perhaps Bobby Clarke, the Soviet players all strained to see for themselves what this legendary bad man, Dave Schultz, looked like.

Closer to home, Dave even became a semi-matinee idol, and the "singer" of a "hit" single called "The Penalty Box." It was a "doo-wah" record which went something like, "How long? How long? How long can you keep me in the penalty box?" I don't recall much more than that, but I'm curious to know how many copies of that record are still in existence. Certainly not nearly as many as Dave's *other* records, the ones in the *N.H.L. Record Book.*

Like so many wild on-ice (or on-field) characters, if you ever met Dave *off* the ice, you would be thrown off balance, not by his famous left hand, but by the fact that he was such a "nice man"— quiet, even introverted, mannerly, kind, soft-spoken—just exactly the opposite of his beastly personality *on* the ice. Fortunately for me, I personally knew only Dave's kindly Dr. Jekyll side, but I did get a close-up view of his brutal Mr. Hyde side once, too. And once was enough for me.

I was waiting in the tunnelway during the last few minutes of a game, preparing for the post-game show. Dave had been ejected from the game, and he was standing just a few feet away from me, jawing at the opposition and wanting to get back onto the ice. I thought I'd try to pacify him, and, at the same time, keep him out of further difficulty, so I said, "Come on, Dave. You'd better go to the dressing room. Go on, Dave."

I then suddenly realized that, so intent was Dave on getting at his prey, he wasn't even aware that I was there. And in my orange Flyers jacket I was hard to miss! (I wasn't called the "Great Pumpkin" for nothing.) It didn't take me long to figure out that, for once, I'd probably be better off keeping quiet.

It was that kind of intensity and singleness of purpose that made Dave so tough to fight. He was one of those rare beings who is not the least bit concerned with self-preservation. Dave didn't care if you blackened his eye, or broke his nose, or tore his ear, as long as he could eventually get a grip on you and then hurt you back. Believe me, those are the last guys you want to tangle with. In fact, Dave almost always lost the first ten seconds or so of his fights, absorbing all kinds of punishment while he tried to get a hold on you with his right arm, so he could then pummel you into submission with his left.

That's why it was so surprising when Dave knocked out Montreal's John Van Boxmeer with one punch. Not the quickest guy in the world, Van Boxmeer threw his arms down to get rid of his gloves, and as soon as both arms went down, Dave drilled him, and Van Boxmeer fluttered to the ice like a mainsail at sundown. Dave was as surprised as anyone else, and that's why he just stood there, looking embarrassed and rather lost.

When Dave got even more carried away than usual, he was invariably warned by the league to *stop*. After one such warning, Dave committed an infraction which caused referee Art Skov to raise his arm for a delayed penalty. Just before the end of the play, Dave circled back and skated hell-bent for the penalty box, where he was comfortably seated by the time Skov blew his whistle to stop play. Skov reached out, ready to point to Dave and designate the penalty, but Dave was already out of Skov's sight in the penalty box. The fans had seen what had happened and were laughing about it, but Skov was angry because he couldn't find Schultz anywhere. Finally one of the linesmen whispered in Skov's ear, and, foolish as it had made him seem, there was nothing Skov could do about it, because Dave had done just what he was supposed to do—"Go directly to the penalty box"—like a good little boy.

Even after fight-filled terms with the Kings, the Penguins, and the Sabres, Dave was still a Broad Street Bully at heart, and Philadelphians accepted him as such, at least until Dave's book, *Confessions of an Enforcer,* was published. The book turned out to be an unfortunate undertaking for Dave, because in it he ripped the Flyers for what they had "forced" him to do, in particular for "having to fight Clarke's battles for him." The book was promoted in sensational fashion, but it was less than warmly received, especially by the fans of Philadelphia and, of course, by the Flyers organization, from which Dave was suddenly estranged.

It was a very unhappy situation for Dave, because a gap was created that will never be completely closed. However much money Dave made from the book, it will never come close to compensating him for all of the difficulty it has caused him. Dave had bit the hand of the team and the game that had fed him so well, and forgiveness would not come easily. Even more of a shame for Dave was that he had to be influenced by his ghostwriter, Stan Fischler, who probably advised him to tell what will sell. And, of course, nothing seems to sell like "inside dirt," whether it be truth, stretched truth, or fiction.

As he had done with Fred Shero, Bob Clarke tried to mend the bridges. First he had Dave back for the Flyers' old-timers game, and then for Clarke's own "night." Happily, Clarke and Schultz were later long-time teammates on the same senior-league hockey team. That fact alone, I believe, says something about the character of both of these men.

Whether he was reviled or revered, whether he was the most scurrilous villain in N.H.L. history or just a clown who wanted to play Hamlet, Dave "The Hammer" Schultz was one of the most significant hockey players of the seventies, and certainly one of the most famous—or infamous. As a man in Chicago put it: "That Schultz! He ought to be thrown out of the league for life! But I sure wish the Black Hawks had him!"

Freddy was the coach, Bernie was the beloved artist, and Schultz was the belligerent bully; but the unquestioned leader of the Cup-winning Flyers was the guy they called, simply

# Whitey

Robert Earle Clarke was known to hockey fans as "Bobby," but to his teammates he was always "Whitey" (because of his pale complexion, especially after his typical overexertion on the ice), or "Angel" (because of his choirboy appearance and/or his devilish style of play) or "Clarkie" (which many still call him, despite the fact that his professional name was changed from "Bobby" to "Bob," to better befit his executive stature as a major-league general manager).

At five feet, ten inches (officially, although I believe he was, and is, less than that), he was not very big, not very fast, and not very powerful; he didn't have a great shot; and he was a diabetic besides. But without him, the Philadelphia Flyers would have been (and still would be) an unrecognizably different team from the team that we know.

There was no special early indication that Clarke would become a "franchise" player. The first report I heard from his first Flyers training camp was encouraging, but not headline material:

"Right now, our number two pick, the kid from Flin Flon, is the best player in camp." Remember, that wasn't saying an awful lot, especially considering the struggling team the Flyers were in 1969.

In his first season, Clarke scored fifteen goals and assisted on thirty more, for a total of forty-five points; not bad for a rookie, but not Rookie-of-the-Year stuff either. However, we who followed the team closely could already see the tenacity and the work ethic which would eventually result in 1,329 career points, seventy per cent of those on assists, in 1,280 games (including playoffs), or well over a point per game for fifteen years.

And where did that all-important work ethic originate? Like Schultz, and Saleski, and the Watsons, Clarke came from Western Canada, where the father of a hockey player was a rough-hewn man, a blue-collar worker with simple tastes and a simple way of life. Clarke's father, Cliff, worked in a copper mine in Flin Flon, a mining town in the deep-cold-north of Manitoba, a town whose one landmark was an 800-foot smokestack to keep the smelting smoke and pollution as high and as far away from the townsfolk as possible. Cliff Clarke's philosophy of life became his son's philosophy of life: "You don't get nothin' for nothin'. Man was born to work, and if you're going to do a job, you might as well do it right."

Nobody did his job any "righter" than Bob Clarke, and that attitude set the tone for the entire Flyers organization. What sounds like the simplest and most *un*remarkable philosophy is truly remarkable indeed, especially in the world of professional sports, where egotism, superstardom, and elitism plague almost every team in every sport. But not the Flyers, thanks to men like Cliff Clarke and his son, Bob.

The exceptionalness of Bob Clarke as a person results from the fact that the most exceptional thing about him is that there *is* no exceptional thing about him, except perhaps his simplicity! There is nothing giant-sized, or even bigger than life, about Bob Clarke. He's still the kid from the small mining town out west, who always understood his role, and who always had a great view of life.

When Clarke first arrived in the big leagues, he was a man of very few words. Like Gary Cooper, those words were usually "yep" and "nope." He was always polite, always honest, and always sincere, but he did not yet have confidence in his ability to communicate. With practice and experience, he became one of the most articulate people I know, with the rare ability to measure each word carefully and to say exactly what he thinks.

At times the revelations he makes about himself, or about his team, or about players on his team, are very pointed, and therefore very difficult. But there is no other way he can tell a story or answer a question, because there is never any smoke-screening or any subterfuge in the life of Bob Clarke. And when he delivered that extraordinarily breathtaking eulogy for Barry Ashbee, he taught me that you don't have to be a professional announcer to be a good speaker. All you have to be is a sincere human being, with command of your thoughts and your language. Never again would I be even remotely concerned about Bob Clarke's ability to communicate.

When I first met him, Bobby was extremely sensitive about the subject of his diabetes. My first impression was that he didn't want anyone to know that he had it, and so it was rarely brought up. Eventually I realized that Bobby felt that way because he never wanted a situation to arise where, if he had a bad game, or a bad stretch of games, people would have sympathy for him because he was "sick." He didn't want anyone saying, "Isn't that terrible! The poor kid's got that terrible disease and they're making him play all that time anyhow. The poor kid has diabetes, you know!" To the contrary, Clarke's philosophy was: "If I have a bad game, or a bad stretch of games, I want people to understand that it was because I was lousy, *not* because I was sick." He was very emphatic about that, and he didn't think it was anything exceptional, so why bring it up? It just wasn't worth talking about. He had lived with it, he had dealt with it, and he had dealt with it very well.

One time when we were in Minnesota, a group that deals with diabetic children asked Bobby to talk with the children, and, a little reluctantly, he agreed, despite the fact that diabetes was a subject he *never* talked about. He was to meet with the children in the stands after the morning skate, but beforehand he had set it up with Joe Kadlec that Joe would come and get him after five or ten minutes to go to the pre-game meal.

Well, Bobby started talking with those kids, all of them about eight to twelve years old, and soon Joe came to get him. Bobby said, "No, no, that's all right . . ."

One of the kids said, "Mr. Clarke, you know I'm a diabetic, too."

Bobby smiled that warm smile of his, and he proceeded to talk on for almost an hour, in his own calm, strong, reassuring way. I'm sure that none of those kids, now adults, have ever forgotten that meeting. Obviously, I haven't either.

I learned early on that Bob Clarke never made excuses about *anything*. There was, simply, *no* excuse for losing. Sickness or injuries? Forget them! Bad breaks or bad calls? They don't matter! They're all part of the game, and they should never be used as a reason for losing. The losses came frequently during Bobby's first three seasons, but he would just say, "We've got to work harder." And they *did* work harder, or at least they kept working just as hard.

Clarke's tenacity and his drive made him the youngest captain, I believe, in the history of the N.H.L. From that point on, the growth and stature of the Flyers, and of Bobby Clarke, came in leaps and bounds. Clarke soon became the most popular Flyer with the fans, and his number "16" became the Flyers' rallying point. It would be hard to imagine any other Flyer wearing that number. Claude LaForge wore it before Clarke, but no one else will ever wear it, now that "16" has joined "1" and "4" in the Spectrum rafters.

The essence of Bobby Clarke is distilled in so many great moments of Flyers history. His first memorable goal came late in October of 1969, and it was also his first goal as a Flyer. With the team trailing by one, and skating short-handed late in the third period, Clarke scored from the left side along the boards against Eddie Giacomin to tie the Rangers. I don't recall my exact feelings at that time, but I'm sure that I had no idea of how many *more* memorable goals there would be from Bobby Clarke.

His first hat trick came in that wild seven-to-six victory over Montreal that I mentioned earlier, and the game-winner was classic Clarke. With a minute left, Bobby came out of the corner and beat both defensemen, Guy Lapointe and Serge Savard, by shooting through his legs with his back to the net to beat Ken Dryden.

Perhaps Bobby's most incredible goal came at the old Detroit Olympia. He was in on a break, but was tripped up, and from a lying-down-sliding position about fifteen feet out, he reached for the puck while on his side and drove a wrist shot over the shoulder of goalie Jim Rutherford, who had been desperately trying to cover the puck.

Clarke's most famous goal was probably his brilliant overtime effort which beat the Bruins in Game Two of the 1974 Stanley Cup Finals in Boston. Perhaps just as famous was the ear-to-ear gap-toothed grin flashed by Clarke later on, when he and Bernie posed with the Stanley Cup.

There were also plays which were not scoring plays, but which were memorable nonetheless. In the Stanley Cup Finals against Boston, Clarke nullified Phil Esposito by hawking him relentlessly, hitting him into the boards, and embarrassing him almost to the point of ridicule by winning seventy-three per cent of the faceoffs. All season long, Espo had logged more than thirty minutes a game for Boston, but in the finals he clearly was exhausted by, and hardly an adequate match for, the exuberant Clarke. As Bobby himself said, "How can you skate if someone's on top of you and hitting you all the time?"

During the 1972 Canada-Soviet series, a play occurred which resulted in Clarke being tagged with an unfortunate international reputation as a chippy, and even a dirty player. The Soviets had taken a commanding early lead in the best-of-nine series, much to the shock of the North American hockey world. But then a Clarke slash broke the ankle of Soviet star Valerie Kharlamov, and the N.H.L. All-Stars rallied behind Clarke and Paul Henderson of Toronto, who eventually won the series with a steal and a goal in the final minute of Game Nine.

Even late in his career, when he wasn't scoring much, Clarke still produced memorable plays, and he could still fore-check with the best of them, a talent he possessed throughout his career. Who could forget the image of the "aging" Clarke as he blasted a defenseman off the puck with a bone-rattling body check, and then calmly fed a perfect pass out front for a last-second game-winner?

During his prime, I recall a game against Detroit in which Bobby had three goals and three assists, for a total of six points. But games like that were extremely rare for Clarke, mainly because he was never concerned with piling up points in one-sided games, unlike the superstars who want to be out there shooting when the score is seven or eight to one, so that they can pad their stats. If he were out there on an occasional shift with a big lead, you could be sure that he was only trying to set up goals for his teammates, not for himself. He always did enjoy his assists more than his goals anyhow, except perhaps for that game-winner in Boston. If the Flyers were leading in the third period, Clarke would play less and less, and he would make sure that the other guys, particularly those who might be struggling, got as much ice time and, therefore, as many shots as possible. "What do I need them for?" he would ask.

Bobby had a similar attitude about money. In the midst of his greatest days, when he signed his first long-term contract, Ed Snider was quoted as saying, "I know my lawyers will hate me for saying this, Bobby, but to tell you the truth, there are guys in this league who can't carry your girdle, and they're making more money than this."

Characteristically, Bobby's reply was, "How much money do I need? It's enough." How many players, or agents, then or now, would say that? Unlike most great players, Clarke wasn't interested in extravagances like fur coats and Rolls Royce automobiles. He wore jeans and drove a Jeep. And that was the style and the standard he set for everyone else on the team.

Bobby also downplayed the many individual awards and accolades he received, and he always pooh-poohed his gigantic role on the team, saying, "I can't go out there alone. The only way I can achieve is with five others on the ice. And I can't play the whole game. It's a *team* game, and I'm just a contributor to the *team*."

As long as Clarke was (and is) around, the key was (and always will be) the *team*. And with *no* superstars. Because if *he* wasn't a star, how could anyone else *dare* to be, even if the inclination were there? Whether you were a fifty-goal scorer, or a plugger, or a non-scoring defenseman, or a fill-in, or a Bob Taylor—everyone was the same. Everyone was a member of the *team,* and that feeling has remained, even after Clarke's retirement as a player, through the continuing leadership of players like Dave Poulin, Mark Howe, and Ron Sutter.

As short as Bobby's career as a player seemed to be, his fifteen years with the Flyers comprised, at that time, the longest term with one team of any professional athlete in Philadelphia sports history. And during that decade and a half, Bobby Clarke was a player unlike any other. There have been great offensive players, and there have been great defensive players, and there have been great leaders; but no player combined offense, defense, and leadership the way Bobby Clarke did. Interestingly, it was only after his offensive skills had waned that he was properly appreciated for his defensive skills, for not until his next-to-last season was he awarded the Frank J. Selke Trophy as the league's best defensive forward.

In previous seasons, Clarke was awarded the Bill Masterton Memorial Trophy (for sportsmanship and hard work), the Lester Patrick Trophy (for outstanding service to the game of hockey in the United States), and, three times, the Hart Memorial Trophy (as the Most Valuable Player in the N.H.L.). He was named a First-Team All-Star, was elected a players association president, and, of course, was voted into the Hockey Hall of Fame. No one was ever more deserving of any of those honors, but the *only* one that Bobby ever really wanted was the one he twice shared with his teammates—the Stanley Cup.

In the diminishing days of Clarke's distinguished career as a player, the Flyers lost a first-round playoff series in three straight games to the Washington Capitals, and Coach/General Manager Bob McCammon was asked to "move up" to general manager so that a new coach could be hired, since it had been determined that the two jobs were too much for one man. McCammon wanted to remain behind the bench. It was agreed that he would move on, presumably behind someone else's bench. That's when Bob Clarke was told, "The general manager's job is there for you now, if you choose to retire now, but we cannot in good conscience hire another guy with the idea of replacing him in two or three years. The job is there for you now; it may not be there for you later."

After carefully measuring his thoughts, his feelings, and the situation, as he always did with every important decision in his life, Bobby Clarke changed from jeans to a suit, put his front teeth in to stay, and became Bob Clarke, general manager. When asked why he had decided to retire as a player—the job he had loved so much—Clarke answered quite succinctly, "I began to realize that the other three centermen on the team were getting more ice time than I was, and there wasn't anything I could do about it."

That somber realization demonstrated once again Clarke's ability to cut to the core of the matter and to see the reality of things, for no one anywhere in the game ever loved the sheer playing of hockey more than Bobby Clarke. He was the first to arrive in the dressing room, along with whatever rookie he had given a ride to that day, and he was the last to leave. And he loved every single minute of it. But he knew that it was time to leave the place he loved so much, and to accept a brand-new kind of challenge.

Many players who have moved up to the front office in other organizations have sabotaged themselves by allowing personalities, friendships, and associations to cloud the harsh judgments that general managers often have to make. Perhaps partly because of his growth and experience as an executive of the N.H.L. Players Association, Bob Clarke carried into the general manager's job a tremendously necessary quality—the ability to unemotionally, even cold-bloodedly, evaluate a situation. And while that may sound almost like a negative characteristic, it is an essential quality for someone in an executive position, especially for someone whose responsibility it is to evaluate the careers of others.

*Top.* Bobby Clarke celebrates his overtime goal in Boston which made the first Stanley Cup possible. The date: May 9, 1974, at 12:01 of overtime. Assists to Bill Flett and Dave Schultz.

*Bottom.* Rick MacLeish steers the Stanley Cup-winning goal past Gilles Gilbert of the Bruins on May 19, 1974. Assist to Moose Dupont, who shot the puck.

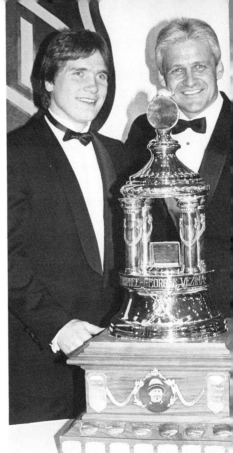

*Above.* Bob "Chef" Taylor (30) in step with his masked friend and co-Vezina winner, Bernie Parent. *Right.* Two Vezina winners: Pelle Lindbergh with his hero, mentor and friend—Bernie Parent.

Reggie Leach looks for someone to celebrate with after his goal has left this goalie in an embarrassing, but not unusual, position for a victim of the "Rifle."

(Photo by Bernie Moser-Dufor Photographers)

The Watson family of Smithers, British Columbia: Joe and Jimmy Watson flank their dad in the locker room following a playoff victory.

Hall of Famer Bill "Arnie" Barber angles in for a shot against the arch-rival Blues. The small 4 on his shoulder is in memory of Barry "Ash Can" Ashbee.

(Photo by Bernie Moser-Dufor Photographers)

Moose Dupont locks antlers with those of Scott Garland of the Maple Leafs during the 1976 playoffs.

(Photo by Len Redkoles)

*Above.* The NHL's all-time scoring leader among goaltenders, Ron Hextall, displays his unique talent.

*Below.* One of the original Flyers, "Fast Eddie" Van Impe, a pre-Clarke captain of the team.
(Photo by Bernie Moser-Dufor Photographers)

The ultimate Hex doll: Ron Hextall, a man who never rests on the ice, uses a break in the action to ward off evil spirits.

*Left.* André Lacroix shows off a few of the chapeaux that were thrown onto the ice to celebrate his hat trick against Vancouver on Nov. 29, 1970.

*Below.* Barry Ashbee: Great player, great coach, great competitor, great friend.

*(Photo by Bernie Moser-Dufor Photographers)*

*Above.* Score! Bob "the Hound" Kelly beats Jim Bedard of the
Washington Capitals for one of his 128 career goals, every one
of which seemed to be an important goal.

*Below.* Look Dad: Gordie Howe's son, Mark, is awarded the
Barry Ashbee Trophy by Barry's son, Danny.

*(Photo by Len Redkoles)*

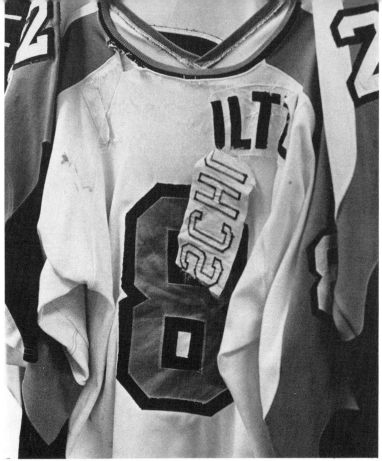

(Photo by Bernie Moser-Dufor Photographers)

*Above.* Dave who? Of the Broad Street what? *Below.* Yes, Dave Schultz does have a pussy-cat side. Here he embraces and kisses every hockey player's dream date, the Stanley Cup.

(Photo by Bernie Moser-Dufor Photographers)

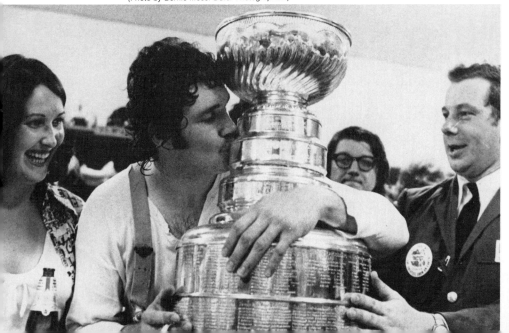

*Above.* Tim Kerr sets up in front of a rude defenseman, awaiting his chance to use a pair of the game's fastest hands.
*Below.* If looks could kill. . .then Dave Schultz would be headed for the pokey instead of the penalty box.
*(Photo by Bernie Moser-Dufor Photographers)*

Kate Smith acknowledges the ovation following one of her incredibly moving performances in the Spectrum.

*(Photo by Bernie Moser-Dufor Photographers)*

The irrepressible Sign Man, with sure signs of spring.

IT'S ALL OVER!

SHAKE HANDS AND LEAVE!

HAVE A NICE SUMMER

START PRAYIN'

YOUR SEASON IS OVER!

THE "GOOSE" IS COOKED!

GIVE UP, YOU HO'SERS

SEE YOU IN OCTOBER

TENNIS ANYONE

(Ron Anzalone Photo)
From one captain to another: Dave Poulin presents Bobby Clarke with a
solid silver stick on Bobby Clarke Night, Nov. 15, 1984.

If ever the right man came along at the right time to take a shot at
succeeding Bobby Clarke as captain of the Flyers, it was Dave Poulin,
who arrived from the University of Notre Dame by way of Sweden.

One way to keep Gary Dornhoefer from taking advantage of his favorite spot on the ice—the goaltender's crease.

Rick Tocchet, that rarest of commodities in the modern game, a man who scores *and* hits.

(Photo by Ed Mahan)

Rival Norris Division GMs: Mike Keenan, now of the Chicago Blackhawks, and Bob Clarke, now of the Minnesota North Stars, during more congenial times in Philadelphia.

Always a diabolical schemer on the ice, Bobby Clarke does a pretty good imitation of Count Dracula.

(Photo by Bernie Moser-Dufor Photographers)

*Above.* The eternally inscrutable Fred "the Fog" Shero in his palacial "office." Extra credit for deciphering the acronym at the bottom of the blackboard. *Below.* The best against the best . . . Ron Hextall thwarts "The Great One," Wayne Gretzky, during the Stanley Cup Finals.

(Photo by Bernie Moser-Dufor Photographers)

Gene Hart or Zero Mostel? In this case it's me a little wetter than normal after a game due to a sudden unexpected spring shower.

*Below.* Reggie "the Rifle" Leach with Paul "Homer" Holmgren riding shotgun against the Minnesota North Stars.

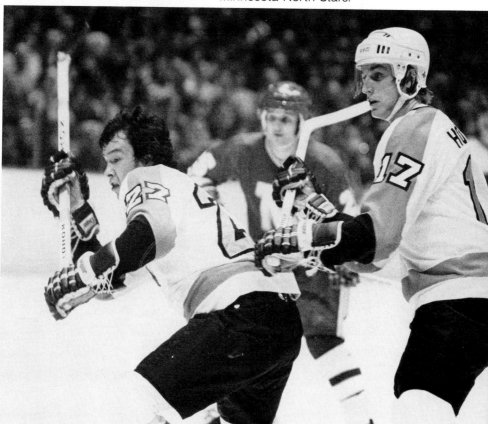

(Photo by Bernie Moser-Dufor Photographers)

Yours truly, on a day no Philadelphian can ever forget: May 20, 1974.

At long last, a City of Winners: The Flyer faithful celebrate their first Stanley Cup.

Bob Clarke loved his teammates—the Bill Barbers, the Dave Poulins, the Brian Propps—but if he ever thought that any of them were dogging it, or that he could improve the team, he would without hesitation make a move for the good of the club. An indication of that occurred the day before the season started in Clarke's first year as general manager, when he acquired two young players, Joe Paterson and Murray Craven, from Detroit in exchange for Darryl Sittler, the unannounced new captain of the Flyers. It was a staggering blow to Sittler, but Clarke realized that, at Sittler's age, he would no longer be able to carry a team to the Cup. So, he went for players who were young enough to some day have their names on the Cup, and at the same time, he opened up the captaincy for a younger player, Dave Poulin.

Later in his first season as general manager, Clarke was asked if he missed being on the ice, instead of having to watch nervously from the press box. I loved his answer: "I don't miss playing as much as I thought I would; but I miss the *contact.*" Not the skating, not the goals, not the assists, not the fighting, but the *contact!* What a surprising and lovely answer!

Robert Earle Clarke—a great person, a great friend, and somebody more than a little special to the Philadelphia Flyers, to the Philadelphia community, and to everyone in the hockey community. Cherish him, because you don't get one like Bob Clarke every ten years, or every fifty years. A franchise is blessed if it gets a Bob Clarke once in its history.

You know how *I* feel about Bob Clarke, but I am obviously somewhat biased. Perhaps you should hold off *your* opinions until you've read some comments I've collected from N.H.L. executives and coaches, and from Clarke's former teammates and opponents.

First, the executives, beginning with the president of the National Hockey League, John Ziegler: "I was at the drafting table, as an executive with the Detroit Red Wings, when we passed him by. It was the biggest mistake we ever made. He was probably the most intense competitor I've ever seen, and one word always comes to mind about Bobby Clarke—'leadership.' He's a leader of people, a leader of men. He's shown it on the Flyers, and with the players association, and he's going to do it in management."

Bill Torrey, general manager, New York Islanders: "I don't think there's ever been a team in the history of the N.H.L. that's had a better leader, and a better competitor, game in and game out, than Bobby Clarke."

Bep Guidolin, former coach, Boston Bruins: "After a faceoff, he didn't let *you* move until *he* moved. The kid was always thinking."

Scotty Bowman, former coach and general manager, St. Louis Blues, Montreal Canadiens, and Buffalo Sabres: "If I'd had Clarke on the Canadiens, we would have won six or seven Cups in a row, instead of just four."

Bob Johnson, former coach, Calgary Flames: "He was an overachiever, and you love to see that type of player. He got everything possible out of his ability, and he had just an outstanding career. If he carries that into the front office, and I'm sure that he will, I feel sorry for all the other clubs in the league."

Craig Patrick, former coach and general manager, New York Rangers: "He's had a great career as a player, and I'm just glad to see a quality guy like that joining the ranks of the league's general managers."

Bob Butera, former vice president, New Jersey Devils: "Bobby Clarke will be a success, no matter what he tries in life. He will be a sensational general manager."

Glen Sather, former coach, general manager, and president, Edmonton Oilers: "He's going to apply the same hard work and class and style that he put in for years as a player to his role as general manager, and he'll make sure that Philadelphia always has a role in the Stanley Cup situation."

Bryan Murray, former coach, Washington Capitals: "Bobby Clarke is a guy who wanted to win, *did* win, and certainly he will *continue* to win, because of the personality and the character he is."

Fred Shero, Clarke's former coach: "Bobby Clarke was the kind of man you'd like your own son to be. Not coincidentally, when he was named captain of the Flyers, that's when the Flyers became a great team."

Pat Quinn, another of Clarke's former coaches: "People of the character of Bobby Clarke, who work that hard, don't fail too often."

Simon Nolet, former teammate, and later, Quebec assistant coach: "Bobby Clarke was the greatest leader I've ever seen in this game, and one of the perfect gentlemen. As I heard many times around the league, 'The only thing wrong against Bobby Clarke is he had some nights the wrong sweater on his back.' "

Orest Kindrachuk, former teammate: "All you had to do was

watch Bobby Clarke, and if you didn't give the same effort he gave, then you weren't doing your job. That's *real* leadership."

Steve Coates, former teammate: "I was here from college as a rookie, and Bobby Clarke took me under his wing. Most superstars wouldn't do that. That was a very special time for me, and he's been a very special friend to me ever since. And I'm only one of the many he's gone out of his way to help."

Terry Crisp, former teammate and later, coach, Stanley Cup Champion Calgary Flames: "I thought I was a pretty good faceoff man, but Clarkie was the best ever. He would slide one hand almost all the way down to the blade of his stick, and then he would use his arms, his legs, his body, his stick, whatever, and he would just tie his opponent in knots. There just never was anyone else with the hockey smarts he had, along with the ability to act on them instantly."

Bob Kelly, former teammate: "Clarkie was truly a person who made you work hard to bring out the best in you, and to just play for the good of the team and the good of the city."

Gary Dornhoefer, former teammate: "What an honor it was to play with and for Bobby Clarke."

You've heard from executives, coaches, and Clarke's former teammates. Now let's try some of the men who played *against* him, starting with Terry O'Reilly of the Boston Bruins: "As a coach, I can appreciate more than ever that the way Bobby Clarke played the game was the greatest example of leadership. He didn't have to say anything; he just played with more intensity than any other player I've ever seen play the game."

Phil Esposito, Boston Bruins, and later, general manager, New York Rangers: "I hated to play against Clarke. It was so frustrating, because I knew that he knew what I wanted to do, and I also knew that he was not only ready to stop my next move, but that he was probably already planning a step or two beyond that."

Bryan Trottier, New York Islanders: "Bobby Clarke had the uncanny ability not only to get under your skin, but to climb into your mind and think right along with you. He had that look in his eye, that toothless half-smile/half-sneer that made you feel as though he could stare right inside of you. He was the most intense competitor I've ever faced off against, and the one I respected the most."

Richard Martin, Buffalo Sabres: "There were times when Clarke would skate back to the bench looking like he was ready to collapse, but then, a few minutes later, he was right back out there setting up the winning goal. Amazing."

Bob Nystrom, New York Islanders: "Bobby Clarke was the most tenacious player I've ever seen on the ice."

Carol Vadnais, Boston Bruins: "Bobby Clarke had everything you'd want in a hockey player. You hated to play against him, but you'd love to have him on your team. That's the biggest compliment I can give to a player—a man I hated to play against, but I'd love to have on my side."

Peter Zezel, St. Louis Blues (traded from the Flyers by Clarke), upon learning of Clarke's dismissal as general manager in the spring of 1990: "He was my idol then, and he's my idol now."

Of all the recollections that have been written and spoken about Bob Clarke, one of my favorites is from Dick Irvin, one of Canada's most respected hockey broadcasters: "The first year Bobby was in the league, I was in an elevator in Vancouver with a friend who was a hockey fan. An unassuming young fellow got on the elevator with a suitcase and glasses, and he didn't look anything like a hockey player. We rode down in silence, and when he got off, I said, 'I think that was that kid Clarke,' and my friend said, 'Yes, I think so.' Well, that unassuming kid Clarke, standing there with his suitcase and glasses, turned out to be the greatest example of how hockey should be played and how a player should conduct himself, both on and off the ice, that I have ever seen."

Montreal's and North America's most respected hockey journalist, Red Fisher, stated simply: "You mention the name Clarke, and you think of words like: intensity, dedication, loyalty, and winner. What more do you need?"

Even Mark Mulvoy of *Sports Illustrated,* never an advocate of the Flyers, grudgingly called Clarke "that tenacious gap-toothed diabetic rink rat, with the guts of ten dozen burglars, who destroyed Bobby Orr and the Bruins."

And finally, to paraphrase Jack Chevalier, the man who originated the term "Broad Street Bullies": "Bobby Clarke may not only have been the Most Valuable Player in hockey, he may have been the Most Valuable Player *in all of sports,* and the greatest leader, perhaps *ever,* in *any* sport. At least, it would be very tough to imagine any better."

On "Bobby Clarke Night," which was just a glorious occasion, the last line came from the honoree himself: "If I had the chance, I'd love to do it all over again."

I know that I, along with just about everyone else who ever saw him play, feel exactly the same way: "If we had the chance, Bobby, we'd *love* to see you do it all over again!"

T he celebration of Philadelphia's first Stanley Cup did not end with the conclusion of the massive parade on May 20. It continued through the summer and fall of 1974, with newspaper and magazine articles, interviews, promotions, commercials, and countless public appearances.

I recall one occasion in particular at Brandywine Raceway in Delaware, when I was invited to be spokesman and Bernie Parent was invited to make a trophy presentation. Well, I couldn't believe it, but it was almost as if the parade were still going on, so overwhelming was the adulation for Bernie. Not only that, but all of the hoopla over Bernie and the Flyers that night precipitated the first million-dollar handle in the track's twenty-two-year history. After all those years, it was a Montreal-born hockey goaltender who put a Delaware racetrack over the top for the very first time.

To me, all of the outpourings of gratitude and affection that the Flyers were receiving were more than understandable. Not only had Philadelphians been starved for a winner, but the Flyers had come from nonexistence to a world championship in just seven years, and there was an unmistakably miraculous fairy-tale quality about the whole story. This was especially so for me, the guy who, just a little more than seven years before, had sat in the dust across the street from Aquarama and watched a hole being dug in the ground for the foundations of a new hockey arena. I could recall trying to picture what it would look like inside, and then watching the first practice, and then trying to explain the new game in town to the relatively sparse crowds in that new building. And now, as I admired my sparkling new Stanley Cup ring, I could cherish it all the more for what it represented to me.

As warmly as the Flyers were received in the Philadelphia area, they were just as icily denounced everywhere else. A veritable barrage of attacks appeared in the national media, always criticizing the "violent" style of the Flyers, the champions of which the N.H.L. could not be proud, and worse yet, the champions for whom the N.H.L. should *apologize*!

Obviously, the Flyers were not totally pristine and guiltless, but the guilty had served their time in the penalty box, more time, in fact, than anyone else had ever served before. Intimidation may have been an element, as it is for most great teams in any sport, but it was just one element among many, the greatest and *most* intimidating of which was the Flyers' relentless, all-out, do-anything-for-the-team, never-say-die attitude. And no team ever played more *as a team* than the Flyers did.

Due to their frequent appearances on national television, as well as cover stories in national magazines like *Time, Newsweek,* and *Sports Illustrated,* the Flyers became the first N.H.L. team to be known from coast to coast. For a while it seemed that the television networks didn't want to show any *other* teams, unless, of course, they happened to be playing against the Flyers. And familiarity definitely bred contempt. It was easy and safe for publications like *Sports Illustrated* to condemn the Flyers, and, in fact, the entire sport, without offending many subscribers—only the ones in the Philadelphia area. And while pretending to "expose" and crusade against the evils of ice hockey, they would shamelessly continue to promote the most violent aspects of pro football, college football, boxing, and even pro wrestling, not to mention baseball's "beanball" wars and any fight that might break out in a basketball game.

To everyone but a Philadelphian, the Flyers were *the enemy,* and even the N.H.L. office openly expressed similar feelings. With all of the attention being showered upon them, it's a wonder that the young and successful Flyers could keep their minds on playing hockey, and that was part of the awesome challenge that they faced next—the challenge of repeating as Stanley Cup Champions.

# That (Almost as) Wonderful Year: 1974-75

As is always the case, even after a Cup-winning season, changes were made before the following season. Bill Flett had slumped from forty-three goals to only seventeen goals, and so, one week after the victory parade, he was traded to Toronto, where he would score only fifteen goals before being waived on to Atlanta.

More than ready to step into Flett's skates was a winger the Flyers had acquired just three days earlier in a trade with the California Seals. In that trade, the Flyers had sent two minor-leaguers and their number one draft choice to California in exchange for a junior teammate of Bobby Clarke's with the Flin Flon Bombers. Clarke and this new fellow, Reggie Leach, had set infinite numbers of records together in the Western Canadian Junior League, and the story goes that Clarke had said, "Get him," even though Leach had been unspectacular during his four years with the Seals and the Bruins, the team that had originally drafted him. (And I've lost count by now of the number of key Flyers who were originally drafted by Boston!)

The acquisition of Reggie Leach completed the only "name" line in Flyers history—the "LCB Line," with Clarke centering for Leach and Bill Barber. Reunited with his (and everyone else's) favorite table-setter, Bobby Clarke, Leach's goal production jumped from twenty-two to forty-five, and Reggie "The Rifle" was just getting warmed up!

Besides Bill Flett, Simon Nolet, who had been with the club since Year One, departed also, as he had been selected in the expansion draft by the new Kansas City Scouts.

Brought up from the minors was a young defenseman, who, in the form of a number two pick, had been thrown in as part of the Parent trade with Toronto. His name was Larry Goodenough (pronounced "good enough"), and, as a Flyer, his nickname of course had to be "Izzy"—when it wasn't "Boris Badenough." Izzy never did have a great year, but he was "good enough" as a young defenseman to team with an *old* defenseman whom the Flyers purchased from St. Louis in September. The *old* defenseman was Ted Harris, a veteran of a ton of great seasons with Montreal, Minnesota, Detroit, and St. Louis. Together, Harris and Goodenough formed a new, solid and reliable defensive pairing for the Flyers.

Also acquired from St. Louis in September, in exchange for a second-round draft choice and an obscure amateur player, was a young goaltender named Wayne Stephenson, whose record in three seasons with the Blues had been a mediocre thirty-one and twenty-seven. To Bob Taylor, this was yet another nail in the coffin, a nail almost as big as the re-acquisition of Bernie Parent had been, because "The Chef" would now be number *three* on the totem pole.

For the season, Taylor's record would be 0-2-0; Stephenson's would be 7-2-0; and Bernie's would be 44-14-10, with a goals-against average of 2.03 and twelve more shutouts—a Vezina season almost as incredible as his *previous* Vezina season had been. It was again obvious that, no matter *who* the other goaltenders were, Bernie was going to play eighty-five to ninety per cent of the games—for at least as long as he remained healthy.

Always looking for an edge, the Flyers opened the season wearing black oval patches with Stanley Cups emblazoned on them. But, after stumbling over the Los Angeles Kings, five to three, in the opener, it was asserted by Bobby Clarke that the players felt uncomfortable flaunting the Cup on the fronts of their jerseys. The Kings would not win again in the Spectrum for a decade or so, and those Stanley Cup patches would never be seen again, except in the 1974-75 team photograph, which had been taken *before* the opening game.

Even without the patches, the Flyers did not fly away from the rest of the league during the first three-quarters of the season. After sixty-one games, the Flyers record was 35-17-9, good enough to lead the Patrick Division, but behind the pace of the rising stars in Buffalo, and behind the pace of the ominously reborn Montreal Canadiens. But hockey fans continued to buy tickets to see the Flyers play. Again, every home game was a sellout, as was every road game except for the five in California, one each in Minnesota and St. Louis (which were both nearly sold out), and two in Kansas City (which never sold out for anybody). Whether or not they were worthy of repeating as Stanley Cup Champions, the Flyers were still the biggest draw in the game.

And like a thoroughbred approaching the homestretch, the Flyers certainly *looked* like Stanley Cup Champions, as they lost only one of their last twenty games. That one loss was an eight-to-two shellacking by, of all teams, the Pittsburgh Penguins. After that loss, in a magnificent finish the Flyers went unbeaten in their final fourteen games and caught up with Buffalo and Montreal, all three teams finishing with 113 points. Because the Flyers had the most wins of the three, with fifty-one (one more than their fifty of the previous season), the Flyers would, for the first time, have the all-important home-ice advantage over any playoff opponent they would face.

In the first round of the playoffs, the Flyers ripped through the Toronto Maple Leafs in four straight, with Moose Dupont assuring the sweep by scoring the final goal to win the fourth game in overtime.

It then looked as though the Flyers' semi-final opponents would be the surprising Pittsburgh Penguins, who were also the last team to have beaten the Flyers, nineteen games before. The Penguins led the young New York Islanders, three games to none, in their quarter-final series, but then the Islanders became only the second team ever to win the last four games of a seven-game series. In Game Seven in Pittsburgh, Islanders Captain Eddie Westfall scored in the final minutes to win it, one to nothing, sending the Islanders on to the semi-finals for the first time.

In the semi-finals, the Flyers blitzed the Islanders three straight times, two of them masterful shutouts by Bernie Parent, to take a three-games-to-none lead. In Game Four on Long Island, the Islanders took a three-to-nothing lead, but the Flyers tied it at three and then apparently won it at the end of regulation on a goal by Reggie Leach. After much discussion, referee Dave Newell decided that Leach's goal had crossed the goal line *after* the buzzer, and thus reprieved, the Islanders went on to win in overtime, four to three.

No matter; with the series returning to Philadelphia for Game Five, it just seemed that the Flyers would now finish it at home. After all, they had lost only one of their last twenty-two games, and they had not lost at home in months. But the Islanders not only won the next game in the Spectrum, they dominated the Flyers, five to one.

Returning to Long Island for Game Six, the Flyers scored first, but the Islanders again came back to win, two to one. For the second straight series, the upstart Islanders had come from three games down to tie and force a seventh game. Long Islanders were delirious, as the legend of the Island was beginning to take shape.

For Game Seven in Philadelphia, Kate Smith was summoned to the rescue, and once again she stirred the Spectrum to an overwhelming ovation. This time, instead of Orr and Esposito getting in on the act, it was Eddie Westfall and goaltender Glenn "Chico" Resch who presented a large bouquet of roses to Kate. But also once again, it was proven that Kate's magic was nontransferable, as before the noise had even begun to die down, Gary Dornhoefer scored on the first shot of the game. The Flyers then scored again and never looked back. Bernie and his boys held the Islanders in check when it counted, and the Flyers won, four to one, but not before we all made a mental note: "Keep an eye on that Islander club, because they look like the Flyers of the future."

While the Flyers were sending the Islanders back to Long Island for the summer (In my mind's eye I can still see Sign Man's "START YOUR BUS!" and "HAVE A NICE SUMMER!"), Buffalo and Montreal were battling in the other semi-final for the right to face the defending champion Flyers in the Stanley Cup Finals. It was a strange series, because the Canadiens won two blowouts in Montreal, while the Sabres, with the home-ice advantage, won four close ones, two of them in overtime, to win the series, four games to two.

If the Flyers had been given their choice, they probably would have chosen the team they got in the finals. Montreal had always given them trouble, home and away, while Buffalo had never won a game in Philadelphia, although Sabres coach Floyd Smith had brazenly stated, "We'll beat the Flyers when we have to." That statement became a rallying cry among the Flyers, who laughed when they heard it.

In reality, the Sabres were no laughing matter. They had a solid defense, and just that season they had traded for goalie Gerry Desjardins, who came through for them with a 2.78 goals-against average. They had great penalty-killing, and they had a super first line known as "The French Connection," featuring Gilbert Perreault at center flanked by wingers René Robert and Richard Martin. That line alone had already scored 145 goals for the season.

During the first two games of the finals in Philadelphia, it was the "LCB Line" that did most of the scoring, while Bernie allowed only one goal in each game. The Flyers won both rather handily, four to one and two to one.

The real drama began during Game Three in the Buffalo Aud, an old building which had been reconditioned for a third deck, but which had *no air conditioning*. It had been a steamy hot May day in Buffalo, and inside the Aud that night it was "Wet City." I mean everything and everybody was dripping, and I suppose that it was the enormous amount of body heat in the building which caused fog to form along the ice. It was also a hot and heavy game, which was tied at four after three periods. Of all the nights for an overtime game, this was not one we would have chosen.

By the time we got into the overtime period, the fog was so thick that no one could see the players, let alone the puck. The action had to be stopped periodically, so that skaters waving white towels could try (not very successfully) to disperse the fog. This primitive attempt at air conditioning was finally abandoned, and the ghostly scene became even more ghastly when, with just a minute and a half left in the overtime period, the red light went on behind Bernie Parent. On the television replay from behind the goal, we couldn't see the puck until it caught the inside of Bernie's pad on the short side and slithered in for the goal that won it for Buffalo, five to four. As the Sabres were mobbing René Robert, we figured out that he must have been the one to credit with the goal.

Inspired by their ethereal victory in Game Three, the Sabres also won Game Four, four to two, and the series was tied at two. But Game Five was back in the clear weather of the Spectrum, where the Sabres again failed to win. This time, to add insult to injury, Dave Schultz scored the first and last goals in a five-to-one blowout, and everyone shuffled off to Buffalo for one last time.

Buffalo had to win Game Six, just to preserve the slim chance of a seventh game upset in Philadelphia. As an emotional kicker, and lacking the services of a Kate Smith, Floyd Smith (no relation to Kate, unfortunately for him) decided to replace beleaguered goaltender Gerry Desjardins with the veteran Conn Smythe winner, Roger Crozier.

There was no fog this time, but it looked like Halloween anyhow, as a live bat swooped and darted about the old Aud. Since it was May 27 and not October 31, the bat was permitted to swoop and dart only until the ever-accurate stick of Rick MacLeish picked it off in mid-air. Buffalo's Jim Lorentz gloved the poor creature and carried it from the arena, much to the relief of many in the audience.

Roger Crozier and Bernie Parent were both perfect through the first two periods, although the desperate Sabres repeatedly stormed Bernie, just the way the Bruins had done the previous year. I still to this day don't know how at least some of the Sabres' laser shots didn't go in, especially during several power plays—both five-on-four and four-on-three. Yes, I suppose I *do* know. It was because Bernie was just that good!

In the opening seconds of the third period, the Flyers sent the puck behind the Sabres' net, where it was controlled by Buffalo defenseman Jerry "King Kong" Korab. Bob Kelly flew down the ice, checked Korab off the puck, and with a quicksilver move, circled in front of the net and stuffed the puck past Roger Crozier. Suddenly, with just eleven seconds gone in the third period, the Hound's glorious play had given the Flyers the one goal they needed.

With about three minutes left, Orest Kindrachuk set up Bill Clement for the clincher, and for the second consecutive year the Flyers had won the finals in six games. This time the score of the final game was two to nothing, instead of one to nothing, but it was still Bernie's game and Bernie's series.

In the final minutes, the Buffalo fans not only graciously accepted the defeat of their Sabres, but they saluted them by standing and chanting en masse, "Thank you, Sabres! Thank you, Sabres!" It was thrilling to me, not only that the Flyers had defied the odds and the "experts," but that the atmosphere in the Aud was so congenial.

In the Aud, like every other building except the Spectrum, I would have expected to hear the Flyers booed, as usual. Far from being booed, the Flyers were applauded as they skated an unimpeded victory lap around the arena with the Stanley Cup. It was as if the Buffalo fans were saying, "Well done, Philadelphia. We didn't think you could do it, but you did it, and we applaud you for it."

I couldn't help thinking, "If a visiting team ever wins the Cup in *our* building, I hope *our* fans will react the same way."

At midnight, before boarding our bus to the airport, I happened to see a young boy go up to Ted Harris and ask him for an autograph. As the veteran of a dozen N.H.L. seasons signed for the boy, I heard him say, "Son, you just saw the last hockey game I'm ever going to play." Ted had played only one season for the Flyers, but he retired a happy man, especially now that he knew his name would be engraved on the Stanley Cup for a fifth and final time.

When we arrived back in Philadelphia, we were greeted by another wild celebration, followed the next day by another magnificent parade. This time, the parade started in center city, at about Sixteenth and J.F.K. Boulevard, and proceeded south along Broad Street to J.F.K. Stadium, where 100,000 fans were waiting to greet their Flyers. It was my son Brian's fifth birthday that day, so, naturally, we told him that the parade was for him!

I recall several details of that day which may seem to be strange ones to recollect. For instance, there we were, for the second straight year, surrounded for many hours by adoring mobs of well-wishers; but one of my main concerns as a parent again had to be: "Where in the world will we ever find a bathroom for the children? Not to mention for *us*!"

Of all the words that were spoken by everyone when we finally made it into the stadium, I think the ones I remember the best were those spoken by Fred Shero, who, when he got to the microphone, told his wife, "I love you!"

And Philadelphia loved the Flyers, perhaps all the more so because no one else did!

A s had been the case the year before, there were many individuals who were responsible for, and who deserve credit for, the winning of the Stanley Cup. Most prominently, Bernie Parent capped off his second consecutive Vezina season with his second consecutive Conn Smythe Trophy, and if anyone had any doubts as to who truly was the most valuable player of the Stanley Cup Play-offs, all they had to do was check Bernie's goals-against—1.89. With four shutouts in the playoffs, Bernie had a total of sixteen for the season, and a total of *thirty* shutouts over the past two seasons. During those two Cup-winning years, Bernie had played the most demanding position in any sport as well as it had ever been played.

Bobby Clarke led the league with eighty-nine assists (among his 116 total points), and was, for the second time, awarded the Hart Trophy as the N.H.L.'s Most Valuable Player. But as Bobby himself liked to say, he couldn't have done it alone, so let's pay tribute to some of the *other* guys who made it all possible, guys like the scorer of the Cup-winning goal—

# Hound

Robert James Kelly of Port Credit, Ontario, was rarely called any-thing but "Hound," or "Muttley," and those names fit him per-fectly, because on the ice he could hound an opponent as well as anyone, and off the ice he was the focal point of tons of fun.

On the ice, Kelly was not just a hard checker and a battler who could throw more punches per second than anyone else in the league, he was a five foot, ten inch, 200-pound human pinball, who came flying off the bench (to the roar of the crowd) and skated so swiftly, and with such reckless abandon, that he seemed to be totally out of control. In fact, just about the only way that Kelly could stop himself was to crash into the boards, or the goal posts, or another player or players; and the other players, whether foe or friend, al-ways came out second best.

There was one other way that Kelly could stop himself, but that was only if he missed everything else, which, of course, was hard to do. I recall one time in particular when he came charging off the bench and made a mad dash into the left offensive circle to check a Red Wing, but he missed the check, got one skate dug into the circle, and like a corkscrew he spun himself around about four times until he almost screwed himself into the ice. That was one of the rare times in my career on the air that I found it extremely diffi-cult not to fall apart in hysterics.

Hound/Muttley was invariably amusing off the ice as well. He and I carried on a running battle of wits, and each of us delighted in giving the other "the business." He would call me the "Mound of Sound," or "Gene, the Dancing Machine," or the "Great Pumpkin," or worse, and he would insist that my pants were flared at the wrong end.

I would retaliate by telling him that he would have to smear lampblack on his balding head (about which he was quite sensitive), so as not to cause too much glare in our camera lens. Or I would insist that he was so dumb that his was the only name on the Stanley Cup that was written in crayon—the name "Muttley," that is.

One of Gary Dornhoefer's favorite riddles was: "What do a school and the Hockey Hall of Fame have in common?" The answer, of course, was: "Bob Kelly doesn't have a chance to get into either one."

One Sunday morning early in his career, Muttley returned from church to the apartment building where he and some of the other single members of the team lived. It was raining hard, so he knocked on the door of teammate Wayne Hillman and said, "You call me dumb, but it's raining and your car is outside with the windows open."

Wayne said, "Well, did you close the windows?"

"I couldn't. The doors were locked!" said Muttley, in his inevitably witty way.

Ed Van Impe and some of the other veterans loved inviting rookies out on "snipe hunts," but never was there a more gullible victim than the Hound. The idea was to go hunting at night with flashlights, presumably for grouse and the like. It was set up in such a way that when Kelly took a shot, there was an awful cry of pain from teammate Earl Heiskala, who, amidst much "blood," was then whisked away in an ambulance. Kelly, of course, was dispatched by the local constabulary directly into court, where he was charged with illegal hunting, carrying firearms without a permit, attempted murder, being an alien without proper papers, and so on. Kelly was sure that he needed thousands of dollars in bail money, and that he'd either be deported or rot in jail, and that his career was definitely over. Meanwhile, of course, his teammates were in an adjoining antechamber, listening to all of this with great glee.

So, if you're ever invited to go on a snipe hunt, take it from the Hound himself, you're probably better off declining the invitation. (A public service announcement from Gene Hart.)

Despite the "treatment" he got from his teammates, Muttley was always ready to do battle for the team. As he charged onto the ice with his instant acceleration, no one ever stirred more immediate attention and more adrenalin for his team in crucial situations. And Fred Shero used him just that way, not as a regular on a given line, but as the designated motivator and/or hit man of the Flyers. Hound's job, and he did it magnificently, was to stir things up, to pick up the pace, to throw the opponent off guard. And that's just what he did at the start of the third period of Game Six in Buffalo, when he bumped Kong Korab off the puck and scored the Cup-winning goal.

After being interviewed as the star of that game, Muttley was fighting his way back through the dressing room, which was mobbed with players, friends, family, press, TV people, and hangers-on, when he saw a small, middle-aged man sitting in his changing-stall area. In the common parlance of athletes and servicemen, Muttley yelled above the din, "Hey, old man, get the _____ out of my locker!"

"Excuse me?" replied the man.

"I said, 'Get the _____ out of my locker!' "

And so, Governor Shapp of Pennsylvania got up and got out of Bob Kelly's locker.

In his ten years with the Flyers, Bob Kelly averaged only about a dozen goals per season. In the first Cup-winning year, he scored only four, and none in the playoffs. In the second Cup-winning year, he scored only eleven, but he had three in the playoffs, and one of those will live forever in Stanley Cup history. Statistically, he was well down the list when compared with his teammates. But if you want to talk about "contribution to winning," the Hound ranked right up there in the highest echelon, along with the Clarkes, and the Barbers, and the Parents.

You were a great team player, a great friend, and a winner to the nth degree, Hound. And you still are a great friend, Muttley.

Hockey players and hockey announcers spend a lot of time waiting in airports, and some of that time is made more palatable by occasional announcements over the public address system, such as, "Paging Mr. Muttley, Mr. Robert Muttley..." or "Paging Mr. Nose, Mr. Hawk Nose..." You know who Mr. Robert Muttley is, and now I'd like you to meet the man they called "Bedrock," or "Cutie," or, more usually, just plain

# Hawk

The Cup-winning Flyers had two great scoring lines. One of them was centered by number 16, Bobby Clarke; the other one was centered by number 19, Rick MacLeish. Clarke and MacLeish were both great centermen, but their styles were as different as milk is from champagne. Neither was very big, but both had tremendously strong legs. Clarke used his to grind away; MacLeish used his to glide away. The rest of Clarke's strength was in his brain; the rest of MacLeish's strength was in his wrists, which were about as big as most men's legs. Clarke would have been a good marathon runner; MacLeish would have been a good blacksmith. In fact, as much as Ricky loved horses, he probably would have loved that job.

Because of his unusual freewheeling, ad-lib style, so different from Clarke's or anyone else's, many thought that Ricky was lazy. It wasn't so much that he didn't put out, but that, like athletes such as Mike Schmidt and Wilt Chamberlain, his talents were so awesome that he could accomplish great deeds without any apparent effort at all. Teammates and opponents alike were simply in awe of the Hawk's ability to skate, to get off a wrist shot, and to simply drive defensemen and goaltenders crazy.

As I mentioned earlier, MacLeish was blessed not only with talent, but also with two linemates who possessed the discipline and the willingness to sacrifice that made them the perfect bookends for the Hawk. No two players in the league could have complemented his style more beautifully than Gary Dornhoefer and Ross Lonsberry did. I can still visualize them now, rotating the puck out of the corner in a triangular pattern, always with the poise and the patience to wait for the Hawk to make his move. It was a great line, especially for a second line, and a wonderful contrast to the feeding center and scoring wings of the first line.

Ricky's talents even included some that no one, including Ricky himself, knew he had. He was challenged to fight one night by Hank Boucha in Detroit, and no one knew how well he would be able to handle himself. We should have known. As they carried Boucha off, bleeding, the battered Red Wing raised his number one finger to the cheers of the crowd. It was the first and only time that I ever saw a "dead gladiator" carried off to cheers. (Detroit was so bad, I suppose, that their fans would have cheered *anything.*) Ricky just blushed and looked embarrassed. I don't believe that he was ever challenged again, by Boucha or by anyone else.

Whether things were going well or not, on or off the ice, Hawk never showed much emotion, one way or the other. It sometimes made it seem as though he didn't really care. But he did. Instead of revealing a frown or a smile, he would just wipe his hand across his face, as if he were wiping off his expression along with his sweat. In joy or in pain, he refused to show it.

One of hockey's most amazing stories (Steven Spielberg, take note!) occurred in the Los Angeles Forum, when Ricky slipped down on the ice and Marcel Dionne appeared to trip over him. Ricky didn't get up right away, and when he did, I noticed as he came off the ice that a trainer was holding a towel around his neck. I assumed that he had been cut, but what a gross underestimate that turned out to be. (If you have a weak stomach, I'd advise you to skip to the next paragraph.) What we hadn't seen (fortunately) and what Ricky hadn't revealed (again, fortunately) was that after Ricky had fallen, Marcel Dionne had actually skated across his throat. Now, in case you didn't know this, a hockey player's skates are every bit as sharp as a well-honed razor, and, in this case, Dionne's skate had gashed Ricky's throat so badly that another fraction of an inch would have severed his jugular vein, and very possibly he would have bled to death before anything could have been done. Fortunately, and just by coincidence, the Flyers' oral surgeon, Everett Borghesani, was making his first West Coast trip with the team, and he hustled down with his ever-ready suture kit and sewed Ricky's neck back together, with a mere eighty-eight stitches.

When we got home, there was a sign in the dressing room that once again displayed the type of gallows humor that hockey players are known for: "What's the difference between Hawk MacLeish and Frankenstein's monster?" In case you haven't guessed, the answer was: "Two stitches."

If that kind of humor didn't have you in stitches, maybe this kind will: Ricky had been named the number one star of a game in Montreal, and he and I were on the ice, across from the television cameras, waiting for the post-game show to begin. Finally, the director gave me the "Go!" and I started in with the usual set-up, "Hi, Gene Hart back at the Forum in Montreal. . ." when I couldn't help noticing that Ricky had placed his thumb against one of his nostrils and had blown his nose on the ice right in front of me. I was somewhat startled, but I carried on.

Next, Ricky pulled the score sheet out of my hand and started to read it. I tried subtly to take it back, so that Ricky would, hopefully, pay attention to the camera. Then I asked Ricky a question, and while I was holding the mike for his answer, he reached down inside his pants and started to scratch his groin. I was thinking, "Oh, my goodness! What do I do now?" but somehow we got through the interview.

About halfway home on the charter that night, Hawk tapped me on the shoulder and said, "That thing we did tonight..."

"What thing?" I asked, innocently.

"That interview..."

"Yes? What about it?"

"Was that on television?"

"Sure, what do you think we were standing out on the ice for?"

"Oh, I thought it was only on radio!"

To say that Ricky was embarrassed would probably be putting it too mildly, but he kept his cool, even when his wife later asked him, "What were you doing, Ricky?"

"Why? Could you see it all?"

"Why, sure! Right on TV!"

I think that a shy, embarrassed blush is about the most emotion I ever saw from Ricky, even in reference to his awe-inspiring talent. I recall his being asked what was the most goals ever scored in a game in which he played, and he shuffled his feet a bit and said, "Thirty-four."

"And how many did *you* score?"

Again blushing, "Nineteen."

He never scored *quite* that many in an N.H.L. game, but if ever anyone had the ability to do that, Rick MacLeish did. He was the first big goal scorer the Flyers ever had, and in his eleven seasons with the team, he scored 381 goals and collected 421 assists, for a total of 802 points, many of them *important* points. But what I'll always remember best about the Hawk is the way he would swoop down the right side, cut to his left past the slot, and unload that fabulous wrist shot. And I'll also always remember that modest little crook of the neck, as he peeked up to see his goal registered on the scoreboard, while wiping away any hint of a smile in blushing embarrassment.

Richard George "Hawk" MacLeish was a pure and marvelous

player, and just one of the great characters who combined to make the Flyers a great team.

**N**ow that you know the Hawk and the Hound, I'd like you to meet the Watson family, specifically Pop Watson's two sons,

# Thundermouth and Chan

The Watson family is from Smithers, British Columbia, which is about as far to the northwest as you can get and still have solid ground under your feet. And how would any family wind up in Smithers? Well, Pop Watson was a genuine settler. He followed the building of the railroad west as far as it would go, and then he followed it north until it stopped in Prince Albert, and then he went a little farther north and settled in Smithers, whose total population, I believe, consisted of the Watson family, six bears, and a school of salmon.

When Pop Watson came to visit his boys in the East, he was like a breath of fresh Canadian Pacific air. He was as big as an ox, and he was honest, sincere, and totally unpretentious. With his beard, his plaid shirt, and his winning western ways, he became quite a hit with everyone he met, including our television audience.

Older brother Joe Watson came about his nickname honestly. As a child I think "Thundermouth" had been vaccinated with a phonograph needle, because he had the rare ability to chatter on incessantly, no matter where he was. Even when he was in the penalty box, he would deliver a painful play-by-play of everything that went on while he wasn't in the game, punctuated by, "Oh, come on, guys!" and "Oh, Holy Jeez!" He was always yakking, and some people thought that he sometimes yakked too much, but he was also the vocal conscience of the team. After a win in a sloppily played game, Joe would say, "We won, but we shouldn't have. We stunk tonight." Thundermouth Watson may have been the first overt tell-it-like-it-is player on the Flyers. And, as such, he was a very valuable asset.

Joe also had the ability to see the light side of a serious situation. During a playoff series in Toronto, a multitude of fights had provoked the ire of the Ontario authorities. At one point, Joe had swung his stick over the penalty box glass and had accidentally clipped a policeman. Said Joe, "Gee, if I go to jail, I hope I get Harold's old cell!" (The reference was to the previous confinement of the owner of the Maple Leafs, Harold Ballard.)

Before Thundermouth got himself in any deeper, he was warned by Moose Dupont, "Don't kid, Joe. Dees time de fan's going to heet de sheet!" With advice like that, how could anyone go wrong?

At one point early in his career, Joe became discouraged with his and the team's lack of success, and he actually planned to retire. Fortunately he was talked into staying, and I know he has never regretted it. If he had left, he would never have had the opportunity of playing on the same team with his brother Jimmy, at least not in Philadelphia. For Joe was instrumental in convincing Jimmy to choose Philadelphia over the W.H.A. franchise in Calgary, which would have been much closer to home for both of them. If they had gone to Calgary, their names probably wouldn't be on the Stanley Cup. But then, without the Watsons perhaps *none* of the Flyers' names would be on the Cup.

They were a marvelous defensive pair—the Watson Brothers, Thundermouth and Chan (so named because of Jimmy's cleft chin). And when I say "defensive," I mean in terms of the old-fashioned team-oriented *defense*-minded defensemen, to whom goals are something to be prevented at all cost, not something to be scored. It is ironic that the Flyers' first goal in their first game in Boston was scored by Joe Watson, who in his two years with the Bruins had scored a grand total of two goals.

We always kidded about the Watsons' lack of scoring ability, and just for them I created the mythical Grizzly Cup, to be awarded annually to the player from Smithers who scores the most goals. Jimmy's strategy was usually successful: "If you could get a goal by Christmas, you were almost a lock." In the five full seasons the brothers played together, Jimmy won the first two years, two to one and seven to six, and Joe won the fourth year, four to three. The other two years were ties, at two and at five. So, overall, Jimmy won two years and Joe won one, with two ties; and if you were to count their total goals over those five years, Jimmy had nineteen and Joe had eighteen.

Later on, Ron "Flocky Hockey" Flockhart moved from Sicamous ("Sic-a-Moose"), B.C., to Smithers, probably just so that he could be eligible for the Grizzly Cup. It was after Joe had retired, and in Flocky's first year he outscored Jimmy, three to two. In his second year, Flocky managed to outscore Jimmy, thirty-three to three, and that was enough for Chan. He retired before anyone could win the cup for a third time.

Before his retirement in 1979, Joe Watson played sixteen games as captain of the Colorado Rockies. He would have played more, but his career was brought to an extremely sudden and horrifying conclusion when he slid into the corner boards feet-first and broke his leg in fourteen places. Even though the doctors were able to get the bones back into the thigh, and wherever else they came from, in time to save his leg, Joe went through a lot of hell in a St. Louis hospital before he was able to get around again.

Obviously unable ever to play again, Joe helped us out occasionally in the broadcast booth. I recall one game when we were back in Colorado, and Joe was doing color for me when he noticed that the Rockies had too many men on the ice. In his typically uncontrolled, but endearing manner, Joe began thundermouthing, "They've got too many men on the ice! They've got too many men on the ice!" I signaled with my hand toward the open mike, and Joe nodded and started to *whisper,* desperately, "They've got seven men on the ice! They've got seven men on the ice!"

After his brief career as a color man, Joe became an unofficial assistant coach for the Flyers and then a scout. He's currently a tremendous addition to the Flyers' advertising department, and, fortunately, he's still never at a loss for words.

Jimmy, after suffering an eye injury during a Team Canada series, and then enduring numerous problems with his back, retired more quietly from hockey to begin a new career in the Philadelphia area.

To me, Joseph John "Thundermouth" Watson and James Charles "Chan" Watson will always be a memorable pair. Even though they could play together for only five seasons, they were five of the best seasons in Flyers history. And of all the images that depict the pure thrill of victory, there is no greater picture in my mind than the picture of the two Watson brothers proudly surrounding their dad in front of the Stanley Cup.

A fter two consecutive Stanley Cups, the theme for the next season was "Hat Trick in '76." And what better way to spend a day in the merry month of May during the Bicentennial Year than with a parade down Broad Street to celebrate a third consecutive Stanley Cup? At least that was the goal.

# That (Not Quite as, but Still) Wonderful Year: 1975-76

The only major personnel change following the second Cup-winning season was the trade of Bill Clement to the lowly Washington Capitals in exchange for their top draft choice. With that choice, the only overall number one choice the Flyers have ever had, center Mel Bridgman became the first player chosen in the N.H.L. draft. It was a move reminiscent of the Montreal Canadiens, who for years had made a practice of trading surplus parts to the league's have-nots in return for top draft choices.

Other than that, the Flyers were obviously loaded with enough talent to have won two straight Cups, so why mess with success? You never want to break up a winning combination; you just want to enjoy it! And there was still a definite feeling of euphoria about the Flyers as they began their chase for Cup Number Three.

But it didn't take long for the euphoria to turn to concern. Early in the season, Bernie Parent noticed some pain in his arm, which was diagnosed as a disk problem at the base of his neck. Even though Bernie would have to miss a good part of the season, it was obvious that surgery was necessary. This was the first serious tear in the Flyers' royal fabric, but the word was that Bernie would be back, and in the meantime, Wayne Stephenson and Bob Taylor would take over in goal.

As a back-up to Stephenson, Bob Taylor had won three games and lost one when he and Ed Van Impe were traded in mid-season to Pittsburgh for goaltender Gary Inness, who had played well for the Penguins in the playoffs of the previous season. The Chef finished his career in Pittsburgh with a record of no wins and one loss for the Penguins, before moving into the broadcast booth in Philadelphia.

As Wayne Stephenson's new back-up, Gary "Inch" Inness won two and lost none. Of the remaining seventy-four games, Bernie played eleven, with a record of 6-2-3, while Wayne played all of the others, with a rather extraordinary record of 40-10-13 and a goals-against average of 2.58.

Despite his excellent record, I always felt that there was a little gap between Wayne, who was an accountant by training, and the rest of the club. And while Wayne was, I believe, a bit aloof, his aloofness was not improved by the constantly nagging thought, "When is Bernie coming back?" Or even worse for him, "Just wait 'til Bernie gets back!"

All things considered, Wayne never did get the credit he deserved during his five-year stint with the Flyers. Always overshadowed by Bernie, Wayne's overall record for the Flyers was nevertheless an outstanding 93-35-19. When Bernie was forced to retire in 1979, it seemed that Wayne's big chance had finally arrived, but he held out for more money during training camp and he was exiled to Washington for a third-round draft choice. After two losing seasons with the struggling Capitals, Wayne retired in 1981, still the possessor of an excellent career record (with St. Louis, Philadelphia, and Washington): 146-93-48 and a 3.06 goals-against average.

No matter who was in goal during the 1975-76 season, the Flyers once and for all put the lie to the "fact" that people didn't want to see their style of play. For the third consecutive year, every Flyers home game was a sellout, and the only non-sellouts on the road were: one in California, two in Atlanta (around 15,000 both times), three in Kansas City, and three in Minnesota (which had hit rock bottom, with only twenty wins for the season).

The Flyers also had no trouble selling out an exhibition game on Jan. 11, 1976. Granted, it was no ordinary exhibition game. In fact, it was a game that had been anticipated for months, with the rallying cry, "The Russians are coming! The Russians are coming!"

Two Soviet teams, the Soviet Wings and the Soviet Army, had been touring North America and playing against selected N.H.L. teams. The Wings had concluded their four-game series with only one loss, a wild one in Buffalo. The Soviet Army was undefeated, their closest game having been a come-from-behind three-three tie against the Canadiens in Montreal. Overall, the N.H.L.'s record was an unimpressive 1-5-1, as the eighth and final game approached. And that final game would be an internationally televised event, featuring the undefeated Soviet Army against the defending Stanley Cup Champions, the Philadelphia Flyers.

The game was to be played on a Sunday afternoon, but the Flyers had begun psyching themselves on Thursday night, immediately following their last game before the Russian game. I can recall how quiet the dressing room was that night, except for the always-encouraging words of Joe Watson. There were some normal pre-game concerns: They knew that the Russians were great; and they knew that they would have to face the awesome Soviet Army attack without their own ace in the hole, Bernie Parent. But Wayne Stephenson had been playing well, and the Flyers were truly looking forward to this tremendous new challenge.

The league and the media were looking forward to it, also. The officials and the writers who had previously condemned the Flyers were now saying, "Good luck, Flyers! We're pulling for you!" Those people who had given so little credit to the Flyers for the qualities they obviously possessed in winning over 100 games and two Stanley Cups during the past two years were now saying, "You have to win it for the league!"

With typical Flyer pride, the team's always-vocal conscience, Joe Watson, answered that with, "Screw the league! We're going to win it for ourselves!" To a man, the Flyers knew that, as champions, they represented the league, and they were proud of that, but, more than anything else, they wanted to win this one for themselves.

On Friday afternoon, there was to be a joint luncheon honoring the two teams at the Spectrum's Ovations restaurant. Early in the week, Ed Snider, knowing that I had some knowledge of the Russian language, had said to me, "Gene, come up with a Russian phrase or something that I can say at the end of my speech on Friday."

I came up with the Russian translation for, "Good luck to all on Sunday," and Mr. Snider asked me to write it out phonetically for him, which I did. Every time I saw him for the rest of the week, he would practice that Russian sentence with me, repeating it over and over with great intensity, always making sure that he had it exactly right.

At the luncheon, I said a few words in Russian and then introduced all of the players from both teams, particularly enjoying the pronunciation of all those wonderful Russian names. As I mentioned before when I was discussing Dave Schultz, old number 8 got the biggest rise out of the Soviet players and officials, one of whom told me afterward, "We are not timid. We also have our bad man like Dave Schultz. Ivan have already forty penalty minutes!" I didn't have the heart to tell him that Dave sometimes had that many minutes in one game, or even one period!

After I was finished showing off my fluency in Russian, Ed Snider gave his speech in very proper English, and at the end he said, "Thank you very much," and sat down. I was disappointed that he hadn't remembered to use the Russian sentence I gave him, or that he was afraid he wouldn't get it right. After the luncheon, he came over to me and grabbed me by the lapels, and with even more fire in his eyes than usual he said, "I want to tell you, Gene, I appreciate what you did, and I wanted you to know that I didn't forget it. It's just that I looked at those cold sonofabitches, and I couldn't say to them, 'Good luck on Sunday.' "

There has never been a hockey game, other than perhaps a Stanley Cup final game or an Olympic final game, that created so much interest. There were, of course, numerous protests from various ethnic and religious groups. Ed Snider knew that there would be, and he handled them beautifully. As much as he may have disliked the Soviets (and their teams soon became unwelcome in the Spectrum), the Soviet Army team was to be his guest on that Sunday afternoon, and no one should ever abuse a guest. It was agreed that protests would be allowed until the Soviets came onto the ice, but at that time, all protesters would leave and all uncomplimentary signs would come down. In general, this policy was adhered to, except for some signs in Russian, and some blood on the steps of the Spectrum.

The game was played without further protests of that nature, but not without protests of a *different* nature. About midway through a scoreless first period, Ed Van Impe came out of the penalty box and threw a hard check at Valerie Kharlamov, the same star winger whose ankle Bobby Clarke had broken four years before. Kharlamov went down as if he'd been shot, and while it may have been a hard check, it wasn't *that* hard! In fact, Bill Barber had earlier dealt a tougher blow to one of the Soviet defensemen along the boards, without causing any such theatrics. But this time, the Russians went after referee Lloyd Gilmour and linesman Matt Pavlich, a Ukrainian who understood some Russian. In a situation such as this, "Sign Man" Dave Leonardi usually held up a sign which read, "TELL IT TO THE JUDGE!" This time he held up, "TELL IT TO THE CZAR!"

Since the Soviets could not be satisfied by the czar or by anyone else at the moment, they protested in the best way they knew how. They simply walked off the ice and refused to return, much to the consternation of everyone, including Marv Albert and yours truly on the national telecast.

While we were trying to figure out what to do next, we filled some air time by panning over some of the Russian signs in the stands and discussing what they meant. Marv would say, "What does that one say, Gene?" and I would answer with, "The Flyers will emerge victorious!" or "Soviets, go home!" or "The Flyers are the best in the world!" until we got to one that prompted me to say, "Gee, Marv, I just can't quite make that one out." During the next commercial break I said, "Marv, I couldn't tell you what it said on the air."

"Why? Was it dirty?"

"No, it said, 'Lenin was a fag!' "

Meanwhile, in the Russians' dressing room, since the czar was still unavailable, the Soviet Army coach was protesting to N.H.L. president Clarence Campbell: "We play no more. Your team de Flyer make it damage on our players. We play no more."

President Campbell replied, "Then you won't get any money."

The Soviet coach thought for a second, but only for about a second, and then said, "We play. With all de money we fix de damage."

So, after a long hiatus, the Soviets returned to the ice, chagrined at having to back down, and further annoyed by a two-minute minor penalty for delay of the game. After the next faceoff, it took the Flyers no more than thirty seconds to score, as Reggie Leach deflected home a shot from the point, and the Spectrum exploded with the loudest ovation since Kate's last visit. Later in the first period, Rick MacLeish broke away and blew a wrist shot over goaltender Vladislov Tretiak's left shoulder, and the Flyers led, two to nothing, after one period.

The coup de grâce came early in the second period. With the Russians on the power play, Don "Big Bird" Saleski took a bullet shot from the right wing. Tretiak stopped the shot, but left the rebound out in front for the trailing defenseman, Joe Watson. Thundermouth took Sign Man's advice, "INSERT HERE!" and the Flyers led, three to nothing. The Russians finally got a goal on a point shot, but the Flyers were clearly dominating the game, and they led, three to one, after two periods.

In the third period, Izzy Goodenough added a power-play goal from the right point, and Sign Man held up, "NEXT GOALIE!" With a four-to-one lead, there was no way the Russians were going to come back. Fred Shero's strategy of not chasing them through all of their fancy looping and circling was working to perfection. The Flyers simply lined up four men across the blue line and dared the Russians to come to them. Since they couldn't get past the blue line, and since they had no idea of how to dump and chase, the Soviet offense was absolutely stymied. Late in the game, the Russians were still back in their own zone, looping and circling and throwing pretty passes to one another, while the Flyers calmly blockaded center ice. Wayne Stephenson played superbly, but he was hardly tested, as the Flyers outshot the Russians, forty-nine to thirteen.

With Shero's brilliant coaching technique, and with a typically marvelous team effort by everyone concerned, the Flyers deserved their glorious victory. Not only had they won two straight Cups, with their sights dead-set on a third, but they had also soundly whipped the team considered by many to be the best in the world. Could there be any question as to what team truly deserved to be called "best in the world"? As Sign Man so succinctly put it at the concluding buzzer, "BRING ON MARS!"

Hypocritically, many of those who had vilified the Flyers now praised them for beating the hated Russians. But even after that dominant victory, the Flyers still took more than their share of rips from the "experts," such as Dave Anderson and Robin Herman of the *New York Times,* both of whom berated the Flyers for their roughness. When Robin Herman called the Soviet Army game "the most vicious sports event I have ever seen," I really blew my cork, and not only because the game wasn't even *remotely* vicious. I was incensed mainly because I was so sick of seeing excellence detracted for the mere sake of detracting, and by what manner of authority?

The next time I saw Robin Herman, I went up to her and said, "Do you know what you are? You're such a dimwit! You've just detracted from a great team effort and a victory that this team deserved. They've won two Cups, they've played brilliantly even without Bernie Parent, and you've found nothing better to do than to berate them. Why the hell don't you go write about a sport you know? 'The most vicious sports event' you've ever seen! How many sports events *have* you seen? Six?" No one in the Flyers organization could say those things, but I thought they were deserved, so I really zapped her. And I didn't feel a bit bad about it afterward. In fact, I felt good about it. And I still do.

The victory over the Russians was one of the most successful of many successful home games for the Flyers during the 1975-76 season. In fact, the Flyers' home record of 36-2-2 was (and still is) the all-time best in N.H.L. history. Montreal once had only one loss at home, but no team other than the Flyers has ever had seventy-four points at home in one season. Overall, the Flyers finished the regular season with a record of 51-13-16, for 118 points, their highest total ever. They had run away from the rest of the Patrick Division, and the rest of the Campbell Conference, but one team in the Wales

Conference surpassed even the Flyers' record: The Montreal Canadiens record was an incredible 58-11-11, for 127 points.

Bobby Clarke had the best individual point total of his career, with 119. Eighty-nine of those were assists, tying his own pre-Gretzky record for a centerman. Besides leading the league in assists again, Clarke also scored thirty goals and won his third Hart Trophy as the league's Most Valuable Player. He also came closer than any other Flyer ever has to winning the Ross Trophy, which is awarded to the league's leading scorer. That was won by Guy Lafleur, who had 125 points, 6 more than Clarke. Lafleur played the full eighty-game schedule, and I always felt that if Clarke hadn't had to sit out four games, he probably would have had at least 6 more points, as hot as he was that season. Clarke also led the LCB Line to an N.H.L. record of 141 goals in the regular season, and 27 more in the playoffs, for an astounding total of 168 for the year.

This time around, the playoffs would be a little different, and a lot more trouble. The past two years, the Flyers had breezed through the opening round, in four straight over Atlanta and in four straight over Toronto. This time the opening round would be against a much better Toronto club, with an absolutely awesome power play to throw at the penalty-prone Flyers and their reshuffled goaltenders, Wayne Stephenson and the recently returned, but still shaky Bernie Parent.

The Flyers won the first two rather easily in Philadelphia, but the Maple Leafs tied the series by winning two squeakers in Toronto. The Flyers again coasted in Philadelphia, seven to one, but the Maple Leafs tied it again by winning in Toronto, eight to five. In that game, the Flyers killed themselves with tons of penalties, while the Leafs' power play of center Darryl Sittler, wings Errol Thompson and Lanny McDonald, and pointmen Borje Salming and Ian Turnbull gleefully pounded power-play goal after power-play goal past Bernie Parent, who suffered through the worst game of his career. Ian Turnbull had been the only defenseman ever to score five goals in one game, but this time Darryl Sittler became the only player, other than Montreal great Maurice Richard, to score five goals in a playoff game.

Every game of this series was won by the home team, so, fortunately for the Flyers, Game Seven was played in Philadelphia, where the Flyers again won easily, seven to three.

In the semi-finals against Boston, the Flyers again had the home-ice advantage, but only until the Bruins shocked everyone by winning the first game in the Spectrum, four to two. It was only the third time all season that the Flyers had lost at home. Game Two in Philadelphia was tied at one goal apiece after regulation, but former Bruin Reggie Leach scored in overtime to win it for the Flyers.

In Boston, the Flyers came alive and staggered the Bruins by winning the next two games, and then finished off the series with a flourish in Philadelphia, winning six to three, with five of the goals by Reggie Leach, who scored in every way imaginable—booming slap shots, little tap-touches, and even a poke-checked pass over the shoulder of poor Gilles Gilbert. It was just a magnificent performance, similar to Darryl Sittler's in the first round, and in a span of just seven games, the number of five-goal scorers in a playoff game had been tripled. More importantly, the Flyers had beaten the Bruins, four games to one, and they were in the Stanley Cup Finals for the third consecutive year.

The final opponent this time would not be the Bruins, whom the Flyers had just knocked out; and it would not be the Sabres, whom the Islanders had knocked out; and it would not be the Islanders, whom the Canadiens had knocked out; it would be the only team that had finished ahead of the Flyers in the regular-season standings, and therefore the only team which could have the home-ice advantage over the Flyers in the playoffs—the Montreal Canadiens. And these weren't just the Montreal Canadiens, but one of the *greatest of all* Montreal Canadien teams. To read down their roster is, as Freddy Shero pointed out, like reading down an All-Star roster:

| | |
|---|---|
| Goaltenders | Ken Dryden (42-10-8; 2.03)<br>Michel "Bunny" Larocque<br>(16-1-3; 2.46) |
| Defensemen | Guy Lapointe<br>Jean Potvin<br>Larry Robinson<br>Serge Savard<br>Don Awrey<br>Pierre Bouchard |

Centers                Peter Mahovlich
                       Doug Risebrough
                       Jacques Lemaire
                       Doug Jarvis

Left wings             Steve Shutt
                       Yvon Lambert
                       Bob Gainey
                       Murray Wilson

Right wings            Guy Lafleur
                       Mario Tremblay
                       Yvan "The Roadrunner"
                         Cournoyer
                       Jim Roberts

Coach                  Scotty Bowman

From the opening faceoff in Montreal Bobby Clarke and rookie defenseman Jack "Buck" McIlhargey set up Reggie Leach, and after just twenty-one seconds, the Flyers led, one to nothing. Later in the first period Ross Lonsberry scored, and the Flyers led, two to nothing, after one period. It looked then as though the Flyers would get their necessary one win in Montreal, and their "Hat Trick in '76."

In the second period, two of the least-fancy Canadiens, Jimmy Roberts and Larry Robinson, scored to tie it at two. Five minutes into the third period, Gary Dornhoefer fed Izzy Goodenough, and the Flyers again had the lead, three to two. Midway through the period Jacques Lemaire tied it at three, and it stayed that way until a minute and a half left, when Steve Shutt sent Guy Lapointe down the left wing. Lapointe cannonaded a shot along the ice which beat Wayne Stephenson, and the Canadiens had salvaged the victory, four to three.

In Game Two, Ken Dryden and Wayne Stephenson (both of whom played every game) kept it scoreless until late in the second period, when, on a Flyers' power play, Lemaire stole from Goodenough and scored short-handed. In the third period, Guy Lafleur boomed a shot from just inside the blue line for a two-to-nothing lead, but Dave Schultz cut it to two to one, with two and a half minutes left. In the final minutes, Jimmy Watson had two good chances to tie, but he missed an open net on one, and Ken Dryden stopped the other. Montreal had won the first two at home, both of them one-goal thrillers.

Not to worry. The Flyers were going back to the Spectrum, where they were indomitable, having lost only three times in fifty-two games, counting the playoffs and the Soviet Army game. But there was a subtle difference this time, and not just because Bernie was, in reality, unavailable. An even more significant change resulted from an injury to Rick MacLeish, which not only left the Flyers with only one scoring line in tact, but which enabled Scotty Bowman to double-shift his two best defensive centers, Doug Jarvis and Doug Risebrough, on Bobby Clarke. The LCB Line continued to score, but Bowman's strategy had to take its toll on Clarke, the man who had single-handedly worn out Phil Esposito in previous series.

In the first period of Game Three in Philadelphia, Steve Shutt scored early, but Reggie Leach came back with two more, and the Flyers led, two to one, after one period. Shutt scored again early in the second period to tie it at two, and it remained that way until midway through the third period, when everyone realized that the next goal could make or break the season. Would it be Leach, or would it be Shutt who would win it with his third goal of the game? It would, of course, be neither, as Murray Wilson set up Pierre Bouchard, of all people, for his first goal of the playoffs, and only his second of the *season*. As so often happens in the World Series or in the Stanley Cup Finals, it's the guy you least expect who wins it for you, as Bob Kelly had done the year before.

In Game Four, Leach once again scored within the game's opening minute, but five minutes later Shutt scored again, and it was tied at one. Montreal's new scoring machine, Pierre Bouchard, then broke the tie, but Bill Barber retied it at two just before the end of the first period.

In the second period, Barber and Clarke set up Moose Dupont for the go-ahead goal, but from that point on, Bowman's clever double-shifting shut down the LCB Line, and with it the Flyers' offense. The only hope now, a slim one indeed, was to shut down the Montreal offense for the rest of the way. But with just eleven seconds left in the second period "Roadrunner" Cournoyer scored to tie it at three.

The third period was, for the first time in the series, all Montreal, as Guy Lafleur and Peter Mahovlich scored to put the Canadiens ahead to stay, five to three. Suddenly it was all over, and in just four shockingly short games.

As I had hoped would happen, but certainly *not so soon,* the fans in the Spectrum reacted just as the fans in the Buffalo Aud had reacted at the conclusion of the preceding season. They applauded politely, and with the proper degree of well-earned respect, for the team which had only been able to hang on for a tie against the Soviet Army, but which had now clearly replaced the Flyers at the pinnacle of the hockey universe.

The Flyers' three-year dominance in the N.H.L. had been ended by a well-balanced Montreal team of incomparable excellence, a team that ranks with the great teams of all time in any sport. Not only could the Canadiens outscore anyone, but they could outskate, outcheck, outdefense, outstrength, outfight, and outgoaltend anyone as well! They not only overmatched the undermanned Flyers, but they would dominate everyone else in hockey for the next three seasons, as they would roll virtually unchallenged to four consecutive Stanley Cup Championships.

The Flyers' royal fabric had not only been torn, the foundations of Camelot had been cracked, and Camelot itself was now starting to crumble in the twilight. The feelings of concern, which had replaced the feelings of euphoria, were now turning to feelings of sorrow at the signs of decline in the once omnipotent Broad Street Bullies. But only in Philadelphia.

E ven in defeat, a member of the Flyers was awarded the Conn Smythe Trophy for the most valuable player in the Stanley Cup Playoffs for the third consecutive year. This time it would not be awarded to Bernie Parent (who did not even play in the finals), but to a pure goal scorer and only the third player from a non-Cup-winning team ever to win the Conn Smythe—a guy known to his teammates as

# The Rifle

Archibald Alexander "Archie" Leach was born in Bristol, England, came to the United States at a youthful age, had his name changed to Cary Grant, and eventually became quite a successful movie actor.

Reginald Joseph "Reggie" Leach was born in Riverton, Manitoba, came to the United States at a youthful age, had his name changed to Reggie "The Rifle" Leach, and eventually became quite a successful goal scorer after joining the Flyers by way of the Flin Flon Bombers, the Boston Bruins, and the California Seals. In fact, The Rifle had to be one of the most astute thefts by the Flyers' astute general manager, Keith "The Thief" Allen, who had acquired a giant of a scorer at very little cost to the Flyers.

After scoring two, thirteen, twenty-three, and twenty-two goals in his previous four N.H.L. seasons, The Rifle fired in forty-five in his first season with the Flyers, followed by eight more in the playoffs. But that was nothing compared with season number two (1975-76), when Reggie rifled in sixty-one goals during the regular season and nineteen more during the playoffs, for the uncanny total of eighty goals in one season! It was the highest-scoring season ever for a Flyer forward, before or since. The nineteen playoff goals were equalled once by Jari Kurri of Edmonton, but never surpassed by anyone.

No Flyer, past or present, has ever shot like The Rifle. Tim Kerr has marvelous wrists, soft hands, and is great around the net, but no Flyer has ever had the long-range and all-around accuracy of Reggie Leach. In fact, even including Hull, Bossy, Gretzky, and Kurri, I've never seen anyone fire with such intensity, such confidence, such clarity of purpose, and such accuracy as The Rifle. As a right-handed right-winger, always with the right shot at the right time, Reggie was the ultimate sniper.

Strangely enough for a man with such a big shot, Reggie always used a small-sized stick with a small-sized blade. "The smaller the stick, the better the control," he would say. He also said that he always tried to shoot for the outer edges of the goalie's pads, unless he were going for the "five hole." And at least for me, he's responsible for bringing to prominence the term "five hole." The first time I asked him about it, he explained, very logically, that the upper-left and upper-right corners of the net were the number one and number two holes, and that the lower-left and lower-right corners were the number three and four holes, and that the area between the goaltender's legs was the five hole. "As soon as I wind up to shoot," said Reggie, "the goaltender has to move to cover the long or the short side, or he has to come out, and while he's moving he's most vulnerable between the pads." Unlike anyone else I ever saw, Reggie made an art of putting the puck through the "five hole."

His next-most-favorite play was to draw the goaltender to the near-side post by taking the puck deep down the right side. Then, all he had to do was bank it off the long-side post and into the net! So simple, so logical, and so few could ever do it!

In his eight seasons with the Flyers, The Rifle collected 583 points, on 230 assists and 353 goals, or an average of forty-four goals per season. When he slumped to "only" twenty-six goals in 1981-82, Reggie was released and signed by Detroit. For the Red Wings Reggie could score only fifteen goals, his fewest since his first year with the Seals twelve seasons before. So, before they could start calling him "The Popgun," Reggie retired, his dignity and his nick-name still in tact.

Because of his American Indian heritage, Reggie was also nicknamed "The Chief," not to be confused with "The Chef," Bob Taylor. It was a joy to see his off-season association with tribal members, who were involved in working with the problems of alco-holism, as well as working with various sports programs. He also became involved with a junior hockey club in Billings, Montana, which was sponsored by his Indian friends in order to learn how to operate a hockey franchise.

Most of his time, though, Reggie spent, and still spends, in his adopted home, Philadelphia, where he will always be remembered, not just as an awfully good guy, but as the guy who scored eighty goals in one season, and who played right wing on one of the great-est lines in the game's history.

Of the 168 goals scored by the LCB Line during the 1975-76 season, Reggie "The Rifle" had eighty, Reggie's childhood pal Bobby Clarke had thirty-two, and the other fifty-six belonged to the guy they called

# Arnie (Piggy)

William Charles "Bill" Barber of Callander, Ontario, was the left-handed left-winger of the LCB Line, a First-Team All-Star, and the Flyers' third, but least publicized, 100-point man. To his teammates, he was never William, or Bill, or Charles, or Chuck, or even Barber. He was Arnold Pigeletti, or Arnie, or Piggy, or Pig. When Reggie

Leach would leave at night, his farewell line to Bill and Jennie Barber would be, "See you, Arnie, and good night, Mrs. Pig."

The Flyers have had a lot of great rookies over the years, but officially, no "rookies of the year." Arnie probably came the closest in 1972-73, when he was brought up from the Richmond Robins after scoring in seven of the eight games he played for them. He then had a tremendous rookie season for the Flyers, but he was beaten out for the Calder Trophy by the more experienced Steve Vickers of the Rangers and, of course, by the New York press. Most voters go by the statistics, and they *were* close:

|  | Goals | Assists | Points |
|---|---|---|---|
| **Steve Vickers** | 30 | 23 | 53 |
| (Playoffs) | 5 | 4 | 9 |
|  | 35 | 27 | 62 |
|  |  |  |  |
| **Bill Barber** | 30 | 34 | 64 |
| (Playoffs) | 3 | 2 | 5 |
|  | 33 | 36 | 69 |

It is my contention that Arnie had a stronger and better rookie season. Whether or not he should have been awarded the Calder, he certainly enjoyed a stronger and better overall career than Vickers, and, like Bobby Clarke and every other Flyer, he certainly enjoyed the only award that ever really mattered to him—the Stanley Cup. And when the time finally came, he also appreciated being voted into the Hockey Hall of Fame, where he rejoined former teammates Clarke and Parent.

As a player, Arnie was one of those rare creatures who had *no* weaknesses. If he was ever criticized, it was only because he did his job so efficiently and so well that he was taken for granted, especially among his flashier and more flamboyant compatriots. He always performed well, but there was little flair in what he did, and without flair, flash, and flamboyance, one could overlook his consistent excellence despite his high numbers. But if you saw him play day in and day out, as I did, you could see that the man some people called "colorless," or even "dull," was one of the most valuable players in the game, and that his total lack of color was a strength, not a weakness, because, like Clarke, he was the ultimate team player.

My exciting interviews with Arnie would usually go something like this: "Bill, your father's been arrested as a Soviet agent, your mother's been convicted for running a still, and your two children are in a reformatory for smuggling dope. How do you react to all of that?"

"I'm just trying to help the team make the playoffs, Gene."

Fortunately, Arnie's family never gave any cause to ask such questions, but no matter what the situation, Arnie's answer would have been about the same. His other favorite reply was, "I'm just happy to be here, Gene." And the Flyers were certainly happy to have him.

After Arnie signed his first long-term big-money contract, some people wondered if he would coast a little, and just try not to get hurt, the way so many professional athletes do. No way. Arnie played just as hard and as well as ever. He may even have played a little better, difficult as that was to believe, because he was secure in the knowledge that the team needed and wanted him, and it was his job to repay the team for its confidence in him.

As with the Watsons, and Schultz, and Saleski, and Clarke, it was easy to see where the character of an Arnie Barber came from. To a man, their fathers were big, strong, burly, tough, working outdoorsmen, who shared great pride in their sons who had gained such prominence in *the game*. At playoff time, it was always a joy to see these men enjoying their time together in Philadelphia, talking about their sons and the playoffs. And it was just as much of a joy to see how proud the sons were of their dads. And what a marvelous relationship of equality all of these men, young and old, shared together!

Arnie Barber enjoyed an amazingly productive decade-plus in Philadelphia. In his eleventh and final full season he had forty-five goals and forty-four assists, for a total of eighty-nine points in eighty games. Then, during his twelfth season with the Flyers, his career was suddenly ended by a serious knee injury. He tried for several years to rehabilitate the knee to the point where he could play again, but it was just not to be. Despite losing who-knows-how-many years to the injury, Arnie still wound up his career as the Flyers' all-time leading left wing, and as the Flyers' all-time leading goal scorer. The final numbers for his twelve years, all of them with the Flyers, were 473 goals and 518 assists for 991 total points in 1,032 games, including playoffs. And if those numbers seem surprisingly high to you, it's only because all the time he was racking them up he was only quietly doing what was expected of him, and what he expected of himself.

And Arnie's years were so much more fruitful than those of so many players who might score more, but who were not the defensive star he was, or who were not as willing to help the team in every capacity. For Arnie Barber not only scored goals, and more of them than any other Flyer in history, but he played hard, he killed penalties with the best of them (also scoring more short-handed goals than any other Flyer), he played every position on the power play, and, at times, he even played as a defenseman. In fact, at one time or another he played every position except goaltender, and number seven probably would have been good at that, too. For a while Arnie was captain of the Flyers, and later he was even head coach of the Hershey Bears, before returning to Philadelphia where he is now a Flyer scout, assistant coach, consultant, bottle-washer, Director of Pro Scouting, and whatever else is needed at the time.

Arnie Barber was a giant, one of the great all-time wings, and one of the great all-time all-around team players. He now enjoys a lesser, but still important role with the Flyers. And the key word is "enjoys." As Arnie likes to say, "I'm just happy to be here."

**A**nother guy who is "happy to be here," and in a number of different capacities, is another former captain (after Lou Angotti, before Bobby Clarke) and a leader of the Flyers right from the beginning. He's the guy they called (and still call)

# Fast Eddie

Edward Charles Van Impe of Saskatoon, Saskatchewan, was a five foot, ten inch, 205-pound defenseman, who, in his first and only season with the Chicago Black Hawks, was second to Bobby Orr in the voting for N.H.L. Rookie of the Year. When he was selected by the Flyers in the expansion draft, Eddie was not anxious to leave the Black Hawks, who at that time were by far the best team among the original six, even though third-place Toronto had won the Cup that year.

As a rookie in Chicago, Van Impe had scored eight goals in three-quarters of a season. In his next ten seasons, including playoffs, he would score only twenty more, for an average of two per season. Bobby Orr he was not, but, in his own end of the ice, he was a rock.

Like so many N.H.L. defensemen, including Flyers Tom Bladon and, later on, Behn Wilson, Van Impe suffered through a tough stretch of games. Every time something went wrong for the Flyers in the Spectrum, Eddie, who was usually on the ice in difficult situations, would be booed. As unfair as it was to boo a competitor like Eddie, he took it like the man that he was, and he battled and survived to the point where he became a kind of Philadelphia folk hero. Eventually, whenever he would carry the puck into the attacking zone, Eddie would be cheered by the Spectrum fans, who realized and appreciated what a rare event they were witnessing.

Eddie was also a kind of folk hero to the other Flyers, especially on the team bus. He would smuggle bottles of beer onto the bus under his coat, like a high school kid, and I recall one night when he lost his balance while climbing up the steps of the bus and he banged into the side of the stairwell. We could hear the "clink, clink, clink" of the smashed bottles settling into the bottom of Eddie's coat pocket as he made his way, clinking and dripping, toward the back of the bus.

I'm not sure whether it was because of the beer or not, but, as you learned earlier from Bernie Parent, Eddie was a master at gaspassing. In fact, he was the Flyers' undisputed King of Flatulence. As a result, Eddie was not only the "butt" of many jokes, but also a world-class record-setter not found in the *Guinness Book of World Records*. On the bus Joe Watson would categorize one blast from another by noting how far away from Eddie you had to move: "Holy Jeez! Holy Jeez! It's a seven-seater! No, its an eight-seater! Holy Jeez!" Just for the record, Eddie's own personal best was a fourteen-seater.

As a defenseman, Eddie was not only flatulent, but also smart, tough, mean, and unbending in front of the net. His skating ability was extremely limited (hence the nickname "Fast Eddie"), but he was a tremendous asset, because he realized his own limitations, he knew exactly the breadth of his ability, and he would *always* play to that capacity.

If I had to pick one word to describe Eddie's defensive style, it would be "mean." I recall one time when he drilled an opposing forward in the corner and then told Bernie, "I guess that takes care of Tannahill."

Bernie said, "That wasn't Tannahill. It was Oddleifson."

Yes, sometimes "Too-Fast Eddie" would zap the wrong guy, but usually he would zap *somebody*. And, like Moose Dupont and others, he could take it as well as dish it out. In fact, the courage of many a hockey player, particularly a hockey player like Eddie Van Impe, is hard to understand unless you're part of the game.

I remember one incident as if it were yesterday, and even though it happened more than twenty years ago, it's still a tough story for me to tell. But here it is: The Oakland Seals were in Philadelphia, and during a first-period power play, Oakland point man Wayne Muloin wound up to take a slap shot. Van Impe went down to block the shot, and my God, it was frightening, because the full force of the shot hit Eddie right in the mouth.

As with the others—Ashbee, Parent, MacLeish, and later, Bob "The Count" Dailey who fractured his ankle in Buffalo—it was hard to know what to say on the air. As a broadcaster, you just cringe, and you know that you can't say anything off-color, and you can't just stop, either, because the people at home want to know what's going on, especially the wives and other members of the player's family. It was obvious that Eddie was seriously injured, but how seriously we wouldn't know until later.

We all felt a little better later on, when, despite the blood on his jersey, Eddie returned to the ice and played the rest of the game. After the post-game show, I saw Eddie coming up the steps to the main floor of the Spectrum, and he was neatly dressed with coat and tie and overcoat. There wasn't much expression on his face, and he was walking with his lovely wife Diane, who was kind of a mother confessor for the other Flyers' wives, and, I'm sure, a great comfort to Eddie that night.

What I never realized until the next day was that Wayne Muloin's shot had literally shattered Eddie's mouth. Three or four teeth on the lower jaw and seven on the upper jaw had been smashed, and after being sutured up to stop the bleeding, Eddie had gone back out and finished the game. After I saw him coming up the steps, Diane had taken him to Lankenau Hospital where he had the shattered remnants of those ten or eleven teeth surgically removed.

I visited Eddie several days later, and, as before, no one would ever have known how much pain he was suffering. The next thing I knew, Eddie was back, taking his regular shift on defense, and not saying much one way or the other, since his jaw was wired shut. And don't ask me how his liquid diet affected his "flatulence factor," because Bernie never mentioned it. At least not on the air.

The amazing aspect of pain, as endured by hockey players, is that, unlike most other sports, all of the players have at some time or another played in pain, and often *very great* pain. Some, like Barry Ashbee, never played any other way. Since it's something that every player learns to endure, nothing special is made of it. There is no sympathy, and none is expected. The conventional hockey wisdom dictates that this is not a time for tragedy, but for comedy, such as when Bobby Clarke asked, "Hey, Doc, did Moose cry?" and when Moose responded with, "No, but de Mooze make faces!" Another time, when Bob Taylor was banged up and his bones were aching terribly, Clarke asked, "What's the matter, Doc? Didn't the Chef drink enough milk when he was a kid?"

One time during practice, a wickedly hard shot hit goalie Gary Inness squarely in the shoulder. It was like one of those old "Tom and Jerry" cartoons when the cat is smashed flat up against the wall and then slides down onto the floor. Gary's gloves dropped off, and he then slid down onto the ice in obviously excruciating pain, while the other players gathered around him and argued over whose shot had done the damage. MacLeish yelled, "I got him!" and Leach yelled back, "No! It was *my* shot that got him!" and so on. Some might call that "sick" or, at least, "insensitive," but it's also the means, as a rule, by which hockey players pass off the *fact of pain.* Some of the exceptions to the rule were Ashbee, Parent, and Van Impe. When an injury is that serious, it's not funny even to a hockey player.

Eddie Van Impe absorbed a lot of punishment during his nine seasons with the Flyers, and he gave his all during every one of those seasons. After being traded with Bob Taylor to Pittsburgh, Eddie played only twenty-two more games over the next two seasons before returning to Philadelphia to go into the commercial insurance business. And, thankfully, I know him even that much better since he has done color on Flyers broadcasts.

All of the players, past and present, have tremendous respect for Eddie, as, of course, do I. He is the classic case of the journeyman who reached a level far above that, because of the intensity with which he played, and because of the pride that enveloped his game, and because of his Clarke-type work ethic—the ethic that teaches, "You go out and give as much as you've got, all of the time, regardless of how you feel." Eddie, like Bobby, did just that.

Fast Eddie, old number two, was a prototypical Flyer—hardnosed, tough, and unyielding, but with a great sense of humor and with great personal character and integrity. It's fun to have him in the Philadelphia area, and it's fun to have him back with the Flyers family. And he speaks quite well through his new teeth!

# The Not-So-Wonderful Years: 1976 to 1979

During the 1976-77 season, Bernie Parent gave a decent impersonation of his former Vezina-winning self, with a record of 35-13-12, a goals-against average of 2.71, and five shutouts. Principally because of Bernie, the Flyers won their fourth consecutive Campbell Bowl as the best in the West or the best in the Campbell Conference, but for the first time in four years there were no Flyers named to either the First or Second N.H.L. All-Star Teams. And the attrition of Cup-winning players continued: Dave Schultz took his hammer to Los Angeles, pepper pot Terry Crisp retired to coaching, and still-young defensemen Izzy Goodenough and Buck McIlhargey were sent to Vancouver in exchange for a lumbering six foot, five inch, 220-pound defenseman named Bob "The Count" Dailey. More importantly, the horrifying news of Barry Ashbee's leukemia hit the team at playoff time.

The grief-stricken Flyers' quarter-final opponent was, for the third consecutive year, the Toronto Maple Leafs. The two prior series had been won by the Flyers in four straight and in the seven-game-home-team-wins-all conflagration of the previous season, but this time it appeared that the tide had finally turned, as Toronto shockingly won the first two games in Philadelphia. It was the first time that the Leafs had ever won two straight in the Spectrum, and it seemed as though the gloomy Flyers were heading for a quick execution in Toronto, Barry Ashbee's home territory.

In Maple Leaf Gardens, the Flyers were just thirty seconds from a third loss, when, with their goaltender pulled for an extra attacker, Rick MacLeish stole a clearing pass from Borje Salming and drove a shot from the right circle past goalie Mike Palmateer. That tied it at three, and Reggie Leach then won it in overtime for the Flyers' first victory of the series.

Game Four in Toronto appeared to be another certain win for the Leafs, as they led five to two in the third period. Much to the delight of the hooting Toronto fans, I was headed downstairs for the post-game show, warning everyone within listening distance, "I'll be back!" And, by Heaven, that's exactly what happened, as Tom Bladon, and then Bobby Clarke, and then Mel Bridgman all scored during the final minutes to tie it at five. And then, in overtime, Rick MacLeish won it for the Flyers, six to five. Astoundingly, the visiting team had won all four games to date, after winning *none* the previous season.

In Game Five in Philadelphia, the home team finally won a game, a two-to-nothing shutout. In Toronto for Game Six, the Flyers did it again, coming from behind to win, four to three, on a goal in the last minute and a half by, of all people, Jimmy Watson, who didn't even win the Grizzly Cup that year.

Despite Barry Ashbee's sad plight, the Flyers had come back to defeat the Leafs in six games, mostly on the kind of emotion and pure guts that "Ash Can" had exemplified.

But in the semi-finals against Boston, the Flyers again lost the first two at home, and they were two of the toughest losses imaginable. In the first, trailing three to nothing after two periods, the Flyers changed goaltenders, replacing Wayne Stephenson with Bernie Parent. In the final thirty seconds, with Bernie pulled, Bobby Clarke scored to tie it at three, and it looked like 1974 all over again. In overtime, however, Bernie tried to scoop away the rebound of a Rick Middleton shot, but the puck caromed off his stick and into the net, and suddenly, Boston had won, four to three.

The second game was just as painful, as a four-all tie was broken in double-overtime, when Terry O'Reilly beat Wayne Stephenson to win it for the Bruins, five to four. In the Spectrum, where it had previously been almost impossible for visiting teams to win, the Flyers had now lost four of five playoff games, and it was time to go to Boston for the next two.

In Boston, the Bruins finished off the series by completing the first four-game sweep over the Flyers since six years before, when the Black Hawks had accomplished the same trick. The Bruins went on to the finals against Montreal, while the beaten Flyers returned home, drained, to wait out the final days of Barry Ashbee.

**T**he next season (1977-78), Bernie's record again improved, this time to 29-6-13, with a goals-against average of 2.22 and a league-leading seven shutouts. But Bernie could play "only" forty-eight games, and Wayne Stephenson, with a record of 14-10-1, did not fare as well. As a result, the Flyers could accumulate "only" 105 points and thus were supplanted as Patrick Division and Campbell Conference champions by the New York Islanders, who had 111 points.

As a second-place finisher, the Flyers for the first time had to play a best-of-three "preliminary round" in the playoffs, so the opponent this time would not be the Toronto Maple Leafs, but the Colorado Rockies. It was the first and only playoff appearance for the Kansas City/Colorado franchise before it was moved to the New Jersey Meadowlands to become the New Jersey Devils. The Flyers won both games that were played, but not before our old friend Doug Favell of the Rockies had concluded his last full N.H.L. season with some sensational goaltending.

In the quarter-finals, the Flyers continued their hex over the Buffalo Sabres by winning the first two in the Spectrum. The Sabres won Game Three in Buffalo, but the Flyers came right back to take Game Four, allowing the Flyers to clinch the series at home in Game Five. The Flyers were clearly better than the Sabres, and they were in the semi-finals for the sixth consecutive year.

But in the semi-finals, the Bruins once again proved their superiority over the Flyers. This time the first two games were in Boston, where the Bruins won both. The Flyers won Game Three in Philadelphia, but just as the Flyers had done to the Sabres, the Bruins came right back to take Game Four, before finishing off the series in Boston in Game Five. Once again, the Bruins were in the finals against Montreal, while the beaten Flyers limped home to lick their wounds, and to make some momentous changes.

Six more members of the Stanley Cup teams would be gone before the start of the next season: Gary Dornhoefer retired; Joe Watson was made captain of the Colorado Rockies; Ross Lonsberry, Tom Bladon, and Orest Kindrachuk were packaged to Pittsburgh for a number one draft choice. But the biggest departure story was that of Fred Shero. The coach who had said, "We'll walk together forever," had walked away, only to reappear the following season behind the bench of the New York Rangers.

**F**or the 1978 draft, the Flyers were awarded an additional number one draft choice from the Rangers, in partial payment for New York's meddling with Fred Shero. With that pick, the Flyers selected a "rink rat" named Kenny Linseman from the Birmingham Bulls. With Pittsburgh's number one (for the traded trio of Lonsberry, Bladon, and Kindrachuk), the Flyers selected a six foot, three inch, 210-pound "pit bull" named Behn Wilson. It would be hard to find a more controversial pair of draft choices than those two.

To replace Fred Shero as coach (as if anyone really could have done that), the Flyers named Bob McCammon, who had illustrious credentials as head coach of the Maine Mariners, the minor-league franchise that the Flyers had cleverly bought and developed in Portland. McCammon was familiar with most of the young players in the Flyers organization, but he had never dealt with Linseman or Wilson, not to mention the remaining Stanley Cup stars, such as Clarke, Barber, MacLeish, Leach, Dupont, and Parent. Entering the 1978-79 season, I think it is safe to say that Bob McCammon was intimidated by the N.H.L. in general, and by the older Flyers in particular. Likable and decent a human being as he was, McCammon's record through the season's first fifty games was an un-Sheroic 22-17-11, and he was asked to trade places with the coach who had taken *his* place in Maine, Pat Quinn.

After nine seasons as a defenseman for Toronto, Vancouver, and, mostly, Atlanta, Pat Quinn had been brought to Philadelphia the year before by Fred Shero, who wanted Quinn as an assistant coach. When Shero left, Quinn felt that he was the logical successor, but when McCammon was chosen instead, Quinn agreed to coach in Maine while awaiting his chance to coach in the big time. He didn't have to wait long.

So, with McCammon back in Maine, and with Quinn back in Philadelphia, the Flyers' record over the season's last thirty games was an improved 18-8-4, but that was not good enough to make up for their slow start, and they were buried in second place behind the Islanders, 116 points to 95. Worse yet, they finished just four points ahead of Fred Shero's third-place New York Rangers. But even that ominous realization paled by comparison with the terrible news that, because of a freakish late-season eye injury, Bernie Parent would never play again.

Due to the abrupt and sad ending of Bernie's career, the Flyers brought up three different rookies to share the goaltending responsibilities with Wayne Stephenson. Here are the 1978-79 regular-season records of the five goaltenders who wore the orange and black that year:

|  | W L T | G/A Ave. | Shutouts |
|---|---|---|---|
| Bernie Parent | 16-12- 7 | 2.70 | 4 |
| Wayne Stephenson | 20-10- 5 | 3.35 | 2 |
| Rick St. Croix | 0- 1- 1 | 3.08 | 0 |
| Pete Peeters | 1- 2- 1 | 3.43 | 0 |
| Robbie Moore | 3- 0- 1 | 1.77 | 2 |

Robbie Moore was listed at five feet, five and a half inches and 155 pounds, but I don't believe he was that big. Whatever his diminutive size really was, it was he who was chosen to share the playoff burden with Wayne Stephenson. As it turned out, Stephenson lost all three of his playoff starts, while Moore won three of five, but Robbie would never again appear in a Flyer uniform. In fact, he would appear in only one more N.H.L. game, a loss with Washington four years later. Counting playoffs and that loss with the Capitals, his lifetime N.H.L. record was a commendable 6-3-1.

In the preliminary round of the playoffs, it was Vancouver's turn to shock the Flyers, as the Canucks won the first game in Philadelphia. The Flyers came back to outgun the Canucks in Vancouver, and again in Philadelphia, but it was not an impressive series victory for the Flyers.

For the quarter-finals, Fred Shero brought his upstart New Yorkers to Philadelphia, and, although they outplayed the Flyers throughout the first game, the Flyers managed to win, three to two, on an overtime goal by Kenny Linseman. But that was only the prelude to perhaps the worst smacking, and the most painfully humiliating playoff series in Flyers history. Anders Hedberg was dazzling, Ron Greschner was magnificent, and the Flyers were rendered impotent, as the Rangers embarrassed the Flyers four consecutive times—seven to one in Philadelphia, five to one and six to nothing in New York, and eight to three in Philadelphia.

For the first time in seven years, the Flyers would not be in the semi-finals. More importantly, for the first time in seven years, the Flyers clearly *did not belong* in the semi-finals.

While Montreal was defeating Boston (again) in the semi-finals, Freddy's Rangers beat the Islanders in six, with their only two losses coming in overtime. The Islanders would not lose another playoff series for the next four years.

In the finals, Freddy outfoxed the Canadiens in the first game, but then Montreal rose to the occasion by winning the next four to wrap up their fourth consecutive Cup. I recall the end of the final game in Montreal, when the Canadiens threw their gloves into the stands and gently passed their sticks over the glass to the fans, a lovely custom which has since been discontinued.

For the Flyers, it had been a most trying time. The tragic loss of Barry Ashbee had been followed by the sudden end of the brilliant career of Bernie Parent. There had been numerous retirements and trades, and there had even been a mid-season coaching switch. And before another season would begin, Wayne Stephenson would become a Washington Capital, and Don Saleski would become a Colorado Rocky.

It was always strange to see the members of the Flyers' Cup–winning teams when they returned to Philadelphia in foreign colors, and especially in the colors of a fledgling expansion team. The first time I can recall that happening was when Simon Nolet returned. I'll never forget when he was recognized as the new captain of the Kansas City Scouts, and the fans in the Spectrum gave him a warm standing ovation while his teammates left a small, but noticeable gap on either side of him, so that he could be more readily singled out for a well-deserved tribute.

Later, when Joe Watson returned, an early stoppage of play brought this simple scoreboard message to the attention of the fans: "JOE WATSON, CAPTAIN, COLORADO ROCKIES." And, of course, the ensuing ovation brought a tear to the eye of Old Thundermouth, as well as to the eyes of many others.

Unfortunately, there were tears and mixed feelings for many others as well. For, of the twenty-eight men who had played or coached on the Flyers' two Stanley Cup-winning teams, twenty-one were now either retired or with other N.H.L. teams or, in the case of Barry Ashbee, deceased. Remaining were just these seven:

|  |  |
|---|---|
| **Defensemen** | Moose Dupont |
|  | Jimmy Watson |
|  |  |
| **Forwards** | Bobby Clarke |
|  | Bob Kelly |
|  | Rick MacLeish |
|  | Bill Barber |
|  | Reggie Leach |

In what seemed to have been no time at all, the Flyers had slipped from the summit of the sport all the way down to rock bottom, or at least so it seemed to the Flyers themselves, and to their fans. Apparently, it was time to start all over again.

# Third Period
# 1979 to the Present

# Year of the Streak: 1979-80

It was a deceptive collection of players that had been assembled by general manager Keith Allen and by Pat Quinn, who was beginning his first full season as coach of the Flyers. At the start of the 1979-80 season, it didn't appear to be a distinguished team in any way, and certainly not the kind of team that figured to start a streak, let alone the all-time longest unbeaten streak in the history of professional sports. There were enough good forwards for three decently solid lines, but the defense and the goaltending looked decidedly suspect. And unbeaten streaks are usually founded upon great defense.

Here is the motley crew of Flyers who would somehow manage to survive thirty-five consecutive games without a loss:

|  |  | Season's Record | G/A Ave. |
|---|---|---|---|
| **Goaltenders** | Pete Peeters | 29- 5- 5 | 2.73 |
|  | Rick St. Croix | 1- 0- 0 | 2.00 |
|  | Phil Myre | 18- 7-15 | 3.57 |

Phil Myre (pronounced MEER), after a string of mediocre (or less) seasons with Atlanta and St. Louis, had been acquired in the off-season as a back-up for Wayne Stephenson (who had not yet been sent off to Washington, but who would be gone before the start of the season).

| | |
|---|---|
| **Defensemen** | **Moose Dupont**—In his last season with the Flyers |
| | **Jimmy Watson**—With five goals, unchallenged for the Grizzly Cup |
| | **Bob Dailey**—"The Count" |
| | **Behn Wilson**—In his second unpredictable season |
| | **Frank Bathe**—A journeyman acquired two seasons before from Detroit |
| | **Norm Barnes**—A twenty-six-year-old "rookie" |
| | **Mike Busniuk**—A rookie |
| | **Blake Wesley**—A rookie |
| **Forwards** | **Bobby Clarke**—Really an assistant coach as well as a player |
| | **Bob Kelly**—In his last season with the Flyers |
| | **Rick MacLeish**—In his next-to-last season with the Flyers |
| | **Bill Barber**—Counting playoffs, an "average" fifty-two goal season |
| | **Reggie Leach**—"Only" fifty-nine goals |
| | **Mel Bridgman**—Captain of the team |

**Kenny Linseman**—In his second unpredictable season

**Paul Holmgren**—A six foot, three inch, 210-pound right wing acquired three seasons before as a free agent, following the demise of the W.H.A.'s Minnesota Fighting Saints

**Al Hill**—Had set an N.H.L. record with two goals and three assists for five points in his first game, but then had scored only five more goals in his next three seasons

**Dennis Ververgaert**—Acquired from Vancouver during the previous season and welcomed by the Moose

**John Paddock**—A journeyman who had played only five games the previous season

**Tom "T.J." Gorence**—A second-year hustler

**Brian Propp**—An impressive rookie, with thirty-four goals and forty-one assists for seventy-five points

From this nondescript roster, only Brian Propp survived for long as an active Flyer. Of course, Bob Clarke and Bill Barber later moved "upstairs," as did John Paddock, to become assistant general manager. Also, of course, Paul Holmgren, who enjoyed one of his few relatively injury-free seasons (and his only thirty-goal season) during the year of the streak, is now head coach of the Flyers.

Unfortunately, as a player "Homer" is remembered mainly for his team-leading totals in penalty minutes, an even 1,600 of them in nine years of combat, but he should also be remembered for his strong, quiet leadership and for his willingness to sacrifice his body for the sake of the team. From his first season with the Flyers, when he suffered a freak and career-threatening eye injury, to his last season, when he suffered through an amazing assortment of different ailments, any one of which would have sidelined an ordinary player, Homer served as the perfect example of the kind of team player the Flyers are known for.

Besides Holmgren, a number of other Flyers had to have "career years" in order to make such a unique season possible. This was most apparent with goaltenders Myre (eight straight non-winning seasons) and Peeters (had played in only four previous N.H.L. games, and only one of those was a win), not to mention a defensive corps loaded with unknowns, most of whom would *remain* unknown.

And there was another "career year," the year enjoyed by the cerebral defenseman-turned-law-student-coach, Pat Quinn, who got just about everything there was to be had from his cast of a few leading men and a dressing room full of understudies, and who became the second Flyers coach to win the Jack Adams Award, as N.H.L. Coach of the Year. As Fred Shero, the Flyers' first Coach of the Year, had made clear, there is a lot more to coaching than line-changing, although during a game the coach's prime responsibility is just that—preparing the next line and/or defensive pair to go out at the right time, whether on the fly or at the first stoppage of play, and depending upon the rotation being used by the opposing coach. Through countless even-strength, short-handed, and power-play situations, for an unbelievable thirty-five straight games, Pat Quinn obviously called on the right players at the right time.

This often overlooked but exceedingly important part of the game is difficult to follow on television, because the cameras have to stay with the puck, but the next time you see a game in person, try to watch for the line-changing opportunities, which usually occur a couple of times for every elapsed minute on the clock, and any one of which can make or break a game. After a stoppage of play, of course, the home team always has the *last* line change, and that is one of the elements of the "home-ice advantage," and one of the factors that makes the game of hockey that much more interesting in the arena than it is on television.

For the first four or five games of the 1979-80 season, there was absolutely no hint of the incredible string of events that was in store for us. The season opened on a Thursday night at the Spectrum, against a team that was soon to have a destiny of its own, the New York Islanders. The Flyers came out flying, with four goals in the first two periods, while the Islanders could manage only two goals in the game against Phil Myre, who was named number one star in his first game as a Flyer. The final score was five to two, and Flyers fans had something to be happy about, at least until Saturday night, when the Flyers were in Atlanta for the season's second game.

Three of the original Atlanta Flames (from the expansion draft of 1972) were defenseman Pat Quinn and goaltenders Phil Myre and Dan Bouchard. All three had been teammates for at least five years. Myre and Bouchard had been colleagues, but they had also been rivals for the starting job, and they had not been happy people together in Atlanta. Now they would be facing each other at opposite ends of the ice—not just in practice, but in a regular-season N.H.L. game. It was not to be a pleasant experience for Myre.

Before a near-sellout crowd of screaming Flames fans, Atlanta's Brad Marsh (another Flyer-to-be) and Eric Vail scored early for a two-to-nothing lead. Kenny Linseman cut it to two to one, but then the Flames scorched the Flyers for *seven consecutive goals*, shelling Myre out of the game in the process. Paul Holmgren managed a goal during the final seconds, but that only changed the final score from nine to one, to nine to two, and a score like that looks disastrous from any angle, especially for the Flyers' already suspect defense, which had completely fallen apart.

After two games, the outlook was not only unpromising, it was downright bleak. I wonder what kind of odds you might have had, if you were to have placed a bet at that point in October that the Flyers would not lose another game in the year 1979! I suppose you would have been locked up for even attempting such lunacy! But, crazy as it sounds, the Flyers' next loss would not occur until three months later, in January of 1980.

The first game of the streak was an odd one. It all started on a Sunday night, the next night after the big blowout in Atlanta. The Flyers were leading Toronto, four to two, with about a minute left. With two men already in the penalty box, Pat Quinn threw an extra forward on the ice, reasoning that the Flyers couldn't be penalized any further than they already had been. Referee Ron Hoggarth invoked an obscure section of the rule book, and for the first time in Flyers history a penalty shot was awarded. Lanny McDonald converted the penalty shot, but the Flyers still won, four to three, and the streak was under way. Why or how, I'll never know! In fact, after about twenty games without a loss, and as the streak continued to build upon itself, I recall someone asking me, "How are they doing it?"

I also recall answering, "Darned if I know! But it certainly is fun!"

In the whole course of those thirty-five games without a loss, only about three games stand out vividly in my memory. One of those took place in early December when the Los Angeles Kings came to the Spectrum, where they had not won in more than five years. The Kings were 12-8-5 and the Flyers were 17-1-6 for the season, but the white-hot Triple-Crown Line (Marcel Dionne centering for Charlie Simmer and Dave Taylor) had the Kings in front, three to nothing, after the first period. It appeared that the streak would end at twenty-two, an impressive but not extraordinary number. But then the Flyers came up with the most explosive period of the streak, and one of the most memorable of all time.

It started with a minor penalty to Charlie Simmer, during which it took Reggie Leach just six seconds to score the Flyers' first goal. Twenty seconds later, Leach rifled in his second goal, and shortly thereafter Kenny Linseman tied the game at three. Then Dennis Ververgaert and Bill Barber added the fourth and fifth goals, all five of which were scored within the first 8:03 of the period. Jimmy Watson, the unopposed Grizzly winner, scored shorthanded later in the period, and the Flyers led, six to three, after two periods.

Within a three-minute stretch of the third period, the Flyers poured in three more scores, on goals by Linseman (his second of the game), Bob Dailey, and Leach (for the hat trick). That made it *nine straight goals* for the Flyers before the Kings closed out the scoring with a late goal that made the final count nine to four. Instead of dying at twenty-two, the streak was very much alive at twenty-three.

The record for most consecutive games without a loss had been twenty-eight (by the Montreal Canadiens), and to tie that record the Flyers had to come from behind against the Pittsburgh Penguins, another team which usually caused them no problems, especially in the Spectrum. The Penguins were 11-9-10 and the Flyers were 20-1-8, but Pittsburgh goaltender Greg Millen had a one-to-nothing shutout until a power play with four minutes left in the game. Then Kenny Linseman passed from the left corner to the far side of the net, where Behn Wilson appeared to kick the puck into the goal, at least according to the protesting Penguins.

In studying the replays, it was ascertained that Wilson had stopped the puck with his skate, and then, as it rolled toward the goal line, he was able to get his stick on it just enough to tap it past Millen for the Flyers' only goal of the night. It wasn't pretty, but it was enough to give Pete Peeters and the Flyers a one-to-one tie instead of a loss, and the unbeaten streak was still alive at a record-tying twenty-eight.

To break the record, the Flyers would have to battle not only the odds, but also another long-standing jinx, for the next game would be on Saturday afternoon, Dec. 22, 1979, in the Boston Garden, where the Flyers had won only four of thirty-four games. What better place to set an all-time record which is still unmatched, and really unchallenged, in the history of professional sports!

The Bruins' record was 18-8-5, and the Flyers' record was 20-1-9. The Boston goaltender, surprisingly, would not be Gerry Cheevers, but Gilles Gilbert, whom the Flyers had victimized six seasons earlier in the Stanley Cup Finals. And for the Flyers, the goaltender would not be the undefeated rookie, Pete Peeters (11-0-4), but the veteran Phil Myre (9-1-5), whose only loss (and the *Flyers'* only loss) had been the rout by his former Atlanta teammates in the season's second game. Peeters would later extend his personal unbeaten streak to twenty-six, a record for a rookie goaltender, but none of those games would be as memorable as that Saturday afternoon game in December, when, as a Boston newspaper writer put it, "On this day in the land of Longfellow, and on a site known as Boston Garden, the Philadelphia people defeated the Boston warriors in a great and wonderful battle."

In the first period, Bobby Clarke scored unassisted and Bill Barber scored on the power play, for a two-to-nothing lead. Early in the second period, Kenny Linseman fired one in from the right circle, and the Flyers were up, three to nothing. But then, at the three-minute mark of the second period, Tom Songin scored for the Bruins, and one minute later Mike Milbury scored, and suddenly it was three to two, and the Garden crowd was roaring. Thirty seconds later came perhaps the biggest goal of the entire streak, as Mike Busniuk fed that clutch goal scorer, Jimmy Watson, who, from the top of the left circle, whistled a shot past Gilbert, a shot which deflated both the crowd and the Bruins.

Phil Myre and the Flyers' defense held off the Boston onslaught for the rest of the game. As for the offense, despite having only eighteen shots for the day, one of those shots became a clinching goal midway through the third period by Bob Kelly, and the Flyers won with a flourish, five to two. The all-time unbeaten record was theirs, with an unprecedented twenty-nine straight.

At the end of the game, the Boston fans gave the Flyers an ovation, which was a wonderful tribute from some of the same folks who are perennially known for giving Philadelphia teams a rough time. Like the Montreal, Buffalo, and Philadelphia fans before them, they had recognized and appreciated a very special sports happening.

As the jubilant Flyers flocked around Phil Myre, I recall in particular Pat Quinn making his way through the mob to congratulate his former Atlanta teammate. I also recall Boston's Gerry Cheevers (whose post-game philosophy was, "I never shake hands after a game, because I don't believe in it!") making it a point to loop around the ice just to give a subtle little tap on the rump with his stick to Myre and to Quinn. It was a marvelous little gesture of congratulations from one pro to two others for a remarkable achievement.

For Phil Myre, whose excellent goaltending had led the Flyers to this victory (and to so many others of the twenty-nine in a row without a defeat), it had to be one of the two or three shining moments of his fourteen-year career in the N.H.L. If Sign Man had been there, he probably would have held up, "MYRE-LY MAGNIFICENT!"

Once past the record-setting twenty-ninth, it seemed as though the streak might just go on forever. After thirty, and thirty-one, and thirty-two, and thirty-three, and thirty-four, and thirty-five, the rest of the league was left with thoughts like this one from Carol Vadnais, then of the Rangers, "Don't worry! We'll get another shot at the Flyers in April!"

After all, the standings at the end of the season couldn't look much more ridiculous then they did in January. Here's the way the Campbell Conference stacked up at about the season's mid-point:

### Patrick Division

|  | Won | Lost | Tied | Points |
|---|---|---|---|---|
| Philadelphia | 26 | 1 | 10 | 62 |
| N.Y. Rangers | 17 | 16 | 7 | 41 |
| N.Y. Islanders | 15 | 16 | 6 | 36 |
| Atlanta | 14 | 18 | 5 | 33 |
| Washington | 10 | 23 | 6 | 26 |

### Smythe Division

|  | Won | Lost | Tied | Points |
|---|---|---|---|---|
| Chicago | 15 | 13 | 12 | 42 |
| Vancouver | 15 | 18 | 7 | 37 |
| St. Louis | 14 | 19 | 6 | 34 |

|          | Won | Lost | Tied | Points |
|----------|-----|------|------|--------|
| Winnipeg | 12  | 23   | 5    | 29     |
| Colorado | 12  | 23   | 3    | 27     |
| Edmonton | 9   | 20   | 9    | 27     |

Besides the single digit in the Flyers' loss column, which for months looked like a newspaper misprint, there were several other items of interest to be gleaned from those standings, as the N.H.L. entered the decade of the eighties. First, other than the Flyers, there were only two teams in the conference with winning records, and they were both twenty or more points behind. Second, the *worst* record in the conference belonged to the Edmonton Oilers, who were already thirty-five points behind the Flyers at mid-season. Of course, it was the *first* season in the N.H.L. for the four surviving members of the now-defunct W.H.A.—Edmonton, Winnipeg, Quebec, and Hartford—all of whom would finish among the also-rans during their first few years in the N.H.L. Third, and perhaps most interestingly, the team of destiny, the New York Islanders, had a losing record at mid-season, a distant twenty-six points behind the Flyers.

With the streak at thirty-five, the Flyers traveled to Minnesota, where an all-time Met Sports Center crowd of 15,962 was in place and howling, "Let's go, Stars!" a full hour before the game was to start, and long before the North Stars had even skated out for warm-ups. The Minnesota franchise had been struggling for several years, but general manager "Sweet Lou from the Soo" Nanne had considerably strengthened the team of late, principally through a merger with the failing Cleveland Barons, and there was an unmistakable aura of success about the Met that night.

The Flyers, who have always relished playing before large and vocal audiences, appeared to be on their way to thirty-six in a row when Bill Barber opened the scoring early in the first period. But midway through the period the North Stars converted the first of their eight power play opportunities of the night, and a minute later they scored again. Before the period was over, the Stars led, three to one, and the Met crowd was tasting blood.

In the second period, Paul Holmgren apparently closed the gap to three to two, but the Flyers had been whistled for a penalty just as the puck was entering the net, and the goal was disallowed. During the ensuing power play, the North Stars scored again, and then again, for a five-to-one lead, and that was it for the game and the streak. Goaltender Gilles Meloche turned away the Flyers' last thirty shots, and the Stars went on to win by a score of seven to one. At least there was no doubt about the losses at either end of the streak!

To me, the most memorable part of that game was the reaction of the Minnesota fans throughout the last ten minutes, during which their North Stars, the team re-born from oblivion, ran out the clock on the most extraordinary streak in the history of professional sports. The building was in a constant state of bedlam, which grew and grew, as if in celebration of "V-E Day" and then "V-J Day" all in the same night.

With the pressure of the streak behind them, the overachieving Flyers lost only ten of their final forty-three games, for a record of 48-12-20 and the most points in the N.H.L. Since there were four "new" teams in the league, the playoff pairings were determined on the basis of seeding the top sixteen teams, with number one playing number sixteen, number two playing number fifteen, and so on. Divisions and conferences did not enter into the seedings. Here is how all of the teams ranked in 1980, the first year of the merged leagues:

**The playoff teams:**                                           Points

| | | |
|---|---|---|
| 1. | Philadelphia | 116 |
| 2. | Buffalo | 110 |
| 3. | Montreal | 107 |
| 4. | Boston | 105 |
| 5. | New York Islanders | 91 |
| 6. | Minnesota | 88 |
| 7. | Chicago | 87 |
| 8. | New York Rangers | 86 |
| 9. | Atlanta | 83 |
| 10. | St. Louis | 80 |
| 11. | Toronto | 75 |
| 12. | Los Angeles | 74 |
| 13. | Pittsburgh | 73 |
| 14. | Hartford | 73 |
| 15. | Vancouver | 70 |
| 16. | Edmonton | 69 |

**And the non-playoff teams:**

| | | |
|---|---|---|
| 17. | Washington | 67 |
| 18. | Detroit | 63 |

| 19. | Quebec | 61 |
| 20. | Colorado | 51 |
| 21. | Winnipeg | 51 |

The top-seeded Flyers were hungry for another Cup, while their first playoff opponents, the sixteenth-seeded Edmonton Oilers, were anxious to prove their worthiness as an N.H.L. team. They were not yet the team that would eventually become the most fearsome offensive power in the history of the game, but they had a high-scoring kid named Gretzky (whom they had acquired during the previous season from the Indianapolis Racers), and they had Don "Murder" Murdoch (whom they had just acquired from the Rangers), and they had a promising youngster named Mark Messier, and they had a veteran goaltender named Ron Low, who was playing brilliantly for them.

The first of four playoff rounds was to be a best-of-five series, with the first two games in Philadelphia. In the first game, the Flyers got off to an early two-to-nothing lead, and it looked as though it would be an easy series. But the Oilers tied it before the end of the first period, and after a scoreless second period, Don Murdoch scored midway through the third to give the underdog Oilers a three-to-two lead. With less than two minutes left, Rick MacLeish saved the Flyers from further embarrassment when he tied it and sent it into overtime. In the extra period Bobby Clarke won it for the Flyers, four to three.

In the second game, Don Murdoch again gave the Oilers a lead, but Behn Wilson tied it, and the Flyers scored four more unanswered goals for a five-to-one win and a two-games-to-none lead in the series.

For Game Three, the Flyers flew to Edmonton, but without Kenny Linseman, who was terribly sick with the flu. Not to be denied, Linseman later got to Edmonton on his own, and despite his illness he suited up for the game, although he was able to play only in sporadic shifts.

The Northlands Coliseum was sold out for Edmonton's first N.H.L. playoff game at home, and the fans were treated to one of the great games in playoff history. With four minutes left in the first period, Wayne Gretzky scored the game's first goal, and a minute and a half later, Mark Messier scored short-handed for a two-to-nothing Edmonton lead after one period. Behn Wilson scored in the second period, and Brian Propp scored in the third to tie it, while

Phil Myre shut out the Oilers through both of those periods, as well as through the overtime period which followed.

About three minutes into the *second* overtime period, Gretzky and Murdoch were suddenly breaking into the Flyers' zone two-on-one. Murdoch took a perfect pass from Gretzky and drilled a shot to the long-side corner, but Myre just managed to get his skate on it to deflect it wide. As Murdoch said later, "I hit it right on the button, and I got it right where I wanted to, but Myre just made a super save." The puck then ricocheted out of the corner to Jimmy Watson, who found Kenny Linseman at center ice. Linseman skated into the right circle, where he turned defenseman Pat Price just enough to slide a backhander into the long side for the game-winner.

Most of the Flyers streamed out to Linseman, who was so exhausted from his illness that he literally had to be lifted up and carried off the ice. While most of the forwards were attending to Linseman, the defensemen surrounded Phil Myre, who may have played the greatest 83:56 (the game's official length) of his career. It was, at the least, his second shining moment, the first having been the record-setter in Boston.

Although the Flyers had swept the series, three games to none, two of the three games had gone into overtime, and there were magnificent challenges and skills throughout. Ron Low was brilliant for Edmonton; Phil Myre was even better for Philadelphia. Wayne Gretzky had some marvelous moments for the Oilers; Kenny Linseman had his most glorious moment for the Flyers.

When Kenny Linseman was drafted from the brawling Birmingham Bulls, it was expected that there would be *many* glorious moments for him with the Flyers. That was not to be, and for a number of reasons. First, when he arrived in Philadelphia, there was the unfair inference that he was the next coming of Bobby Clarke, and he was in no way, shape, or form a Bobby Clarke, either in style or in substance. Not that anyone else was either, but Linseman was promoted in that fashion and there was, of course, no way he could live up to that kind of billing.

Linseman was a talented player, quick like a darting bee and with the sting of a whole nest of hornets, but it was his chippy Mickey Rooney–style little-tough-guy attitude that hurt him more than it helped him. They didn't call him "The Rat" for nothing. He had come from an extremely difficult family situation, and his rough background had made it difficult for him to relate to his teammates, so he insulated himself from the rest of the team. As a result, he was never close to his teammates, and they were not close to him. That self-imposed gap made life in the big leagues harder for Kenny than it needed to be. The fans also sensed that he was more of a lone wolf than a team guy, and that made him unpopular with them as well.

On the ice, it seemed that for every step forward Kenny would make with his quality of play, he would take two steps backward with his trouble-making antics. In his four seasons of discontent in Philadelphia, there was almost a geometric progression (or retrogression) of misconduct, which eventually short-circuited his first term with the Flyers:

| Season | Goals | Penalty Minutes |
|--------|-------|-----------------|
| 1. | 5 | 23 |
| 2. | 22 | 107 |
| 3. | 17 | 150 |
| 4. | 24 | 275 |

Penalty minutes per se will not necessarily get you traded, but many of Kenny's minutes represented the "bad kind," including gross misconducts and the sort of uncalled-for activities that had the officials constantly looking for him. His unfortunate reputation was based upon incidents such as the one that took place during the 1982 playoff series against the Rangers. Anders Hedberg had knocked Kenny down, and Kenny had retaliated by spearing Hedberg. The Flyers were ahead when that happened, but the Rangers rallied to win, inspired, some believe, by their desire for revenge against "The Rat."

After the 275-minute season, Linseman was traded (along with Greg Adams and first and third-round draft choices) to Hartford for Mark Howe (and a third-round choice, who turned out to be Derrick Smith). The Whalers immediately traded Linseman to the Edmonton Oilers, who later traded him to the Boston Bruins, where he eventually seemed to settle in more comfortably, for a while; or at least until the season of 1989-90, when he was traded *back* to the Flyers.

At any rate, in the 1980 playoffs Linseman's glorious last-gasp goal had finished off the Edmonton Oilers and had propelled the Flyers into the quarter-finals against the archrival New York Rangers of Fred Shero. The Flyers, of course, were still smarting from the embarrassing defeat inflicted by Shero's Rangers during the quarter-finals of the previous season, when Kenny Linseman had won the first game in overtime, which had only incited the Rangers to a sweep of the next four, during which the Flyers had been out-scored, twenty-six to five.

This time it would be the rookie Pete Peeters in goal against the Rangers' hot goaltender, John Davidson, who always seemed to do his best work in the playoffs. Game One in the Spectrum was a classic goaltenders' duel, with seventy-two shots and only three goals. Rick MacLeish scored the first, and then, two minutes after the Rangers had tied it in the third period, Behn Wilson scored to win it for the Flyers, two to one.

In the second game, Holmgren, Barber, and MacLeish gave the Flyers a three-goal lead before Peeters allowed another solitary New York goal. Reggie Leach then scored short-handed, and the Flyers won easily, four to one.

With the Flyers leading two games to none, the series moved on to New York, where Pete Peeters was again unconscious, this time shutting out the Rangers, three to nothing, with goals by Bob Dailey, Barber, and MacLeish. After three games, Peeters had yielded a total of only two goals, and even John Davidson wasn't up to that standard. And how many times have you heard that it's the "hot goaltender" who wins in the playoffs?

Game Four was a slightly different story, as Ranger Ron "Doogie" Duguay scored a goal in each period, Phil Esposito (later to become the unfortunate general manager of the team) added his only goal of the series, and the Rangers squeezed out a much-needed four-to-three win, which was also the first loss for Pete Pee-ters in the playoffs.

The Flyers had wanted a sweep, but back in Philadelphia they got the next-best thing, as Pete Peeters and the Flyers' defense again shut down the Rangers, while Al Hill, Behn Wilson, and Paul Holmgren took care of the scoring. Ron Duguay managed a mop-up goal, his fifth of the Rangers' paltry total of seven goals for the five-game series. So, the Flyers won the game, three to one, and the series, four to one.

This time the fickle finger of fate had pointed Fred Shero to-ward the exit, never again to return to the playoffs, while the Flyers, after a one-year absence *because of* Shero's Rangers, were in the semi-finals for the seventh time in eight years. And the getting there was all the sweeter for having turned the tables on Freddy and his New Yorkers.

The Flyers' semi-final opponents this time would be the surprisingly reborn Minnesota North Stars, the team that had so convincingly ended the Flyers' unbeaten streak. To reach the semi-finals, the North Stars had beaten the best that Canada had to offer. First, they had swept the Toronto Maple Leafs, which wasn't all that amazing. But what they had done next *was* amazing, for they had defeated the four-time Stanley Cup Champion Montreal Canadiens in a seven-game series, even though Montreal had owned the home-ice advantage.

And that's not the whole story either, because after the North Stars had shocked everyone by winning the first two games in Montreal, they had apparently blown their opportunity by losing the next two in Minnesota. Montreal won Game Five and appeared to have everything back under control, but then Minnesota won Game Six, and suddenly it was a one-game series, with that one game to be played in the Montreal Forum.

That game was the only close game of the seven. In fact, it was tied at two as the clock ticked into the last minute of regulation time. Then, to the disbelief of all, the winning goal was illuminated on the *visitors'* side of the scoreboard, and Montreal's dream of a fifth consecutive Stanley Cup was over. It would be the suddenly radiant North Stars, not the Canadiens, who would be traveling south to Philadelphia for the semi-finals.

The semi-final series began with the craziest first period of playoff hockey that I've ever heard of. The sky-high North Stars were leading, three to one, when the Flyers scored three goals in less than two minutes, one by Tom Gorence and two by Kenny Linseman, to take a four-to-three lead after just one period. The North Stars then scored the *next* three goals, for a six-to-four lead, before Paul Holmgren cut it to six to five. That was the final score, and it appeared that the Stars were on their way to the Stanley Cup Finals, where they *would* go the following year.

The second game brought the Stars back to earth somewhat, when the Flyers blew them out, eight to nothing, but the next two games would be in Minnesota, where the fans in the Met would be seeing (and screaming for) their team for the first time since their joyous victory in Montreal. In the second period of Game Three, the Flyers led, four to nothing, thanks to a hat trick by Bill Barber and an additional goal by Mel Bridgman. It appeared that the Flyers were home free and that the North Stars had fizzled out, but all of that changed very quickly.

First, on a Philadelphia two-man advantage, the Stars scored two short-handed goals in less than a minute, and the score was four to two. Then on a Minnesota two-man advantage, the Stars scored again. Instead of four to nothing, the score was suddenly four to three, and the cries of, "Let's go, Stars!" were deafening. If it had not been for another clutch performance by Phil Myre, the Flyers might have blown the game and perhaps the series right then. But Myre hung on through an aggressive third period by Minnesota, and through a ton of Minnesota power plays, until Bill Barber ended the drama with a short-handed goal, his fourth score of the game.

In Game Four, the North Stars had ten more power-play opportunities, but could not take advantage of any of them. In fact, the Stars had a total of forty-four power-play opportunities during the series, but could score only five power-play goals. Thanks to two *more* goals by Bill Barber and to the marvelous goaltending of Phil Myre, the Flyers managed not only to survive, but to win both games in the madness of the Met.

Back in the friendlier surroundings of the Spectrum, Game Five was strictly no contest. The Flyers led, seven to three, after two periods, and that's the way it ended. The Flyers had won four straight after losing the first game at home, and for the fourth time (and for the first time in four years), the Flyers were in the Stanley Cup Finals—this time due in good part to the goaltending of Louis Philippe Myre, the journeyman who had been acquired from St. Louis as a back-up, in exchange for two minor-leaguers.

For Phil Myre, it was obviously the best year of his career. In fact, it was the *only* truly illustrious year of his career. Not only did he enjoy those three shining moments against Boston, Edmonton, and Minnesota, but his overall record, including the playoffs, was 23-8-15. Just compare that record with his record of the two previous seasons, which was a combined 22-54-16!

Myre's record the following year with the Flyers would be 6-5-4, before he would move on to Colorado and then to Buffalo, where his combined record would slide back to 8-25-3. He would retire after that, a veteran of fourteen seasons with six N.H.L. teams, beginning with Montreal back in 1969. I'm sure that if he had the chance, Phil would trade just about all of those seasons put together for another "MYRE-LY MAGNIFICENT" one like the Year of the Streak.

During the 1980 Stanley Cup Finals, Phil Myre was not to be much of a factor, as Pat Quinn elected to go with the rookie, Pete Peeters, in every game but one. The opponent was the new "Team of Destiny," the New York Islanders, who, on the way to the finals, had beaten Boston and Buffalo, both of whom had been seeded ahead of them. In both of those series, the Islanders had won the first two games on the road, and now they would be playing the first two games of the finals in Philadelphia, where they had to win at least once in order to capture their first Cup.

As it turned out, a dead-even first game was the key to the entire series. In the first period, a goal by Mel Bridgman was answered by Mike Bossy. In the second period, a Denis Potvin score was answered by Bobby Clarke. The third period was scoreless until Rick MacLeish gave the Flyers a three-to-two lead with seven minutes left. Then, with less than four minutes left in regulation time, a power-play goal by Stefan Persson sent the game into overtime and set up the first of many disputes in this series, when referee Andy van Hellemond called Jimmy Watson for holding Bob Nystrom.

The argument wasn't whether or not Nystrom was held, but with the timing of the call, as such penalties are not usually called in overtime unless the foul is particularly flagrant, which this one was not. At any rate, with one second left in the penalty, Denis Potvin took a pass from behind the net and scored the winning goal, and perhaps the deciding goal of the series for the Islanders. The Flyers' power-play defense, which had been so brilliant against Minnesota, had yielded the tying and winning goals, and the Islanders would score thirteen more power-play goals in the next five games—more than enough to tip the scoring balance in their favor.

Game Two was a sparkling effort for Philadelphia. Paul Holmgren became the first American-born Flyer to record a hat trick, and the Flyers won handily, eight to three. But the Islanders had already accomplished what they had set out to do, which was to win one game in Philadelphia.

On Long Island the New Yorkers really pasted the Flyers in Games Three and Four, six to two and five to two, to take a three-games-to-one lead in the series. The Flyers then returned the disfavor, six to three in Philadelphia, featuring two goals by Rick MacLeish. But the Flyers were still faced with the unappetizing task of returning to and winning on the Island, in order to even the series and bring it back home for a seventh game in the Spectrum.

Game Six, the famous (or infamous) "Offsides Game," was

one of the most thrilling and memorable games in Stanley Cup history. It was played on Saturday afternoon, May 24, 1980, and it left all of the participants, and most of the television viewers, with a distinctly unpleasant taste in their mouths.

The first period was a microcosm of the entire series. Reggie Leach scored first, but Denis Potvin tied it with a shot which may or may not have been taken with his stick above shoulder level. That play was controversial, but not nearly so controversial as the one which came just two minutes later, when Butch Goring took a pass two feet offside outside of the Flyers' zone, then carried it back into the zone and found Brent Sutter in front of the net for a two-to-one Islander lead.

Linesman Leon Stickle later admitted that he had not been enough of a stickler on Goring's obvious offsides play, but by then it was too late to do anything about it. Unfortunately for Stickle, the fans in the Spectrum have never let him forget his costly oversight.

With one minute left in the period, Brian Propp tied the score at two, but the second period belonged to the Islanders. First Mike Bossy and then, with fourteen seconds left, Bob Nystrom scored, to make it four to two after two periods. For the battered and weary Flyers, the season appeared to be over, and for the Islanders, the Cup appeared to be theirs.

But the Flyers were not dead yet. Less than two minutes into the third period, Bob Dailey, who was playing despite an injured and unusable arm, scored to make it four to three. Four minutes later, John Paddock, who had scored only three goals all season, tied it at four, and suddenly the Islanders' first Cup was not such a sure thing.

For the next twenty-one minutes, including seven minutes of overtime, the tension in the Nassau Coliseum, and in living rooms throughout the Delaware Valley, was nearly unbearable. Finally, at the charmed overtime clock reading of 7:11, Bob Nystrom put the puck past Pete Peeters and became "Mr. Overtime" for the Islanders.

Instead of taking the series back to Philadelphia, there was no more series to take back, and all by the margin of an offsides call that never came. The Flyers, who had fought back so valiantly, were a staggered and shattered bunch in the dressing room after that game. They were burned out, washed out, and wrung out. And now they were just plain *out*.

The season which had begun on such a high note, with the most successful streak in history, had ended on a note so low as to be almost inaudible. For the second time in four years, the Cup had not only eluded the Flyers in the finals, but they were to serve as a stepping stone for another team's rise to four straight Stanley Cups. It was, I believe, the most disappointing finish to any season in Flyers history.

And with the subsequent departures of Bob Kelly to Washington and Moose Dupont to Quebec, just five seasons after their second Stanley Cup there were now only five Flyers remaining from that last Cup team:

Defensemen             Jimmy Watson

Forwards               Bobby Clarke
                       Rick MacLeish
                       Bill Barber
                       Reggie Leach

If you'll recall for a moment the Flyers' *first* season of success, which also happened to be their first season of *existence,* that season was followed by a four-year period of limbo, a period noteworthy mainly for the manner in which an eventual Stanley Cup contender was built. Similarly, following the success of their thirty-five-game unbeaten streak and of their surprise appearance in the 1980 Stanley Cup Finals, the Flyers were to endure a *second* four-year period of limbo, another period noteworthy mainly for the manner in which *another* consistent Stanley Cup contender was built.

The building process actually began during the Year of the Streak, when first-round draft choice Brian Propp came to the Flyers from the talent-laden Brandon Wheat Kings. Besides Propp, three other keys to the future were either drafted or signed that year, players who would not become Flyers until several years later. Drafted after Propp were a tough Western Canadian forward named Lindsay Carson and a young goaltender from the Swedish national team named Pelle Lindbergh. Not drafted, but signed as a free agent was a big forward from Kingston, Ontario, named Tim Kerr. No one could have known it then, but those four would play pivotal roles in the future success of the Flyers. And there were many more to come.

By the time Bobby Clarke, the last of the Cup players, would retire, most of the parts for a new-model Stanley Cup contender would be in place.

# Rebuilding Years: 1980 to 1984

For most teams, periods of rebuilding are trying times of painful ineptitude. Not so for the Flyers, who, during their next four seasons (1980-81, 1981-82, 1982-83, and 1983-84), never dropped lower than sixth overall in the N.H.L. hierarchy. But despite their continued excellence, at least by comparison with *most* of the teams in the league, the Flyers were victimized by fan psychology, and rather normal fan psychology at that. For as I see it, there are five stages of development in the evolution of a sophisticated sports fan:

1. With the start of a new franchise, the charter fans are willing to accept almost anything, including terrible seasons, as long as the effort is there. Everyone is content with minimal successes, such as beating an old-guard club here and there, and possibly getting close to a playoff position.

2. After a while, the fans are less content with mediocrity and hungrier for real success. At this stage they become less forgiving and more critical of their team.

3. As a team develops into a true contender, the fans begin to taste and smell a division or conference title, and they become even hungrier, and often more unruly—sometimes even bloodthirsty.

4. When championship success is finally achieved, there is a glowing pride among the fans. As after a wonderful feast, they are satisfied, perhaps satiated, and more benevolent towards all.

5. Eventually, success is no longer hoped for; it is expected. Any lessening of success is met with disenchantment, or worse—boredom. This is especially true when excellence has been sustained over a long period of time. Winning becomes routine, and the fans

become blasé and spoiled. I recall one season when the Flyers' home record was 36-2-2, but to awaken the fans there had to be a shutout, or a hat trick, or a battle royal.

Most fans are stuck at some arrested stage of development between Stage One and Stage Five. (In fact, some of those fans *deserve* to be arrested!) And then there are the fans of the Bruins, and the Flyers, and the Canadiens, and the Islanders, and perhaps now the Oilers. It takes a lot to get them excited, compared with the fans in Washington, for example. This is not meant as negative criticism, but merely as recognition of human nature.

While the Flyers were rebuilding, the Islanders took over the Patrick Division during the 1980-81 season, the season after they had won their first Cup by beating the Flyers in the finals. The Islanders would not relinquish the division title until the Flyers were rebuilt and ready to take it back from them. In fact, for sixteen seasons (from 1972-73 until 1988-89), only two teams won the Patrick (or the old Western) Division—the Flyers and the Islanders.

After the departure of good old Phil Myre, the Flyers used two goaltenders for the 1980-81 season—Pete Peeters, whose record was 22-12-5, and Rick St. Croix, whose record was 13-7-6 and who started nine of their twelve playoff games that year.

In the preliminary round of the playoffs, the Flyers had the home-ice advantage over Quebec and won the series, three games to two, with the home team winning every game. That set up a quarter-final series with the Calgary Flames, who hadn't won a game in Philadelphia in four years, and who usually made an early exit from the playoffs. But not this time.

With the home-ice advantage again, the Flyers won the first game rather easily, four to nothing, and it looked like another early snuffing for the Flames. But then Calgary surprised everyone by winning the next three games, all of them by one goal, and suddenly the Flyers had to win three straight just to survive.

The Flyers breezed through Game Five, nine to four, and they squeezed through Game Six in Calgary, three to two. But in Game Seven in Philadelphia, Calgary goaltender Pat Riggin, with a lot of help from a gutsy shot-blocking defenseman/captain named Brad Marsh, stoned the Flyers, four to one. It was yet another disappointing finish for Philadelphia and its ''Stage-Five'' fans.

Following the disillusionment of 1980-81, the Flyers put their past further behind them by engineering several major trades. First and most shockingly, they dealt Rick MacLeish (along with Don Gillen, Blake Wesley, and first, second, and third-round draft choices) to Hartford for Ray Allison (a former junior linemate of Brian Propp), Fred Arthur (a capable defenseman, but one who would soon retire to pursue safer ways of making a living), a first-round choice (Ron Sutter), and a third-round choice (Miroslav Dvorak).

Next came a rare exchange of team captains, as Mel Bridgman was sent to Calgary for the defenseman's defenseman, Brad Marsh, the guy with no speed, no skating ability, and no scoring punch, but the guy who had just played such a large part in knocking the Flyers out of the playoffs.

Then there were the acquisitions of two more free agents, goaltender Bob Froese (pronounced "Froze") from St. Louis and winger Ilkka Sinisalo from Finland, both of whom would later become important members of the Flyers' club.

And then, in the middle of the 1981-82 season, the Flyers acquired the long-time superstar of the Toronto Maple Leafs, Darryl Sittler, in exchange for minor-leaguer Rich Costello and a second-round draft choice.

If anything certain came out of that 1981-82 season, it was that the Flyers were not afraid to make changes, and there was one more big change to come. With just eight games left in the regular season, the Flyers were in third place behind the two New York teams, with a record of 34-29-9, and, at least in the eyes of management, Pat Quinn seemed to be losing control of the situation. So, after compiling a four-season record of 141-73-48 and a playoff record of 22-17, Pat Quinn was replaced by the man Quinn had replaced, Bob McCammon, the man who had replaced Quinn in Maine, where McCammon had coached originally, before he was first promoted to coach the Flyers, until he was replaced by Quinn.

Have you got all of that straight? Anyhow, with the playoffs just two weeks away, McCammon was back behind the Flyers' bench, and Pat Quinn was gone.

Except for eight games, the goaltending during 1981-82 was again handled by Pete Peeters (23-18-3) and Rick St. Croix (13-9-6). The other eight games served as an introduction to the N.H.L. for the rookie from Sweden (by way of Maine), Pelle Lindbergh (2-4-2).

This time Pete Peeters got the call in the playoffs, which were being played for the first time under another new format. The preliminary round now became the divisional semi-finals, in which the third-place Flyers were to face the second-place Rangers, with the first two games to be played in Madison Square Garden.

Peeters and the Flyers won the first game handily, four to one, and the home-ice advantage switched over to the Flyers. The Rangers romped through the second game, seven to three, but Game Three was the key to the best-of-five series.

In Philadelphia, with the series tied at one game apiece, the Flyers were leading, three to nothing, when Kenny Linseman created the aforementioned rallying point for the Rangers by spearing Anders Hedberg. New York retaliated with three solid goals and a fluky fourth goal, for a four-to-three win.

New York's momentum carried over to Game Four, when the Rangers built a six-to-two lead. Bobby Clarke and Bill Barber closed the gap to six to five with a memorable three-goal surge, but the Rangers held on to take the game, seven to five, and the series, three to one.

It was another distasteful finish to a Flyer season, all the more so for having lost two straight heart-pounders to the detested Rangers, and both of them in the Spectrum. "Stage Five" lived on.

**B**efore the next season (1982-83), Jimmy Watson retired, and Reggie Leach drifted off to Detroit, leaving only Bobby Clarke and Bill Barber as survivors from the Cup-winning years. By this time the Flyers had also become convinced that, despite their high hopes, Kenny Linseman was just not their type of player, especially after the ugly incident against the Rangers in the playoffs of the previous season. So, Linseman was sent to Hartford, and to Philadelphia came Mark Howe, who not only filled a need for a mobile defenseman, but who eventually would become the Flyers' *greatest* defenseman.

As part of the *previous* deal with Hartford (for Rick MacLeish), the Flyers' first pick in the draft (and the league's fourth overall) was Ron Sutter, the fifth of six Sutter brothers to play in the N.H.L. The sixth Sutter, Ron's twin brother Rich, was drafted by Pittsburgh and then acquired by the Flyers in an early-season trade which reunited the twins in Philadelphia, at least for a few years.

Winger Dave Brown was brought in to add some muscle, and another great defenseman-of-the-future, Brad McCrimmon, was acquired from Boston, where he had been the Bruins' number one draft choice in 1979. Before that, McCrimmon had been another of Brian Propp's teammates on the Brandon Wheat Kings.

To get McCrimmon, the Flyers gave up goaltender Pete Peeters, who, after a wonderful rookie season (37-10-5, including playoffs) during the Year of the Streak, had been having his troubles during the two seasons which followed (48-33-8, including playoffs). In his first year with Boston, Peeters would enjoy another great season (40-11-9), before again leveling off and again being traded, this time to Washington.

The other half of the goaltending tandem of Pete Peeters and Rick St. Croix (the latter with a six-season record of 42-32-16) was traded during the 1982-83 season to Toronto for Michel "Bunny" Larocque, the former Canadien. But Larocque was to serve only as veteran insurance behind the two rookies who had taken over the position, Pelle Lindbergh and Bob Froese, also known as the "Gumper" and "Frosty." (The derivation of the nickname "Frosty" is obvious; "Gumper" is derived from the famous gnome-like goaltender, Lorne "Gump" Worsley, who played from 1952 through 1974 for the Rangers, Canadiens, and North Stars.)

In his first season in North America, Pelle Lindbergh had been a First-Team All-Star for the Maine Mariners, as well as the American Hockey League's Rookie of the Year and Most Valuable Player. He had even received unprecedented honors from the state of Maine. Now he had been selected by the Flyers as the guy who could win championships for them, and in his first full season in the N.H.L. his record was a promising 23-13-3, with a goals-against average of 2.98.

As was to be the too-often-told story of *his* career, Bob Froese was cast as the back-up. His record as a rookie was 17-4-2, with a goals-against average of 2.52.

Although the Flyers (with a record of 49-23-8) finished first in the Patrick Division for the regular season, the N.H.L.'s new playoff format meant a divisional semi-final rematch with the fourth-place, but still dreaded Rangers (35-35-10). This time the series started with the Rangers in Philadelphia, against the Flyers' newest playoff goaltender, Pelle Lindbergh. And this time the Rangers quite literally added insult to the injury of the season before, as they won the first two in the Spectrum and then finished off an embarrassing three-game sweep by ripping the Flyers in New York, nine to three.

Not only had the Rangers won six consecutive playoff games against the Flyers, four of those in Philadelphia, but they had humiliated the Flyers during the final rout by laughing and having just a gay old time at their expense. That attitude left an aftertaste of bitterness, and that bitterness always seems to renew itself whenever these two teams meet.

**D**espite the decidedly sour ending to the 1982-83 season, one fortunate development did emerge from the rubble. Toward the end of the Maine Mariners' season it had been decided that some help was needed up front for the A.H.L. playoffs, so the Flyers contacted their man in Sweden, Ted Sator, who was coaching there at that time. Sator recommended an undrafted Notre Dame graduate whom he had discovered in Sweden, and who was then playing for him. He was, in fact, one of two English-speaking players on Ted's team. To this day, he contends that he always knew when Ted was angry with him, because that was the only time Ted spoke to him in English.

The young man's name, if you haven't guessed, was Dave Poulin, and he and his lovely wife Kim had decided to end their European hockey adventure and return to their home territory of Chicago, where Dave had already tentatively accepted a position in business. For a few extra dollars, the Poulins were persuaded to stop off in Maine on their way west, and since the Flyers also needed some help up front, Dave was brought up to Philadelphia for the final two games of the regular season. In his N.H.L. debut in Toronto Dave scored two goals, and then in the playoffs he was one of the few bright spots for the Flyers, with four points in the three-game sweep by the Rangers.

For the 1983-84 season, Dave decided to give full-time hockey another try, this time in Philadelphia. As a rookie in the N.H.L., Dave not only scored thirty-one goals, but he also proved to be the young leader who, at the start of the following season, would replace Bobby Clarke as captain of the Flyers. Perhaps it was only appropriate for a team populated by such important free-agent discoveries as Tim Kerr, Ilkka Sinisalo, and Bob Froese, that the captain, too, should have been acquired as a free agent.

In the spring of 1983 the Flyers had no number one draft choice, but four future Flyers were drafted nonetheless, three of them "underagers": Peter Zezel (in the second round), Derrick Smith (third) and Rick Tocchet (sixth). All three lived near the same suburb of Toronto, called Scarborough, but all three had lived separate lives, and only since all three were drafted by the Flyers have the three families become particularly close. Interestingly, all three are also examples of the polyglot melting pot that is part of the fascination of hockey. Zezel's parents were Yugoslavs whose name had been Zezelj. Tocchet's parents were from Germany, by way of Italy, and originally their name had been Toket, which explains why Tocchet is pronounced "Tocket" (rhymes with "Rocket") and not "Toe-shay." Smith's parents were from England, and when asked why "Derrick" was not spelled the English way—"Derek"—Derrick replied, "I guess my dad liked oil wells!"

Also drafted (in the eighth round) was another European Flyer-of-the-future, Per-Erik (nicknamed, of course, "Pelle") Eklund, like Pelle Lindbergh, a young Swedish star.

As astute as the Flyers were with free agents and the draft, they also remained active on the trading front, acquiring defenseman Doug Crossman from Chicago along with a number two draft choice (who later turned out to be winger Scott Mellanby) in exchange for Behn Wilson, the defenseman who never quite became the superstar he was expected to become. After five seasons of some cheers and many boo's with the Flyers, I think that I will best remember Behn as he was once caricatured in a skit, asking his coach who had just waved him onto the ice, "What do you want? A goal, an assist, or a knockout?"

During the 1983-84 season, Pelle Lindbergh was again the number one goaltender, but in a mid-season exhibition game against a team of Soviet all-stars, his wrist was fractured, and Bob Froese again proved to be a more-than-worthy replacement. For the season, Froese had a record of 28-13-7, while Lindbergh, who wasn't as sharp after returning from his injury, had a record of 16-13-3.

Late in the season, another sad departure occurred, when a serious knee injury forced Bill Barber to the sidelines. Despite his tireless efforts in attempting to rehabilitate the knee, Barber reluctantly had to hang up his skates, leaving only one Stanley Cup–winning Flyer still on the ice, and that, of course, was Bobby Clarke.

Clarke must have realized that his playing days were also numbered, especially when Coach/General Manager Bob McCammon sent him to Florida for an enforced vacation, in order to recharge his batteries before the playoffs. After fifteen seasons of all-out effort (the only kind of effort Clarke knew anything about), the vacation may or may not have helped him in the playoffs, but it didn't help the Flyers to avoid another embarrassing three-game sweep in the divisional semi-finals, this time to the Washington Capitals.

As awful as it had been to lose six straight playoff games to the New York Rangers, it felt even worse to lose three straight to the Caps, who had never before won a playoff series of any kind. Worse yet, the Flyers were not really competitive in any of the three games, losing four to two and six to two in the Cap Centre, and five to one in the Spectrum.

That game in the Spectrum marked the last of nine consecutive playoff losses for Bob McCammon. It also marked the end of his career as coach of the Flyers (with a commendable regular-season record of 119-68-31 over four seasons, but with a playoff record of only 1-9).

The McCammon Era was over, as was the Era of Bobby Clarke, hockey player extraordinaire. But the New Era of Bob Clarke, general manager, was about to begin.

# That Wonderful "Fresh-Start" Season: 1984-85

When Bob Clarke was named general manager on May 15, 1984, he knew that there was an abundance of young talent already in the organization. He also knew that his first priority was to find the proper leadership for that young talent. Nine days later, after a series of secret meetings and other assorted globe-trotting machinations, it was announced that the Flyers' new head coach was to be a young man named Mike Keenan, an unknown, or at least an unknown in Philadelphia. But as Clarke knew very well, Fred Shero had also been an unknown—until he was named coach of the Flyers.

Mike Keenan's background as a coach showed success at every level, from Junior "B" championships in the Metro Toronto League to the Calder Cup Championship of the American Hockey League. After winning the Calder with the Rochester Americans, a farm club of the Buffalo Sabres, Mike could see no opportunity for a vertical move, so firmly entrenched in Buffalo at that time were such stalwarts as Scotty Bowman, Jim Roberts, and Red Berenson. So, Mike made a horizontal move to the University of Toronto, where he coached the Varsity Blue to the Canadian Collegiate Championship in 1983-84. And that's when Bob Clarke came calling.

My first impression of Mike Keenan was one of discipline, and that was a characteristic which was felt by all. Compared with Bob McCammon, Keenan was a martinet, and Bob Clarke had recognized the importance of such an approach with a team so young. But Keenan was not just a disciplinarian, he was a modern-day "high-tech" coach who brought with him to the Flyers organization the ultimate in the use of computers, satellites, video replays, and dry-land aerobic training. Under Keenan and Physical Conditioning and Rehabilitation Coach Pat Croce, every Flyer was exposed to the highest form of training, and every Flyer was (and still is) trained to perform at his maximum level.

This intensive preparation applied to the mental and psychological aspects of the game, as well as to the physical aspects. Keenan broke the N.H.L. season into eight ten-game segments, and at least once every ten games he met privately with every player for the purposes of personal evaluation and of goal-setting for the next ten games. Also, equal monetary bonuses were awarded to each team member for each ten-game segment, with the amount dependent upon the team's won-loss record during that ten-game stretch.

As surprising as Clarke's choice of coach had been, it paled by comparison with the trade he made the day before the season started. The team's veteran superstar and future Hall-of-Famer, Darryl Sittler, was expected to be named captain of the young Flyers, which seemed only logical to everyone, including Sittler. But instead of being named captain, Sittler was sent off to Detroit in exchange for two more youngsters, Murray Craven and Joe Paterson, both of whom would play key roles in the success of the Flyers' season, while Sittler would suffer through one final injury-plagued year with the struggling Red Wings. The team captaincy, of course, was bestowed upon a young, but well-deserving Dave Poulin, one of the true gentlemen of the game, and a player who had come so very close to retiring "undiscovered."

With the departure of Sittler, the Flyers were suddenly the youngest team in the league, and by a wide margin. There was a great deal of speculation as to how the Flyers would fare with a rookie general manager, a rookie head coach, a rookie assistant coach (E.J. McGuire), and a roster full of rookies and other unproven young players. In fact, just about the only N.H.L. experience in a leadership role belonged to Ted Sator, who was serving as an assistant coach for a second season, before moving on to become head coach of the New York Rangers and then the Buffalo Sabres, and who now serves as an assistant coach with the Boston Bruins.

Despite the lack of experience, there was no shortage of inspiration during the early going, as Bernie Parent became the first member of the Flyers to be inducted into the Hockey Hall of Fame, and future Hall-of-Famer Bobby Clarke was honored with a memorable night. After Clarke's number "16" was retired, and Bobby spoke of doing it "all over again," Kate Smith's "God Bless America" was played for the sixty-sixth time before a Flyers game. Naturally, the Flyers won, running Kate's all-time record to 55-9-2.

Thus properly inspired, inexperience did not seem to bother the Sutters, nor the rookies—Zezel, Tocchet, and Smith. And on defense, Brad McCrimmon came of age, and Mark Howe was simply superb. Offensively, the Flyers showed early on that they could score, as they poured in thirteen goals against Vancouver, tying a club record which they had set during the previous season against Pittsburgh. And Sign Man was in rare form, with "ILKKA SCORA GOALA," and "KERR-PLUNK," and "PROPP-ERLY DONE," or "SNAP, CRACKLE, & PROPP."

Pelle Lindbergh had a sensational season, with a record of 40-17-7 and a goals-against average of 3.02. Bob Froese was sensational, too, when he got the chance, with a record of 13-2-0 and a goals-against average of 2.41. Lindbergh became a First-Team N.H.L. All-Star and was named the first winner of the Bobby Clarke Trophy as the Flyers' Most Valuable Player. Even more impressively, he became the second Flyer to win the Vezina Trophy, the first having been his goaltending coach, Bernie Parent.

With such spectacular performances as these, the Flyers burst through the N.H.L. season with fifty-three wins, the most ever in Flyers history. And for turning the youngest team into the winningest team, Mike Keenan became the third Flyers coach to win the Jack Adams Award, as N.H.L. Coach of the Year.

As pleased and proud as Mike Keenan, and Bob Clarke, and everyone else felt about their exciting young club, the Flyers would still have to prove themselves in the playoffs, where they had lost nine straight games, six of those to the New York Rangers, who, as fate would have it, were once again the Flyers' opponents in the first playoff round. With the first two games in the Spectrum, and with the Flyers leading three to nothing in the first period of Game One, it seemed that the ugly old days were just that, the ugly old days. But, inexorably, the Rangers came back, and in the final minute of regulation time Ranger ghosts of playoffs past returned to haunt the Flyers, as Anders Hedberg scored, wiping out a four-to-three Philadelphia lead.

Eight minutes into overtime, Mark Howe ended the suspense with the goal that won it for the Flyers, five to four. After that, things went more smoothly, as the Flyers swept the series by winning the next two, three to one and six to five. In New York, the final game was highlighted by a marvelous four-goal outburst in the second period by Tim Kerr, who set N.H.L. playoff records for most goals in a period (four) and fastest four goals by one player (8:16). The ghosts were gone, at least for the time being, and it was time to move on to the Patrick Division Finals and to that other New York team, the Islanders—the team that had reigned as champions of the division ever since they had overtaken the Flyers on their way to four consecutive Cups.

Pelle Lindbergh started the series in royal style, by shutting out the Islanders, three to nothing, in the Spectrum. The Flyers also won the next two before the Islanders finally showed that they weren't going to go quietly, winning Game Four in New York, six to two.

Game Five in the Spectrum was a beauty, as the Islanders were determined to take the series back to New York for a sixth game. Goaltenders Lindbergh and Kelly Hrudey were both magnificent throughout, with the only goal occurring in the second period, when Peter Zezel bumped Hrudey, allowing Ilkka Sinisalo to score. As the clock wound down in the third period, and as the crowd chanted, "Pel-le, Pel-le, Pel-le," I can recall thinking aloud, "If this game ends at one to nothing, it will be a tribute to the championship qualities of both of these teams." And that was just the way it did end, with the Flyers winning the series, four games to one, and recapturing the Patrick Division Championship from the team that had taken it from them.

For the eighth time in thirteen seasons the Flyers were in the Stanley Cup Semi-Finals, which were now called the Conference Finals, or, to be more exact, the Prince of Wales Conference Finals, since the Patrick Division had been moved from the Campbell Conference to the Wales Conference. The opponents were the swift and tough Quebec Nordiques, and the first two games were to be in

Quebec, once a home-away-from-home for the Flyers, but not any longer.

The first game was a tight-checking, low-scoring, classic example of playoff hockey, and it was won by the Nordiques, two to one, on an overtime goal by Peter Stastny. The Flyers retaliated by winning the next two games, both by the score of four to two, before Quebec took back the home-ice advantage with a five-to-three win in Philadelphia.

With the series tied at two games apiece, the fifth game was in Quebec, and it was a stunner. A second-period power-play goal by the Nordiques was the only score until the third period, when Joe Paterson tied it for the Flyers. Then, with four minutes left in regulation time, Brian Propp and Murray "Crafty" Craven broke two-on-one into the Quebec zone, with Craven scoring the goal that won it for the Flyers, two to one. Who knows what effect the presence of Darryl Sittler might have had during the playoffs, but the ironic fact remains that the only two goals scored by the Flyers in the pivotal game of the Conference Finals were scored by the two young players for whom Sittler was traded.

Game Six in the Spectrum stands out clearly in my mind, mainly because of one of the singularly most exciting, dramatic, and wonderful moments in Flyers history. With Philadelphia leading, one to nothing, in the second period of another marvelously hard-checking game, the Flyers made the tactical error of committing consecutive penalties, which left them two men short against the dynamic Quebec power play. But instead of allowing the Nordiques to tie, that priceless gift from Notre Dame via Sweden, Dave Poulin, exploded the game and the Spectrum with one of the most extraordinary goals ever scored in an N.H.L. playoff game. Playing on the point of the Flyers' three-man defensive triangle, Poulin intercepted a pass, streaked down the ice, and blew a shot past Quebec goaltender Mario Gosselin. It was the only two-man-short playoff goal ever scored by the Flyers, and if ever a goal ended any hope a team had of winning, it was that one. The Nordiques sagged, Doug Crossman added a third goal, and Pelle Lindbergh earned his third shutout of the playoffs, as the Flyers won the game, three to nothing, and the series, four to two.

The Flyers had won the Prince of Wales Trophy and their fifth conference title in the eleven years that the league had been structured by conferences. Also for the fifth time, but for the first time since the Streak Year of 1980, the Flyers were in the Stanley Cup Finals.

Awaiting the Flyers in the finals were the defending Stanley Cup Champions, the Edmonton Oilers, the team which had dethroned the New York Islanders in the finals of the previous season, and the team that virtually everyone had picked to repeat as champions. With their Big Six of Wayne Gretzy, Jari Kurri, Glenn Anderson, Mark Messier, Paul Coffey, and Grant Fuhr, and with a dozen or so grinders, Glen Sather's playoff-hardened Oilers were more than a match for the young, inexperienced, and now injury-depleted Flyers.

For the rugged Quebec series had taken its toll on five of the Flyers' most important players: A collision in the corner had put Brad McCrimmon out for the rest of the season with a separated shoulder; a recurring knee injury had rendered leading scorer Tim Kerr a non-factor; a sore shoulder limited the effectiveness of Ilkka Sinisalo; damaged ribs made simple movements difficult for Dave Poulin; and a banged-up knee hindered the super-mobility of Pelle Lindbergh.

Although the first two games were to be played in Philadelphia, the next three were to be played in far-off Edmonton, which meant that if the Oilers could win either one of the first two in the Spectrum, they could then finish off the series by winning the following three in the Northlands Coliseum. In Edmonton, the Oilers were accustomed to being treated as royalty; in Philadelphia, the Oilers were greeted with something less than royal treatment. As Coach Sather put it, "That's Philadelphia—scrapple and boo's!"

In the first game of the finals, the Flyers kept the pressure off Pelle Lindbergh and won easily, four to one. But that just seemed to awaken the slumbering giant, as the Oilers took the second game, three to one, and then flew happily back to Edmonton, where they did indeed finish off the series by winning the next three, four to three, five to three, and, in an embarrassingly shaggy concluding game, eight to three.

Much to the delight of Glen Sather, who had maintained that no team could win the Cup with a Swedish goaltender, the ailing Lindbergh had been replaced for the fifth and final game, and for the first time in the playoffs, by Bob Froese, who deserved a better fate. Lindbergh's playoff record had been twelve and six, with a brilliant goals-against average of 2.50, but he was clearly suffering in Edmonton. And unfortunately for Froese, his only chance in the playoffs didn't arrive until after the Cup had really already been decided.

For Lindbergh, for Froese, for all of the Flyers, it was a sad and seedy ending to an otherwise wonderful season. The Oilers made it no better with a fight near the end of the game and with a refusal by Sather to shake hands after the game.

For the league's youngest team, which had come so far as such a long shot, the marathon season was finally over. But like the first Flyers team to make it to the semi-finals in 1973, there was an almost tangible feeling of eager anticipation about the future. Like the players and coaches themselves, I just couldn't wait until the following season, when this young club would get another shot.

# Season of a Thousand Heartaches: 1985-86

In the spring of 1985, I was carrying my bags through the Newark Airport when I was struck with a sharp pain just off the left-center area of my chest. It was enough to stop me in my tracks, and it left me standing there struggling for air with long, gasping breaths. All indications were that something was seriously wrong—something more than just the usual polluted air from the oil refineries of North Jersey.

The pain was severe enough to make me want to check into it, so I underwent the usual stress test. I was positive that the important question was not whether or not I had a disease, but how severe the disease would be. Much to my surprise, I was told that nothing was seriously wrong, and that I may have had an arthritic shoulder which had been aggravated by the stress of carrying my bags. I said, "Thank you very much," and left thinking how amazing it was that I did not have heart disease, especially considering the way I had dissipated myself over the years. I don't mean that I had been a drinker or anything like that, but I had been a bad eater, and I had been through a number of other physical disorders. No matter how bad the news, I would not have been surprised at anything I was told.

During the summer the pains returned, and they not only continued to persist, but they became more severe and with more lasting effect. In September it was determined on an angiogram that I had 90 per cent blockages in what they call the left anterior descending. The doctors referred to my problem, in a mildly joking way, as "the widow-maker."

It was agreed by Doctors Edward Viner and Jeff Hartzel, the Flyers' and my doctors, that I might be a candidate for angioplasty, the means by which the arteries are cleared by a small balloon, which not only has a Roto-Rooter-reaming-out effect, but which also flattens the evil plaque against the walls of the arteries. This procedure might reduce a 90 per cent blockage to, say, 30 per cent, which, in medical terms, is fine. So, we all agreed to schedule angioplasty for Friday, October 4, just six days before the opening of the Flyers' season.

If the angioplasty worked, I would be able to go home the next day, in plenty of time to prepare for the opener on Thursday and the start of the season I had been so eagerly anticipating. Of course there was always the outside chance that I might need bypass surgery, in which case I would be in the hospital a lot longer. In either case, I was extraordinarily well briefed about what to expect by the people at the University of Pennsylvania Hospital, where the deed was to be done.

During the two hours of the angioplasty, I was completely conscious and quite aware of areas of pain, but having been so well prepared, I understood everything that was happening. Finally, the doctor at my side, Dr. John Hirshfeld, leaned over and said, "We're going to wait for fifteen minutes and see what happens."

After fifteen rather anxious minutes, I next heard, "We're having a little problem. I think we ought to do the surgery."

I had known that surgery was a possibility and that I would have to make that determination then and there and not go back to my room and think about it for a couple of days. So, without further ado, I said, "O.K.," and I was wheeled into the operating room.

For those of you who have never had bypass surgery, it's quite an interesting experience! I was fully awake when I arrived in the O.R., and there was a veritable army waiting for me there. I recognized Dr. Clark Hargrove, and I asked him, "What did you do, sell tickets?"

Dr. Hargrove explained that there was no room for paying customers and proceeded to introduce the various battalions of his army. First, off my left leg, was the surgical team that would remove the vein from my leg that would be used in the bypass work. A second surgical team would open my chest cavity and do the necessary work there. A third team would be operating the heart-lung machine. A fourth team was in charge of anesthesia. And there was, of course, a fifth team of support nurses.

"How many people are there?" I asked.

"Sixteen," I think he said.

After scraping the hair off my chest and performing some other housekeeping chores, it appeared that we were ready to go. Dr. Hargrove looked at me and said, "All set?"

The broadcaster in me could no longer be restrained, and I said, "Just a minute, please." Lying there on my back, looking up at that large circular light with which we have all become so familiar from movies and television, and just before departing for Never-Never Land, I said, "Live! From the Hospital at the University of Pennsylvania, it's time for . . . 'Bypass Surgery'! And now let's go down to gurneyside and Dr. Clark Hargrove."

He said, "This is serious."

I said, "O.K. I'll be good."

"Before you go," he said, "do you have any tickets for Thursday's game?"

"I'll tell you when I wake up," I said.

I did wake up, thank Heaven, but in a strange and misty kind of atmosphere. I was in a kind of stupor, sort of a mild semiconscious euphoria. I had no idea how long I'd been unconscious, or how long the operation had taken, or how it had gone, or where specifically I was now located. Obviously, I told myself, since I was thinking and semi-awake, things must have gone well enough, or at least well enough for me to remain alive a little longer. I was aware of voices around me, but I couldn't open my eyes to see where I was.

Finally I was advised that I was in the recovery room, and I was reassured by hearing my wife's voice and then the doctor's voice saying that everything had gone fine. I was appreciative of that, and then I heard another voice saying, "Gene, God bless you. I'm here, Father Casey." The good father is the infamous unofficial chaplain of the Flyers, who is generally seen at the games wearing a Yankees jacket, and whose main claim to fame is a superb imitation of the enigmatic Fred Shero. In my closed-eye awareness of his presence, I heard the voice of Father Casey say, "Gene, I'm really sad right now."

I said, consolingly, "No, don't be, Father. They said it all went off pretty well."

He said, "No, not that, Gene. While you were being operated on, the Yankees lost the pennant."

When I got back to my room, I gave thanks for the extraordinarily well-disciplined hospital staff and went to sleep. It seemed that I'd barely been asleep for any time at all when I became aware that someone was shaking my shoulder and that a female voice was saying, "I gotta do things for you, Mr. Hart."

"Who are you?"

"My name is Cheryl."

"What time is it, Cheryl?"

"Five A.M."

"Cheryl, what did you wake me up at five o'clock for?"

"Well, you see, Mr. Hart, the people on this floor are surgeons, and they gotta be in the O.R. at seven o'clock, and that means I gotta do my stuff before they do their rounds at six."

So, five o'clock was the time for medication, blood pressure, blood samples, taking my pulse, and whatever else had to be done. While Cheryl was going through her maneuvers, I could feel her grabbing my right wrist, the wrist on which I have a large area of scar tissue—the result of an old skate cut. I could sense her feeling around on that scar tissue, trying to locate a pulse. Finally she said, "Oh, Mr. Hart, I've got bad news for you."

"What's that, Cheryl?"

"If you don't give me some pulse in five seconds, you dead."

One doesn't want to laugh in a situation like that, and risk opening up the large incision in one's chest, so I said, "Try the other wrist, Cheryl."

"O.K., Mr. Hart."

"Is that better, Cheryl?"

"Well, I guess you not dead."

Not only was I not dead, I was out of the hospital in a week. I still marvel at the fact that, despite all of the dissipation that I'd done to my body, those doctors were able to correct that really seriously damaging potential killer and have me out of there in seven days.

And what an incredible seven days it was. In fact, thanks to so many good people, it was the best possible week I could have spent in a hospital. The medical staff was wonderful, and the outpouring of fruit and flowers and mail made my room look like a combination orchard/greenhouse/Hallmark shop.

On my next-to-last day in the hospital, which was the day before the season opener, Mike Finocchiaro brought a camera crew into the room to tape a little piece to run before the game. That made my adrenalin flow, and I got up and seemed tremendously healthy, and alive, and bright, and full of energy—especially considering the trauma of the week before. But all of that energy faded quickly, and the nurse abruptly ended the session by saying, "O.K., everybody out!"

My roommate, who was a lovely middle-aged gentleman, watched all of that hoopla with interest, but I had been concerned about bothering him, so I said, "This must be very disturbing for you."

I felt better about it all when he said, "No, I haven't had so much fun since my wife and I went to Disneyland in 1970!"

Once you're out of the hospital, they tell you to get out and walk for exercise. I remember very well the day after I got home, which was exactly one week after the operation, when I walked half-way around the block. What I remember was not the pain, which was limited, but the fatigue I experienced, as whatever energy I had just seemed to drain from me so quickly.

I was definitely not yet ready to broadcast a game, not even a home game. I had never missed one before, and I didn't know quite how I would react to watching on television. After all, the only Flyers game I had ever seen on television was that one in Pittsburgh for which I'd done the color from my hospital bed. All the rest I had seen live. But I wasn't feeling too lively on the night of the opener, at least not until they showed a shot of the Spectrum message board, which read, "GENE, GET WELL SOON! WE LOVE YOU!"

I had been told that I might be able to return to work sometime in December, and that I wouldn't be able to travel until January, but I was already wheeling and dealing in my mind to get to a game against Quebec the following Thursday, even though it would be less than two weeks from the date of the operation. I told my wife, "We're going to go to that game." Everyone told me that was outlandish, but after all of the turmoil of the past two or three weeks, and the month of anguish before that, I felt that I needed some spark, and I thought that going to a game might be just the thing, even if it wasn't just what the doctors ordered.

So, we went. To save a few steps, I was driven down the tunnelway to the ground floor of the Spectrum, and I then walked down the corridor toward the dressing rooms, greeting a number of people who were more than a little surprised to see me there so soon. I didn't want to bother the players too much, so I just leaned into the dressing room and waved.

Just as I was closing the dressing room door, the Flyers' physical therapist, Pat Croce, spotted me, and in a response so typical of him, he came over, grabbed me by the shoulder, and said, "Gene, Gene, it's so great to see you!" while instinctively punching me twice in the chest. The punches didn't really hurt me, but I was startled, and still being rather shaky, I fell against the wall.

Pat, realizing that he had just hit a bypass patient squarely in the bypass, started to apologize and fluster and fumble to a degree that I found tremendously funny, and as I was leaning against the wall laughing, I started to slide down the wall. I was trying not to laugh any more, because it made my chest hurt, and I finally said, weakly, "Pat, please don't let me fall on the floor." And, like a good physical therapist, Pat didn't.

Anyhow, I saw the game, and I was thrilled—so thrilled that I decided that I was going to work a game. I pointed to Sunday, November 3, on the schedule, which was one month before I was supposed to return to work, and one month, less a day, after the date of the surgery. Our own Ebeneezer Scrooge and assistant to the president, John Brogan, said, "Oh, no you're not!" and I remember telling him, "John, when I came out of the O.R., with the intravenous in my arm, and with tubes coming out of my nose, and out of my rectum, and out of all of my other orifices, including the large new one in my chest, which was still bleeding, with all of that going on, at that very second I looked and felt better than you do right now, so leave me the heck alone and let me work!"

Finally, there was a compromise plan which I didn't fully appreciate: They would let me work that game, but only the second period. I figured that if I could work one period, I could work the whole game. But they didn't want to wear me out, so we agreed that I would take over at the start of the second period, after my dear friend Mike Emrick had worked the first. Of course I thought, "Fine! Once I get behind the microphone, I'm not going to leave!"

When the big night arrived, and I started the second period, I was surprised that I was as sharp as I was. After all of those days of sitting at home, and just letting the hours go by, and not sleeping very well, it was exhilarating to be back at work.

At the first break in the action, I was writing some notes on my score sheet, when I noticed that the crowd was applauding, so I looked up at the message board and saw: "WELCOME GENE

HART BACK TO THE MICROPHONE!'' I waved, and the fans stood and welcomed me back with the kind of extended ovation that I thought was reserved only for very special players in the Flyers organization, or for Kate Smith!

All of the letters of concern which I had received in the hospital meant so much to me that it is hard for me to express, but that warm welcome in the Spectrum, which indicated acceptance of me as a person, had to be one of the most satisfying moments of my life. At first, it had startled me, as Pat Croce had done, but then it slowly warmed the cockles of my newly repaired heart, and as I finished the second, and then the third periods of that game, I was more exhilarated than ever.

I was feeling good not only about myself, but about the team, because Pelle Lindbergh and the boys were playing marvelous hockey. In fact, by the following Saturday, they had won eleven of their first thirteen games, and their last nine in a row. That Saturday night, Bob Froese started in place of Pelle and beat the Bruins, running the Flyers' record to twelve and two, with ten wins in a row. Better yet, the team would now have four well-deserved days off to rest and prepare for their next game, which would be on Thursday night against the two-time Stanley Cup Champions, the Edmonton Oilers.

I, too, was looking forward to the time off. I knew that the extra rest would do me good, especially since I was still having trouble sleeping through the night. There was the continuing discomfort of having to sleep on my back, and, naturally, there was still some pain in my chest, so the best I could hope for was to get snatches of sleep every couple of hours. But that Saturday night after the Boston game, I was tired enough to sleep fairly well.

When I awoke on Sunday morning, I felt rather good—a little stronger and peppy enough—even though it was only six A.M., for my Sunday morning specialty. At the risk of sounding like the ultimate egotist, my Sunday morning specialty is to go down to the kitchen, fix some hot tea, open the *New York Times,* and do the crossword puzzle—in ink, of course! As I sipped my tea and perused the puzzle, I couldn't help thinking that all was right with the world. How lucky I was, and how glorious the world appeared to be on that Sunday morning!

And then, at 6:30, the phone rang. My first reaction was, ''Oh, my goodness, which one of my children's teen-age friends is calling at 6:30 on Sunday morning? For Heaven's sake, why don't they let us sleep?''

I wish it *had* been a call like that, but it wasn't. It was, instead, a call which started a flood of thoughts and emotions which were so difficult, and which are *still* so difficult, that they are almost impossible to explain. As had been the case when we learned that Barry Ashbee had leukemia, suddenly the importance of the Stanley Cup and all of that seemed to diminish into nothing.

"Gene, this is John Paul Weber at WIP. Do you know anything about Lindbergh being involved in an accident?"

"No, why do you ask?"

"Someone claiming to be a policeman from South Jersey said he saw his Porsche all wracked up."

Realizing that there weren't too many cars around that resembled the Gumper's Porsche, and also realizing that this sounded as though it might be more than just the usual fender-bender, I decided that I would risk the ire involved with what might turn into an early Sunday morning wild goose chase. "I'll call around and check into it," I said, with more than a little bit of apprehension.

None of the team officials I called had heard anything, but then a radio news bulletin announced that Pelle Lindbergh had been in an auto accident and had been hospitalized, and that his condition was not yet known. I figured that if anyone would know about his condition, the Flyers' (and my) physicians would know, so, at about seven A.M., I called Dr. Ed Viner.

"Ed, gee, I hate to be bothering you so early in the morning. . ."

"You're calling about Pelle?"

"Yes, was he in an accident?"

"Yes, he was."

"How bad?"

Then he said something that will stick forever in my mind: "It's the worst."

Dr. Viner then had to ring off in order to leave for the hospital, but I had heard more than enough. Because of my postoperative condition, I still wasn't able to drive, so I asked my wife to drive us to the hospital.

When we got there, we saw Murray Craven coming out, looking very dejected. He nodded, and we nodded, all of us realizing that it was one of those peculiarly awkward times when no one knows quite what to say.

In the emergency room we saw Ed Snider, John Brogan, and

Mike Keenan. During his first year-plus as an N.H.L. coach, Keenan had been a Stoic tower of strength, almost inscrutable in his emotions. But now he had a look of pain in his eyes that told us that something truly terrible had happened. In my mind I remember telling myself, "It can't be so bad that he won't get better. Can it?"

Then we were told that Pelle's brain stem had been moved, and that they were still working on him. Although no one actually said so, it was becoming apparent that what they were *really* saying was, "The injury indicates that Pelle is brain dead."

Through the next few days, we visited the hospital for considerable stretches of time. When it was officially announced that Pelle was brain dead, I still refused in my mind to admit that it was so. After all, I had seen him in his hospital bed, with his fiancée Kirsten seated beside him, and he looked pale, but, for want of any better words, he didn't look that badly off. There was bandaging on one leg and on one arm, but there was not a lot of other noticeable damage to his body. The most frightening aspect was not the sight of Pelle lying in his bed, but the "beep...beep...beep" sound of the heart-lung machine that was keeping his body alive. I can remember very clearly sitting there, in tears, hoping that a miracle might happen and that Pelle would pop up again, smiling.

Pelle's mother had been visiting him before the accident, and she had been on hand through all of this, while his father's trip from Sweden was being expedited by the Flyers. When the family had been reunited, it was decided that Pelle's greatest gift would be to have his heart, liver, kidneys, and whatever other organs removed for use in other people or for research. It was noted by some that this action was consistent with the "pragmatic" philosophy of the Swedish people. That may be so, but it was also a terribly difficult time for Pelle's family and fiancée, who were told that Pelle would have to be kept alive, or at least breathing, for several days until his organs were removed, and that after that, they would never see him again.

On Wednesday I called Dr. Viner to ask him how everything was going. He said, "It's over."

As if the ordeal of Pelle's death weren't enough for his family to withstand, also horribly difficult for them was the issue of alcohol, which had been introduced early on and which had since become *the* story of the town. In Sweden, drunken driving is not only newsworthy, but a disgrace akin to mortal sin. The people who caused the most pain to the Lindberghs were those who said, "He was just another drunk driver, and it's a good thing that he's off the road, so no one else will be killed." Statements like that were unfair to the memory of this vibrant young man, who, by all accounts of Flyers past and present, was one of the least likely to be involved in an incidence of driving while under the influence.

One of the lessons to be learned from this is that it's not just the overt and obvious drunk who is dangerous. There are so many of us who drink in circumstances where we don't know that we might be impaired, or when we are under situations of stress, that it's really only blind luck that we don't find ourselves in a coincidental and unexpected situation similar to that which struck Pelle. And in retrospect, there was such a string of coincidences involved on the night of Pelle's accident, that I think the story warrants telling. So, bear with me, please, while I relate those coincidences, the absence of any one of which would probably have prevented this tragedy:

1. After a number of consecutive games, Pelle did not play against Boston on Saturday night, and he was, therefore, fully rested.

2. Through some quirk in scheduling, the Flyers, who almost always play home games on Sunday nights, played Saturday night, but were *not* playing on Sunday.

3. In fact, they were not playing again until five days later, on Thursday night—also unheard of.

4. After fighting back from his injuries of previous seasons, and after the long pre-season grind and a dozen or so games of the regular season, Pelle was feeling rested and strong. With no curfew, either by the club or self-imposed, and with no more games for five days, he stayed out later than usual.

5. Pelle drove his sedan home to King's Grant in Marlton, New Jersey, where he learned that some friends from Sweden were visiting and that they were at the Coliseum, about fifteen minutes away, which not only housed the Flyers' practice and training center, but other facilities as well, including a restaurant and cocktail lounge.

6. Pelle decided to join his friends, but this time instead of taking the sedan, he took his small, fiery, $150,000 Porsche, which was Pelle's proudest material possession. It was a magnificent car which could fly like the wind, and Pelle loved driving it.

7. At the Coliseum Pelle drank beer with his friends, how much beer I don't know. I do know that it was far more than he usually drank, but not so much that he was noticeably impaired.

8. Also present at the Coliseum during the early morning hours was Ed Parvin, Jr., the son of the Flyers' unofficial real estate agent. Ed and his lady companion had been driven to the Coliseum by someone else, so they were without a car.

9. Good guy that he was, Pelle offered to drive them home.

10. The seating arrangement in the Porsche had Pelle behind the wheel, with Ed in the passenger's seat and with Ed's lady companion on the console between Pelle and Ed. (If the passenger's seat is sometimes called the "death seat," I don't know what being seated on the console should be called, besides "stupid.")

11. Off the three of them went, in the opposite direction from where Pelle lived, and on a road that Pelle had never driven before.

12. On that seemingly straight and safe road, just a minute or two from the Coliseum, there is one banana-shaped curve—a very difficult curve to judge when driving at night.

13. At the arc of that curve, there is a school with an elevated lawn in front, so that a retaining wall is necessary along the road. There are no other walls along that road. (In fact, there are hardly any walls in all of South Jersey.) If Pelle had been anywhere else on that road and had missed a turn, he probably would have ended up on someone's lawn. But the fates provided that the world's number one goaltender, with the greatest reflexes on earth, entered that unfamiliar curve at a high rate of speed and crashed into the wall.

14. If he had hit the wall at an angle, he would have careened off and caused some damage to the car, but probably no one would have been killed. And he would have hit just that way except for a

break in the wall to accommodate a set of steps. Instead of careen-
ing off, the Porsche struck the corner of the wall next to the steps,
and instantly Pelle was brain dead.

If Pelle had played for twenty-five more years, surely that series of coincidences would never have occurred again. And remove
just one of those fourteen factors. . .

Thinking about all of this did not relieve the grief that was felt
by me and by everyone else who knew Pelle. My wife and I cried,
especially at the terrible waste and stupidity of it all. Here was I,
who had dissipated myself and done a lot of stupid things; but
thanks to medical science, I was given a second chance. And here,
on the other hand, was this twenty-six-year-old young man, with his
whole life in place and doing everything right; but due to just one
simple error in judgment, his life was over. They say that the good
die young; but with good people like Barry Ashbee and Pelle Lindbergh, no matter how old they are, they're still too young to die.

The team was, of course, in a state of shock. So many of them
were so young that most had probably never experienced a death in
the family. The players and coaches met every day to grieve together, and to talk things out together, and to practice together,
however grimly. Already a closely knit group, they became an even
more tightly interdependent team, as together they faced this new
and unprecedented challenge.

The Thursday home game against Edmonton, which was to
have been a glorious confrontation of the two best teams in hockey,
now took on an insignificant meaning, and it had even become a
kind of burden for both teams to bear. The members of one team
were suffering under the stress of their goaltender and dear friend
having been killed; the other team was suffering with the thought of
having to play in this aura of uncomfortable grief.

Glen Sather offered to postpone the game, but the Flyers replied, "No, let's play it. Pelle would have wanted it that way."
Sometimes, I think, that's a convenient excuse to play a game. But
in this case, I'm sure it was a justifiable reason. And perhaps the
most appropriate tribute was the ceremony which took place on the
ice before that game, on Thursday, Nov. 14, 1985. Actually, more
than a ceremony, it was a memorial service for the Flyers' beloved
Pelle, the guy they called

# The Gumper

As a participant in the ceremony honoring Pelle, I don't ever recall having a harder thing to do than maintaining control of my emotions that night. It was, after all, just six weeks after my bypass surgery, and I was still shaky and still extremely moved by Pelle's death. But with the Stanley Cup Champion Edmonton Oilers lined up on one blue line, and the Flyers on the other, I took the microphone at center ice and began to speak from the heart:

"My good friends, what was to have been a shimmering evening of spectacular hockey, with the two greatest teams in the professional game, has become instead a deeply more personal occasion, as we, the Flyers family, the team, the organization, and, especially, you fans, gather to grieve over the loss of one of our own. But really, since Pelle Lindbergh's entire existence exuded nothing but the positive things in life, what I'd like to do this evening is to make the theme of our ceremony not the mourning of his death, but the celebrating of a life that we in Philadelphia were privileged to share."

At this point, I was relieved to hear a warm and loud round of applause.

"Please, first, let me assure you, particularly you youngsters, that our sorrow will diminish, and it will be replaced with rich memories that are part of the legacy that Pelle leaves us. The sorrow is going to ease, and we will endure, because that's really the marvel and the essence of life in its continuation. And when you talk of life, what a life filled with triumphs and achievements!

"I think it all goes back to 1967, when Pelle was eight, because in that year a team called the Flyers was born. And in the ensuing years this young Swede began to formulate a dream. In that dream, he wanted to make a trip to North America, to play hockey, and to conquer the toughest position in the world's toughest game. As he became a teen-ager, the dream began to refine itself even more: Pelle now wanted to meet that challenge in a place called Philadelphia, because there he had an idol who had already become a legend in this building. And it was his dream to become the best and to have his name on the Vezina Trophy alongside the name of his idol, Bernie Parent."

More applause, this time for Bernie, who was standing nearby.

"And so the work began: the Swedish National Team, the Olympics, and then, fate magically intervening, he was drafted by Philadelphia. And it took three years, and a superb relationship between the old legend, Bernie, and the new one, Pelle.

"I think that a marvelous part of this story is in the finest tradition of the melting pot of this country, when last year this Swede —with the help of a fellow countryman, a Czech, a Finn, Americans, and Canadians—had a spectacular year. And that team drove him to the top of the mountain, culminating last spring in Canada when his idol presented him with the highest achievement that could be given to him, the Vezina Trophy; and, finally, his name was there."

More applause.

"And so, that far-fetched hundred-thousand-to-one dream that began so long ago and so many thousands of miles away came true. He was the best. He was admired on two continents, he was honored in his homeland, and he was loved in Philadelphia. Add to that the personality and the marvelous manner that endeared him to everyone with whom he came in touch. And he was able to share all of this with a fiancée who was able to make his every day a joy, and a young lady whose courage and strength this past week have been magnificent.

"And then, add to all of that the ultimate—the ultimate triumph that, posthumously, through the miracle of transplant, he has given life to two people this week."

An ovation.

"It is the fulfillment of a life far beyond what any of us in this building can expect or hope to achieve in a lifetime twice or three times his twenty-six years; as Dave Poulin said yesterday, 'Pelle is indeed to be envied.' And in a sense, I think all of us here should be envied; because of the blessing of kind circumstance, we were permitted to be a part of this extraordinary person's life; and so, all of us in this building owe fate, and the Gumper, our eternal gratitude."

More applause followed, and after a touching invocation by Father John Casey, I again took the microphone, this time to introduce Pelle's family, and then his eulogist:

"Friends, I think you should know that the entire Lindbergh family is here tonight with Pelle's fiancée Kirsten, and they, along with the players and coaches and management of the Flyers, would like to thank each of you for your kind expressions of sympathy. Your support at this extraordinarily difficult time was so much appreciated.

"There was nobody more thrilled in all of hockey that a two-syllable chant in this building was changed from 'Bernie' to 'Pelle.' He said earlier in the week that losing Pelle was like losing a son, and I think there would be no more appropriate spokesman now than Bernard Marcel Parent."

Another ovation.

"Thank you, Gene. Mr. and Mrs. Lindbergh, Kirsten, friends and fans of Pelle, as I stand before you tonight, I feel that our hearts are one. Every single one of us has lost someone we respected, someone who made us very happy, and someone who made us awfully proud. Every single one of us has lost a friend, a man who loved hockey, a man who loved his family, and a man who loved the fans. No single moment in my entire career has been as difficult as this one. For this one is filled with flashbacks of one of the most memorable and positive relationships the game of hockey could ever produce. Flashbacks of a young, boyish goalie from Sweden, who relied on me to teach him how hockey in America is played. Flashbacks of how this same young, boyish goalie brought to my own life a sense of purpose and accomplishment. The papers have said that I was his hero. I wish I could tell you how much I admired him. . . I wish I could have only told him this. . .told him how much I admired him and how much I cared about him. . ."

As Bernie hesitated and wiped away a tear, the crowd helped to fill the pause by applauding.

"A goalie stands on a very lonely island, and I'm grateful that I was able to share some of that island with him, but for too brief a period. Pelle Lindbergh had become, without question, one of hockey's greatest goalies. And when death defeats greatness, we all mourn. And when death defeats youth, we mourn even more. But as we mourn, we must strive to define those qualities that Pelle left behind that can give us strength throughout this period, and beyond. I personally feel, and the team also feels, that Pelle Lindbergh left a legacy to all of us. . ."

More applause.

"Pelle Lindbergh had a sense of determination second to none. His spirit, his will, was made of iron. His ability to bounce back from defeat and setbacks will always be imprinted in my memory. His determination to become the best goalie in the National Hockey League was totally evident to all of us who knew him. And when he became the best, his superstar status did not go to his head. Pelle was still Pelle. Behind that white mask, and behind that super talent, was a boy—young, naive, and sensitive—whose friendly twinkle and engaging innocence drew people to him. Pelle was friendly, likable, anxious to please. He loved the fans, and he loved kids. When he signed autographs he knew he was making the fans happy, and that made him happy. Most of all, Pelle loved life, and the saddest thing about this tragedy is that while his positive attitude and love for life helped him to overcome defeat, it could not defeat death. But in a way, he has. Pelle is already giving life to others in what Mike Keenan has appropriately called 'the ultimate save.' "

More applause.

"Pelle, . . . You will always live . . . in our hearts. . . Pelle, we miss you."

Another ovation, the longest one of all.

Then, there was just one last thing that I wanted to say:

"There is one journey left for Pelle, to return to his beautiful Sweden, where a nation waits to greet its son. And that country, and his last trip, brought to my mind the last stanza of a familiar and haunting poem by Robert Frost:

> The woods are lovely, dark, and deep,
> But I have promises to keep,
> And miles to go before I sleep,
> And miles to go before I sleep.

"Indeed he has miles to go before he sleeps, but on the journey the affection of thousands of us, and the love of his teammates, will act as silent escorts, and will, we pray, make the Lindberghs' family peace . . . and Pelle's sleep . . . deep, enduring, and serene."

Following the playing of the National Anthem of Sweden, which concluded the ceremony, the crowd, one last time, chanted, "Pel-le, Pel-le, Pel-le. . ."

At that moment, I couldn't help thinking of all the people in the Delaware Valley who were probably crying, including the children who had been lucky enough to be Pelle's neighbors, and with whom he loved playing hockey on a nearby frozen pond. They must have been crying. I certainly was.

**A**fter Bernie's wonderful eulogy, and the beautiful Swedish anthem, and the chanting, and the tears, the ice was cleared, as if to give everyone fifteen minutes to regain composure. Both teams were told, "The best thing you can do, and the best tribute to Pelle, is to give us a whale of a game." And both teams gave us just that.

Adding further drama to the situation, Bob Froese had been injured and was not able to play. So, amidst all of this turmoil and grieving and the confrontation between the Flyers and the Oilers, up from Hershey to take Pelle's place (as if anyone could even hope to do that) came young Darren Jensen, a veteran of exactly one N.H.L. game—a seven-to-nothing loss during the previous season. And, of course, Jensen came up with the kind of performance which usually occurs only in one's dreams.

At one point during the second period, with the Flyers leading one to nothing, "The Great One," Wayne Gretzky, whirled down the ice on a short-handed break-away, but Jensen stoned him, one on one. I can recall looking across the arena to Kirsten and Mr. and Mrs. Lindbergh, and they were standing and applauding Darren Jensen. I can also recall thinking, "How, with all of the grief of a son dying the day before, can they cheer and applaud like that?" Then I realized that they were cheering and applauding Pelle's team for what they considered to be a tribute to Pelle, and rightfully so!

After the game, which was won by the Flyers, five to three, Pelle's father came down to the Flyers' dressing room to congratulate the players. With no knowledge of English, and with no way to verbally communicate with the players, Mr. Lindbergh nevertheless shook hands with them all and quite obviously *did* manage to communicate with them all. "Pragmatic" Swedes? I prefer "wonderful."

For the rest of the season, Pelle's locker remained empty except for a small Swedish flag at the top, where Pelle had placed it at the start of the season. Also for the rest of the season, Pelle's teammates wore his number "31" embroidered in black on the shoulders of their jerseys. And also for the rest of the season, I worked all of the games, home and away, because under the circumstances, it just didn't seem to me that anyone else should broadcast the games but the regular team of Gene Hart and Bobby Taylor.

Despite the constant reminders of their loss, and despite the emotional wringer that they had been through, the Flyers continued to win. On Sunday night, just three days after the Edmonton game, the Flyers extended the Islanders into overtime and then beat them, five to four, on a goal by Murray Craven. It was their thirteenth consecutive win, a new club record. Even during the thirty-five-game unbeaten streak of 1979-80, the Flyers had not gone through thirteen straight games without at least one tie.

As the victories continued to come, so did the individual honors. The Flyers' all-time left winger and all-time leading goal scorer, Bill Barber, was honored with a "night," while right winger Tim Kerr became the first Flyer to score fifty goals in three consecutive seasons (fifty-four, fifty-four, and fifty-eight goals), after three less-than-sensational injury-plagued seasons (twenty-two, twenty-one, and eleven goals). Kerr also set a new N.H.L. record for power-play goals in a season, with thirty-four. As Sign Man put it, "Kerrific!" And, as Mike Keenan put it, "Tim Kerr has the best touch around the net in the N.H.L. You might get an argument from the people on Long Island about Mike Bossy, or the people in Edmonton about Jari Kurri, but I don't know what kind of scientific tools you could use to judge it."

The only former player who would belong with that exclusive company would probably be Phil Esposito. As they used to say about his ability to score from around the goaltender's crease, "Sixty of his goals wouldn't add up to one good Bobby Hull slap shot!" But like those dribbling infield singles in baseball, they all look like line drives in the next morning's box scores!

On defense, Mark Howe was again superb. For the second time he was named a First-Team N.H.L. All-Star, and he was also awarded the Bobby Clarke Trophy as the Flyers' Most Valuable Player. Even more impressively, he won the league's Emery Edge Award, for the best plus-minus rating in the N.H.L. Mark finished the season with a rating of plus eighty-five (meaning that in even-strength situations he was on the ice for eight-five more goals scored by the Flyers than were scored against them). It was the second-highest rating ever, after Wayne Gretzky's plus ninety-eight in 1984-85. Second to Howe in 1985-86 was Mark's defense-partner, Brad "Beast" McCrimmon, with a rating of plus eighty-three, but it was only fitting that Howe should come out on top, since the award was to be presented by Mark's father, Gordie. Along with everything else, Mark Howe also became the all-time leading scorer among Flyer defensemen, in just his fourth year with the team.

After the staggering loss of Pelle Lindbergh, the fortitude of many members of the Flyers organization shone through. But the one player who had to endure the most out of that almost impossible situation was Bob Froese. There is a camaraderie among goaltenders that is altogether different from that of any other players in any other sport. From the time they were with the Maine Mariners together, Bob Froese and Pelle Lindbergh had been not only colleagues, but friends—as well as competitors for playing time. For whatever reasons, Froese seemed always to have been relegated to the secondary role as Pelle's back-up. Competitor that he was, Frosty would have done almost anything to have become number one. Now the job was his, but in the most distasteful possible manner. Not only had he won the position by default, but he had been left standing nearly alone on the goaltender's already lonely island, with only a raw and virtually untested rookie as his back-up.

In the spring, to give Froese someone a little older on whom he could lean, the Flyers traded a third-round draft choice for the oldest player in the league, Glenn "Chico" (after his resemblance to the main character in the old television series, "Chico and the Man") Resch, a veteran of thirteen seasons with the New York Islanders, the Colorado Rockies, and the New Jersey Devils. The records of the Flyers' four goaltenders during the 1985-86 season were as follows:

|  | W L T | G/A Ave. | Shutouts |
|---|---|---|---|
| Pelle Lindbergh | 6- 2- 0 | 2.88 | 1 |
| Bob Froese | 31-10- 3 | 2.55 | 5 |
| Darren Jensen | 15- 9- 1 | 3.68 | 2 |
| Chico Resch | 1- 2- 0 | 3.21 | 0 |

Despite all of the pressure that was exerted upon him, Bob Froese performed magnificently. His 2.55 goals-against average was the league's best, and, along with Darren Jensen, he shared the William M. Jennings Trophy, for the N.H.L.'s best combined goals-against average. Bob Froese not only led the N.H.L. for the season, but he ended the year with the best career winning percentage (.731) of any active goaltender in the league.

The Flyers led the Patrick Division (and the Wales Conference) for most of the season, but near the end they blew an eleven-point lead and saw the Washington Capitals take over the top spot. Unwilling to settle for second, the Flyers came on again down the stretch, beat Washington on the season's final night, five to three, and won the division title for the third time in four seasons, and for the ninth time in their nineteen-year history. The victory was their fifty-third of the year, tying the club record which they had set during the previous season, and giving Mike Keenan 106 wins in his first two seasons as coach of the Flyers.

It had been an emotionally draining and grueling year, and in the division semi-finals against the New York Rangers the Flyers were hollow examples of themselves. It was, once again, those guys in blue who did them in, but this time the hero was goaltender John Vanbiesbrouck, who would win the voting for the Vezina Trophy (over Bob Froese, who would finish second) with his stellar performance against the Flyers.

In the first game in Philadelphia, the Rangers easily took away the home-ice advantage with a six-to-two win. The Flyers then won a squeaker, two to one, and the series moved on to the Garden, where the Rangers again coasted, five to two. Just when it appeared that the Rangers would wrap it up in New York, the Flyers romped through a seven-to-one blowout, and the series headed back to the Spectrum for the fifth and deciding game. By this time, as it turned out, the Flyers had little left, and Vanbiesbrouck and the Rangers finished them off, five to two.

It had to be a satisfying victory for the man who was then coach of the Rangers, Ted Sator. The former Flyers assistant coach had been passed over for the head coaching job, when Mike Keenan was chosen instead. Sator's knowledge of the Flyers' players, systems and schemes certainly didn't hurt the Rangers' chances of pulling off the upset—especially against a Flyers team which had been through such a season of gut-wrenching tension.

And so, the year that was supposed to have brought the Flyers and the Oilers together again in the Stanley Cup Finals saw not only the Flyers, but the Oilers, too, eliminated in the early rounds of the playoffs. It was a strange ending to the strangest and most emotional year I've ever experienced.

**T**here is a hockey term which summarizes not only the abrupt conclusion of the Flyers' season, but also the sad underlying tone of the entire year. That term is

# Sudden Death

The Stanley Cup is hockey's symbol of excellence—not only excellence, but the highest standard of excellence—and that is what everyone in hockey strives for. But what stands out in my mind through the years, including several Stanley Cup years, are not the Cups, or the goals, or the saves, or the games, but the *people* who play the games. It is, after all, *people* who make sports exciting, and when people are stricken, it leaves such an empty feeling. And when good people like Bruce Gamble, and Bernie Parent, and Barry Ashbee, and Pelle Lindbergh are stricken, the hurt goes on for a long time.

But as I tried to say to the youngsters on the night of the ceremony for Pelle, time goes on, and wounds are healed, and the pain diminishes, and the good memories of good people remain with us. And forever indelibly etched in my mind will be the character of the two men to whom this book is dedicated, two marvelous examples of that kind of character for which the Flyers have stood all these years. Although Ash Can and the Gumper were taken from us far too soon, their sense of humanity remains with us today, and it is that sense of humanity, and the humanity of the game, that I cherish the most.

Barry Ashbee's death was not only mourned, but was turned into a positive force, a force which continues today in the form of fund-raising for the Barry Ashbee Leukemia Research Laboratories. Another cancer research fund was requested by the parents of Pelle Lindbergh, but an additional positive force which resulted from Pelle's death was the increased awareness of another pervasive threat to our nation, the threat of death due to driving while under the influence of alcohol.

Pelle Lindbergh was not, per se, a drinker, or a drunk, or a drunk driver. He was someone, like so many of us, who was slightly impaired and who was, therefore, not using the best of judgment concerning alcohol and a car. This is a striking problem for Philadelphians, for Pennsylvanians, for New Jerseyans, for Americans, for North Americans—and it has been a problem for generations. As drinking proliferates, and as ownership of cars increases, and as cars become matter-of-fact possessions of teen-agers, the number of people that we kill on the road is immense and horrifying.

Years ago, most of us didn't drive as kids. So, if we drank, which many of us did, we'd stumble and fall down, or maybe we'd fall off a bicycle or something silly like that, but it wasn't usually tragic. But today, we think nothing of gambling with the speed of an automobile. And today our automobiles are so easy to control that we can be lulled into a false sense of security, especially while we are listening to a beautiful stereo system under almost soundproof conditions. Even though we may be moving at fifty-five miles per hour or more, we are blissfully unaware that in a case of emergency we are not going to be able to react properly. And so, we do ourselves in, or we do other people in, or both.

So often as a school teacher, I read stories in the newspapers, and they're all pretty much the same, listing the names of one, two, three, or four youngsters, with the following line: "_____ were in a car last night that failed to negotiate a curve and hit a tree. _____ were killed, and _____ were seriously injured." With all of my years of experience, I translate that as, "Four (or however many) teen-agers, drunk or high, were going like hell in a car and blew themselves out." In cases like that, or in the case of Pelle Lindbergh, or even in the case of Lenny Bias, when people tend to be harsh with their criticism I just think, "It's such a terrible, terrible price to pay for one mistake."

That "one" mistake is made thousands of times every day, while many of us stand by and listen as someone laughs about how he got home "blind." And we listen as someone else brags about his capacity to drink. And we listen as someone else tells us, "Oh, I don't know how I was able to drive the car. It must have been on automatic pilot!" And we stand by, thereby giving our tacit approval, while these people carelessly take the lives of thousands and thousands of others, to the extent, as one judge put it, that "we have permitted sociably acceptable murder."

As a result of the Lindbergh incident, a young lady from a high school in South Jersey called me to ask about the possibility of my giving a speech to a growing S.A.D.D. chapter at her school. I told her that I'd love to come, and I did enjoy the opportunity of speaking to, and with, so many fine young people.

To my horror, the following weekend I read that the young lady who had invited me to speak had been struck down, along with three other students, by a drunken driver. Two of the students were not seriously injured, another had almost been killed, and the young lady who had invited me *had* been killed. The driver pleaded guilty and was sentenced to five years in a New Jersey prison.

Stories like that do not register upon the national consciousness. But if the P.L.O. or Lebanese or Libyan terrorists had machine-gunned those children on the road, this country would have erupted in violence. And if three thousand teen-agers had been machine-gunned, this country would have demanded reprisals, in order to prevent the reoccurrence of such attacks. And if twenty-three thousand Americans had been gunned down, we would probably have started World War III. And yet, every year in this country three thousand teen-agers and twenty-three thousand other Americans are killed as a result of drunk driving. And what do we do about it?

In the past several years we've had Americans hijacked and kidnaped and murdered to the degree that eight million people were terrified of traveling outside of what we consider the safe confines of the United States. We were frozen in fear because of what happened to a few dozen people. But what about the thousands we kill every year who are only traveling within their own "safe" neighborhoods?

If it seems as though I'm giving a speech, that's because I am. Since that first request to speak in January of 1986, I've been attempting to act as an unofficial spokesman of sorts, not as an expert on driving or drinking or alcohol, but just as an articulate person who is trying to express his own thoughts and feelings about what he gathered out of that incident which struck the Flyers so severely—the death of Pelle Lindbergh.

I had been aiming my speeches directly at drinkers until I realized that this message should also go to non-drinkers and near-drinkers, because we are the targets as well. We all have to understand that there's nothing *inherently* wrong with drinking. At the risk of having this book banned by most parents, I say, "Drink, and God bless you!" Even if you are an excessive drinker, that's your prerogative. If you want to pour it in your ears, and in your nose, and take it intravenously, and then fall over in a stupor every day of your life, that too is your prerogative—however stupid and unattractive it may be. But most of the sane people I know who are thinking seriously about this problem say, "*If* you drink, please, just honor us and other people by *not* getting behind the wheel of a car."

I think often of the young lady who started me speaking on this subject, and of the drunk driver who killed her. Afterwards in court, he was, of course, remorseful and contrite. When he was sentenced, he said, "Her death will be on my mind the rest of my life." That may be true, but unfortunately, the people we're killing don't have the option of thinking about *anything* for the rest of *their* lives.

The Flyers, and the Hart family, and many other families were tortured for weeks and months by their sadness over the unnecessary death of a friend. I hope that never has to happen to you.

With all of the disappointment and despondency which followed the 1985-86 season, I reminded myself that we live in a world which is filled with sorrow and with frightening prospects, and that we *should* feel sorrow sometimes, and that we *should* be frightened sometimes; but I also reminded myself that we must always retain the element of hope. To me, hopes and dreams are a large part of the glory of life, and they are also a large part of the marvel of sports.

Like most fans, at first I just sat there and resented the fact that "my" team had been unfairly ambushed, and I resented my idle state, and I wondered, "What will the world come to? And when?" Then, as I started to settle down and think more logically, and as my anger and dejection diminished a bit, I could sense a smile replacing my scowl, because I once again remembered and understood that, as bad as everything seems, and as down as you feel, you only have to wait a few months before the excitement of a new season begins to grow again.

And sure enough, in September there we were, ready to begin our twentieth season, and to begin the drive for a tenth division title, and a ninth semi-final, and a sixth final, and a third Stanley Cup. The memory of Pelle Lindbergh was still there, but Mike Keenan and Bob Clarke were back at work together, and the rest of the gang was all there, fit and raring to go. And the owners were there, and my broadcast partner, Chef Taylor was there, as were so many of the fans. The sad memories lingered, and they still do, but there was also a feeling almost of enchantment, because we had a chance to start all over again, to strive for excellence, to shoot for the glory, to go for that Cup. And all anyone can really hope for is another chance. Barry Ashbee and Pelle Lindbergh didn't get that chance, but in a sense, we honor them by our continuing drive for excellence.

In 1986 a third beloved member of the Flyers family had died —Kate Smith. To honor her memory, and to inaugurate the 1986-87 season, a video recording of Kate singing "God Bless America" was played on the Spectrum's new six-sided "ArenaVision" scoreboard, and the fans reacted almost exactly the way they had when Kate had been there in person. The queen is dead. Long live the queen!

Before the opening faceoff of the Flyers' twentieth season, each member of the starting line-up presented a commemorative plaque to his counterpart from the original line-up which the Flyers had started in the Spectrum's first N.H.L. game in 1967. For the record, the six starters for that first Flyers home game were: Ed Hoekstra (number 18), centering for left wing Leon "Cheesie" Rochefort

(9) and right wing Bill "Sudsy" Sutherland (11), with Joe Watson (3) and Jean Gauthier (5) on defense and Doug Favell (1) in goal. And before you correct me on those numbers, Favell did wear number "1" before Bernie (who was then number "30"), and Joe Watson wore "3" before he switched to "14," and Sutherland wore "11" before he switched to "10." Now that's *real* trivia! And I love it!

Also for the record, league president Clarence Campbell dropped the first puck between Ed Hoekstra and Pittsburgh's Art Stratton, who was traded to the Flyers later during that first season. And as you may recall from "The First Period," Bill Sutherland scored the game's only goal, and the first ever in the Spectrum, when he lifted a rebound of a Rochefort shot over Penguin goaltender Les Binkley at 2:59 of the third period.

However, the hardest part of that first game for Sutherland was not scoring the goal, but getting into the building before the game. Sudsy and several of his young teammates had been stopped at the gate by one of the Spectrum's new security guards and had been asked for their tickets. "But we're players," they said.

"I don't care who you are. Nobody gets in here without a ticket," replied the guard.

The rookie Flyers finally got around the rookie guards by finding an unattended gate and sneaking in. "It was kind of like being barred from your own party," said Sudsy.

But enough trivia from 1967. For the 1986 opener, there were also some new players in the Flyers' line-up, and fortunately, they had no trouble finding their way into the building. On defense, there were twenty-year-old J.J. Daigneault (who had been acquired from Vancouver in a trade for Rich Sutter and defenseman Dave Richter) and eighteen-year-old Kerry Huffman (the Flyers' first-round draft choice). In goal, surprisingly, was another rookie, twenty-two-year-old Ron Hextall, a sixth-round draft choice from the Brandon Wheat Kings back in 1982, and a third-generation N.H.L. player; his grandfather was Hall-of-Famer Bryan Hextall of the Rangers, who is perhaps best remembered for scoring the winning goal the last time the Rangers won the Cup in 1940; his father was Bryan Hextall, Jr., of the Rangers, Penguins, Flames, Red Wings, and North Stars. Mike Keenan's decision to start Hextall in goal was surprising, partly because it had been assumed by most that Bob Froese would start the opener, and partly because of the high-powered nature of the Flyers' opening night opponents, the Edmonton Oilers.

As it turned out, Ron Hextall's debut was definitely one for the book! The very first shot of the first period of the first game of the N.H.L. career of Ron Hextall was posted on the new scoreboard as an Edmonton goal. That was also Edmonton's last goal of the night, as the Flyers won another chiller over the Oilers, two to one. Hextall's record was 1-0-0. Kate Smith's went to 56-9-2.

Two nights later at Washington, Hextall again started and again allowed only one goal, as the Flyers easily routed the Capitals, six to one. The Flyers have had a tradition of early-season success, due in good part to the advantages of superior conditioning, and this time, despite the unpredictability of a rookie goaltender, they began their season with six consecutive wins—the best start in their twenty-year history.

And thus was inaugurated a new era in Flyers' history, a crazy-quilt up-and-down seesaw kind of an era...

# The Hex:
# Tall-Hexed-Tall-Hexed Era:
# 1986 to the Present

Perhaps the tone of this new era had been set at the pre-season media luncheon, when general manager Clarke had declared, "It is time for this team to do something." Hmmm. Let's see now, the team had gone to the finals just two years before and had won fifty-three games and a Patrick Division title in each of the two previous seasons. What was left to do?

Just as he had always done during his playing days, Clarke had been thoughtful, matter-of-fact, honest, and blunt. While everyone else may have been trying to gain respectability, the Flyers' mission was nothing short of winning the Cup for a third time.

Even before the arrival of Ron Hextall, the Flyers had become an odd team, due not so much to bizarre behavior, but due to the odd fact that the odd years were winning years and the even years were not so productive. Little did we know at the time, but this odd-even-odd-even phenomenon was to become even more phenomenal during the Hextall Era. A year of standing *Tall* would inevitably be followed by a year of being *Hexed: Tall-Hexed-Tall-Hexed-Tall*...

In another sense, the advent of the Hextall Era represented a continuation of the Flyers' history of great goaltenders, which began with Parent, and continued through the early careers of Pete Peeters and Bob Froese, and then through the Roman candle career of Pelle Lindbergh. Most teams would have been thrilled to have developed even *one* goalie like any of those, and the Flyers have been blessed with *five,* as well as many other good ones. And, of course, in hockey, success as a team starts with the most important (and the only sixty-minute) position, goaltender.

The advent of the Hextall Era also meant the hexing of one of the aforementioned five fabulous Flyer puckstoppers, Bob Froese. As Hextall continued to play, and play well, Froese kept quiet—at first. But those close to the team knew that eventually he would lose his cool. It finally happened when he made it known that he was "not mentally prepared to play."

When Mike Keenan learned of this, Froese was not permitted to dress, even as a back-up, for sixteen games. He finally played in early December, beating Vancouver, six to three. However, when his post-game speech revealed that he was "playing for himself," it became clear to all that he would soon be playing (or not playing) for a team other than the Flyers.

In deciding whether to play Froese or Hextall, the Flyers quickly determined that it was more important to give Hextall the only quality he lacked, experience, because it was felt that he, not Froese, was the goaltender who could help them to achieve their ultimate goal—the Cup. By the middle of December, Hextall's record was a robust 19-6-2, with a 2.53 goals-against average. And exactly one week before Christmas, Bob Clarke surprised everyone, not because he traded Bob Froese, but because he traded him to the Flyers' playoff nemesis, the New York Rangers, for a virtually unknown Swedish defenseman and a number two draft choice.

Obviously Clarke had been hoodwinked by the Rangers, who needed a reliable back-up for John Vanbiesbrouck, and who got a first-line player in exchange for a so-so, rather aged piece of excess baggage, just because Bob Froese had expressed his unhappiness with being a back-up. Or was it the Rangers who were hoodwinked by Clarke?

As a member of the Flyers' management team stated, "Look at it this way. We were getting rid of Froese because we thought the way to be successful in the playoffs was to go with one guy. Like we did with Bernie. Like the Islanders did with Billy Smith, the Canadiens with Ken Dryden, the Oilers with Grant Fuhr, and even last season, the Canadiens with Patrick Roy.

"Look at it our way. We were beaten by the Rangers in the playoffs last season by Vanbiesbrouck. We were more worried about Vanbiesbrouck than Froese. And maybe if we traded Froese there, Vanbiesbrouck wouldn't be so sharp.

"We needed a good defenseman, and we thought Kjell Samuelsson would help. We also considered that maybe we could upset the Rangers' hot goalie. Maybe we figured that Froese would screw up the Rangers."

The "so-so" Swedish defenseman, Kjell (pronounced "Shell") Samuelsson, was anything but ordinary. At six feet, six inches, and 235 pounds, the Stalk-Stork-"Killer Flamingo" was not only one of the biggest, if not *the* biggest player in the N.H.L., but along with all of that size he had a ranginess which made him extremely difficult to play, especially around the net. As ex-everybody Ron Duguay put it, "Playing close to Samuelsson is like swimming in a bed of seaweed." He might have added, "with an octopus lurking nearby."

Like most Swedes, he was not known as a punishing player, and during his first months in Philadelphia the opposition really went after him, mercilessly running at him to test his courage. We had no idea of his temperament either, until he had his nose broken, and he came back right away, and fought through all of the rough stuff, and eventually became, quite literally, Mark Howe's right-hand man, and part of the Flyers' top defensive pairing, upon whom the team would depend in crucial situations.

Led by a defense bolstered by the addition of Ron Hextall, and then Kjell Samuelsson, along with the outstanding play of defensive stalwarts Brad Marsh, Doug Crossman, Brad McCrimmon, and First-Team N.H.L. All-Star Mark Howe, the Flyers allowed only 245 goals, the league's second-best total, and only four more than Montreal's league-leading total of 241. After Bob Froese took his 3-0-0 record up the turnpike to New York, the Flyer goaltenders' records ended up looking like this:

| | W | L | T | G.A. |
|---|---|---|---|---|
| Ron Hextall | 37 | 21 | 6 | 3.00 |
| Chico Resch | 6 | 5 | 2 | 2.91 |

As so often happens when a team has a great defense, the offense soared also, with a Wales Conference–leading 310 goals, 114 of those by the line of Poulin, Propp, and Kerr. And if you listed Wayne Gretzky in a league of his own, Tim Kerr was the N.H.L.'s leading scorer, with a second consecutive fifty-eight-goal season, and a fourth consecutive season of fifty or more.

Along with all of those flashy statistics, the most important one was the Flyers' tenth division title, and by the relatively huge margin of fourteen points over the second-place Washington Capitals. In fact, only one team in the entire league had more points than the Flyers, and that was the reigning superteam, Gretzky's Edmonton Oilers, who finished with 106, just 6 better than the Flyers' even 100. The oddsmakers had those two teams, the N.H.L.'s two *best* teams, destined to meet in the Stanley Cup Finals for the second time in three seasons. But first, of course, one has to look at the playoffs as a whole new season, with sudden death lurking around every corner.

The hauntingly familiar first-round playoff opponent was, naturally, that most natural of rivals, the New York Rangers, featuring the goaltending tandem of Vanbiesbrouck and Froese. No team takes greater joy from beating another than the Flyers and the Rangers take from beating (or better yet humiliating) each other. And now they would meet in the playoffs for the eighth time since their first playoff meeting in 1974, when the Broad Street Bullies upset the Broadway Blues on the way to their first Cup. Since that time, the Flyers had all too often stubbed their toes on the Rangers, and as recently as the previous season, when the hated New Yorkers had won the deciding and, for the Flyers, season-ending game in Philadelphia.

The outlook again appeared grim when, in Game One in Philadelphia, Vanbiesbrouck shut out the Flyers, three to nothing. But then the Flyers and Ron Hextall came on with gusto, gaining a split in Philadelphia, and then a split in New York, as Hextall avenged the earlier shutout with a three-to-nothing shutout of his own in New York. Along the way, Bob Froese also won one, and then lost one, for a split against his former teammates.

The Flyers took a three-to-two lead into Game Six in the Garden, where the Flyers atoned for some historically horrifying final games against the Rangers, who, of course, had always seemed to go out of their way to rub salt into the Flyers' wounds. This time the Flyers reveled in a five-to-nothing victory, with Hextall earning his second shutout of the series, one more than he had recorded during the entire regular season.

The Flyers relished the early emptying of the Garden, whose occupants apparently could not bear to witness their idols being hopelessly outclassed by the detested Flyers. The Flyers also relished the expertise of their rookie goaltender against his grandfather's team, along with the realization that they apparently had indeed made the right choice when they had decided that their best hope for a Cup was not with Bob Froese, but with Ron Hextall in goal.

Unlike the Edmonton Oilers, who had quickly dispatched their first-round opponent, the Flyers paid the price of a six-game series against an archrival. Captain Dave Poulin had suffered a painful cracked rib, J.J. Daigneault a severely sprained ankle, Murray Craven a broken foot, and, although it was not publicly known at the time, the Flyers' biggest gun, Tim Kerr, was playing with a badly damaged left shoulder.

Against the Islanders in the Patrick Division Finals, Kerr collected a hat trick in the first game, but later in the series his shoulder popped out for good. Not only had his glorious season ended, but so had his glorious run of four consecutive fifty-goal seasons.

"I guess it was my fault," said Kerr, who had been wearing a harness to help hold his shoulder in place. "Maybe I should have called it quits earlier and maybe had an operation earlier. But I wanted to play so badly. And I figured if I could just get some strength, I could help."

Following Kerr's super show in Game One, in Game Two the Islanders got a goal in the final seconds for a two-to-one win and a split in Philadelphia. The Flyers won twice on the Island to lead the series, three games to one, but then lost at the Spectrum and again on the Island, and for the second time, a Flyers-Islanders series would be decided by Game Seven in Philadelphia.

In 1975, the Flyers had won the seventh game of the semi-finals, four to one, on the way to their second Cup. In 1987, the result was similar, thanks in good part to Dave Poulin, who had his rib cage pumped full of painkiller, and who then made the key passes on two of the Flyers' three first-period goals, which initiated a five-to-one victory.

For the second time in three seasons, and for the ninth time in their twenty-year history, the Flyers were headed into the Stanley Cup Semi-Finals, or, in this case, the Wales Conference Finals. The opponent this time would be the league's best defensive team, the Montreal Canadiens, a team the Flyers had met twice before in the playoffs, neither time with much success. In the 1973 semi-finals, the Flyers' *first* semi-finals, Montreal had won four straight, following an overtime loss in Game One. In the 1976 finals, Montreal had swept all four games, although all four had been tantalizingly close. Overall then, Montreal had won eight of nine, and eight straight in playoff competition against the Flyers.

There was good reason for a feeling of trepidation, and not just because of the Flyers' poor playoff history against the Canadiens. For, once again, the Flyers had paid a stiff price for not wrapping up a series quickly, as the seven games with the Islanders had added Tim Kerr to the list of wounded, and Dave Poulin had returned to that list following his courageous captain's effort in Game Seven. Outwardly, the Flyers were optimistic about their chances against Montreal, but beneath the surface there was real concern.

"What is it? What is it that makes these things happen to us?" Mike Keenan had asked. "Do we live wrong or something? Our captain and our leading goal scorer. Two years ago, it was the same thing. What is it? You don't like to cry injury, but Jeezus Murphy, this is crazy. This is bad, bad, bad..."

The feeling was that it was going to take a miracle to get past Montreal and reach the finals.

Again, the Flyers could manage only a split in the first two games in the Spectrum, where their playoff record was now a meager seven up and six down. The only victory resulted from a wacky, somewhat fluky goal in overtime of the first game. It was scored by Ilkka Sinisalo, who always seemed to specialize in game-winning goals. This particular one, though, was probably the slowest goal ever scored in N.H.L. history. It was a little bleeder which just trickled...trickled...trickled...and took so long to cross the goal line that I almost wondered why the whistle didn't blow for delay of game. At any rate, the puck finally trickled across the line, and the Flyers survived, four to three.

In Game Two, the Canadiens ripped the Flyers, five to two, and it was the Habs who now held the home-ice advantage, as the underdog and undermanned Flyers traveled to Montreal for Game Three. Matters looked even grimmer in that game, as the Flyers fell behind, two to nothing, a score that could have been four or five to nothing, had it not been for the brilliance of Ron Hextall.

Then, with Brian Propp continuing to turn his reputation as a playoff bust into one of playoff hero, and with little Pelle Eklund turning on his jet-skates, the Flyers bounced back to win Game Three, four to three, and then their second straight in the Forum, six to three, with Eklund getting the only playoff hat trick ever by a Flyer against Montreal.

And speaking of Pelle Eklund, the diminutive eighth-round 1983 draft choice out of Stockholm, Sweden, I am sorely pressed to think of a Flyer who offensively so dominated any playoff series. Perhaps Reggie Leach in 1976 against Boston; perhaps Billy Barber in 1980 against Minnesota; but no Flyer ever had a more magnificent offensive series than Pelle Eklund in 1987 against Montreal.

Once again, though, with a three-to-one lead in the series, and a chance to wrap it up in Philadelphia, the Flyers could not finish off an opponent early, as Montreal won for the second straight time in the Spectrum, and by the identical score of five to two. That carried the series back to the Forum, where everyone, including me, felt that there was absolutely no way that the Canadiens could lose three straight to the Flyers, or to anyone else, ever!

It was an unseasonably hot, muggy day in Montreal for Game Six, and the Flyers had an unreasonably hot, muggy greeting for the host Canadiens, even before the first puck was dropped. First, a little background on the pre-game games people were playing. Montreal's Claude Lemieux had a ritual of shooting the puck into the opponent's net at the end of the warm-up, and for four games the Flyers had tried out different methods of thwarting him. This time, Flyer tough guy Ed "Boxcar" Hospodar tried to unnerve him by throwing punches at him.

Since this came about at the end of warm-ups, most of the players were in the dressing rooms. Doug Crossman had even been in the bathroom, attending to a nervous pre-game habit. When he rushed back onto the ice to join his teammates, he was wearing not a uniform and skates, but a robe and slippers.

The Flyers' leader in penalty minutes, Rick Tocchet, made it out of the dressing room, but he was then physically restrained by conditioning coach Pat Croce, one of the few members of the Flyers' entourage who could manage such a feat. Another Flyer who missed the ensuing fracas was Ron Hextall, and not because he *meant* to miss it. He was headed off by Mike Keenan, who had literally thrown himself against the dressing room door. If any Flyer was to be tossed, Keenan wanted to make sure that it would *not* be *this* Flyer. Hextall promised that he wouldn't get into a fight, but Keenan prevailed, as he inevitably did.

Since all of this excitement had occurred during warm-ups, some twenty minutes before game time, there were no officials in attendance, at least not at the start of it all. Probably for that reason, only Ed Hospodar was banished. But the Flyers' outdated reputation for "Broad Street Bullyism" (if not downright goonery) was rekindled by the Montreal media, as well as by the media of every other N.H.L. region.

Eventually a hockey game broke out, as they say, and another superior effort by Eklund and Hextall disposed of the Canadiens, four to three. The picture in my mind's eye that summed it all up was a scene during a Montreal time-out in the game's final seconds. After this exhausting six-game series, Larry Robinson had just slumped down on the ice, crumpled up like a rag doll, or a straw man, totally spent, totally limp.

It was that kind of series, and it was one of the great moments and memories in Flyers history, for the Flyers had done something no other visiting team had ever done in the long history of the playoffs: They had won all three games of a series in Montreal. In three playoff series against the Canadiens, the Flyers had lost six of seven at home, but had won four of eight in the Forum, a building where they had hardly won that many in twenty years of regular-season competition.

The prize for out-toughing Montreal was a trip to the Stanley Cup Finals, for the sixth time in the fourteen years since the Flyers' first finals and first Cup in 1974. The ultimate opponent, for the second time in three years, would be the Edmonton Oilers. It was a fascinating matchup, for, as Detroit coach Jacques Demers put it, "The Oilers have the most talented players in hockey, but the Flyers are the best *team* in hockey."

Unfortunately, however, the "best team" was again missing some of its key people. As had been the case in the finals of two years before, Dave Poulin was injured, and Tim Kerr was out. Also hampered by various physical problems were Ilkka Sinisalo, Ron Sutter, and Peter Zezel. It figured to be an all-Edmonton series.

But, hurting or not, as Mark Howe said, "Forty guys are going to be out knocking heads, doing whatever they can. The team that wins, they're going to remember this for the rest of their lives. The team that doesn't, they're going to remember that, too, for the rest of their lives."

All of us who were privileged to be there will remember it, also. It was that good. As Frank Dolson wrote in the *Inquirer,* "It's rare that ice hockey—or any other sport—soars to the heights that the Flyers and the Oilers attained during this championship series.

At a time when both teams should have been dragging, they were storming, pushing themselves to the limit and, seemingly, beyond. It wasn't necessary to be a hockey fan to get caught up in this drama. . ."

And, as Wayne Gretzky put it, "There are three parts to the season—the regular season, the playoffs, and the Stanley Cup Finals. And when you get to this point, there is nothing mentally or physically that should stop you."

The drama began in the very first game in Edmonton. The Flyers outshot the Oilers and carried a two-to-one lead into the third period. But then, for the first time in ten playoff games, and for just the second time *all season,* they lost a game they had led after two periods, four to two.

Game Two was another tight one, which was won, three to two, on a goal by Jari Kurri well into an overtime period.

The Flyers came home realizing that they had to win, at worst, four of five against the world's "most talented" hockey club. The sense of impending doom became almost overwhelming when the Oilers fired out to a three-to-nothing lead in the second period of Game Three at the Spectrum. Then, just when the outlook was at its gloomiest, the Flyers began "Amazing Comeback Number One." Consecutive goals by Murray Craven, Peter Zezel, Scott Mellanby, Brad McCrimmon, and Brian Propp resulted in a satisfying must win, five to three.

In Game Four, the Great Gretzky was *too* great, and the Oilers shut down the Flyers, four to one, in the Spectrum. The series definitely appeared to be over. Down three-to-one in games, the Flyers needed to win three straight, two of those in Edmonton, where they had won only one of six previous playoff games.

Worse yet, Flyer-haters were handed even more anti-Flyer ammunition when, late in the game, Ron Hextall lost his poise and slashed forward Kent Nilsson with a two-hander across the front of the leg. Nilsson went down, everyone was aghast, and Hextall was assessed a major penalty. Nilsson soon returned to play, but that incident had everyone fuming, fussing, and fighting once again.

Returning to Edmonton for Game Five, that city was ready to celebrate. A victory parade had already been planned, and the P.A. announcer greeted the crowd at the Northlands Coliseum with, "Are you ready?"

Both the crowd and the Oilers appeared to be, as, for the third straight game, the Oilers took a two-to-nothing lead in the first period. Then came "Amazing Comeback Number Two," capped by a third-period goal by Rick Tocchet for a four-to-three victory. Once again, Ron Hextall had been superb in goal, despite being taunted all night long by the Edmonton crowd, who wouldn't let him forget the slashing incident of the previous game.

Back to a friendlier crowd for Game Six, the *thirteenth* playoff game of the season in the Spectrum. The night began with a video-taped "God Bless America" by Kate Smith, a charm that had worked in Game Three. And once again, the Oilers took their by-now-traditional two-to-nothing lead.

In both finals against Philadelphia, Edmonton had played marvelously, not only on offense, but on *defense*, a fact easily obscured by all of their highly publicized firepower. In Game Six, the Oilers again shut down the Flyers' offense, and were leading, two to one, after two periods, and midway into the third.

Then, with the clock dwindling, Brian Propp, who had enjoyed a marvelous series, banged a power-play goal over the right shoulder of Grant Fuhr, and "Amazing Comeback Number Three" was underway. Moments later, with the Flyers pressing in the Edmonton zone, and with the crowd on its feet, the puck kicked off the boards and slid back toward the blue line. The Flyers were changing their defensive pairing at that moment, and flying off the bench from the other blue line came J.J. Daigneault, who took two or three strides and, as he hit the blue line, wound up and blew a long shot from just inside the blue line along the left-wing boards. The puck flew past the left knee of Scott Mellanby, through the screened Fuhr, hit the post on the long side, and went in.

The Spectrum, long noted for its noise quotient, absolutely exploded. It was an extraordinary moment for me and, of course, for J.J., whose smallish stature had perhaps precluded his being a top-line N.H.L. defenseman. But he had always worked diligently, and despite not having been played a lot by Mike Keenan, he had come through with that one bright shining moment, which was just enough to give the Flyers that near-miracle third rousing comeback win, three to two.

This beautiful series between the number one and number two teams in the N.H.L. would now return to Edmonton, and for the first time in seventeen years, the league had a seventh game in the Stanley Cup Finals. It was such a special occasion that, the night before the game, an entourage of players from the 1974 and 1975 Cup teams flew into Edmonton on invitation from the Flyers. In all, fourteen former Bullies were in attendance for the Flyers' first and only Game Seven of a Stanley Cup Final series.

Said Mark Howe, "All we've done the last two games is just try to pretend it's the seventh game." It was no longer necessary to pretend. For the fourth time in the playoffs—including the seventh game against the Islanders and the previous two games against the Oilers—the Flyers were in a must-win situation. They had learned not only to live with pressure, but to thrive on it, and to let it inspire them to new heights.

For the Oilers, pressure was a new thing to deal with, and no one knew how they would react, especially when, for the first time in the series, the Flyers recorded the first goal. Implausibly, with an early five-on-three power play, Murray Craven had scored, and there were thoughts of, "Could it actually happen? Despite all of the injuries and other adversity? Why not? A team of destiny, right?"

Well, almost. But not quite. With one of those absolutely electric plays that leaves you (or at least me) almost breathless, Gretzky, Messier, and Anderson worked a perfect triangular passing pattern, and Messier scored to tie the game. From that time, it became a matter of attrition, with neither team yielding.

As the game wore on, Edmonton appeared to be stronger and stronger, especially defensively, while the Flyers appeared to be frailer by comparison. The Oilers' marksman, Jari Kurri, made it two to one in the second period, as the season headed into its concluding period. By then, the Flyers were but a hollow shell of themselves, totally drained, with only Hextall's gallant effort holding them in the game.

With less than three minutes left, Glenn Anderson fired through the five hole on Hextall, the score became three to one, and everyone knew that it was finally over. The Oilers were champions again, after a simply wonderful seven-game series in which the better team had eventually won, but not before they were hammered, scratched at, and battled to the limit by a fierce underdog. To me, that series reflected everything that's good about sports, and about those two teams, and about the game of hockey.

Not only had the Flyers taken the "most talented" team in hockey to the final minutes of Game Seven, it had also become obvious that the Conn Smythe Trophy for the M.V.P. of the playoffs would be awarded for the fourth time ever to a member of a team that did *not* win the Cup. Ron Hextall would become the second Flyer to be so honored, the first having been Reggie Leach in 1976.

And for you trivia and numerology buffs, both wore Flyer uniform number "27."

After his valiant series of series against the playoff nemesis Rangers, followed by the Islanders, Canadiens, and Oilers—the only three teams to win the Cup since the Flyers had last won it in 1975—no choice other than Hextall would have made any sense. I was thinking, "What a wonderful way to end the best playoff series and first seven-game final in memory, if the fans could put aside the one moment when the young man lost his poise and did something foolish. If, when the announcement comes, they could just forget the slash and give a salute of 'well done,' with a little applause for a performance which had been not just gutsy and glorious, but positively breathtaking!"

The Edmonton fans blew it, I thought, by booing the inevitable announcements of Hextall's name as number one star, and then as Conn Smythe winner. It was a shaggy, sad, and disappointing note by some fans who missed a marvelous moment, and thereby took a little edge from their own victory. After all, if you can't be gracious in winning it all, when can you?

And so, a few hours before the arrival of the month of June, the N.H.L.'s longest season was over. And how long was the longest? If you count pre-season, it was 116 games long: 10 pre-season; 80 regular season; and 26 playoff games, 2 shy of the maximum possible of 28 playoff games.

In the most difficult and demanding sport we know in North America, the Flyers had played twenty-six pressurized playoff games in fifty days, or an average of one every-other-day for seven weeks, plus travel. Another way of looking at twenty-six post-season games is that they comprise the equivalent of one-third of a season. They were also four games *more* than the previous playoff record for any N.H.L. team. No wonder that the Flyers' legs were like so much black and blue jelly by the time the curtain finally fell.

As Flyer scout Reg Higgs put it, "You know the playoffs are too long when three guys suffer broken bones in the playoffs—and come back to play again."

Sinisalo, Craven, and Poulin did that, although Poulin had trouble enough breathing, not to mention taking a hard check into the boards, or delivering one, which he never hesitated to do. Sutter, Crossman, and Zezel also played hurt. And, of course, as Mike Keenan pointed out, it could be argued that the Flyers would have won if their leading scorer, Tim Kerr, had been able to play at all against Edmonton, even if only on the power play. As it turned out, the first of Kerr's multiple and complicated shoulder surgeries was performed after the season, and Kerr's damaged shoulder would never regain its previous strength.

"This was the hardest Cup we ever won," said a man who should know, Wayne Gretzky. "When we were leading three-one in games, everybody was saying: 'Where's the parade? Where's the party?' Then, all of a sudden, it was three-three. We had a chance to go from the best team ever to goats. Well, we had to play the game of our lives to win, and we did it."

Edmonton coach Glen Sather called the Flyers "a terrific hockey team" and added, "If this game had been in Philly, I think they probably would have won."

So, are the playoffs too long? Or is the much-maligned regular season too long? Well, the Oilers earned that seventh game at home by winning the regular-season point total over the Flyers. That was what Mike Keenan had been pushing for all season, pushing *too hard* many said, especially some of his own players. Draw your own conclusions. It's a certain bet that the season will *not* be shortened.

In the dressing rooms after the game, the winners were ecstatic and grateful. The losers were momentarily crushed, not because of the money the defeat had cost them, but because of the defeat itself.

It was refreshing to see professionals play the game for the sake of the game, for the sake of their teammates, and, even for the sake of the fans. Win or lose, those forty or so hockey players had put on a fabulous show, and along the way, they had shown just how much some pros really do care.

Ron Hextall cried unashamedly, as did Murray Craven, and even the veteran, Mark Howe, who doused his head with water so that the cameras wouldn't detect his tears. Said Howe through all of that emotion, "We fought like crazy to get back in the series, and we fought like crazy tonight. It just wasn't to be."

Rick Tocchet added, "I just think we ran out of gas, put it that way. I feel empty a little bit. I feel disappointed. But I also feel proud to be part of this hockey team. I just want to go around this room and hug every guy."

Somewhere in the course of the four-and-a-half-hour flight home that night, the mood of the team began to lighten. Finally, the players were able even to laugh amongst themselves. After all, they knew that they were young and good and on the way to getting even better. In their minds, this Stanley Cup thing wasn't over with.

As Ron Hextall explained on the plane, "We gave it our best, played our hearts out, and there's nothing we can do about it now. This has been the best year of my life, because we've got a great bunch of guys who dedicated themselves totally to hockey. All we have to do now is look forward to next year.

"We have a lot of good young hockey players. We have a great base. We have a great team that's going to be here a lot of years."

It was a happy team and a happy Ron Hextall who walked off the plane the next morning carrying the Conn Smythe Trophy. Rightfully, the Flyers were given a hero's welcome by the several thousand who greeted them at the airport. In return, the Flyers told the waving faithful that they would not rest until the Stanley Cup was back in Philadelphia.

I can't recall another time that any team was so universally praised when it didn't win. It was a special and appropriate measure of credit and adulation for a team that had given its best. I remember thinking, "May it always be so!"

W hile the many memories of that first season of the Hextall Era blur with time, the memories of Hextall himself stand out in bold relief. Even after that most vivid of memories, the mindless slashing of Kent Nilsson, Hextall simply shrugged off the torrent of criticism, never permitting it to affect his concentration. Amazingly, he just seemed to become even more efficient and even more tenacious.

It was a truly remarkable performance by a truly remarkable young player. And since we've already named an era after him, we really should say a little bit more about the man his teammates call

# Hex

After leading the Hershey Bears to the Calder Cup Finals during the previous season, Ron Hextall was named a First-Team American Hockey League All-Star *and* A.H.L. Rookie of the Year.

After leading the Flyers to the Stanley Cup Finals the following season, Hextall was named a First-Team National Hockey League All-Star, but he was *not* named N.H.L. Rookie of the Year. Luc Robitaille of Los Angeles won that particular Calder Cup, just as New York's Steve Vickers had won over Bill Barber in 1973.

Why? Probably for the same reason that Pete Peeters failed to win following the Year of the Streak. And before that, Rick Mac-Leish. And before that, Bobby Clarke. In fact, the Calder Cup is one of the very few awards which has never been won by a Flyer.

The voting process may have something to do with that. Each N.H.L. team is represented by the votes of three writers. That gives the Flyers three votes to start with, but it gives the New York press six votes (for the Rangers and Islanders), or nine, if you count the nearby North Jersey Devils. And the Flyers have never been especially popular in New York.

As a rookie, Ron Hextall did, however, collect his share of *other* awards and accomplishments. Among them were these:

- Thirty-seven wins, a record for a Flyers rookie, and the fourth highest ever for an N.H.L. rookie goaltender

- Flyers record for assists by a goaltender

- Led the N.H.L. in: Wins
  Save percentage
  Games played
  Minutes played

- N.H.L. record for penalty minutes by a goaltender (104)

- N.H.L. All-Rookie Team

- N.H.L. First-Team All-Star

- Only rookie to be named to the All-Star Team and to Team Canada for Canada Cup Series vs. Soviets

- Vezina Trophy as N.H.L.'s best goaltender

- Including playoffs, new N.H.L. record for games played in a season (92), surpassing Bernie Parent's record (90) in Flyers' first Cup season (1973-74)

- New N.H.L. playoff record for minutes played (1,540)

- Tied N.H.L. record for playoff wins (15)

- Bobby Clarke Trophy as Flyers' Most Valuable Player (for the first of three consecutive seasons)

- Conn Smythe Trophy as N.H.L.'s Most Valuable Player in Stanley Cup Playoffs

Perhaps some day Hextall will be able to appreciate all of this. But when asked about the Conn Smythe Trophy following Game Seven, he had everything in perfect perspective, as he answered with red-rimmed eyes and a shy, quavering voice, "It's a great honor, but I'll trade it for a Stanley Cup any day." He went on to express his feelings about Glenn Anderson's clinching goal, which had sent him, literally, to his knees: "It was a hard shot, a tough one to stop, but I wish I would have done it, because I was trying to keep our team in the game. But after it went in, I realized our season was over.

"I feel tired, because we lost. If we had won, I wouldn't be feeling so tired. And this trophy would have meant a lot more if we had won the Cup."

Rick Tocchet expressed the feelings of his teammates about Hextall when he said, "He was like God out there. I thought fate would give it to him. I really did."

But a couple of nearly perfect plays by the Oilers had intervened, and when it was over, Hextall had lumbered into the Flyers' dressing room and wept.

"He was pretty broken up," said Glenn "Chico" Resch, the thirty-eight-year-old veteran who had spent the season serving not just as Hextall's back-up, but as the rookie's mentor and father figure as well. "He was too emotional to even say anything. You know, it's usually the guy who gives the most who releases the most emotion afterward."

Resch had been an avid student of goalies past and present, and an ardent collector of hockey memorabilia. And in this, Resch's final season, Hextall may have given the old veteran his most vivid memory of excellence. "Some of this stuff may sound corny, but I don't usually talk out of emotion," Resch said. "But Ronnie is probably the most graceful goalie who has ever played the game. And I'm not just talking about his stopping the puck, I'm talking about the way he moves across the crease. It's like ballet.

"I mean, if there was ever a guy you can run a tape of and put music to it, it would be Ronnie. I know one thing, I'm keeping the tapes of his performances in the playoffs, and if I ever get to a point where I can teach young goalies, I'm going to show them these tapes and tell them, 'This is the standard, guys, try to reach it, but I doubt if you can.'

"Let's face it, he was our Gretzky. In all my years, and there's been a lot of them, I've never seen a guy give so much, night in and night out. I'm telling you, this kid is going to be the best in the league for at least another ten years."

And if, as Chico put it, Hextall was the Flyers' Gretzky, how did Gretzky himself feel about Hextall? When asked about him following Game Seven, the Great One merely repeated his earlier assessment, that the Flyers' rookie goaltender was "probably the best goalie I've ever faced."

And how did an upstart rookie get so far so fast, playing what I believe to be the toughest position in all of sports? I think that the story of the arrival of Ron Hextall was best told by Ken Rappoport of the Associated Press:

### 'Hex' Marks the Spot of Flyers' Future Success

When Ron Hextall came to the Philadelphia Flyers' training camp, he had to overcome obstacles that few rookies have ever faced.

For one thing, he carried the burden of a well-known family name that included a grandfather, father, and uncle who preceded him with some hard-nosed exploits in the N.H.L.

For another, his competition included Bob Froese, an award-winning goaltender of the previous season who had helped the Flyers gain the second-best record in the league.

On top of that, the Flyers' management put an extra hex on Hextall with praise that bordered on hyperbole, comparing this lanky twenty-two-year-old who hadn't yet started an N.H.L. game with such Hall of Famers as Ken Dryden.

Pressure? No sweat, as it turned out.

With all of that on his shoulders, Hextall simply went out and won the number one goaltender's job, making Froese essentially redundant. Froese was eventually traded to the New York Rangers, completing a stunning victory for the relatively untested Hextall.

More remarkably, Hextall quickly rose to the top of the goaltending ranks statistically in the N.H.L., leading all of his colleagues in victories and goals-against average.

If the rest of the Flyers are surprised by all this, it hasn't been evident.

"He's a very mature kid," Captain Dave Poulin said, "and it shows both on and off the ice. If you think about it, it's pretty incredible, to be thrown into the limelight like he has and to handle it like he does.

"A lot of that could have come from his parents, from his dad playing in the league and having been exposed to the league."

Hextall's father is Bryan Hextall, Junior, who played for five N.H.L. teams in eight years and left the game in 1976 after compiling a record of 99 goals and many more minutes in penalties. His uncle,

Dennis, left the game in 1980 after racking up 153 goals and a few more opponents with his fists. Together, the tough Hextall brothers amassed 2,136 minutes in penalties.

It is Ron's grandfather, however, who is the Hall of Famer in the group. Bryan Hextall, Senior, recorded twenty or more goals in seven of his eleven N.H.L. seasons, and will be remembered by history-minded Ranger fans as the player who scored the winning goal when the team last won the Stanley Cup, in 1940.

If Hextall brings any of the family characteristics to his game, it is a sense of competition, he says.

"Everybody in my family has been competitive," Hextall says, "and I'd like to think that I'm competitive. I have a lot of energy, and when I play well, it's usually because I'm aggressive."

In Hextall's case, that might be construed as the understatement of the year. Prowling like a wired-up tiger in front of the net, Hextall doesn't stay still for a second. Even when the action is at the other end of the ice, he's constantly smashing his stick against the pipes of the net and against his leg pads.

"It's a superstition, something I started as far back as I could remember," Hextall says of his habit of striking the pipes with his stick. "I like to roam a little bit between whistles. Besides that, I go from corner to corner. It's part of my game."

Also part of Hextall's game is his willingness to come way out to play the puck and handle it, almost as if he were a sixth skater on the ice. Observers say this is his best aspect as a goaltender.

"He moves the puck better than any goaltender in the N.H.L.," Darcy Regier, a scout for the New York Islanders, says. "And when you scout Philadelphia, it becomes a very, very big factor in how to stop him. A big part of how you forecheck and how you're going to carry the puck into the Flyers' zone revolves around how to keep the puck away from him.

"It's unbelievable. You can't shoot around him, because he gets out and he stops it and he plays it. They scored two power play goals one time we played them this year, and one of the goals was a result of him moving the puck right up the middle and catching us on a line change. It's one of his best strengths as a goaltender. Obviously he has to be able to stop the puck, too. He's very quick, stands up, has so much size and takes advantage of it."

As far back as Hextall can remember, he wanted to be a goaltender, and it didn't have anything to do with family tradition, either.

"I used to throw a sock up the stairs and stop it on the way down," Hextall remembers. "I think I was two or three years old at the time."

His intuitive sense for hockey was further fortified by the life of a "hockey brat," as he likes to call it.

"The traveling around with my dad showed me the lifestyle of a professional hockey player," Hextall says. "I decided very early in life that's what I wanted to be and went for it."

It didn't take him long to make the grade. Ron was sixteen when he led the Brandon, Manitoba, midgets to the provincial championship in that Canadian district. The Flyers selected the six-foot-three, 175-pound Hextall in the sixth round of the 1982 draft.

He spent two more seasons in Brandon, played with Kalamazoo, Michigan, in the International League in 1984-85, and was promoted to the Flyers' Hershey affiliate in the American Hockey League the following season. At Hershey, he won thirty games, as he led the Bears to the Calder Cup finals and was named A.H.L. Rookie of the Year.

Then came his big chance in Philadelphia. Mike Keenan started him on opening night against the Edmonton Oilers, and Hextall allowed only one goal in a two-to-one Flyers' victory.

"It was definitely a test for me, but I was confident that day," Hextall said. "Sure, we were playing the Edmonton Oilers, a great team, but we have a great team, too. It wasn't me against the Oilers, it was the Flyers against the Oilers. It was twenty guys out there pulling the same way."

Keenan felt he had opened himself up to criticism by putting his unvarnished faith in a rookie goaltender. But, he said, "It's a decision we felt very comfortable with."

Apparently so did Hextall.

The man the Flyers would ask to play more than sixty games in the regular season alone was "all ribs and mustache," in the words of goaltending coach Bernie Parent. "But he's as tough a kid as you'll see. We were sure he could carry the load."

Ironically, the very man the Flyers were most worried about suffering an injury was one of the few who *didn't* succumb to some misfortune.

When I think of Ron Hextall, then or now, I picture a tall, lean, angular, almost gaunt figure, although he is somewhat less gaunt now, at 190-plus pounds, than when he was listed at 175. A true-to-life image of the Grim Reaper, with enormous strength in his wrists and arms, he works around the crease in such a menacing manner that there is a halo not of six feet, but of sixteen feet, into which no one dares to penetrate without the fear of being disarmed, or perhaps dislegged.

Besides his threatening defensive posture, he maneuvers the puck so well, and handles it so often, and shoots with such authority, that he is an important element not just of the team's defense and penalty killing, but of the offense as well, including the power play.

And added to all of those *physical* attributes, and they are more diversified than those of any other goaltender who ever lived, there is his unique personality. His aggressiveness, his feistiness, his brash and challenging nature are all extremely rare qualities for a goaltender. And those qualities, in turn, make him a team leader, also extremely rare for a goaltender.

Those same qualities make him a villain in the arenas of most N.H.L. cities. He has not only created a new style of goaltending, but he has also prompted a new style of derisive cheer, if you can call it that. For, after a goal or two, the crowd in the Garden (and most other enemy buildings) will begin to chant in an irritating sing-song kind of tone, "Hex-tall...Hex-tall...Hex-tall..."—the facetious counterpoint to "Bernie...Bernie...Bernie..."

With the orange arrow on his black helmet pointing straight ahead at the opponent's goal, Hextall seems almost to bask in the sound of this new ritual. Or is the arrow pointing back at the fans? Or forward toward the future? Or tauntingly toward his own five-hole?

No matter where his arrow and his head will direct him, Ron Hextall is a hockey player unlike any other, ever. Let's appreciate him for that. Let's *not* remember him just for the occasional loss of poise, but for the positive things that only he can do.

One of those positive things occurred in the Spectrum on Dec. 8, 1987. The Flyers were leading Boston, four to two, in the final minutes of a satisfying comeback win over the ever-competitive Bruins. As they desperately tried to get back into the game, the Bruins dumped the puck into the Flyers' zone and pulled their goaltender. Hextall swung behind the net, picked up the loose puck, and moved it out to the left side of the net. He then wristed the puck out of the zone and toward center ice.

In all of my fifty-or-so years of following hockey, I had never seen anything like what I now sensed was about to happen. I called in a broadcaster's kind of semi-hysteria, "It might be...*IT IS!* Ron Hextall has become the first goaltender *ever* to actually score a goal by shooting the puck into the opponent's net!"

As for making that call for the other side, Fred Cusick, the Boston announcer, who is even older than I am, said that he thought he'd never live to see it, let alone call it.

As they comprehended the significance of it all, the players erupted and swarmed around Hextall to congratulate him. I also recall the odd sight of referee Andy van Hellemond pointing at Hextall, not for a penalty this time, but to credit him for a goal.

It was a shot literally heard 'round the world, because, like its instigator, it was unique, a one-time-only kind of thing. It had happened before in the *minor* leagues, and Billy Smith of the Islanders had once been *credited* with a goal, but no N.H.L. goaltender had ever before actually shot a puck into the opponent's net.

In Smith's case, there had been a delayed penalty called, and, as is customary, the Colorado Rockies had pulled their goaltender. Smith had steered the puck into the corner, and from there a Rockies' centering attempt had slid all the way back into their own net. Since Smith was the last Islander to touch the puck, he was credited with the goal.

We all knew that some day some N.H.L. goaltender would probably score a legitimate goal. We also knew that if *anyone* were to do it, it would most likely be Hextall. He himself had talked about the possibility, saying, "If I ever try it, I want to be sure the situation is right. If we're on the power play, or have at least a two-goal lead, in case I blow it, we won't blow the two points along with it."

Actually seeing it done was *not* that imposing a sight! Because it had never been done before, there had been the anticipation of a "wonder-what-it's-going-to-be-like?" kind of miracle. But how do you describe something that is so unlike any other sporting feat? It's not like a 100-yard touchdown run, or a titanic home run onto the roof of Yankee Stadium, or a mile run in world-record time.

It's just a hockey player sliding a puck 180 feet into an empty six-by-four-foot net. It just doesn't look that difficult! In fact, I'd say it looks about as spectacular as rolling a bowling ball down the alley and hitting some pins—not *all* of the pins, mind you, just *some* of them!

Nevertheless, history was made, and the Flyers froze the moment, by turning the scorecard into a burnished-in-metal plaque which was later presented to all of the players. I have one on the wall next to my desk. It shows each of the scores in that five-to-two win over Boston, including the utterly unique last one: "#7, 3d period, 18:48, F [for Flyers], Hextall [#1], unassisted, even-strength goal."

Those who were there to see Hextall score that first goaltender's goal thought that it probably wouldn't be the last time that he would do it. They were right.

And it also wouldn't be the last time that he would do something that only one man could do. There may be other goaltenders, eventually, who will equal, or even surpass his expertise. But there will never be another Ron Hextall!

Here's a salute to you, Hex! You're a one-of-a-kind original!

**A**fter that lovely year of standing *Tall* all the way to the final minutes of Game Seven of the Stanley Cup Finals, there followed, inevitably, a not-so-lovely even-numbered and therefore *Hexed* year—1987-88. But the ugly implications of the calendar's jinx did not prevent the Flyers' management from viewing the coming season through the usual set of rose-tinted lenses.

Stated Vice President and General Manager Bob Clarke in the team's pre-season publicity, "We're a far more mature hockey club than we were three years ago when we went to the Finals with the youngest team in pro sports. Players like Craven, Smith, Tocchet, Zezel, and Sutter are still in their early twenties, but they have a great deal of experience under their belts, including two Stanley Cup Finals.

"Plus, guys like Hextall [age 23], Eklund [24], Daigneault [22], and Mellanby [21] are just in their second or third seasons, and figure to get better and better.

"Both last season and in 1985 when we went to the Finals we had serious injury problems, but that's no excuse. Our goal is to win the Cup, and I believe this team has the ability to do it. They know how close they came last year...and what it took to get there."

Mike Keenan, who had recorded his 150th win faster than any other coach in N.H.L. history, was similarly optimistic about the team's prospects for building upon the remarkable achievements of the previous season. Said Keenan, "Our objective is to repeat the success that we attained over the course of the past three regular seasons and climb that final rung of the playoff ladder. I know that it will be quite a challenge, but I'm confident that we have the type of personnel on this team who can respond to that type of challenge."

Unfortunately, that rosy party-line did not take into account some significant changes in the make-up of the Flyers. First, the N.H.L. had suspended Ron Hextall for the season's first eight games, as punishment for his overt and embarrassing slash of Kent Nilsson on national television.

Since Chico Resch had finally hung up his pads, during the summer Bob Clarke had acquired, first, Mark Laforest from Detroit, and then, Wendell Young from Vancouver. It was those two who were in goal for the season's first eight games, instead of Ron Hextall. And instead of the best start ever with Hextall as the new Man, the Flyers clunked off to one of their worst starts ever, 4-6-2, quite unlike the 6-0-0 and 10-2-0 of the previous season.

There were some other changes as well. Craig (like all other players with any American Indian blood, known as "Chief") Berube (pronounced "Buh-ROO-bee"), a tough young man who was signed as a free agent in 1986, replaced Ed Hospodar as the team's "Chief" enforcer.

On defense, Clarke brought in the veteran Willie Huber for one last go around the league. He also brought in some youth, when Kerry Huffman was given a full shot, rather than just the brief look he got at the start of the previous season, when he had been almost as surprising a rookie starter as Ron Hextall had been.

In fact, Huffman himself had been as surprised as anyone else, when he was summoned to the principal's office from his Wednesday afternoon science class in his high school in Peterborough, Ontario, one fine October afternoon. He was sure that he was in big trouble, until the principal told him, "You'd better go home. The Flyers have called you up."

The next night he was in Philadelphia, playing against Wayne Gretzky and the Edmonton Oilers. And how's that for culture shock?

These changes in themselves probably wouldn't have made a lot of difference, but there were several other important people missing. One was the team's leading scorer, Tim Kerr, who missed virtually the whole season, or, to be exact, seventy-two of eighty games. Instead of fifty-eight goals, he would score three, or just two more than would be scored by Ron Hextall.

I had been keeping track of a new statistic, "man-games lost to injury," and the Flyers would reach a new team record of 244 during that season. It was a statistic which was destined for even greater prominence in the *next* even-numbered-Hexed year of 1989-90. In those two seasons, unfortunately, I certainly had enough practice keeping track of my new stat.

Another important missing person was due not to injury, or suspension, but he was sorely missed nonetheless. And he was gone not just temporarily, but permanently. That would be Brad Mc-Crimmon, who had the gall to become involved in a contract dispute with the Flyers' management, and who was then traded before the season to Calgary for two draft choices, a first and a third-rounder.

With McCrimmon as an integral part of their defense, the Flames soared to the league's best record for the next two seasons, so that the draft choices the Flyers would receive in return were as low as they could possibly be. And how much of that was because of

McCrimmon? Could the Flames have won the Stanley Cup without McCrimmon? Maybe, but probably not.

Not only had one of the anchors of Calgary's Cup team been "stolen" from the Flyers for two mediocre draft picks, but the Flyers' defense would be lacking one of its most reliable anchors. And all, it has been suggested, not because of money, but because of a personality clash between McCrimmon and/or his agent and the Flyers' chief negotiator, Bob Clarke.

McCrimmon's agent had apparently informed Clarke that Brad "wouldn't be happy here any more," and the Flyers have never appreciated any kind of distraction from their team's long-established image of "one big happy family." This particular impasse resulted, ironically, in the first suggestion of trouble, or of a move that wasn't the smartest, or even of a *bad* move, since Bob Clarke had accepted his new role as one of the heads of the "family."

It had always been assumed that much of McCrimmon's effectiveness with the Flyers was due to his having been paired most of the time with Mark Howe. Later, in retrospect, it became apparent that McCrimmon was every bit as effective in Calgary, even without Mark Howe. And you can be sure that McCrimmon was missed by Howe, or at least until he and Kjell Samuelsson became accustomed to one another.

When Ron Hextall returned from his suspension, he never quite achieved his sharpness of the year before, probably in part because of all of the changes on defense. Nevertheless, his record was impressive, although not quite so impressive as that of his rookie season:

|  | W | L | T | G.A. |
|---|---|---|---|---|
| Rookie season (1986-87) | 37 | 21 | 6 | 3.00 |
| Second season (1987-88) | 30 | 22 | 7 | 3.51 |

Hextall's record for the season was more impressive when compared with the *team's* record of 38-33-9, just five games over .500, and a fall from second place overall in the N.H.L. to ninth.

Without Tim Kerr, the team's offensive stats also fell off. Brian Propp and Murray Craven tied for the team scoring lead, each with seventy-six points, and the only thirty-goal scorers were Craven and Rick Tocchet. The latter also became a trivia item, as the first Flyer ever to accumulate thirty goals and 300 penalty minutes in the same season (with 31 and 301).

Since no one else seemed to want to win the Patrick Division, the Islanders came out of oblivion and won it almost by default. The Flyers and Capitals tied for second, each with eighty-five points, which meant that they would face each other in the first round of the playoffs.

The season series between the two, and the resulting home-ice advantage in the playoffs, came down to the season's final game in the Spectrum. The Flyers needed a win, but the Caps needed only a tie to earn the advantage. Former-and-future Flyer Pete Peeters and the Caps got the tie, two-two, and thus won the home-ice advantage.

The Philadelphia-Washington I-95 series would be the second in their history, and the first since the embarrassing three-game wipeout by the Caps in that not-so-wonderful even-numbered year, 1984. Tim Kerr returned to give it a go, but he would manage only one goal in six games, and he was not really much of a factor in any of them.

The Flyers won the opener in the Cap Centre, four to two, thus earning the desired split on the road, despite losing the second game, five to four. They also won Game Three in the Spectrum, four to three.

In Game Four, the Caps led, four to one, in the third period, but the Flyers stormed back to tie and then win in overtime on a goal by Murray Craven, five to four. The Caps, whose playoff history had been anything but glorious, appeared to be dead and buried, down three games to one. The Washington media had the Caps "choking again," and there just seemed to be no way that they could possibly win three straight to take this series.

The Caps won Game Five, five to two. No problem. The series would return to the Spectrum for the Game Six clincher.

The Caps didn't just win Game Six in Philadelphia, they hammered the Flyers, seven to two. Uh, oh...Back to the Cap Centre for Game Seven.

No problem again. Propp and Howe scored early, and before anyone could believe it, the Flyers were leading three to nothing, and had apparently overcome the home-ice advantage that they had lost to Washington in the regular season's final game.

If any single game was ever a microcosm of an entire seven-game series, this was it, for, unbelievably, the Caps came back to tie and then lead in the third period, four to three. Brad Marsh then retied it for the Flyers, and we were headed for the ultimate in sudden death—overtime in Game Seven.

Once before the Flyers had been eliminated from the playoffs by an overtime goal, in 1980, when Bob Nystrom had won the Cup for the Islanders. This time, the overtime period was all Washington, as the Caps poured in shots from every angle on Ron Hextall, who held them off as long as he could. Finally, on a missed Flyers' defensive change, Dale Hunter, possibly Philadelphia's least-favorite opposition player, got a break up the middle of the ice, charged in all alone on Hextall, and scored the game and series winner.

For the Caps, it was the sweetest moment in their history. For the Flyers, it was not just sudden death; it was Capital punishment.


**T**he even-numbered year had ended, with the Flyers again failing to survive the first round of the playoffs. The following year, an odd one, would certainly have to be better.

But first, as a residue of 1988, there was now an undercurrent of speculation over Coach Keenan's job. Something about his win total dropping in three seasons from fifty-three to forty-six to thirty-eight.

It was tough to read at the time, without the perspective of history, but had a downward spiral begun? And, if so, whose fault was that? The suspension's? The injuries'? The players'? The coach's? The management's? All of the above? None of the above? Some of the above? Or wasn't there any downward spiral to worry about?

From the beginning, Mike Keenan was (and still is) a bottom-line guy. Through his first three seasons, the bottom line had been good: an average of more than fifty wins per season, three Patrick Division titles, and two trips to the Stanley Cup Finals.

In fact, Keenan might have been the first coach who *lost* two finals and was still perceived as a winner. In a none-too democratic way, he got things done, at least until now.

Along the way, ribs had cracked, backs had fractured, knees and shoulders had popped. But Keenan kept cracking his whip. And getting results.

Finally, after four seasons of what had been viewed as cruel and inhuman punishment, Mike's unbendingly harsh drill-sergeant's technique was wearing thin on many of his players. At various times, virtually *every* player had been enraged by him. Even his assistant coaches had been wounded by his demanding ways.

Concern over all of this naturally spilled over to the front office, to the Sniders and Bob Clarke. To Clarke, there was a very serious decision to be made.

How much of the team's retrogression in total wins had been the result of the growing disinterest of the players, and of their growing distaste in playing for Keenan? And how much had been due to a possible lack of quality players? The dividing lines between who or what might have been to blame were further clouded by all of the turmoil which accompanied this kind of thinking.

More and more, it was felt that Keenan was "too tough," or "too dictatorial." More and more, he was referred to as "Iron Mike," or behind his back, as "Dolf," short for "Adolf," an infamous dictator of another era. While that might have been overstepping the bounds of good taste, the similarity in their mustaches lent credibility to the caricature.

Actually, Keenan's appearance, demeanor, and methods more closely resembled those of Scotty Bowman, for whom he had worked in the Buffalo organization—even to his ingenious practice of keeping his cool during a game by chewing on his own private supply of ice cubes. Although Bowman had been considered a coaching genius in St. Louis, Montreal, and Buffalo, he had also infuriated several armies of people, mostly his own players.

Both Bowman and Keenan had a way of looking down their noses, as if trying to keep their glasses from falling off, even when not wearing any glasses. In Mike's case, he wore contact lenses most of the time, and maybe that had something to do with the arrogant tilt of his head. And maybe not.

I recall one game, it was a tense game, and in the final seconds Mike called a time-out. With all of his players encircled about him and awaiting his instructions, Mike just stared down his nose at them, saying nothing.

Another time, near the end of that crucial semi-final playoff series against Montreal, Mike called a team meeting for early in the morning. When everyone was assembled, he told them that there would be no practice that day. Dismissed.

After observing Keenan's dealings with his players for a while, one of the old Broad Street Bullies just shook his head and said, "If he'd treated us that way, somebody would have laid him out cold."

In the minor leagues, and in college, and in juniors, Keenan literally *drove* his players toward improvement and excellence. But in those situations, he had a whole new gang of recruits every three years or so with which to work. Not so in the N.H.L., where, without that constant turnover of players, the same approach eventually wears thin.

No one ever questioned the hours or the devotion Keenan gave to his job. In game preparation, in fitness, in practice sessions, he seemed tireless, almost inhumanly so at times.

If you went to the Coliseum at eight A.M., he was there. If you went at ten P.M., he was there. After a tough game, it might be well past midnight, and one of the last cars left in the Spectrum's security parking lot would be Mike's silver Mercedes coupe, a gift from the team when Keenan's Flyers had reached the Stanley Cup Finals for the first time.

Mike Keenan was (and is) a man dedicated, above all else, to winning, almost to the exclusion of all other facets of life. For example, after living in Cherry Hill, New Jersey, for four years, he had no idea where the Cherry Hill Mall was. That would be almost like a native of India not knowing where the Taj Mahal was.

In his naive way, he would sometimes try a psychological lift for the players. Once during the playoffs against New York, he asked me if there might be a show in town that the players would like to see. I suggested one, and he treated the entire team, a lovely and very expensive gesture on his part.

Another time, in Edmonton, we had one of those six P.M. Sunday games, which means that we're all out around nine P.M., in time for a late meal. Mike decided to spring for a team dinner and asked Joe Kadlec to track down a likely restaurant.

With the new methods of training and nutrition, pasta is now the "in" food, so Joe lined up a neighborhood Italian restaurant about four blocks from the Northlands Coliseum. It was a lovely little place, with fifteen or sixteen tables, checkered tablecloths, Chianti bottles with candles in them, as well as bottles with beer, wine, and soft drinks in them.

All of the tables were set, and we were all comfortably seated, when Mike, impatient to get things moving, said, in effect, "I wonder what's going on back there?"

I, curious to see what the kitchen was like, volunteered to find out. Through the swinging door, it was like fairyland. The whole family—grandmother, grandfather, children of all ages—everyone was cooking and getting things ready, and everyone was obviously thrilled to have the famous Flyers team there. They were preparing a feast to do an old-country Roman proud, starting with handsomely lined-up plates of a glorious antipasto.

As I was admiring all of this, Mike came barging through the door and said, "When're we going to eat?"

The owner replied, politely, "Oh, any minute now. Don't worry, we'll be starting to serve any minute..."

When we had returned to our table, I said to Mike something like, "Well, how do you like it?"

"I don't know. We came here for a team dinner, and all they've got is cold cuts."

I realize that this is a somewhat shaggy dog of a story, and I tell it only as another small example to show that here's a guy whose dedication to hockey is so complete that it's left him a little out of touch, not just with the fact that antipasto begins a classic Italian meal, but with much of what most people consider everyday parts of everyday living.

At any rate, after many long executive meetings, it was determined that Keenan's style was having a detrimental effect on his players. Bob Clarke had two choices: Extend Keenan's contract and risk mutiny, or make a move in a different direction and see if someone else with a softer touch might be able to rejuvenate the club.

We often hear that nonsense, "When the players are unhappy, they fire the coach, and that's not fair." Well, fair or not, that's part of being a coach, and, in this case, Bob Clarke got the credit for hiring Keenan, and he took the blame for firing him.

As Clarke later explained, "The relationship between Mike and the players had deteriorated to almost zero. But I liked Mike. I think our relationship is still good. We're friends. I think he understood why I had to do it. Obviously, he didn't like it. I'm sure there has to be resentment."

When the decision was made known, I can assure you that it startled and stunned and deeply hurt Mike Keenan. We all knew that his talents would be welcomed elsewhere, so that it was not a matter of employment or *un*employment. But for the first time in his life, Mike had been fired, and he took it badly.

In retrospect, there is irony in the fact that Keenan was fired because he was too tough, and, several years later, his successor would be criticized for not being tough enough. Either or neither may be true.

It reminds me of an old Bette Davis movie, in which she sings in a stage-door canteen about the absence of men during wartime: "They're either too young or too old."

It seems that, in my experience in the N.H.L., coaches are either too tough or not tough enough. It's a rare one who finds the happy medium, and who doesn't meet with at least some disgruntlement.

Like the proverbial cat, Keenan quickly landed on his feet in Chicago, where he met with almost the same kind of instant semi-success he had brought to Philadelphia. Was this a case of *déjà vu,* or had Keenan "mellowed," as some have suggested?

Mellow or not, it didn't take Keenan long to develop a Flyer-like Blackhawk club. No matter who they are, everyone hits, and everyone plays to the hilt, or they don't play.

Of course, we also have heard some of the same complaints: "The coach is too tough, too demanding, too dictatorial." A repeat performance?

Some of the Flyers felt a breath of fresh air when it was announced that Paul Holmgren would be their new coach. Of course, he was new to them only as a *head* coach, having served as an assistant to Keenan since the time that Ted Sator had left to become head coach of the Rangers.

Not only was "Homer" everyone's friend, from Bob Clarke on down, he was also the answer to a new trivia question: "Who is the only N.H.L. head coach whose entire playing and coaching career— through juniors, scholastic, college, and professional—has been with American teams?" For, prior to becoming the first former Flyer player ever to be named the team's head coach, he had grown up, lived, and played in Minnesota, including for the University of Minnesota, and for both of that state's professional teams, as well as for the Flyers and for Team U.S.A.

Named as Holmgren's assistants were two more "good guys"— Andy Murray, as tactician, or strategy coach; and Mike Eaves, as spiritual leader and motivator, or to be the "rah-rah" guy that Holmgren was never comfortable being.

Along with the coaching changes came other changes. The power play improved dramatically, partly because it was stressed in practice, something that had *not* happened under Keenan, amazingly enough. Probably more importantly, Tim Kerr played in almost seventy games, instead of *missing* seventy-some. As a result, he scored forty-eight goals, instead of three.

On defense, the changes continued. Goalie Wendell Young was shipped to Pittsburgh for a third-round draft pick in 1990, and Greg

Smyth was sent to woeful Quebec for young defenseman Terry Carkner, who would become not only a regular, but an assistant captain.

Another formerly key defenseman, Doug Crossman, was granted his wish and traded to Los Angeles, in exchange for defenseman Jay Wells, one of the few Kings ever to be known more for his fists than for his finesse. As for Crossman, he had always danced to the tune of a different piper. As he once told me, "Gene, the trouble with this organization is that they don't believe in the free spirit." As for Doug's definition of "free spirit," I didn't ask.

During the season, the changes continued to come. J.J. Daigneault was sent to Montreal, while Moe Mantha arrived from Minnesota, as well as Al Secord from Toronto. Dave Brown, whose future in Philadelphia was limited by his reputation as a Jack Tatum–like assassin, was exiled to Edmonton, in exchange for Keith "Woody" Acton and a future draft pick.

The biggest trade came at Thanksgiving time. Rick Tocchet and Peter Zezel had been promoted as the Flyers' super-eligible "matinée idols." That didn't faze Tocchet, but it was felt that Peter's progress had been hindered by his glamorous image, which he himself had not fostered, but, good-bye, Peter; hello, Mike Bullard, a former fifty-goal scorer for Pittsburgh, who had also scored forty-eight in his one full season in Calgary, before being traded to St. Louis for two months or so.

Then, just prior to the trading deadline in early March, the Flyers acquired goaltender Ken Wregget from Toronto for two number one draft choices, one of them having come from Calgary in the McCrimmon deal. Those two draft choices would turn out to be N.H.L. picks number fifteen and twenty-one.

Wregget had been considered expendable in Toronto, partly because he was sick with mononucleosis, and partly because he was sick of the non-support of a team that didn't understand the term "defense." Bob Clarke figured that the Flyers could afford to wait until Wregget recovered his good health, and then, Heaven forbid, if Hextall should ever be sick or injured...

At the beginning of the season, it appeared that the Holmgren-for-Keenan move had been a good one, as the Flyers won five of their first six games. But after that, they won only five of their next twenty-one, and for the remainder of the season, they were never able to rise any higher than three games above .500.

In the end, they struggled to wind up with a record of 36-36-8, just barely able to salvage the tradition of never having had a losing season in the seventeen years since 1971–72. In the yearbook, the line about "X" number of "consecutive winning seasons" had to be slightly edited.

All things considered, Ron Hextall's record remained quite remarkable:

|  | W | L | T | G.A. |
|---|---|---|---|---|
| Rookie season (1986-87) | 37 | 21 | 6 | 3.00 |
| Second season (1987-88) | 30 | 22 | 7 | 3.51 |
| Third season (1988-89) | 30 | 28 | 6 | 3.23 |

Following the third-place finish of the previous season, the Flyers this time slipped one more notch, to fourth. They were still well ahead of New Jersey and the Islanders for the final playoff spot, but they were now *behind* the third-place Rangers, and *behind* the Pittsburgh Penguins, who finished second, thanks in good part to Mario Lemieux.

Finishing on top with a late surge were the Washington Capitals, who finally won their first title of any kind. In doing so, they broke another long-standing tradition, by becoming the first team other than the Flyers or Islanders to win the Patrick Division since that division was formed in the mid-seventies.

And so, into the playoff breach once more came the Flyers, although it appeared not to be for long, as once again their first-round opponent would be the same team that had defeated them the year before, Washington. And this time the first-place Caps would be the clear-cut favorites, while the fourth-place Flyers would be the obvious underdogs.

In Game One in the Cap Centre, the Flyers led, two to nothing, but lost, three to two. In Game Two, Brian Propp's third-period goal won for the Flyers, by the same score.

In Philadelphia for Game Three, the home-ice advantage was recaptured by the Caps in overtime, four to three. Game Four was the *only* game of the series which was decided *before* the final minutes, as the Flyers won handily, five to two.

Back to the Cap Centre for Game Five, with the series tied at two games apiece. And *this* one would be one for the books.

Washington led, five to four, in the third period, but the Flyers came back and tied it at five. Then Pelle Eklund put them ahead, six to five. Kjell Samuelsson made it seven to five, and then came the shocking coup de grâce.

Ron Hextall, the man who had so often frustrated and even intimidated the fore-checking of the Caps, by firing the puck out of the zone, became the first goaltender ever to score a playoff goal. I can still vividly recall seeing Pelle Eklund, from thirty feet away, signaling "Score!" with his stick in the air, as he watched the puck head dead-on into the net. Hextall's second career goal had added a bit more lustre to his legendary status, but, more importantly, the Flyers had won, eight to five, and now led the series, three games to two.

Even though Game Six was to be in the Spectrum, there was no indication of a fold by the Caps. After all, they had won three of the last four playoff games there. And sure enough, the game was tied at three in the third, and it was there for the taking.

As so often happens in such a tight playoff situation, it took a break to win it. With Washington's Pete Peeters protecting the short side, Rick Tocchet threw the puck out of the left corner. Somehow it squeaked inside Pete's pads and across the line for the goal that won the game, four to three, and the series, four games to two.

With Washington's reputation for "never making it out of the Patrick Division," the upset victory by the experienced Flyers didn't exactly set the league on its ear. But next they would face a greater challenge in Lemieux, Coffey, Barasso, and Company, a.k.a. the Pittsburgh Penguins, who had breezed past the Rangers in four straight.

In Pittsburgh, the Pens won the opener, four to three, but in Game Two, the Flyers gained a split, when Tim Kerr broke a two-two tie with a game winner. The series appeared to be a carbon copy of the previous one, when the Pens regained the home-ice advantage with an overtime win in the Spectrum, four to three. But again, as in the previous series, the Flyers evened things at two games apiece by winning Game Four rather handily, four to one.

Game Five in Pittsburgh was *un*like anything in the Washington series. In fact, it was unlike any other game in any series ever played!

First, the new "Great One," Mario Lemieux, scored four goals in the first period, tying Tim Kerr's single-period playoff record, and the Pens led, six to one, after one period. Already, thoughts were turning toward Game Six in Philadelphia. Those thoughts didn't change much, as the Pens ran the score up to nine to three, after two.

In the third period, the seemingly dead-and-buried Flyers, believe it or not, scored four unanswered goals, and it was suddenly a nine-to-seven game. And but for a missed empty net, it would have been nine to eight.

When the Flyers pulled their goaltender, Lemieux did *not* miss the empty net. His fifth goal of the game gave him a total of eight points for the evening, the most ever against the Flyers in post- *or* regular-season play. His five goals in a playoff game also tied the N.H.L. record set by Montreal's Richard in the forties, and tied in 1976 by Toronto's Sittler *against* the Flyers and by Reggie Leach *for* the Flyers.

In one of the wildest scoring barrages in Stanley Cup playoff history, the Pens won by a football score, ten to seven, and the Flyers had to be stunned, as they headed back to Philadelphia, trailing three games to two.

If the Flyers *were* stunned, it didn't show in Game Six, which they won easily, six to two. Back to "The Igloo" in Pittsburgh, for another one of those delicious "no-more-tomorrows" seventh games.

The first news from Game Seven was, almost, the worst of all possible news: Due to a knee injury, Ron Hextall had been scratched from the line-up. In his place would be Ken Wregget, coming off his bout with mononucleosis and into his first meaningful game for the Flyers, who had acquired him less than two months before, in case of just such an emergency.

Thanks to a brilliant and gallant performance by the game's number one star, Wregget, the Flyers led, two to one, in the third period. Then ex-Pen Mike Bullard made it three to one. When Pittsburgh pulled its goaltender in the closing minutes, I can recall saying, "There goes Mellanby...toward the empty net...*BANG!* We're going to Montreal!"

For the second time in three years, there would be a Philadelphia-Montreal semi-final series, the Flyers' *tenth* semi-final (or conference final) in the seventeen years since their *first* semi-final in 1973, which was also against the Canadiens.

The first game in the Forum was dominated by Ken Wregget, just as the previous game against Pittsburgh had been. Again, Wregget allowed just one goal, and that was late in the game, after the Flyers had already scored twice.

Both of the Flyers' early goals were short-handed, by Derrick Smith and by Ilkka Sinisalo. Montreal's goal came on a power play which, for a change, led to a score by the team which supposedly had the advantage. Rick Tocchet then made the final score three to one.

The marvelous performance by Ken Wregget and the Flyers was, unfortunately, only part of the story. The game had also been marked by a much-disputed non-call in the first period.

Since this controversial play occurred far behind the on-camera action, I didn't see at first what had happened, except that, as I glanced back, there was Brian Propp, lying unconscious on the ice near the boards. While we were waiting for Propp to be carried off, we could ascertain quite clearly from slow-motion replays what had happened:

As play headed up ice from the Flyers' defensive zone to Montreal's offensive zone, and as Propp skated toward center ice from behind the play, out of the corner in full pursuit came Canadien defenseman Chris Chelios. Chelios caught up to Propp and literally left his skates to deliver a raised elbow squarely into Propp's skull, which, as a result of that blow, was then driven the remaining six inches or so directly into the glass. Medical diagnosis: concussion.

Since the officials hadn't seen it, no penalty was called. But after seeing the replays, there was no question in my mind that Chelios had deliberately lined up Propp and had equally deliberately tried to hammer him. It was a clear-cut bad, even vicious, check, designed to hurt.

"How can you read Chelios's mind?" you might ask.

Well, I contend that you do not hold your elbow up that high, at shoulder height or above, and you do not leave your skates, and you do not charge a guy who's only a foot or less from the boards, and then say, "Gee, I didn't think he'd hit the glass." What else could he hit?

Paul Holmgren was worried that his team might retaliate, so he gathered everyone around him and told them, "No, no, no!" The Flyers listened, they played a disciplined game, and they won.

Unfortunately for them, and for whatever reason, from that point on the Canadiens took charge of the series. The Flyers could manage only one goal in the next three games, as Chelios, Robinson, Roy, et al., were simply too much defensively for the Flyers' un-Propped-up offense to penetrate.

Montreal won Game Two, three to nothing, and then, in Philadelphia, they twice embarassed the Flyers in front of their own fans, by scores of five to one, and again, three to nothing. With shutouts by Montreal now almost expected, the Flyers still refused to give up.

In Game Five in the Forum, the Flyers carried a one-to-nothing lead into the final minutes, but a late Montreal goal tied it. In overtime, Captain Dave Poulin scored to keep the Flyers alive, and the series headed back to the Spectrum one last time.

In Game Six, the Flyers scored twice, for a meager six-game total of eight goals. Looking back, it was amazing that the Flyers could carry that series to a sixth game, but Montreal won both the game and the series, and both by a count of four to two.

Two years before against the Canadiens, the Flyers had lost two of three at home, but had won all three in Montreal. This time, the Flyers had won two of three in Montreal, but had lost all three at home. Strangely, the Flyers' all-time playoff history against Montreal looks like this:

| | W | L |
|---|---|---|
| In Montreal | 6 | 5 |
| In Philadelphia | 1 | 9 |

My memories of the 1989 playoffs will revolve about four players. Offensively, Tim Kerr enjoyed the best playoffs of his ten-year career, with twenty-five points in nineteen games. Not far behind was Chris Chelios' target, Brian Propp, with twenty-three points in eighteen games, a total that he had topped only once, in 1987, with his team record of twenty-eight points in twenty-six games.

The other two memorable players were the two goaltenders, Ken Wregget and Ron Hextall. Unfortunately, as in 1987, the latter will be remembered more for another "incident" than for his goaltending prowess.

While the Flyers had not retaliated against Chris Chelios in Game One, they had obviously seethed over it ever since. Then, in the season's final game, down four to two, and with only a minute or two remaining, all the hell in Hextall broke loose.

A most polite, withdrawn, almost introverted fellow off the ice, Ron Hextall saw Chelios coming down the side to his right, and he saw red. He ran into the corner, threw a swing at Chelios, and missed. Then he tried to clunk him with his blocker.

It might have been funny, if it hadn't been so shocking. And the legend continued to grow...in all directions.

Unlike Chelios in Game One, Hextall received a game misconduct penalty for his overt and awkwardly uncontrolled attack. Some complained that, with a minute or two left, Hextall had, for all intents and purposes, conceded victory to Montreal in favor of gaining a measure of revenge against Chelios. Whatever, it was an embarrassing moment, and it will stain what should be remembered as a quality effort by the Flyers in a tight, hard-nosed series against some very heavy odds.

As unfortunate as the ending of the playoffs had been, the relative success of the Flyers in the playoffs had also had some unfortunate, but at that time, unforeseen aspects:

First, it had diverted attention away from a lackluster .500 season. After all, the new philosophy, or rationalization, seemed to be: It doesn't matter what happens during the regular season, just so we make the playoffs; then we'll turn on the juice and go on to the semi-finals, and maybe even the Cup.

Second, hiding somewhere not-too-far-beneath the veneer of their playoff "success," there might have been some rust spots, some chips, some chinks, and possibly even some deep holes in the armor of the valiant and vaunted Flyers. And lurking just over the horizon was that evil, even-numbered year—1989-90.

# That Evil Year: 1989-90

As usual, the upcoming season had the Flyers billed as the ultimate blend for success. It was a team anchored by a solid nucleus of proven veterans, highlighted by a group of rising young stars, and enhanced by a crop of talented newcomers.

Bob Clarke and Paul Holmgren were banking on the fact that the team that went 36-36-8 during the previous regular season had been transformed into the powerhouse that had ousted Washington and Pittsburgh from the playoffs, and had taken the league's best defensive team to six games in the conference finals.

That wasn't the case, partly because that team lost its three-time most valuable player even before the season opened. For attempting to take the law into his own hands against Montreal, the league had again chastised Ron Hextall with a suspension, this time for the season's first twelve games, instead of the eight games he had sat out at the start of the 1987-88 season.

In light of Hextall's impending absence, some pre-season

finagling shuffled the goaltending corps several more times. First, Pete Peeters was signed as a free agent from Washington, where his previous season's record had been a very respectable 20-7-3, with a goals-against average of 2.85. It was an interesting ploy to bring Pete back to Philadelphia, where it was assumed that he would be content to spend his waning years as a back-up to Hextall.

With Hextall returning soon, and with Peeters now in the fold, and with Ken Wregget now healthy, and with young Bruce Hoffort down in Hershey, Bob Clarke traded Mark Laforest to Toronto for two future draft choices. It was assumed by many that, following Hextall's suspension, Wregget would also be traded, possibly for some additional scoring punch, preferably on the left wing.

But before the Flyers could cash in their blue chip, there were suddenly some other goaltending problems to settle. Before training camp, Ron Hextall had emotionally, even tearfully, announced that, despite the fact that he had a few years left on his long-term contract, he felt that conditions had changed so drastically since the contract had been signed that he was certainly now worth a lot more, and he wanted to deal with the Flyers on that basis. Ill-advisedly, I believe.

Analyzing the situation in retrospect, it seems to have been an unwise decision, probably made by Hextall's new agent. After all, any time someone wants to negotiate, or re-negotiate, it should be done from a position of strength. Hextall's position was anything but that:

1. He had previously signed a long-term contract.

2. He had to miss the season's first twelve games in any case.

3. The Flyers now had two other veteran N.H.L. goaltenders, in Wregget and Peeters, plus a promising youngster in Hoffort.

4. Hextall's proposition had been presented almost as a demand, rather than as a request. As such, it was almost as if he were waving a red flag in the face of the Flyers' management, and there was just no way that they were going to deal with it.

In my view, had Hextall's representative politely (not obsequiously, just politely) suggested to the Flyers that he hoped to be able to sit down with them in order to iron out a new, more equitable pact, I think that they would have answered, "Of course, let's try that."

Instead, Hextall and his agent came up with, "I'm not going to play unless we get this thing re-written," and the die, unfortunately, was cast. As a result, the season began with a goaltender who was not only unpresent, but unsettled, unstrung, unhappy, and unsure about any part of his future—except that he wouldn't be playing for at least the first twelve games.

I think that Ron and his representative finally realized that their position was not only weak, but mired in quicksand. At any rate, Ron eventually returned, saying, "We'll deal with this later."

Two years before, when Hextall missed the first eight games, the Flyers never seemed to recover from their horrendous start. That, of course, was one of those even, or Hexed years.

One year before, *with* Hextall, they had started off well, winning five of their first six games. That was one of those odd years.

Now, in another Hexed year, they got off not only to a worse start than before, they got off to *the worst* start in their entire history. For the first time ever, they lost their first three games. They won just one of their first eight, and two of their first ten. Many of the so-called experts had given up on the season before Hextall had even appeared in his first game.

When Hextall finally did return, he became part of the team's best stretch of the season. From nowhere at the end of October, the Flyers, during the next thirty games, posted a 16-10-4 record that actually had them in first place by Christmas time.

Three months later they were back to nowhere. What happened? Rather, what didn't happen?

Rarely can anyone point to one game as the "turning point," or the "being-turned-around point," where a downward slide is suddenly out of control. But I think I can point to one, or perhaps two, in this season.

Two days before Christmas, the Flyers began a major road trip, one of those painfully long, winding journeys during which you just don't want to get hurt too badly. It started out on an up-note, with a five-to-three win in Montreal.

Then, in Edmonton, a scoreless game in the third period turned when a couple of clearing passes hit the referee and sat down right in front of the Flyers' goal. So, despite one of their better efforts ever in the Northlands Coliseum, the Flyers lost, two to one.

The next three games went about as well as could be expected, as the Flyers clobbered the Kings in L.A., six to three, and then tied the next two, in Vancouver and Calgary. Two ties on the road, after all, equal one win at home, or anywhere else, but these two were so-called "bad ties," since the home team had come from behind both times.

So far on the trip, the Flyers were 2-1-2, with no disasters yet, but then came the game in question. In St. Louis, they were playing a superb defensive game and were leading, two to nothing, after two periods. The road trip was looking good, as the Flyers appeared to be coming out of it on the plus side.

Then came the third period in St. Louis. The Blues scored four unanswered goals, and the Flyers appeared helpless, and worse yet, hapless. They did come back to tie on Dave Poulin's second goal of the game, but then, as would become so characteristic through the rest of the year, they were burned on a two-on-one in overtime, and lost, five to four. Some losses are more painful than others, but when you go from a two-to-nothing third-period lead to a five-four loss, you really feel as though the bottom has dropped out.

The final stop on the trip was in Chicago, where Mike Keenan's Hawks again hammered the Flyers, eight to five. For the trip, the totals read: Two wins, three losses, and two ties. But that was only the beginning of the bad news.

An absolutely terrible string of games followed, at home and away, during which the Flyers continued their problem of giving away late leads and losing by one goal. They really appeared to bottom out with an overtime loss at home to lowly Vancouver.

The Flyers finally stopped what could have been a record-tying tenth consecutive loss, with a win over Winnipeg. But they followed that with another one-goal loss at home, this time by a score of two to one to Boston. Oddly enough, the Flyers played the eventual Stanley Cup–finalist Bruins three times during the season, and all three were two-to-one losses.

From several games above .500 at the season's mid-point, the Flyers had started the second half of the season with but one win in twelve games. Then came the *other* game in question.

In the beloved Cap Centre, where there are often as many Philadelphia fans as there are Washington fans, the Flyers fell behind in the second period and then appeared, quite literally, *to quit.* Yes, I said *"quit,"* and I repeat that, because it was indeed something that I had never, ever seen before from *any* Flyer team.

Back in the Spectrum came a home stand, during which the Flyers seemed to level out their slide somewhat, but they still struggled, even in the rare instances when they had large leads. And they seemed utterly incapable of winning two games consecutively.

I knew, the team knew, we *all* knew that changes would have to be made, somehow, somewhere. They began, actually, in December, when Ron Sutter was named captain in place of Dave Poulin, and Terry Carkner was named assistant captain in place of Mark Howe. It was explained at the time that this was a way of giving some respect and responsibility to the younger players, who would lead the club into the future.

In Dave Poulin's case, it had to hurt. As he stated later, "I don't know if bitter was ever the right word. I was disappointed. I wore that uniform proudly, and I was very proud to be captain. I think a lot of my success has to come from the fact that I was proud and took things personally. That's the only way I can be successful. I *lived* the game in Philadelphia as well as played it there."

I think that Dave's chest may have bled a little when they pulled that "C" from his jersey. I think that the Flyers as a team bled a little, too.

In early January, Bob Clarke tried to shake up the troops with some trades. First, he sent a fourth-round draft choice to Edmonton for a tough mucker-winger named Normand Lacombe. Unfortunately, Norm was to play in only eighteen games, because Clarke later appealed the trade, contending that the Oilers had misrepresented Lacombe's health. Also unfortunately, the appeal was unsuccessful.

In mid-January came not just a shaker-upper, but a true jolt to everyone, when it was announced that former captain Poulin had been traded to Boston for former-Flyer Ken Linseman, both of them thirty-one-year-old centermen. It was undeniable that Poulin's role and statistics had been diminishing as his age was increasing, but the same was true of Linseman.

Was Clarke admitting that drastic measures were needed? Or was this a true effort to "bolster the offense," as was reported? I thought that two *other* elements may have entered into Clarke's thinking.

First, realizing what a sharp person Dave Poulin is, and with the Flyers on the downside during his waning tenure, Clarke may have thought that Dave would want to retire at the end of the season and enter the world of business, where he had been offered some fine opportunities.

Second, the Flyers may have been stocking forwards for an upcoming major trade.

As for the "Rat," Linseman, I don't think that Clarke ever regarded Kenny very highly, although Linseman had obviously matured and mellowed in Boston. It was like trying to renew an unsuccessful old love affair. And how often does *that* work?

And as for bolstering the offense, Linseman ended up with just five goals in twenty-seven games. He also suffered the ignominy of being benched for the first time in his entire career. In his *two* careers with the Flyers, Linseman had regressed from "the next Bobby Clarke" to one of the nails in Clarke's coffin.

Just prior to the trading deadline in early March, Brian Propp was also sent to Boston, in return for a number two draft choice. The eleven-year veteran, the Flyers' second-all-time left winger after Bill Barber, had been selected by the fans to start in February's All-Star Game, despite having missed twenty-five games due to an odd, even bizarre injury.

I believe that Propp's affliction is called "Butcher's Hand," but it should be called "Butcher's Block," because it consists of a blood-clot blockage in the palm of the hand. After microsurgery and a period of rehabilitation, Propp returned and immediately recorded seventeen points in his next twenty games. But management decried his penalty-killing and hustle, and like Linseman, he was scratched by Holmgren for not working hard enough.

The Bruins already had the league's best record, but were seeking that added edge which might bring them a Cup. With Poulin, and then Propp, Boston had acquired the Flyers' (and the league's) major penalty-killing team of the eighties. The Bruins were expecting a defensive edge from them, but they got an offensive edge as well, as both Poulin and Propp were useful on the power play, an aspect of Poulin's game, at least, which had been pretty much unused in his last several years in Philadelphia.

Every time I saw those two perform so well for Boston during the playoffs, my battered old heart felt a little twinge. If the Flyers couldn't be there, at least it was good to see two *recent* Flyers in the Stanley Cup Finals again! I must say, though, that it looked odd to see them in gold and black, instead of orange and black, and with a "B" instead of a "P" on their chests. And no "C" on Poulin's.

I just wish that they'd had the chance to face Mike Keenan in the finals. Almost, but not quite! Our old friends, the Edmonton Oilers, made sure that *that* wouldn't happen!

Three days after the Propp trade, rough and rugged defensive veteran Jay Wells was sent to Buffalo for rough and rugged young winger Kevin Maguire. But, as might have been expected, Maguire was able to play in just five games, before a knee injury ended his season.

One of the oddest injuries involved Scott Mellanby at a Canadian resort during the summer. While trying to protect a friend during a bar fight, Scott's arm was severely lacerated by broken glass.

Following surgery and extended rehabilitation, Scott never did regain the strength in his grip to be an effective scorer. After two consecutive twenty-plus goal-scoring seasons, he could manage only six for the year.

Besides Propp, Maguire, and Mellanby, two other regular wingers were hobbled by injuries, and they also never came near their season average for goals. Those two were Derrick Smith and Tim Kerr.

After undergoing a *sixth* operation on his left shoulder, Kerr missed most of the first half of the season. His value to the team was illustrated by the fact that, *after* the surgery, he racked up thirty-five points in his first twenty-five games.

In all, Tim Kerr played in only forty games, or exactly one-half of the season. He totaled twenty-four goals and twenty-four assists, still approximately a fifty-goal, one hundred-point pace over a full season. In other words, Tim Kerr was still one of those rare players who is worth a goal or more per game. And during his absence, the Flyers had lost a dozen games by just one goal.

Perhaps the *worst* injury in terms of affecting overall team play was Mark Howe's bad back. The only Flyers defenseman (and one of the few in the N.H.L.) with both a scoring touch and the composure and ability to withstand tough times in his own zone, Howe went out for good in January, when the herniated disks in his back became just too painful to bear.

In the forty games he played, Howe had twenty-eight points and, more importantly, he lent an air of confidence and consistency to his teammates. In fact, during those forty games, the Flyers' record was 19-16-5, with a goals-against average of 3.2.

*Without* Howe, they were 11-23-6, with a goals-against of 4.4. And their penalty-killing went from 86 per cent (the best in the league) to a mediocre 74 per cent. And numbers aside, along with Ron Hextall, Howe was the only player who was able to hide some of the Flyers' blemishes and warts, including, especially, their growing inability to come out of their own end of the ice.

Besides all of the time missed by the wingers, and precisely one-half of the season missed by both their big scorer and by their long-time bellwether defenseman, now enter at the top of the I.R. the name "Ron Hextall." And if you had to compile a list of the three people the Flyers could *least* afford to miss, it would have to be those three, with Hextall at the top. So, of course, he missed *more* time than anyone else!

Following his twelve-game suspension and his brief but emotionally charged contract dispute, Hextall was supposedly set to return for Game Thirteen, in Toronto in early November. The timing seemed appropriate, since he was replacing an ill Ken Wregget.

After two periods of action, Hextall was out again, this time with a groin pull. And back in came Ken Wregget, ill or not.

Five games later, Hextall returned again, for Game Eighteen on Long Island. He won the battle against the Islanders, four to three, but he lost the war with his injured groin. He would not appear in goal again for the Flyers until the middle of February.

Long before that, when the groin seemed to have recovered, he agreed to play himself back into shape at Hershey. Almost predictably, in his first game there, the groin did not pull, but a hamstring did. He was now not only an injured Flyer with a bad groin, but a wounded Bear with a torn hamstring.

Forty-three games after his last appearance for the Flyers, Hextall again returned against the Islanders, and again he beat them, three to two. Five games later, against the Rangers in early March, he was injured for a *fourth* time, and this time it was, realistically, for the remainder of the season.

After having played more than sixty games per season for three consecutive seasons, this time he played in a total of only eight, and some of those were not full games. His record for the season: four wins, two losses, and a tie; also two left groin-muscle pulls, one right groin-muscle tear, and one left hamstring pull.

So, after four seasons, Hextall's career record looked like this:

|                          | W   | L  | T  | G.A. |
| ------------------------ | --- | -- | -- | ---- |
| Rookie season (1986–87)  | 37  | 21 | 6  | 3.00 |
| Second season (1987–88)  | 30  | 22 | 7  | 3.51 |
| Third season (1988–89)   | 30  | 28 | 6  | 3.23 |
| Fourth season (1989–90)  | 4   | 2  | 1  | 4.15 |
| Career totals            | 101 | 73 | 20 | 3.24 |

While Hextall was missing, the Flyers' defense allowed almost 300 goals, but that was not entirely due to the absence of Hextall and Howe. It was due also to the injury problems of Ken Wregget, who played fifty-one games and won a career-high twenty-two, but who missed eleven others, including four crucial ones in the season's final days. Diagnosis: Not one, but *two* hamstring pulls.

And there were other problems in the net, as third-string goaltender Pete Peeters showed why Washington had given up on him. Aside from a three-to-nothing shutout of Toronto in mid-February, the Flyers' *only* shutout of the season, Peeters' record was 0-13-5.

Fourth-string prospect Bruce Hoffort played eight games for the Flyers, the same number as Hextall played, and his record was a promising 3-0-2. Overall, the Flyers' season goaltending stats displayed a list four times longer than their list of thirty-goal scorers; and that doesn't even include trainer Sudsy Settlemyre, who suited up once, but never got in a game:

| | W | L | T | G.A. |
|---|---|---|---|---|
| Ken Wregget | 22 | 24 | 3 | 3.42 |
| Pete Peeters | 1 | 13 | 5 | 3.74 |
| Bruce Hoffort | 3 | 0 | 2 | 3.65 |
| Ron Hextall | 4 | 2 | 1 | 4.15 |

As one N.H.L. executive put it, "When Ron Hextall is not in the net, the Flyers' transition game goes into the toilet. If any organization loses a goalie the caliber of Hextall for seventy-two games, I don't care if you've got Toe Blake behind the bench, you're not going to win."

In case you didn't know, Toe Blake was the legendary Montreal Canadien coach, and the hockey equivalent of Green Bay's Vince Lombardi.

And how did Hextall himself react to all of the turmoil surrounding his absence? First, regarding the actions which led to his suspension: "Anybody who has ever played hockey in a championship series knows how emotional and intense the game can become. If I have a good game, a lot of it comes from my emotional attitude. Unfortunately, some bad things can come from it, too."

Then, regarding his injuries: "Any injury can become chronic, but I don't think that is my case. I hurt the same muscle only twice, and I had just one pull in all my years of junior hockey. I don't consider those injuries career-threatening, and I'm not worrying about them. I'm not really changing my routine. I wasn't doing anything wrong last season. All those injuries were flukes, as far as I'm concerned.

"It was a very tough time for me. It's tough enough to sit there and watch your teammates play night after night, but it's even tougher when they're struggling."

Next, as for whom or what to blame: "It doesn't bother me to take the blame. I'm used to taking the blame. I know that once you become a key player on a team, and I consider myself to be that, that you have to share the blame. I've never shunned that.

"But is it justified? I don't know. Who is to say how I affected the team? All I know is that, for me, the team comes before anything else. Players don't play for a general manager. They don't play for the coach. They play for the team. People ask me, 'Who comes first, your wife and kids or the team?' I say, 'Both of them have a time. When I'm on the ice, the team comes first. At home, it's my wife and kids.' "

Finally, as for the future: "I'm looking forward to next season, because I see some new blood coming in. I want to see some young guys who are hungry. Look how well Edmonton did this year, winning the Cup with a young team. Our club has to be picked near the bottom next year, but we'll still have high expectations.

"You know, I'd sooner be on a team with more heart than talent than the other way around. It's like the 1987 team. We had heart. We didn't win the Cup, but it was a rewarding season because of the way we played."

Have you heard enough about injuries? Sorry, I'm not through quite yet. After all, injuries were undoubtedly the biggest reason for the team's collapse.

To their credit, the management and players refused to blame their poor showing on their lack of manpower. But, speaking of manpower, or lack thereof, do you remember that new statistic of mine: "man-games lost to injury"? Well, the Flyers not only led the N.H.L., with 387, they also surpassed their previous club record by 143 games.

When asked about this ugly number, Paul Holmgren replied, "I hate to use injuries as an excuse, and I'm not going to start now. At times we played, as a whole, up to our potential. Most times we didn't, and that was the reason for our inconsistency. We all have to share the blame.

"Hockey is a violent sport. Things are done at a high rate of speed. Most of the injuries we had this year were probably unavoidable, no matter what we did. It's part of the game. It's the nature of the sport.

"It's tough, though, to get any real chemistry when you're using that many people. The line-up is different every night."

As a result of all of that line-up juggling, when you looked in the daily paper for the list of the N.H.L.'s leading scorers, only one Flyer appeared in the top twenty-five, which is as far as the published list goes. That was Rick Tocchet, who finished fifteenth, with thirty-seven goals, a career-high fifty-nine assists, and a career-high total of ninety-six points. Not bad for a sixth-round draft choice.

Other than Tocchet's personal best season, and Tim Kerr's productive half-season, the only other plus for the year offensively was Pelle Eklund, who established himself as a solid two-way player, rather than just a power-play specialist. And he was particularly brilliant in the second half of the season, when the pressure was greatest.

But the statistics of those three—Tocchet, Kerr, and Eklund— were the only numbers which recommended the Flyers for anything but elimination.

Pragmatically speaking, the Flyers (except for Tocchet and Kerr) did not get big performances from their big forwards. And, of course, they did not get big hits from their small forwards. As a result, the Flyers were a team with a split personality: The big guys couldn't score, and the little guys couldn't hit!

So, on every line change, Paul Holmgren had to make a choice between the two, and he never did have a complete Flyer-type team on the ice at the same time. In fact, he never had on the ice a consistent image of *any* kind, except perhaps a consistently inconsistent one.

All of this brings me to one last point regarding this even year of even more injuries than ever before: For a half-season or more, and/or especially during the all-important final weeks of the season, the Flyers were missing their best forward line of the eighties— Poulin, Propp, and Kerr; their all-time best defenseman—Mark Howe; their All-Star goaltender—Ron Hextall; *and* his newly accomplished back-up—Ken Wregget. That group, with one more defenseman added, would make a pretty fair All-Star Team!

In fact, if you'll allow me to throw in the promising rookie, Jiri Latal, who also missed a major portion of the season due to injuries, I'll play my all-injured team against yours any day! And just as long as my guys are healthy again, I'd bet my all-hurt team would lay some hurt on your all-hurt team every time!

Incredibly, with all of that turmoil and adversity, the Flyers were still struggling for a playoff spot until the season's next-to-last game. And they missed out in the oddest way, while the Islanders squeezed in, also in the oddest way.

The Islanders entered the final week of the season with a record of 1-15-4 in their preceding twenty games, but somehow still managed to make the playoffs. How? Two reasons:

1. The Penguins lost Mario Lemieux to injury, and then went winless in their last twelve on the road and their last eight overall. They finished fifth in the division.

2. The Flyers, needing only a point here or there, couldn't get them, going winless in their last five games. Ironically, it was the Islanders themselves who, on the last Saturday night of the season, officially eliminated the Flyers, six to two. The Flyers finished sixth in the division.

So, the Islanders, with their hard-charging stretch drive of 3-15-4, finished fourth in the division, and they were in the playoffs. The Penguins were not. And, of course, the Flyers were not.

The news from Hershey was similarly discouraging. Three years before, when the Flyers had gone to the Stanley Cup Finals, the Bears had not only gone to the finals in the A.H.L., but they had won the Calder Cup with twelve straight wins. It was the first time in professional playoff history that *any* team had won twelve consecutive games.

Now, in 1990, the Flyers and Bears had almost identically poor records, and neither team made the playoffs. It was one more indication of how thin the talent had become in the Flyers organization.

Following their Saturday night elimination by the Islanders, there still remained one final game, a Sunday night game against Detroit in the Spectrum. So, we all turned our clocks ahead (for Daylight Saving Time), and on April Fool's Day, also known as All Fool's Day, 1990, the Flyers played the first and *only* meaningless game in the entire history of the franchise.

It was a very odd feeling for me, and for the players, and for the subdued members of the audience. "How fortunate we've been," I recall thinking, "that this has never happened before: No playoff implications for either team; only future draft implications. Ugh!"

Had the Flyers lost, they would have jumped ahead of Detroit in the selection order for the draft. Fittingly, the teams tied, three-to-three, giving the Red Wings the third pick, and the Flyers the fourth.

As expected, the Flyers weren't interested in losing, only in giving some prospective future Flyers some N.H.L. ice time. Rookie goaltender Bruce Hoffort played the entire game, and another rookie, Craig Fisher, was given a regular shift as a centerman. It probably meant something to them, but it didn't mean much to anyone else.

During the season-ending awards ceremony that night, young Gord Murphy was named winner of the Barry Ashbee Trophy as the Flyers' best defenseman, and Rick Tocchet was awarded the Bobby Clarke Trophy as the Flyers' Most Valuable Player. For Ron Hextall, it was the first time in his five years as a professional athlete that he was *not* named his team's M.V.P.

As close as the Flyers had come to making the playoffs, just two points away to be exact, it was officially recorded as their *lowest finish ever,* because for the first time ever in *any* division, they had finished dead, *blunk[1]* last. In the cellar. The other two times they had missed the playoffs (1970 and 1972), they had finished in a fourth-place tie, and had been eliminated by a tie-breaker.

Only three teams in the N.H.L. finished with fewer points than the Flyers' total of seventy-one. The league's five worst teams, and the only non-playoff qualifiers, were these:

| Team | Points |
|------|--------|
| Pittsburgh | 72 |
| Philadelphia | 71 |
| Detroit | 70 |
| Vancouver | 64 |
| Quebec (last *again*) | 31 |

By comparison, the worst of the playoff *qualifiers* were these:

---

1. *"blunk"*—the sound of a rock striking, after a long fall, the bottom of a well.[2]

2. Since we spent all of that time in school learning about footnotes, I thought we should use at least one or two.

| Team | Points |
|------|--------|
| N.Y. Islanders | 73 |
| Los Angeles | 75 |
| Minnesota | 76 |
| Washington | 78 |
| Toronto | 80 |

Do you detect some so-called "parity" in those totals?

Further, only two Patrick Division teams had winning records. And there was a spread of only fourteen points from the Rangers' division-winning total of eighty-five to the Flyers' last-place total of seventy-one.

Unfortunately, however, there were some other very ominous notes for the Flyers:

1. Not only had their once expert penalty-killing slipped into mediocrity, their once-vaunted power play was ranked among the league's bottom third.

2. They had lost a total of twenty games by one goal, while winning only nine.

3. Only once all season had they won a game that they trailed after two periods.

4. Nine times they had *not* won a game that they *led* after two periods.

5. In overtime games, they won just two of eighteen.

6. Against teams in their own fading division, they had won just thirteen of thirty-six games.

7. In games at the Spectrum, where they had once Bullied everyone, they were 17-19-3, the worst home record in their history.

8. They had lost a club-record thirty-nine games.

9. And, most importantly, for the first time in eighteen years, the dream of a Stanley Cup had ended before it had even begun.

# Low...
## Lower...
### Lowest

Even before the 1990 season finale against Detroit, general manager Bob Clarke had made several points perfectly clear:

"In hindsight, I should have traded Dave Poulin for a younger player or a draft choice, like I did with Brian Propp and Jay Wells. If I thought we weren't going to make the playoffs, that's what I would have done.

"But no one's going to give you a young player who can do the same things as one of your thirty-one-year-olds or give you a high draft choice. We just didn't have the depth to make the right deal. At the beginning of the season, our only excess was in our goalies. And that was no longer an excess when Hextall held out and then got injured. So I lost the option of trading a goalie.

"Considering all the diversity he faced, I thought Paul Holmgren did a pretty good job. Things got screwed up for him right from the start of the season, when Hextall became a holdout. That was the first of what became many disappointments this year.

"I think a coach should share the responsibility when he doesn't use his players properly. But when it comes to putting out a solid effort every game, that's the responsibility of the player himself. It's not always the coach's fault. One thing we learned this season is which players hung tough when things went bad and which ones didn't.

"Ken Wregget was one of the bright spots for us this year. But, obviously, he doesn't give us the extra dimension Hextall gives us with his stick-handling. I also thought Rick Tocchet, Ron Sutter, Murray Craven, and Pelle Eklund had good years. They give us a pretty good nucleus.

"When you don't make the playoffs, you know that changes have to be made. *Changes will be made,* and, for sure, we will have a younger club. We're committed to a youth movement."

Bob Clarke also stated that one thing that would *not* change would be the identity of the man behind the Flyers' bench, as both Paul Holmgren and Clarke himself were committed to and looking forward to the challenge of rebuilding the team. At the same time, club president Jay Snider sent word through a team spokesman that he would reserve comment on club matters until later in the week.

As the Flyers finished the season's final team meeting, Clarke criticized the players for taking advantage of Holmgren's easygoing methods, and he blamed the club's many injuries on players who were more interested in looking like Greek gods than in being in condition for hockey. He added these statements for publication:

"Paul's got to get tougher with the players. Some of them [bleeped] on Paul.

"Players today are almost into bodybuilding. They don't need to look good on the beach. They have to look good on the ice. They need their muscles to be more functional."

The evening after the final game, I was entering the studio at WIP for my usual Monday night's "Hart on Hockey" show, when lovable Howard Eskin, as he was ending his shift, spotted me. Before he could fully insert his needle, I simply played taps on my kazoo over his introduction.

The theme of the show that night was similar to what Ray Parrillo had written in the *Inquirer:* "Blasphemous as it may sound to Philadelphia's hockey fans, the New York Islanders probably did the Flyers a favor on Saturday night by drawing a curtain over their Stanley Cup playoff hopes.

"Now, at least, the Flyers can't camouflage their decline with a successful playoff run, as they did last season, when they finished .500 during the regular season, then advanced to the Cup semi-finals.

"Now the aging Flyers know beyond doubt that they must be reshaped with an infusion of youth and with some trades. After all, they had been in a steady decline since the end of the 1986–87 season before the bottom dropped out when the Isles eliminated them from playoff contention."

I don't think any of us dared to guess that night how deep the changes would go. My emphasis during the show was on the upcoming draft, which reputedly would yield the best crop of prospects in recent years. And realizing that Bob Clarke had accumulated seven (*never enough,* in his estimation) of the first forty-seven choices in that draft, including the fourth pick overall, I delighted in discussing the possibilities involved.

The last time the Flyers had an equally lofty choice was in 1982, when they selected Ron Sutter, now captain of the team. I enumerated all of the players who would be available through the first four or five picks this time, and every one of them just happened, happily, to be a big, rangy, creative centerman, which also just happened to be one of the Flyers' greatest needs.

Despite the dismal ending of the season, and the rather limited options for a major trade, I was feeling quite good. After all, the late-season agony was over, the draft looked ultra-promising, and one of my favorite people, Fred Shero, had rejoined the family. In other words, I was just starting to feel as though there might be a tomorrow after all for the Flyers, and for me.

That was on April 2. Just two weeks later, on Monday, April 16, there came an aftershock that was far more devastating than anything that had preceded it.

At the start of the season back in October, just six months earlier, imagine the odds you could have had on this parlay:

1. The 76ers would win the N.B.A.'s Atlantic Division Championship.

2. They would beat a good Cleveland team in the playoffs and then face Michael Jordan and the Chicago Bulls in the next round.

3. The Flyers would *not* make the playoffs for the first time in eighteen years.

4. The "Ultimate Flyer," Bob Clarke, would be fired.

I would have said, as the Phillies' folksy Rich Ashburn would have put it, "You can bet your house it won't happen." I guess that's why I'm not a betting man.

On Tuesday, April 17, the *Inquirer's* front-page headline blared: "Clarke Is Fired as Flyers GM." The *Daily News* trumpeted, in its bold and clever fashion: "Hero's Unwelcome."

The lead story of that heavy news day was summarized thus: "After serving six seasons as general manager of the Philadelphia Flyers, Bob Clarke, who personified the Flyers' smoldering work ethic, was fired last night because of what team president Jay Snider termed their "fundamental differences" over the future direction of the team.

" 'After much discussion over many months, it became apparent that Bob and I have fundamental differences concerning the future of the team,' Snider said. 'Though we both have the same goals —winning our division and the Stanley Cup—we disagree on the best way to attain those goals. Plus, putting personal feelings aside, I felt it was necessary to make a change.

" 'This is the most difficult decision I've ever had to make.' "

Probably no more shocking jolt has hit the city of Philadelphia than the dismissal of the man who had been without question the most popular, the most admired, and the person to receive the most affection of any sports figure in the history of the city.

It was, obviously, a blockbuster of a story, and one which dominated the newspapers, the talk shows, and all of the TV news programs. The *Inquirer* alone, besides its front-page lead, ran five other articles on the front page of the sports section, then five more the following day, and so on, for weeks.

The furor, and the deep feelings of the notoriously cynical Philadelphia press would perhaps best be represented by these four sentences from Frank Dolson: "It's never pleasant to see a fallen hero, least of all a hero of Clarke's magnitude in this city.

"It would be hard to find anyone who taught us more about how sports should be played—and about how sportsmen should act —than Bobby Clarke. That's what hurt most about his firing on Monday—the realization that he, of all people, deserved to go out with a blare of trumpets, a standing ovation, a heartfelt thank-you, not a boot in the rear.

"On this day, of all days, we should remember Bob Clarke, the player, his face scarred by those fifteen years of high sticks and flying elbows and digging unhesitatingly into the corners, not the Bob Clarke in the gray flannel suit."

Many writers phrased in different verbiage this thought from Paul Holmgren: "No matter what direction they take from this point on, the Flyers will never ever be the same."

Holmgren also added a personal note: "I let Bob down."

On Channel 10's eleven o'clock news, sports director Al Meltzer ended his closing commentary with this: "In my long career, I respected him more than anyone else I've ever covered in hockey, no, make that in all of sports. I have four daughters, but if I had a son, I'd want his role model to be Bob Clarke."

Two days later, on his morning radio show, Tom Brookshier said, "I was in shock all day. They might as well change the team's uniforms, like the L.A. Kings did when they got Wayne Gretzky."

The aftershocks continued to reverberate around the N.H.L., as the news reached and touched players, ex-players, coaches, and general managers, no matter where they were.

Several Flyers called from Switzerland, where they were playing in the World Championships. A shocked Rick Tocchet said, "I didn't expect that at all. When I think of Bob Clarke, I think of a Philadelphia Flyer forever..."

An equally jolted Mark Howe said, "Bobby Clarke is the Flyers, and the Flyers are Bobby Clarke."

And from Clarke's former teammates:

Bernie Parent: "I wish I could say something, but I don't know what to say. It's such a tough decision for them to make. I just can't get my thoughts together on this right now. Such a good friend."

Joe Watson: "He exemplified what hard work really is and what dedication can do for a person. If there was ever a self-made superstar, boy, there's the guy. He really didn't have a lot of talent, but he made himself into one of the finest players in the game.

"It's hard to fathom what happened to him tonight. I was really taken aback. The GM is in charge of everything; it's his team. I guess he and Jay Snider just didn't get along. So he gets put out to greener pastures."

Bob Kelly: "Everybody was waiting for something to explode. It might have been the best thing for him physically. No question about it, he lived and died with every shift. He died a lot of deaths this year.

"This is just another chapter in his life. It didn't go as well as when he was playing, but that doesn't mean he wasn't a success. It doesn't take anything away from him, and it doesn't tarnish what he did for this city."

Bill Clement: "No one, absolutely no one ever, wanted the Flyers to do well more than Bob Clarke. Bobby Clarke wanted the Philadelphia Flyers to win almost as much as he wanted to live.

"It was a terribly sad thing to see. Believe me, all of the players on those two Cup teams—and I'm one—realize that they owe their two championship rings to Bobby Clarke."

Fred Shero, Clarke's former coach: "The Flyers got spoiled. They won and they won and they won. All that winning made for lousy drafts. They came up with nothing in those drafts. Then you add injuries to Hextall and Howe and Kerr, and that will kill any club...and any coach or general manager."

Mike Keenan, the coach Clarke hired *and* fired: "It's a fine line that you tread sometimes. Last year's Stanley Cup champions, the Calgary Flames, could have lost to Vancouver in the opening round on a breakaway in overtime in the seventh game, and that could have changed the whole history of the Calgary organization.

"You have to live through those situations sometimes to understand them. It's part of sport, and it's part of the excitement of sport."

David Poile, Washington Capitals general manager: "When you think of all that man has done for that franchise, you would think that if anyone had lifetime security, it was Clarke.

"I don't think any general manager in this league feels very good about this move."

Pat Quinn, Vancouver Canucks general manager: "Are the people of Philadelphia upset? They should be. To an outsider like I am now, it looks like a dramatic reaction to one bad season in eighteen.

"The day after the stuff hit the fan, I called Bobby and offered him a job. I said, 'You can come work for me right now.' I know he probably thought it was just a gesture on my part, but I meant it. The offer still stands. He's a good hockey man."

Harry Sinden, Boston Bruins general manager: "Without Ray Bourque we're a very different club than with Ray Bourque. Same goes with Mark Howe. Without Howe they are a very different club.

"And they are a *totally* different club without Howe, Kerr, and Hextall in there. It would not be fair not to take that into consideration.

"People sometimes don't look at the reality of a hockey club. The easy thing is to blame a coach and GM.

"We are all vulnerable to missing playoffs and bad years and such. We are all walking a very thin line these days.

"Maybe there were problems for Clarke about the trades. The Poulin trade was very good for us. And if there were major disagreements, say here between myself and others on trades, I'd be gone, too.

"If it were me, I'd go look for another Bob Clarke."

And from the fans, not just the ones who called in to the talk shows, but also the ones who sent messages to the Clarkes' home:

Along with flowers, came this message: "Every so often, why do I have to be reminded like this that life ain't fair?"

And this representative telegram:

We watched you for 21 years from Section G, Row 10.
We speak what the real fans think:

1. You are the greatest sports hero in Philadelphia in any sport.

2. You have done more for the Flyers organization than any other person.

3. The decision to replace you was one of the all-time worst decisions ever made by a sports owner.

4. Any other N.H.L. team will be delighted to employ you.

5. Your loss to Philadelphia is irreplaceable.

6. Never ever change your ideals or feel cheated.

7. In the long run you will be remembered when your employers will be forgotten.

8. Down the road all will work to your advantage.

9. Thank you for being the best at what you do.

—Two Charter Season Ticket Holders


All books, hopefully, try to find a complete ending. Our assumption was, as we came to the closure of our book, that the end would be the first failure of the Flyers in eighteen years to make the Stanley Cup playoffs: "In the year 1990, in the month of April, the Flyers had reached rock bottom with a thump..."

That would have been the culmination of our long story, along with the idea of beginning anew and starting again to build up the team, as in the expansion year of 1967-68. With new troops, and fresh faces, along with some rejuvenated veterans, we would anxiously await the coming of September, and another run at the Stanley Cup...

The ending, obviously, wasn't to be that simple. But it would become far more significant. For, Bob Clarke's departure would mark not just the end of an "era," a term we've used a number of times already; let's call it, instead, the end of an epoch. And what an epic epoch it was!

But, after twenty-one years, Bob Clarke was no longer a Flyer. Maybe in heart, but not in actuality.

In sifting through the ashes, trying to find meaning and reasons for Clarke's departure, there was obviously more to it than not making the playoffs, or perhaps some failure in drafting and/or trades, or anything else of that nature. More so, it appeared to be the manner in which the Flyers were to be conducted in the future, and the manner in which they would be led into that future.

Piecing all of the stories and comments together, one has to feel that Jay Snider wanted to make a clean overhaul of the club, building with youth as a base, both in Philadelphia and in Hershey. One might project that Clarke may have said, "No, you can't go all kids, because we might wind up as another Quebec, a total failure."

Perhaps Clarke suggested that it had to be done more gradually than Jay Snider wanted it to be done. In any case, Clarke's patience and deliberate style may have been one of the causes contributing to his dismissal.

When on the one hand you have a bottom-line-oriented businessman with a complete overhaul in mind, and on the other hand you have a former player saying, in effect, "Let's go gently into this good future," the man who signs the checks will win every time. Nevertheless, Clarke had to be surprised at what he must have perceived as his own failure.

The analysis of all this, as to the whys and wherefores, could go far into the night. In fact, it did. But the deed had been done, and now one can only reflect in memory on Clarke's time in Philadelphia.

From his arrival in the late sixties through his career as a Hall-of-Fame-caliber player, and then through his second career as a general manager, Clarke's style became the Flyers' style—smart, aggressive, even intimidating. The Flyers were, and probably still are, the most hated team in the N.H.L., because of that style.

Occasionally in recent years, that image may have hurt the Flyers a bit. As Ron Hextall once said, "We are not bullies; we are having to live with the reputation of the teams in the past."

Whether that reputation was legitimate or not, it all started with this young man from Flin Flon who, when he finished only second in the Rookie-of-the-Year voting, stated, "I don't care about personal recognition. All I want to do is help the Philadelphia Flyers be as good as they can be."

From the start, Clarke also understood the supposedly hypercritical Philadelphia fans: "I think the fans here like teams that try hard. They like physical play, and I think they like the idea that if a guy gets knocked down, he's going to get up and battle back. Everybody wants to win, but I think they're not going to give you a tough time if you try your hardest and lose."

With that kind of attitude, it's no wonder that Clarke became the first player ever to receive not just a long-term contract, but a *lifetime* contract. That meant, amazingly enough, that no matter what might happen, Clarke would be paid by the Flyers, even in the unlikely event that he should work for another team.

When he finally retired, or was urged into retirement as a player, and when he then assumed what must have been for him the most frustrating job imaginable, Clarke reflected upon some of his background for that job:

"Playing big-league hockey was just something that I wanted to do more than the next kid. Everybody on the block would play. Some only played three nights a week, some four nights. I was the one that played every night. It was just because I liked to play. . .

"I'm extremely proud of winning the two Stanley Cups. For me, the greatest thing was when you got everybody on the team all pulling together for the same common goal and everybody working as hard and wanting the same thing and then accomplishing that. It's such a feeling. It was like dreamland for three or four years. For me, that was the whole thing.

"It scares me when I hear a player say, 'Well, this is a great contract because, when I'm done playing, I'll never have to work another day in my life.' The guy's going to be maybe thirty-four or thirty-five when he's done playing, and he doesn't want to work the rest of his life? What kind of a person is that?

"It's like loyalty and dedication to your hockey club or your sports team is not considered a strong trait any more. Like Freddie Shero used to say, 'We want people with character, not people who are characters.'

"My wife always tells me that I never look backwards. She says I have an ability to always look forward, to never really look back and carry these things with me."

Fortunately. And hopefully.

After the Flyers' miserable start of what turned out to be Clarke's final season with the team, *PhillySport* magazine in its December issue ran a somewhat prophetic cover story entitled, "The Mid-Life Crisis of Bobby Clarke." In that story, Bill Fleischman included several quotations which take on new meaning in the light of subsequent events:

"I played hockey for a living, and I loved it. But my basic feelings are no different than yours or anyone else's. I have my own worries about my family and whether my kids will be all right.

"The problem we all face raising children is the options that are available for kids today. When I was thirteen or fourteen, in the winter, you played hockey. Kids now have so many things thay can do. Sometimes they don't make a total commitment to the game until it's too late or it's later than you hoped for them.

"I worry if this job is what I want to do the rest of my life. If it isn't, then what's my next step? I was a lucky one, because for fifteen years I got to play hockey. I don't know that anything else in my life is ever going to be that good.

"When you play, the satisfaction is always right there. You've got control over so much of your own destiny. When you're in a management position, you don't have that much control. That's tough to get used to.

"My real problem with the job is, I don't see the big picture three years down the road as much as Jay does. I'm thinking, 'We've got to win tonight,' or 'Why did we lose last night?' "

And from Jay Snider: "His whole life as a hockey player, he was called on to go on the ice and perform. He never was trained how to look into the future, how to proceed on a management basis. He lives and dies with every game. That's part of learning. He's doing a good job.

"We put him in a tough position at first. He's handled it remarkably well, but he's had to struggle to become management-oriented. The great GMs all had a lot of years in the managing end. It was ten years before they hit their peak, but Bob's best years are ahead of him. He's his own worst critic. He wants perfection. If we're not a 100-point team, he looks at it as his fault."

And from Jay's father, Ed Snider: "He's like a lot of coaches who burn themselves out. He eats, sleeps, and breathes the job twenty-four hours a day. Keith Allen used to go home after a loss and forget about it, because he knew there was nothing he could do about it. I'm hoping Bob will stay on a consistent level of happiness."

Even in his last public statement before his dismissal, Bob Clarke, as always, was true to form. At the time, the Flyers were still struggling for playoff survival, when I had the honor of introducing him at the gala Philadelphia Sportswriters' Dinner. He didn't say much, but everyone listened:

"This organization has always based its approach on one word—'effort.' We always felt that if the effort were there, everything else would fall into place. Somehow we've gotten away from that. We're going to get it back."

So simple. So succinct. That's the way his whole career was. A P.R. man's dream.

And speaking of public relations, in which the Flyers have always excelled, it was definitely their all-time toughest time in that area. First, their desperate, but failing struggle on the ice. Then the discussion of a possible move across the river to Camden, New Jersey. And then the firing of the man president Jay Snider still refers to as the "Ultimate Flyer." That's certainly not the kind of P.R. the Flyers would like to have to deal with, but deal with it they did.

As before, rather than listening only to my pontifications regarding Bob Clarke, let's allow the principals to tell the story through their own words, most of them spoken not only for publication, but then widely publicized. Let's begin with Jay Snider, the man who announced the dismissal at a Monday evening press conference, referring to "fundamental differences."

First, some little-known background on Jay Snider, as portrayed by Bill Lyon in the *Inquirer:*

"Jay Snider, in his own way, is said to be every bit the persistent grinder and indefatigable mucker that Bobby Clarke was. Those who have been around Jay Snider in competition describe him as 'incredibly tough mentally.'

"He trained for five years in a karate discipline, attaining the sport's ultimate prize, a black belt, in 1984. The combat was so rigorous, so ferocious, that he was hospitalized, yet he kept coming back for more. At one point, his father urged him to give it up.

"It is not difficult to imagine how that must have motivated him even more, how his heart must have sung.

"The popular notion is that Jay Snider was handed over a hockey team and had not the slightest idea how it worked. But, in fact, he had studied the organization from the ground up. Literally. One of his first jobs had been sweeping Spectrum floors.

"But no matter how mightily he labored, there was always someone out there who thought of him only as a figurehead. No matter what he did, the perception lingered that whatever he had, somehow he hadn't earned.

"Wouldn't that eat at you?

"And then as the hockey team that was in his keeping began to fade, slowly at first, then with increasing momentum, he began to fret.

"He decided, increasingly, to exert his influence.

"And his general manager, a man of not inconsiderable pride himself, did not relish the idea of being pressed into deals or trades, preferred that 'evolution, not revolution' philosophy, preferred to build slowly through the draft, to take some lumps now in exchange for long-term stability and success.

"Perhaps those were the 'fundamental differences.'

"In the stewardship of Bob Clarke, the Flyers, as Snider himself noted, came within one twenty-minute period of winning the Stanley Cup. And they survived the death of goalie Pelle Lindbergh and an uncommon run of crippling injuries to almost every key player.

"But in the last five years their point total also slipped each season. They have been in steady, undeniable decline.

"It has become obvious they had to do something. They have begun with the biggest decapitation possible."

Jay Snider:

"Whether this organization does well or poorly is my responsibility, and I will not sit back. I am not brain dead. My job is not guaranteed, either. I am not happy with my performance this year, and I'm going to do something about it.

"When you finish fourth-worst in the league, if you're satisfied, something is wrong.

"We had a hell of a run in the 1980's. But all teams have a four-to-five-year life. Ours was coming to a close, and I wanted to make some changes so we can have a similar run in the 1990's. We were lacking identity this year. We're in a transition period, and we have to be sure to develop the team that we want. We have a lot to do here.

"My goal is not to make the playoffs. It is to win the division and then the Stanley Cup. Too many teams settle for making the playoffs, and that's why so many teams are stuck at the bottom of the standings. The consolation prize is the draft, and I didn't want to trade for veteran players who might have helped us make the playoffs this year but not be here three years from now.

"I don't like the idea of a veteran taking ice time away from a kid.

"Because Bob and I had private differences does not mean that I want more power than I have now or that I want to be more involved. I have always been involved, and I always will be. I was involved with Bob McCammon and with Bob Clarke, and I will be involved with the new general manager. I'm not comatose.

"He's got to be a good manager of people. He's got to be able to plan ahead. He's got to see into the future and make tough decisions. He also has to stay level. My father is emotional, and I'm emotional. I need someone who can keep their composure in tough situations.

"I think I made a good choice in Bob Clarke. But I had an extraordinary guy, and there aren't many like him. I think there is one in a thousand who could come off the ice and do what he's done. Serge Savard did it in Montreal. I don't think there are any others.

"Bob Clarke has a lifetime contract, and he will always have it. The door has been left open."

Ed Snider (years ago): "He's like a son to me."

Ed Snider (April 1990): "You know, when he took this job, Bob never had a chance to catch his breath, and, believe me, we're still looking at ourselves in the mirror about that. But that's history now.

"The way things went, Bob ended up insisting that Jay fire him. Bob did not want another role in the organization. Keith Allen resigned as general manager to become an executive vice president, and he's a tremendous asset. We thought Bob could do the same. It came down to a matter of pride and competition. Bob lived and died with the team, but what had to be was not what he wanted.

"This was not a personality thing. Their differences just became more pronounced. They had several meetings, and it all culminated on Monday. We all knew we had to do something to turn the team around. It had declined for the past five years.

"The difference was how we should turn things around in the long run. The two had different blueprints, and when they couldn't come to a compromise, it came to this. It was just impossible to continue.

"I can't say how sad I am about what happened.

"I'm worried about Bob. He's chewing tobacco again, and he's a very intense person. He lived and died with the team."

As Bill Lyon summed it up, "You can understand that, understand brother against brother, son against son, can't you?

"After all, doesn't it happen even in the best of families?"

Not until several days after his dismissal, and not until he was sure that his words would not jeopardize the position of anyone else (such as Coach Paul Holmgren or Assistant General Manager John Paddock), did Clarke himself speak out. It was in a press conference before a full encampment of the best of Philadelphia's media—an all-star company representing dailys, weeklys, monthlys, radio, television, you name it. And it seemed that most of those in attendance were there mainly to elicit from Clarke the specific reasons for the split.

No way. The harshest thing Bob Clarke would say about the franchise that let him go was:

"I was loyal. I sacrificed everything, including probably my family, along the way.

"If being loyal to the players was wrong, then I'm wrong."

Over and over, pressed to provide details, prodded for the reasons he was fired, Clarke deflected all of the inquiries.

He would, with an apologetic shrug, whisper, "I can't give you answers to some of the questions you're asking."

Or, he would demur, "I really don't want to talk about what's private between Jay and I. We have to respect each other's position. Throwing mud at each other doesn't solve anything. It was a brotherly quarrel. I like Jay. We just think differently.

"We had some differences of opinion that I hoped we could work out. Jay felt otherwise, and he's the boss...I had absolutely no problems with the Snider family. I just had a difference of opinion.

"I don't think what went on behind closed doors is for public consumption." He later added, "I think Jay is an owner you can be successful with."

And as for Jay's father, Ed, Clarke said, "Mr. Snider was sick over it. He probably took it worse than I did."

As for why he had refused to accept another position within the Flyers organization: "I don't think my pride would let me. And I don't think it would have been good for the organization. The new general manager coming in doesn't need me hanging around."

As for how he felt about it all: "I'm not bitter. I'm disappointed. But I think that's understandable. I think for twenty-one years, everything was terrific, and one day isn't going to spoil that. I've had a tremendous amount of success. I've made great friends. I've made a lot of money. The fans have been outstanding to me. The media has always treated me good.

"My father raised me to be loyal to my employers and to work hard, and I think I brought that to the table. I just lost a job, and I have to look at it that way.

"My pride is damaged, but I'll get another job, and I'll be successful somewhere else."

As for his own future, he was typically understated. Yes, he would stay in hockey. "That's my life," he said plaintively. "That's my love."

Sigh.

Pause.

"That's all I know."

As for whether he'd be interested in coaching:

"No...no..."

When you are known for getting right to the point, *un*like me, you don't need to say a whole lot. And how rare that quality is.

In his simple earthy valedictory, he said: "If we're all loyal to the same cause, we can be successful."

The miner's son from out west definitely had the best perspective of all: "I won't let one day spoil twenty-one years."

Later, with the added perspective of several weeks behind him, Clarke was again asked how he felt about it all:

"I certainly don't consider myself a tragic figure. My career here has been outstanding. Most people, especially in pro sports, either get fired or change jobs once or twice in their careers. I just happened to go twenty-one years before it happened to me, and I'm thankful for that."

And how did his children feel about having him around for a change: "I think I need it more than they do. They were probably better off without me. They're going to play whether I'm there or not. I'm just like any other father."

In retrospect, what probably was most difficult of all for Clarke to accept was that two men, both of whom shared such desire and even fervor for the Flyers to succeed, could not come to an accord agreeable to both. And as for the suggestion that, if they could not agree, Clarke might resign, he admitted to being too much of a competitor for that.

Through the day of dismissal, and then the aftermath of that, and then his own press conference, and even after that, Bob Clarke handled everything, as always, with the ultimate dignity. Every question was answered carefully and deliberately. Every statement was delivered with a calm demeanor, but also with the slightly uncomfortable aura of someone who has never been at ease with public speaking.

Of course, with previous setbacks, he had always exhibited a certain amount of personal pain, as during his extraordinary eulogy of Barry Ashbee, and then in dealing with the death of young Pelle Lindbergh, and more recently, with the firing of Mike Keenan. All of those were distasteful times to him, but they were *team* setbacks, shared equally by all.

Whatever success he had, personal or otherwise, Clarke would always say, "It's the team." And yet, in defeat, he would take the losses personally, as if he himself did not do enough.

This time, for the *first* time, he was reflecting his *own personal* pain, over what he considerd in his own mind to be his *own personal* failure. And that had to make the hurt that much more difficult to deal with.

In fact, when this humble man said, "My pride is damaged," that was the first time in all of the more than two decades that I had known him that he had *ever* referred to his own pride. And, of course, that makes sense, since the only real pride he had ever known was in his team.

# Eternal Optimist: Onward and Upward Again

For the Flyers, no matter who sits in the general manager's chair, and no matter who plays in goal, or anywhere else, winning is expected as much as superior conditioning and hard work are expected. And this formula has resulted in a remarkable record of accomplishment over the years, especially when compared with the rest of the Expansion Class of 1967, of which the Flyers are clearly the class of the class. The records of the other surviving members of that class—the Penguins, the Blues, the North Stars, and the Kings—don't come close.

Of the Original Six, only Montreal has won the Cup since the Flyers became the first expansion team to win it in 1974. Chicago hasn't won since 1961, Detroit since 1955, and the New York Rangers haven't won the Cup since the year of which we are reminded each time they play in the Spectrum, by the sign which reads, simply, "1940."

Despite the lean early years of expansion, and despite their recent difficulties with years ending in even numbers, the Flyers are one of only three N.H.L. teams with an all-time winning percentage over .600, the other two being Montreal and Edmonton. Until 1990, the Flyers had not had a losing season since 1971-72, the last year that Boston won the Cup. In fact, in *all of professional sports,* only the Bruins and the Dallas Cowboys of a few years back have had more consecutive winning seasons during the modern era. And

Montreal is the only N.H.L. team with approximately as many wins as the Flyers during the years since expansion.

That's a lot of games, and a lot of seasons, and a lot of success. And, happily, a lot of occasions for me to exclaim, "Score!"

In eighteen years, I think that even the best teams are entitled to one bad season. And maybe they even *deserve* one! At least the Flyers have never had one of those derogatory nicknames, like the Toronto "Maple Laffs," or the Detroit "Dead Wings!"

In fact, the Flyers have been the most resilient franchise in hockey. Just two years after their previous low point (in 1972), they won the Stanley Cup. And just two years after the death of the Vezina Trophy winner who had led them to the Cup finals, they had *another* Vezina winner who led them *back* to the finals.

Can they be that dynamic again? Only time will tell. And that's why I can't wait, as always, for a new season to begin, so we can all find out together.

This time the Flyers will be a new entity, with a new identity. For the first time in almost two decades, they will be rebuilding from *out of* the playoffs. And for the first time in *more* than two decades, they will be without Bob Clarke.

But the Flyers of the near future will remember Bob Clarke. As assistant coach Andy Murray stated after Clarke's dismissal: "Because of him, I think the team is headed in the right direction. We're going to have a lot of depth here. Bob hasn't sacrificed the future to try and go for it right now. His objective is to go for it all the time, but this team looks solid for the next few years.

"It's unfortunate he's not going to be a part of it, and I'm disappointed he's not going to get any of the credit."

Murray also praised Clarke for bringing to the club through trades: Murray Craven, Kjell Samuelsson, Terry Carkner, Jiri Latal, and Ken Wregget. And he said that Clarke doesn't receive enough credit for drafting and signing youngsters like: Ron Hextall, Jeff Chychrun, Gord Murphy, Kerry Huffman, Murray Baron, Jukka Seppo, Len Barrie, Craig Fisher, Pat Murray, Claude Boivin, Scott Lagrand, Dominic Roussel, and Bruce Hoffort. In fact, at least one or two of those players said that they had signed with the Flyers *because of* Bob Clarke.

Murray concluded, "His record in terms of trades is great. Look at the draft picks we've got this year. This is one of the best years for drafts, and we're in the best position the Flyers have ever been in."

Clarke had indeed gained a strong position for the 1990 draft by collecting a combined total of seven picks in the first three rounds, or seven of the first forty-seven. And most N.H.L. scouts had agreed that it would be the deepest draft in at least four years.

"No doubt, this will be a very critical draft for us," Clarke had said. "It's possible we'll get a player who can help us next year."

Clarke added that the Flyers' most pressing need was for a center-man who can give them thirty-five to forty goals a season. As it turned out, the Flyers feel that they did indeed receive the impact player that they were after, when they chose, with the fourth selection overall, center Mike Ricci (pronounced Ree-Chee), six feet, 180 pounds, from Peterborough, Ontario.

Although slowed during the last of his three junior seasons by a shoulder injury, Ricci still managed to score 116 points in sixty games, was named the Canadian Major Junior Hockey Player of the Year, and was rated number one by the Central Scouting Bureau. He also served as captain of the Canadian World Junior Team. And, therefore, could the inevitable and ironic comparisons with Bobby Clarke be far behind?

Said Ricci, sounding almost like Clarke himself, "It would be a great honor to be like a Bobby Clarke. I only have *one* missing tooth, though. I don't have more than that yet.

"I don't really think about leadership. I just go out and do the best I can and try to win. If that's what leadership is, then that's what I do. But there are a lot of leaders in Philadelphia."

And, as for his injury: "It was overplayed a lot. If I had taken a week off, I would have been one hundred per cent. But I played right through it. It healed, and that's all that counts."

Also at draft time, the Flyers traded Kevin Maguire and an eighth-round pick to Toronto for the Leafs' third-round choice, giving the Flyers not seven, but *eight* picks in the first three rounds. The club was particularly pleased with the variety of skills possessed by its fifteen draftees, as well as by the *size* of many, including that of Mike Ricci.

One problem with recent Flyer teams has been that all of the centermen have been smallish players, especially by today's standards. Not to take anything away from any of their skills, but, ideally, Ron Sutter and Pelle Eklund (and even Woody Acton and Kenny Linseman) are the kind of players who would be far more effective as second, third, or fourth-line centermen.

To make that possible, the Flyers needed a bigger, more physical specimen to play first-line center. And, of course, like number one pitchers in baseball, they don't grow them on trees in the Pine Barrens.

To continue the analogy with baseball, there is a ripple effect with a big stopper as a baseball team's number one pitcher, who, in turn, makes all the rest of the team's starters that much more effective. Likewise in hockey, a big, rangy front-line center would allow a Ron Sutter to concentrate on canceling out the opposition's top-scoring center, while a Pelle Eklund would have even more room to operate against the opposition's third or fourth-line centers.

To throw in another analogy from another sport, even "small" forward Charles Barkley (at six-feet-four, or so) would have trouble operating in the N.B.A., if he had to go head-up against a front line of Akeem Olajuwon, Patrick Ewing, and David Robinson every night.

Besides Mike Ricci and the other seven high picks from the 1990 draft, most of whom will need at least a year or two of seasoning at lower levels of play, there are numerous other forward prospects acquired through previous drafts, trades, and signings. As Bob Clarke said during his final season, "We feel some of our better players are in college or in Europe. Hopefully, they'll be able to step right in and play."

Among those players are center Craig Fisher, of Miami (Ohio); left winger Pat Murray, of Michigan State; center Greg Johnson, of North Dakota; center/left wing Jukka Seppo, in Finland; and left winger Patrick Juhlin and center Niklas Eriksson, both in Sweden.

And, as Paul Holmgren said after the season, "Obviously, Craig Fisher and Len Barrie and Jukka Seppo, guys who are already under contract, are going to be given a long look during training camp, and if they show they can pull their weight at this level, I'm sure they'll stick."

On defense, three youngsters made their presence felt during the 1989-90 season. Gord Murphy, Jiri Latal, and Murray Baron all won significant playing time because of their aggressiveness and puck-handling skills. And, of course, Bruce Hoffort showed promise in goal.

Baron and Murphy were both low-round draft picks, while the rights to Latal were acquired for another low-round pick. In fact, Murphy was a number nine choice in 1985, Baron was a number eight in 1986, and Latal was acquired from Buffalo for a number seven in 1989.

Gord Murphy, the Ashbee Award winner, was one of those rags-to-riches stories you love to see come true. From nowhere, Gordo developed into not only a major-league defenseman, but a legitimate scoring threat, and one of the anchormen upon whom the Flyers of the future will be based.

Perhaps the most interesting story among the younger Flyers belongs to the man whose uniform number and name comprise the answer to this trivia question: In all of major-league sports, who is the only player whose number and name are both palindromes (*i.e.,* like "radar," they read the same forward and backward)?

The answer is: "11, LATAL" (rhymes with "bottle"), as Jiri (rhymes with "cheery") Latal became the second Czechoslovakian defenseman in Flyers history.

The first Czech checker was Miroslav "Cookie" Dvorak in 1982, a player who was appreciated by his Flyer teammates as one of those rare Europeans who always gave his full energy to the team, rather than just coasting for the dollars. A most important distinction between Dvorak and Latal, though, was that Cookie was in his early thirties when he came over here, while Latal was in his early twenties. Dvorak played here for three seasons; Latal will be here, hopefully, for a decade or more.

Some think that Latal may be the successor to Mark Howe. At a minimum, he plays very much like Buffalo's talented Phil Housley, but is a little quicker. And like many Europeans who grew up with a soccer ball, he has remarkable skills afoot, as well as the gifts of great speed and an ability to shoot.

And how did the Flyers find and deliver such a talented young man from a then-Communist country? It's almost an old-fashioned "undercover" story:

First, Andy Murray traveled to Germany, where Jiri was playing in a fall tournament with his Czechoslovakian team. Andy and Jiri somehow met secretly about the possibility of Jiri coming to North America to play for the Flyers. Since Jiri had been in Germany, he had a legal visa, which he then used to come to America, leaving behind his father, his wife, and a young daughter.

Under the more severe Czech regimes of the past, some of the older (or "over-age") players, like Dvorak, would be allowed to come here in exchange for something like $300,000, which was then kept in Czechoslovakia, along with the player's family, so as to lure him back to become a hero of sport and a hockey coach, or whatever. The player eventually got the money, but only to use in his own country.

No country ever wants to lose its young people. But with the newfound freedom in Eastern Europe, if a player wants to leave, it will be increasingly difficult to keep him from doing so.

Fortunately for the Flyers, they were one of the first teams to benefit from the new philosophy in Czechoslovakia. I trust that the rebirth of the Flyers will proceed as quickly as the rebirth of freedom in Eastern Europe!

As further testimony to that freedom, soon after Jiri arrived here, he was joined by his father, his wife, and his daughter. His father eventually returned to the home country, but Jiri, his wife, and his daughter are living here now. And happily ever after, I hope.

During the pre-season, Jiri had to learn about play in the corners, which in North American hockey is very different from the European style. He also seemed to be overmatched defensively at times. But from the start, one thing he knew how to do was to jump into the offensive play and either pass to a teammate or get off a shot himself.

The Flyers thought that Jiri should get some North American experience in Hershey, but director of pro scouting Bill Barber kept saying, "He's too good for that league; He ought to be up here." So, for a while he was like a shuttle train—"up here" Thursday, "down there" Friday, "up here" Saturday. A helicopter might have helped.

After playing full-time for a while with the Flyers, he quickly improved in the areas that needed improvement, and he continued to stir things up offensively. Unfortunately, while stirring things up, he himself got stirred up—specifically, his ribs and shoulder—so that he was really able to play only 40 per cent of the season.

That 40 per cent was enough to show glimpses of a beautiful future career in the N.H.L., especially after a maturing process, which will teach Jiri to be a bit more wary of the more physical game in the smaller rinks of North America. Once he learns when to go up ice, and when not to, and when to protect himself and not leave himself so vulnerable to being drilled by a big body check, Jiri Latal will be ready to become a legitimate force in the N.H.L., rather than a bounced Czech, or even a canceled Czech!

When asked how he and Bob Clarke assessed the future prospects of the Flyers, Paul Holmgren responded, "Whenever we talked about the young guys who were coming, everyone was excited. The organization will move on. I don't think this team is that far away at all from being a contender. In fact, I think we'll be one of the better teams.

"I think Bob did a good job. I think he didn't get enough credit. He's not the type of guy who wants credit or expects credit. I think this organization is going to see a lot of the good things he's done in the last two or three years over the next eight to ten years."

What *will* be the legacy of Bob Clarke? Whereas Bob McCammon never got credit for the players who soon went to the Stanley Cup Finals, will Clarke get credit (or blame) for this promising crop for the nineties?

Well, here's some credit to *both* McCammon *and* Clarke!

And also, of course, the best of everything to the new general manager, Russ Farwell! (The subject of Chapter One, Volume II?)

And to the new GM of the North Stars, Bob Clarke!

And to the new GM of the Blackhawks, Mike Keenan!

In my way of thinking, the stimulation over the speculation will continue, for it's not only the quest, but the questions which fascinate and titillate:

What will happen?

Who will what?

Who will be where?

And who will finish where?

Ah, the questions! They are part of what makes hockey, and sport, so intriguing. I recall asking Keith Allen a long time ago, after the Flyers had won big in Montreal on Saturday night, and then lost to a bad Oakland team at home on Sunday night, "How do you figure it, Keith?"

"If you could figure it, there'd be no reason to play the game."

And isn't it reassuring that we will *always* have a reason to play the game?

And all of the unanswered questions are part of what makes each season truly a *new* season, with new and burgeoning hopes and dreams...

Dreams of new arenas, new players, and new accomplishments. Dreams much like the ones of a quarter-century ago!

And so, we end this book, not at the end of the story, but at the beginning of the story revisited. Because whether I'm blueskying or not, I am, first of all, a fan. Aren't you?

Probably, or you wouldn't have even started this book, let alone finished it.

In any case, whether you're a fan or not, join me in that wonderful anticipation...

For, as Gene Hart always says: "As bad as it may seem at the end of any season, all you have to do is count down the months until September and October, when fall brings another chance to begin the growth again, and to rejoin the quest, not only for a spot in the playoffs, but for an eleventh division championship, and an eleventh semi-final, and a seventh final, and, of course, a third Stanley Cup."

And, one way or another, you know that an odd year is never far off!

And I love it!

# Overtime

I've been told that I inevitably begin a wrap-up of a victorious game with, "And so, my good friends ... " And so, my good friends, I'd like to conclude this unique (for me) venture by sharing with you some of the often-overlooked aspects of the game and the team that I love.

To me, a hockey arena is the closest thing we have to the ancient arena, but the sport itself transcends by far that concept. It is not so much a "throwback" to the past as it is an entirely modern sport, with speed, and intricacy, and beauty, as well as the most basic element, courage. I appreciate all of those relatively obvious facets of the game, as I'm sure you do, too, or you probably wouldn't have read this far!

But there are so many less obvious particulars which I appreciate as well, such as, for example, the relatively recent invention of ice skates by the Dutch! And who ever would have thought of using a frozen rubber disk instead of a ball? And then calling it a "hockey puck"? Even before Don Rickles! I would award that guy (the inventor of the hockey puck, not Don Rickles) a "Hart Trophy" any day! And how about the almost equally essential development of surgical sutures, and of modern dentistry? You've got to admit that Bob Clarke looks a lot different now than he did when he was baring his fangs on the ice!

And that brings us to the modern players' protective equipment, which, theoretically, means "fewer sutures in their futures." Things have changed considerably since the days not so long ago when *no goalie wore a face mask!* (Give Bobby Hull's invention of the curved stick blade an assist on Jacques Plante's invention of the goaltender's mask!) The only problem nowadays is that the suit of protective armor worn by *everyone* in junior hockey is so complete that the officials tend to allow more stick work, which results in the need at the major-league level for more protection than ever, and puts those without all of that protection at a distinct disadvantage. Well then, the argument goes, everyone should wear all of the protection he can get. I agree to a certain extent, but at the same time I don't think it should be *necessary* to encase every player in an armored coating of sterile plastic.

The N.H.L. has made it mandatory for all players entering the league to wear helmets. It's a good idea, of course, to protect one's top end, but what about one's other end? With typical league-legality lunacy, when the Flyers pioneered newly fashioned long pants, which afforded not only a better-fitting uniform, but a more protective uniform, and when the Hartford Whalers then "followed suit," the league in all of its wisdom outlawed the wearing of long pants. Why? Probably because the idea came from the Flyers, and the rest of the N.H.L. (except for Hartford) wasn't yet grown-up enough for long pants! Interestingly enough, long pants are now very popular in junior hockey, but, of course, when the players grow up and join the big boys, they have to switch to shorts!

I wonder what would have happened if the Flyers had continued to wear their long pants, despite the league's rule against them. Would the officials have made them take their pants off and play in their long underwear? Did anything happen to the Maple Leafs when every team was ordered to wear names on their jerseys and Toronto's Harold Ballard flaunted his independence by having blue letters stitched onto the Leafs' blue jerseys? (Eventually, of course, Toronto complied with the rules, but not before Ballard had demonstrated that he took action only when *he* wanted to, not when the *league* wanted him to. This kind of creative thinking last resulted in a Cup in 1967.)

Obviously, as in the N.F.L., names on jerseys help the fans to identify the players, most of whom are now more difficult to recognize because of their helmets and/or face masks. So, for the fans, they're a good thing, even if they aren't good for the sale of programs in Toronto, nor for some players who would prefer to remain anonymous!

Another innovation to be grateful for is the miraculous system whereby miles of refrigerated tubes set in concrete provide a nearly perfect ice surface upon which to skate, except, of course, in the case of the grand opening night of the Philadelphia Blazers! I also appreciate the guys who manage to paint the checkered red line, the two blue lines, and all of those other tricky designs under the ice! And how about Mr. Zamboni's invention of a machine which will resurface the ice—at almost any time, except, of course, on the Blazers' opening night!

I am also thankful for the executive decisions against repeats of such ill-fated public relations fiascos as the fuzzy-suited and fuzzy-brained mascot called "Slap Shot," the third-level section of seats reserved for the "Zoo Crew," the foghorn-voiced cheerleader named "Beer Man Joe," and the between-periods game of "Score-O," which was just a little bit less entertaining than watching the ice being resurfaced. For those of you who don't recall "Score-O," it was an opportunity for some "lucky" fans to make fools of themselves by trying to shoot a puck from center ice at a board which covered the goal, and which had a slot at the bottom that appeared to be just slightly smaller than the puck itself. I think that the contestants were permitted to shoot across the rutty un-resurfaced ice without blindfolds, but from the results as I recall them, I'm not too sure on that point. I remember best the small children who could barely shoot the puck six feet, let alone in the laser-beam-perfect line necessary to hit the jackpot!

All of us, I think, should be grateful to (I'm serious now) the referees and linesmen, who withstand enormous quantities of abuse from the players and from everyone else, and who never enjoy the luxury of a "home" game. They pretend to ignore the personal comments and the threats from the crowd, which they *really do hear* most of the time, but to which they cannot show any reaction. Poor old Leon Stickle, for one! After his famous blown offsides call in the Stanley Cup Finals, he grew a mustache over the summer, and on his next trip to Philadelphia he was greeted in the Spectrum not only by a chorus of boo's, but by a sixty-foot sign with a picture of a gigantic mustache under which was carefully lettered, "WE STILL KNOW WHO YOU ARE!" He tells me he's kept that sign ever since. I wonder where in his house he keeps it!

I am also thankful for all of those good people who work overtime to provide the conditions for success which we take for granted, people like trainer David "Sudsy" Settlemyre and his trusty crew. Like good Moms, they work almost around the clock—

cleaning and mending uniforms, sewing names onto jerseys, and picking up after and catering to the whims of several dozen athletes. *Un*like Mom, Sudsy also does the skate-sharpening, presides over the dressing room, home and away, and has even served as an emergency goaltender, a position he once played for the old Philadelphia Firebirds of the North American Hockey League.

I am grateful also for the insight and acumen, business and otherwise, of the Sniders, Presidents Ed and Jay. And for the enduring work and perspicacity of Keith Allen, whose book of wisdom would be far longer and far deeper than mine. And, of course, I appreciate all of the great players I've told you about earlier, as well as the unsung ones, such as the forwards who come back to help defensively, and the ones who cover for the offensive thrusts of a talented scorer like Mark Howe.

Perhaps most of all, I'm thankful for the fans, including especially the old-fashioned few who still throw their hats into the rink when a player scores his third goal of the night! And, of course, I appreciate those fans I see before every game, as I slowly make my way up the steps toward the Spectrum roof, singing my own semi-operatic version of "Nearer, My God, to Thee."

I'm thankful for *all* of the *good* fans, both at home and on the road, like a little old lady I recall in Kansas City who volunteered to go to court for me after I got myself involved in a fist fight with an obnoxious guy who had been throwing pennies (the cheapskate), beer, beer cans, and beery insults at me while I was trying my best to tape a pre-game show. That good lady's testimony in court not only got me off, but it got her fellow Kansas Citian barred from hockey games for the rest of the season!

And I'm thankful for fans like John Kieran, an intellectual fellow who served on the famed radio show "Information Please," and who loved hockey so much that he wrote poems about it, one of which follows. It's not Robert Frost, but I'm fond of it:

### Give Me Hockey—I'll Take Hockey—Any Time

I'm a fairly peaceful man and a long-time baseball fan,
Always eager when the umpire cries: "Play ball!"
And I jump with joy or terror at each hit and slide and error
'Til some game-deciding tally ends it all.
But the diamond sport is quiet to that reeling rousing riot,
To a slashing game of hockey at its prime;

It's a shindig wild and gay, it's a battle served frappé;
Give me hockey—I'll take hockey—any time.

Once, while crazy with the heat, I coughed up to buy a seat,
Just to watch a pair of boxers grab a purse.
It was clinch and stall and shove, and "Please excuse my glove";
What I thought of them I couldn't put in verse.
But for fighting fast and free, grab your hat and come with me;
Sure the thing that they call boxing is a crime;
And for ground and lofty smacking and enthusiastic whacking,
Give me hockey—I'll take hockey—any time.

I've an ever-ready ear for a roaring football cheer,
And I love to see a halfback tackled low;
It's a really gorgeous sight when the boys begin to fight
With a touchdown only half a yard to go.
But take all the most exciting parts of football, baseball,
    fighting,
And then mix them up to make a game sublime;
It's the hottest thing on ice; you don't have to ask me twice;
Give me hockey—I'll take hockey—any time.

Yes, for speed and pep and action, there is only one attraction;
You'll see knockouts; they're a dozen for a dime;
When the bright steel blades are ringing,
And the hockey sticks are swinging,
Give me hockey—I'll take hockey—any time.

# Roster

Finally, for you numerologists out there, here is the full Cast of Flyers/Characters—by the numbers. And I'm sincerely grateful to each and every one of them:

**Number  Name; Years with Flyers**
Names are listed alphabetically within numbers. (Numbers in parentheses represent other numbers worn with Flyers.)

1    (Number retired to honor Bernie Parent)
Favell, Doug ("Favvie"); 1967-73
Parent, Bernie ("Bennie"); 1967-71, 1973-79 (30)
Wilson, Dunc; 1969-70

2    Dailey, Bob ("The Count"); 1977-82
Howe, Mark ("Bugger"/"Howie"); 1982-
Van Impe, Ed ("Fast Eddie"); 1967-76

3    Bladon, Tom ("Sparky"); 1972-78 (4, 23)
Brossart, Willy; 1970-73 (10, 25)
Brown, Larry; 1971-72

Crossman, Doug ("Cross"); 1983-88
Hillman, Larry; 1969-71
Mair, Jimmy; 1970-72 (25)
Murphy, Gord ("Gordo"); 1988-
Watson, Joe ("Thundermouth"); 1967-78 (14)
Wilson, Behn; 1978-83

**4**   (Number retired to honor Barry Ashbee)
Ashbee, Barry ("Ash Can"); 1970-74
Bladon, Tom ("Sparky"); 1972-78 (3,23)
Goodenough, Larry ("Izzy"); 1974-77 (5, 23, 29)
MacSweyn, Ralph; 1968-72 (19, 21, 24)
Miszuk, John; 1967-70
Suzor, Mark; 1976-77

**5**   Bathe, Frank ("The Bather"); 1977-84 (21, 31)
Boland, Mike; 1974-75 (17)
Cherry, Dick; 1968-70
Gauthier, Jean ("Goach"); 1967-68
Goodenough, Larry ("Izzy"); 1974-77 (4, 23, 29)
Huffman, Kerry ("Huff"); 1986-
Hughes, Brent ("Hugsy"); 1971-72
Lajeunesse, Serge; 1973-75
Lapointe, Rick; 1976-79
Leach, Reggie ("The Rifle"); 1974-82 (27)
Richter, Dave; 1985-86 (34)
Smith, Steve; 1981-82, 1984-85, 1986-87 (24)

**6**   Arthur, Fred; 1981-82
Chychrun, Jeff ("Chick"); 1986-
Dupont, André ("Moose"/"Mooze"); 1972-80 (28)
Eriksson, Thomas ("Tumba"); 1980-82,
    1983-86 (8, 27)
Hanna, John; 1967-68
Hillman, Wayne; 1969-73
Paterson, Joe; 1984-85 (28)
Smyth, Greg; 1986-88 (40)
Stanley, Allan; 1968-69

Wesley, Blake; 1979-81 (8)
Young, Tim; 1984-85

7   Angotti, Lou; 1967-68
    Barber, Bill ("Arnie"/"Piggy"); 1972-85
    Dobbin, Brian ("Dobber"); 1987-   (18)
    Fisher, Craig; 1990-
    Lacroix, André; 1967-71 (15)
    Parizeau, Michel; 1971-72
    Wells, Jay; 1988-90

8   Baron, Murray; 1989-
    Blackburn, Don ("Blackie"); 1967-69
    Eriksson, Thomas ("Tumba"); 1980-82,
        1983-86 (6, 27)
    Hoyda, Dave ("Hondo"); 1977-79
    Mantha, Moe; 1988-89
    Marsh, Brad ("Bradley"); 1981-88
    Morrison, Lew; 1969-72
    Schultz, Dave ("The Hammer"); 1971-76 (25)
    Wesley, Blake; 1979-81 (6)

9   Bailey, Reid; 1980-82 (34, 35, 36)
    Cochrane, Glen ("The Cocker"); 1978-79, 1981-84
        (29, 35, 44)
    Dvorak, Miroslav ("Cookie"); 1982-85
    Eklund, Per-Erik ("Pelle"/"Eeks"); 1985-
    Fleming, Reggie ("Cement Head"); 1969-70
    Kelly, Bob ("Hound"/"Muttley"); 1970-80
    Rochefort, Leon ("Cheesie"); 1967-69
    Sittler, Darryl ("Sit"); 1982-84 (27)

10  Bridgman, Mel; 1975-81
    Brossart, Willy; 1970-73 (3, 25)
    Bullard, Mike ("Bullie"); 1988-90
    Clement, Bill; 1971-75 (15)
    McCrimmon, Brad ("Beast"); 1982-87
    Roupe, Magnus; 1987-88

Schmautz, Cliff; 1970-71
Selby, Brit; 1967-69
Sutherland, Bill ("Sudsy"); 1967-70 (11)
Wright, Larry; 1971-73, 1975-76 (15, 20, 21)

11    Flockhart, Ron ("Flocky Hockey"); 1980-83 (43)
Gendron, Jean-Guy; 1968-72 (20)
Hachborn, Len; 1983-85 (36)
Latal, Jiri; 1989-
Saleski, Don ("Big Bird"/"Bird"); 1971-79 (25)
Seabrooke, Glen; 1987-
Sutherland, Bill ("Sudsy"); 1967-70 (10)
Ververgaert, Dennis; 1978-80 (28, 43)

12    Dornhoefer, Gary ("Dorny"); 1967-78 (24)
Kerr, Tim; 1980-
Paddock, John ("Too Tall"); 1976-77, 1979-80, 1982-83 (21, 32)

13    Michayluk, Dave; 1981-83 (35)

14    Hannigan, Pat; 1967-69
Linseman, Kenny ("The Rat"); 1978-82, 1989- (18, 26)
Nolet, Simon; 1969-74 (17, 21, 22)
Propp, Brian ("The Propper"); 1979-90 (26)
Sutter, Ron ("Coyote"/"Twin"); 1982-
Watson, Joe ("Thundermouth"); 1967-78 (3)

15    Clement, Bill; 1971-75 (10)
Crisp, Terry ("Crispy"); 1972-77 (29)
Daigneault, Jean-Jacques ("J.J."); 1986-88
Hill, Al ("Wacko"); 1976-82, 1986-88 (28, 36, 37)
Lacroix, André; 1967-71 (7)
Lucas, Danny; 1978-79
Mickey, Larry; 1971-72
Peters, Garry; 1967-71
Sulliman, Doug; 1988-

Sutter, Rich ("Twin"); 1983-86
Taylor, Mark ("Tails"); 1981-83 (35)
Wright, Larry; 1971-73, 1975-76 (10, 20, 21)

**16**   (Number retired to honor Bobby Clarke)
Clarke, Bobby ("Whitey"/"Angel"); 1969-84 (36)
LaForge, Claude ("Pepsi"); 1967-68

**17**   Berube, Craig ("Chief"); 1986-   (34, 43)
Boland, Mike; 1974-75 (5)
Hale, Larry; 1968-72 (19, 23)
Hicks, Wayne; 1967-68
Holmgren, Paul ("Homer"); 1975-84
Hospodar, Ed ("Boxcar"); 1984-85, 1986-87
Nolet, Simon; 1969-74 (14, 21, 22)
Osburn, Randy; 1974-75

**18**   Carson, Lindsay; 1981-88
Dobbin, Brian ("Dobber"); 1987-   (7)
Hoekstra, Ed; 1967-68
Lawless, Paul; 1987-88
Lesuk, Bill; 1970-72
Linseman, Kenny ("The Rat"); 1978-82,
    1989-   (14, 26)
Lonsberry, Ross ("Roscoe"/"The Rabbit"); 1972-78
Paiement, Rosaire ("Rosie"); 1967-70 (19, 20)
Preston, Yves; 1978-79, 1980-81

**19**   Allison, Ray; 1981-87 (36)
Bergen, Todd; 1984-85 (42)
Bernier, Serge; 1968-72 (21)
Hale, Larry; 1968-72 (17, 23)
Heiskala, Earl; 1969-71
MacLeish, Rick ("Hawk"/"Cutie"/"Bedrock");
    1971-81, 1983-84
MacSweyn, Ralph; 1968-72 (4, 21, 24)
Mellanby, Scott; 1985-
Paiement, Rosaire ("Rosie"); 1967-70 (18, 20)

Pelletier, Roger; 1967-68
Stratton, Art; 1968-69

**20**    Barrie, Len; 1990-
Gendron, Jean-Guy; 1968-72 (11)
Johnson, Jimmy; 1968-72 (21)
Joyal, Eddie; 1972
Maguire, Kevin; 1990
Paiement, Rosaire ("Rosie"); 1967-70 (18, 19)
Plante, Pierre; 1971-73 (25)
Poulin, Dave ("Moose"); 1983-90 (34)
Watson, Jimmy ("Chan"); 1972-82
Wright, Keith; 1967-68
Wright, Larry; 1971-73, 1975-76 (10, 15, 21)

**21**    Bathe, Frank ("The Bather"); 1977-84 (5, 31)
Bernier, Serge; 1968-72 (19)
Brown, Dave; 1982-88 (32)
Busniuk, Mike; 1979-81 (28)
Carruthers, Dwight; 1967-68
Cunningham, Jimmy; 1977-78
Edestrand, Darryl; 1969-70
Flett, Bill ("Cowboy"); 1972-74
Gillen, Don; 1979-80
Horacek, Tony; 1989-
Johnson, Jimmy; 1968-72 (20)
MacSweyn, Ralph; 1968-72 (4, 19, 24)
Morrison, Gary; 1979-82
Nolet, Simon; 1969-74 (14, 17, 22)
Paddock, John ("Too Tall"); 1976-77, 1979-80, 1982-83 (12, 32)
Sarrazin, Dick; 1968-70, 1971-72 (24)
Secord, Al; 1988-89
Sirois, Bob; 1974-75
Wright, Larry; 1971-73, 1975-76 (10, 15, 20)

**22**    Bennett, Harvey; 1976-78
Byers, Mike; 1968-69

Fitzpatrick, Ross; 1982-84 (32, 34)
Foley, Rick; 1971-72
Gorence, Tom ("T.J."); 1978-83 (36)
Kennedy, Forbes ("Forbsie"); 1967-70
Nolet, Simon; 1969-74 (14, 17, 21)
Schock, Danny; 1970-71
Swarbrick, George; 1970-71
Tocchet, Rick ("The Rocket"); 1984-

**23**    Barnes, Norm; 1976-77, 1979-81 (25)
Bladon, Tom ("Sparky"); 1972-78 (3, 4)
Collins, Bill; 1976-77
Drolet, René; 1971-72
Evans, Paul ("The Crow"); 1978-79, 1980-81,
    1982-83 (25)
Gardner, Dave; 1979-80
Goodenough, Larry ("Izzy"); 1974-77 (4, 5, 29)
Hale, Larry; 1968-72 (17, 19)
Keenan, Larry; 1971-72
Meehan, Gerry; 1968-69
Sinisalo, Ilkka; 1981-90
Stankiewicz, Myron; 1968-69

**24**    Ball, Terry; 1969-70
Dornhoefer, Gary ("Dorny"); 1967-78 (12)
Hoffmeyer, Bob; 1981-83 (34, 35)
Holt, Randy; 1983-84
MacSweyn, Ralph; 1968-72 (4, 19, 21)
McLeod, Don; 1971-72 (30)
Murray, Terry; 1975-77, 1978-79, 1980-81 (25)
Sarrazin, Dick; 1968-70, 1971-72 (21)
Smith, Derrick; 1984-
Smith, Steve; 1981-82, 1984-85, 1986-87 (5)
Zeidel, Larry ("The Rock"); 1967-69

**25**    Acton, Keith ("Woody"); 1988-
Adams, Greg; 1980-82 (36)
Barnes, Norm; 1976-77, 1979-81 (23)

Brossart, Willy; 1970-73 (3, 10)

Evans, Paul ("The Crow"); 1978-79, 1980-81, 1982-83 (23)

Guay, Paul; 1983-85 (34)

Harris, Ted; 1974-75

MacAdam, Al; 1973-74

Mair, Jimmy; 1970-72 (3)

McCarthy, Kevin ("Kato"); 1977-79, 1985-86 (36)

Murray, Terry; 1975-77, 1978-79, 1980-81 (24)

Plante, Pierre; 1971-73 (20)

Potvin, Jean; 1972-73

Saleski, Don ("Big Bird"/"Bird"); 1971-79 (11)

Schultz, Dave ("The Hammer"); 1971-76 (8)

Zezel, Peter ("The Matinee Idol"); 1984-88

**26** Fenyves, Dave; 1987-   (39)

Kindrachuk, Orest ("O"); 1972-78

Linseman, Kenny ("The Rat"); 1978-82, 1989-   (14, 18)

Propp, Brian ("The Propper"); 1979-90 (14)

**27** Cowick, Bruce; 1973-74

Eriksson, Thomas ("Tumba"); 1980-82, 1983-86 (6, 8)

Hextall, Ron ("Hex"); 1986-

Leach, Reggie ("The Rifle"); 1974-82 (5)

Sittler, Darryl ("Sit"); 1982-84 (9)

**28** Botell, Mark; 1981-82

Busniuk, Mike; 1979-81 (21)

Callander, Drew; 1976-79

Dupont, André ("Moose"/"Mooze"); 1972-80 (6)

Hill, Al ("Wacko"); 1976-82, 1986-88 (15, 36, 37)

Paterson, Joe; 1984-85 (6)

Samuelsson, Kjell ("The Killer Flamingo"/ "Sammy"); 1986-

Stanley, Darryl; 1983-84, 1985-87 (29)

Ververgaert, Dennis; 1978-80 (11, 43)

29    Carkner, Terry ("Carks"); 1988-
Cochrane, Glen ("The Cocker"); 1978-79, 1981-84
   (9, 35, 44)
Crisp, Terry ("Crispy"); 1972-77 (15)
Dean, Barry; 1977-79
Fotiu, Nick; 1987-88
Goodenough, Larry ("Izzy"); 1974-77 (4, 5, 23)
McIlhargey, Jack ("Buck"); 1974-77, 1979-80
Stanley, Darryl; 1983-84, 1985-87 (28)

30    Belhumeur, Michel; 1972-73 (35)
Gamble, Bruce; 1970-72
Gillow, Russ; 1972 (DNP)*
Hoffort, Bruce; 1989-
Inness, Gary ("Inch"); 1975-77
Lemelin, Rejean ("Reggie") (DNP)*
McLeod, Don; 1971-72 (24)
Parent, Bernie ("Bennie"); 1967-71, 1973-79 (1)
St. Croix, Rick; 1977-83
Settlemyre, David ("Sudsy") (DNP)*
Taylor, Bobby ("Chief"/"Chef"); 1971-76
Young, Wendell; 1987-88

31    Bathe, Frank ("The Bather"); 1977-84 (5, 21)
Lindbergh, Pelle ("The Gumper"); 1981-85
Myre, Phil; 1979-81
Ritchie, Rob; 1976-77

32    Brown, Dave; 1982-88 (21)
Craven, Murray ("Crafty"/"Muzz"); 1984-
Dunlop, Blake; 1977-79
Fitzpatrick, Ross; 1982-84 (22, 34)
Paddock, John ("Too Tall"); 1976-77, 1979-80,
   1982-83 (12, 21)

33    Bloski, Mike; 1985-86

---

*DNP = Dressed as back-up goaltender, but did not play.

Jensen, Darren; 1984-86
Laforest, Mark ("Trees"); 1987-89
Larocque, Michel ("Bunny"); 1982-84
Mrazek, Jerome ("Moses"); 1975-76
Peeters, Pete; 1978-82, 1989-
Resch, Glenn ("Chico"); 1986-87

**34**  Bailey, Reid; 1980-82 (9, 35, 36)
Berube, Craig ("Chief"); 1986-   (17, 43)
Brickley, Andy; 1982-83
Fitzpatrick, Ross; 1982-84 (22, 32)
Gillis, Jere; 1986-87
Guay, Paul; 1983-85 (25)
Harding, Jeff; 1988-
Hoffmeyer, Bob; 1981-83 (24, 35)
Morosak, Carl; 1985-86
Patterson, Dennis; 1979-80
Poulin, Dave ("Moose"); 1983-90 (20)
Richter, Dave; 1985-86 (5)
Root, Bill; 1987-88 (48)
Williams, Gordie; 1981-83 (35)

**35**  Bailey, Reid; 1980-82 (9, 34, 36)
Belhumeur, Michel; 1972-73 (30)
Cochrane, Glen ("The Cocker"); 1978-79, 1981-84
(9, 29, 44)
Froese, Bob ("Frosty"); 1982-86
Hoffmeyer, Bob; 1981-83 (24, 34)
Michayluk, Dave; 1981-83 (13)
Stephenson, Wayne; 1974-79
Taylor, Mark ("Tails"); 1981-83 (15)
Williams, Gordie; 1981-83 (34)
Wregget, Ken; 1988-

**36**  Adams, Greg; 1980-82 (25)
Allison, Ray; 1981-87 (19)
Bailey, Reid; 1980-82 (9, 34, 35)
Clarke, Bobby ("Whitey"/"Angel"); 1969-84 (16)

Gorence, Tom ("T.J."); 1978-83 (22)
Hachborn, Len; 1983-85 (11)
Hill, Al ("Wacko"); 1976-82, 1986-88 (15, 28, 37)
Lacombe, Normand; 1989-
McCarthy, Kevin ("Kato"); 1977-79, 1985-86 (25)
Roberts, Gordie; 1987-88

**37** Berglund, Bo; 1985-86
Freer, Mark; 1987-  (45)
Hill, Al ("Wacko"); 1976-82, 1986-88 (15, 28, 36)
Lamoureux, Mitch; 1987-89
Tookey, Tim; 1987-89

**39** Fenyves, Dave; 1987-  (26)
Moore, Robbie; 1978-79
Murray, Mike; 1987-88

**40** Smyth, Greg; 1986-88 (6)

**41** Stevens, John; 1987-88

**42** Bergen, Todd; 1984-85 (19)
Nachbauer, Don; 1985-

**43** Berube, Craig ("Chief"); 1986-  (17, 34)
Flockhart, Ron ("Flocky Hockey"); 1980-83 (11)
Ververgaert, Dennis; 1978-80 (11, 28)

**44** Cochrane, Glen ("The Cocker"); 1978-79, 1981-84
  (9, 29, 35)
Huber, Willie; 1987-88 (47)
Stothers, Mike; 1984-86, 1987-88

**45** Freer, Mark; 1986-  (37)
Jensen, Chris; 1989-

**46** Biggs, Don; 1989-

47    Huber, Willie; 1987-88 (44)
        Sabol, Shawn; 1989-

48    Root, Bill; 1987-88 (34)

49    D'Amour, Marc; 1988-
        Gilmour, Darryl; 1987-88

## Head Coaches

Allen, Keith; 1967-69
Holmgren, Paul ("Homer"); 1988-
Keenan, Mike; 1984-88
McCammon, Bob; 1978-79, 1982-84
Quinn, Pat; 1979-82
Shero, Fred ("The Fog"); 1971-78
Stasiuk, Vic; 1969-71

**A**nd now, my good friends, to each and every one of you—
Good day! Good night! And good hockey!